TOP
BOYS

Published by John Blake Publishing Ltd,
3 Bramber Court, 2 Bramber Road,
London W14 9PB, England

www.blake.co.uk

First published in paperback in 2006

ISBN 978 1 84454 276 5

British Library Cataloguing-in-Publication Data:

A catalogue record for this book is available from the British Library.

Design by www.envydesign.co.uk

Printed in the UK by CPI Bookmarque, Croydon, CR0 4TD

7 9 10 8

© Text copyright Cass Pennant, 2006

Papers used by John Blake Publishing are natural, recyclable
products made from wood grown in sustainable forests. The
manufacturing processes conform to the environmental regulations
of the country of origin.

Every attempt has been made to contact the relevant copyright-holders,
but some were unobtainable. We would be grateful if the appropriate
people could contact us.

TOP BOYS

MEET THE MEN BEHIND THE MAYHEM

CASS PENNANT

JOHN BLAKE

Contents

Introduction xiii

 MR M
Aberdeen 1

 JASON MARRINER
Chelsea 77

 ONNO
AFC Ajax ... 19

 SERGEY 'MOWGLI' CSKA
Moscow 99

 SPENNA
Aston Villa 31

 YAUZA CSKA
Moscow 111

 'BRAINS'
Birmingham City 45

 'DOC' CSKA
Moscow 119

 LES MURANYI – 'THE GENERAL'
Cambridge United 61

 JIM 'JINKS' MCTAGGOT
Glasgow Rangers 129

 WOODY
*Halifax
Town* *145*

 RENNO
*Manchester
City* *231*

 PHILLY &
IAN BAILEY
*Hartlepool
United* *163*

 EDDIE BEEF
*Manchester
United* *243*

 COCKNEY
JACKO
Hull City .. *181*

 BOATSY
*Nottingham
Forest* *259*

 COALVILLE
DAZ
*Leicester
City* *199*

 SPENCER
*Oldham
Athletic* *273*

 TOMMY
ROBINSON
*Luton
Town* *215*

 MIKE
*Plymouth
Argyle* *289*

 EDDIE CRISPIN
Portsmouth 305

 COLA
*West Bromwich
Albion 369*

 GREGOR
*Queen's
Park Rangers
.... 323*

 BUNTER
*West Ham
United 383*

 STEVE PARKER
*Rotherham
United 339*

 JELA
*West Ham
United 397*

 TONY
CRONSHAW
*Sheffield
Wednesday 353*

Conclusion 415

Acknowledgements

No book of this nature would have been remotely possible without the assistance, enthusiasm and goodwill of a multitude of people. Above all, I would like to thank each and every one of the 'Top Boys' featured, along with the individuals who made the contacts on my behalf. If there are any whose names I have omitted to mention, I apologise profusely.

Mr M and the lads, plus my contacts John and Trevor T. Onno, I spare the blushes of your partner but good luck to you both. Longy of F-Side, thanks for that email. Rotherham Blade Shaun, no luck with Tony B but Steve proved an interesting guy. Staying up your way, I thank Will for a bed and Cowhorns for my spiked shandy. Blues Brendon, Brains and Keith, my full respect and good luck with that book. To Terry and Paul for contacting the General, who was an interesting meet along with pals Captain & Co – you really can never underestimate anyone. Learned much the same with Migs main man Tommy R. Thanks for that, Virgil and Tuse. Next stop The other Claret and Blues Mr Spenna was a good call, so thanks, Martin. Jason, jog on, I hope you do it, book or documentary, but no love lost with our teams, eh? Mr King, thanks for the Chelsea contact. Yauza, Mowgli, Cashpoint, Doc, Egor, Hohol, Tartan, Troi, The Skull, you CSK are crazy. Good to see you smarten yourselves up in good old London. Up in Glasgow, Big Kirky, always a pleasure, mate, and, Jinks, we hold the copyright on the ICF. As for those I met in the Louden, you are the people. Woody, call me for 2006, 'cos you will find the cheapest room and cheapest beer for sure. Good luck with the new book, Richy Horsley, the call on Mr Bailey was spot on. Two for the price of one, Philly and Ian, my respect to Shaun Tordoff and Cockney Jacko ... wish I'd stayed longer. Coalville Daz, we are sorted for that Rejects gig, leave it to me, pal. Renno and Eddie Beef, funny as fuck and both true Manchester. Thank you, Mr Nicholls. Boatsy, honest interview, you have a good set of lads. Oi! Spencer, you half know how to pick a shirt, pal. Mike, a cool weekend had by all, give regards to the boys. Eddie, you are Pompey through and through; Rob, you are a good mate, you both are. Gregor, fair play to you. Tony Cronshaw – *Rucks and Rock 'n' Roll* – that was a big contribution bookman. Cola, Johnny Payne, whenever you're ready for that beer ... Bunter, do I need say anything? Respect to the family. Little Jela, stay on top, son, you know what I mean. It was a long journey and things do go belly up. A-Company ... what happened, no reply? CSF, you left it far too late. Peter Kelly, hope we can meet again. Darlo Chiz, do something with that answerphone. Southey, it was worth a thought, mate. Hi to Jason and Wes – did you fix your front door, boys? To Para Dave, thanks anyway. So no go with border crew then, Brendon? Likewise, the Thailand Gooner ... football politics, he said. Far, far up north, more no can do as Chris said his son played for the first team, equal tops with another who had a magistrate for an in-law. Finally, rock bottom with no equal was the QE-linked chapter that was pulled when it lost all credibility.

My additional thanks for help on the preparation of this book go to Niomi and Apollo for computer stuff; Press Gang for photocopying; cover photo permission of a Casual Look; authors Lorne Brown and Nick Harvey; production, Mark Hanks and all at Blake Publishing. And not forgetting Mrs Wendy Sanford, who worked so hard for me to transcribe some right dodgy accents and even discovered ten different ways of spelling Thierry Henry.

I also have to add that this book really does come down to the support of my family who have had to put up with being ignored while I worked tirelessly for 18 months. My wife made all the travel arrangements, my son dropped his homework to type out what would have taken me days, and my daughter attempted to guide me through using the computer. I would like to express my debt to Elaine, Marcus and Georgie.

Chapter Dedications

Spenna (Villa):
Martin Smith, Gary Bradley.

Jason Marriner (CFC):
My other half Julie and my son Billy Boy who are everything to me. Like to thank all the old skool Chelsea lads, the likes of Andy Frain, the twins Ian and Dave Simm, you'd never meet a more loyal bunch. R.I.P. Paul Hopping and Nicky Olpin, you are always in my thoughts.

Jinks McTaggot (Rangers):
Barry Johnstone R.I.P. loyal friend.

Ian and Philly Bailey (Hartlepool):
Loads of respect to a one Mark Purdy.

Daz (Leicester):
To my football mad son Nathan.

Tommy (Luton):
To Warren Heath, died too young, R.I.P. pal.

Spencer (Oldham):
Dedicated to Bloorer, Stash and Muz.

Mike (Plymouth):
Message to Tissy – sorry.

Eddie (Pompey):
Dedicated to Keeley and Casey, always everything to me.

Gregor (QPR):
Special thanks to Samantha Kenny for keeping me out of trouble plus all my love to Nicola, Georgia, Lee, Charlie and Vincent. Finally big respect to a true friend, DJ Norman Jay.

Steve (Rotherham):
R.I.P. Trev Jackson, Stan Cutts and Barry Critchley you are all still missed.

Tony Cronshaw (Weds):
For my wife Christine, daughter Samantha and all the lads that were part of the Eastbank Republican Army, plus the OCS and ITI for keeping the spirit alive.

Cola (WBA):
Full respect to lads Johnny Payne, Eamon, Bale, Clem, Peachy and Hoggy.

Bunter (WHU):
Specially for Mal, my children and grandchildren, all my family and close friends. They know who they are.

Jela (WHU):
For all the Ispanedi family, Dad Celal, Savash, Fudia and my mum Rose who has always stuck by me. R.I.P. Derek Hilton, Danny Tyderman, Lee Donner, Shaun and Lol Pearman-Bevan, Peter Wynn and Terry Marchant.

Introduction

Even before England won the 1966 World Cup, the game of Association Football was still the most popular sport in the country. Today, it attracts national media coverage and generates millions of pounds in revenue per season. However, it is also making headlines for all the wrong reasons. Your old favourite, the football hooligan, still appears to be prominent on the scene. How anyone can still be surprised is beyond me; violence and hooliganism have been part of our game for decades. It is ingrained into society; today's big games still bring out all the old faces. The old firms of the '80s are now re-forming in order to keep the pride that they enjoyed as some of the most notorious hooligans in the country. It's class of '84 all over again.

We're all fascinated, whether we're in the front line or just observing it. I had someone from a famous rock band once say to me, 'Cass, I was never part of all that and would run a mile if I had to be. But I support the same team and remember some of the games you've written about and I would sit high up in the main stand and watch it. It was like watching two armies on a hill colliding. Fucking awesome and more entertaining than the match I had come to watch that day, certainly more adventurous – that's for sure.'

Sickening or cold reality? The truth is, people are genuinely fascinated with this phenomenon and its subculture. It's a club you can't buy now. Most lads I knew had no thought of seeing violence or fighting at football, but would accept that it had become the reason for going to football. And they would never

ever refer to themselves as 'hooligans'; it was an unspoken word. The whole thing was that they were young, likely to be single and that was where it was at, that's just what was done at the time. It was part of growing up and becoming a man ... at least, that's what they thought then.

It's probably the most honest description I can give. These are guys who have lived their football and they'll all say the same to a man, even those who have had a brush with death. Like little Jela. They'll all tell you ... those were the days.

Dawn raids, arrest and trial, CCTV and banning orders all testify to the ongoing battle with football hooliganism. They say the hooligan is coming back; well just maybe he has never gone away. What's certain is that, whatever measures are introduced and whatever tactics are adopted, there will always be a group of lads who will push them to their limits.

Well, who are these guys? You can tell a football guy; you know the moment they walk through a crowd or enter a pub that these are not ordinary supporters but football guys. People may think it's the clothes, but it isn't. It's the presence; there's an aura, there is something there. You just know instantly what these guys are.

So, once again, I embark on a journey with a view to interviewing these guys for their lively, honest, unbiased experiences from their own unique perspectives on going to football. I feel privileged in some way, for I go where no outsider can go. It's a secret world that opens up to me, no doubt on the strength of my own CV, some curiosity and, dare I say it, respect.

That respect can be fragile, though. And the tact is to move fast in conveying very quickly my reason for meeting them. The most important thing is that I am 100 per cent genuine. The moment I lose that, I'm in serious trouble, hand on heart. When I meet these guys for the first time, I enter the unknown, I really do. I don't know if they will see me as Cass Pennant, West Ham and the ICF or simply the author. My aim is always to go as the author; to make the point, I always go alone on a meet. A phone call will obviously have been made beforehand. The only thing

I take with me is my trust in the contact who is either the go-between or the person I intend to interview.

When I get there, I'm faced with the challenge of being on unfamiliar territory. Then the adrenalin rush kicks in, just like in my old days of going to away matches. What's the right way to play this? How many will I be meeting? What will the reception be like? And what about old rivalries – will there still be any grudges to bear? I nervously smile to myself as I find myself buzzing.

I thought those days were long behind me. The fact is, I had personally made the decision to turn my back on violence long before I was fortunate enough to forge a career as an author on football fan culture. Today my written work is a real passion with me, a passion without the violence. Talking to these guys and getting them to open up quite possibly keeps the spirit alive in what is the most reported and misunderstood football phenomenon of our time in social history. I feel as if I am on a mission here. I genuinely seek to know what it all was for these guys and what it meant to them. Was it in any way the same for them as it was for me? That the violence was only part of the story, the only one the public get to hear, or was there a whole big scene going on? A kind of culture, a bond of brotherhood so strong that this male bonding could be the reason why they say that those were the best days. Was there a worthwhile cause behind what they did and was it all worth it?

These are my thoughts as to the sort of questions I would be asking at our first meeting. I cannot know what thoughts go through the mind of my intended interviewees – I've never asked. My guess is they'll be thinking something like 'I'm fucking not happy with what he's said in some of his books ... he don't know it but we've certainly met before ... his friends once did this to one of ours ... we've always rated his firm ... it will be interesting to hear what they really thought of us ... we hear a lot about his lot and they've done this, done that. We'll show Mr Pennant how tight our little mob is, let him see. Let him take it back with him.'

At the end of the day, it comes down to that little word 'respect', and I don't necessarily mean to myself. They know I am meeting them on their terms, their manor and their environment, whether it is in the D-section, F-Side or a loyalist-supported pub in the heart of Glasgow. They are calling the shots from the moment we shake hands until it is time to go – I know that nothing need be said. And there is something else I know, by the presence felt, the aura, the contact made when his eyes will meet mine that first time, there's a look, a begrudging wink, a wry smile, as if to suggest that, indeed, we are the same culture, maybe the same person, with the difference being we were on opposite sides. Sometimes, it will take a few words of conversation but there will at some point come a relaxation between us, which takes the edge out. That's the moment that I know I will be walking away with my interview.

Some of the interviews will push the boundaries to their limits. Brutal in their honesty, brutal in the deed told, all described in their matter-of-fact way. What they reveal is not for the sake of any kudos. These guys have already achieved all of that. The name, the reputation, comes with being part of a firm.

Not all the guys that I've met claim to be top boys; some insisted they be thought of as just one of the lads. Whatever, they still meet the criteria of having taken the call of passion further than most would when following their respective teams. It's a club you can't buy your way into, not even wearing the right clothes. And if you're not part of it, you can't possibly know it. Rarely are the real opinions from the proper faces ever heard. Yet turn the pages and they're all here. Heroes or villains ... once again, you decide.

NAME: MR M
CLUB: Aberdeen
FIRM: Aberdeen Soccer Casuals

'It can never
be what it was,
but the memories
will live on.'

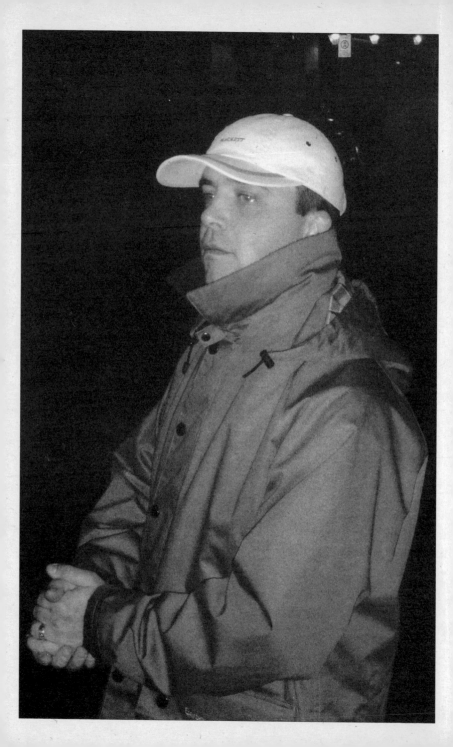

BACKGROUND AND MEET

Now here's a call for me, the ASC – the Aberdeen Soccer Casuals. You know, there was a time we thought everything north of the border was ten years behind, but I heard there was a football casual scene in Scotland long before I picked up Jay Allen's novel Soccer Casual. I would hear of Hibs, Aberdeen and Hearts, but the one that I kept on hearing about was the Aberdeen Casuals. And if you look into the history of the whole thing, then it's common knowledge that the ASC were the first casual firm north of the border.

I flew into the Granite City knowing I was to meet their proper lads, including the Mr M I sought for my interview. I think everyone knows they have something going on with Tottenham's firm and, indeed, it was from the main lad of the Tottenham Massive that I had been given my ASC contact. How big this link is and how it all came about, I still don't know. I did recall that, a few seasons back, a serious West Ham firm with bad intent went to Tottenham and came across 70 Aberdeen half showing out. 'What the fuck's it got to do with you, Jock?' screamed out our infamous one. I'm not sure we got a printable answer, or maybe we misunderstood their accents, but I was about to find out.

And I did find out a few things, too, for I met them in the Monkey House, a modern bar in Union Street, and they weren't that hard to miss. A table of casual dressers positioned in the far corner of the pub where they could see everyone coming in.

More beers were ordered as they quickly pointed out something they were not happy with in the book on the ICF. 'We never joined with United ... we don't go with them. That's Hibs who go Man U, not us, Cass.'

Mr M was born in 1970 and obtained O-levels in English, Maths, Technical Drawing, Art and History. First job and up to the present day is as a painter and decorator. He's married and remembers his first game being the 1979 Cup Final against Rangers with his father.

WHAT HAS BEEN THE MOST LEGENDARY FIGHT OR RIOT YOUR TEAM'S SUPPORTERS HAVE BEEN INVOLVED IN?

Hibs away '84/85 season ... the day Raymond Morrell, a Hibs lad, nearly died. At the time, Aberdeen were the biggest and best in Scotland; Hibs were just beginning to make a name for themselves. Hibs away was always a good one as you knew it would kick off as there was only one way to go to the ground and you had to pass the Hibs mob on Easter Road.

On this day, Aberdeen had around 400 and Hibs 150-plus, but they still came ahead as Aberdeen came down the road. Aberdeen charged at Hibs and most of them done a runner, but a few of them stood but were overpowered and they had to take off, realising they stood no chance. Unfortunately for them, one lad got caught and took a bad beating as the rest of the Hibs mob legged it. Once in the game, the Aberdeen lads started hearing stories about the lad dying and the Hibs fans were singing, 'Murderers ... murderers.' Thankfully, he pulled through out of his coma as, deep down, no self-respecting lad wants anyone to die.

HOW IMPORTANT WAS THE ROLE OF ALCOHOL AND DRUGS? WAS THERE ANY TIME IN YOUR EXPERIENCE EITHER HAD PARTICULAR INFLUENCE?

I would say alcohol is more important because most away games and 90 per cent of the home games involve drinking. The drugs side of things was probably more relevant in the late '80s, early '90s. The drugs had quite an effect on Aberdeen's mob because, up until the late '80s, we had huge numbers and a lot of older lads, but a lot of them drifted away to the rave scene and left the younger lads to carry the torch.

WHO WAS THE MOST VIOLENT, CRAZY SET OF SUPPORTERS YOU EVER CAME ACROSS?

Hearts' scarfers from the early '80s. They never really took to the scene as their support was made up of punks and skins. Before the Casual scene, the Gorgie Aggro were one of the most violent sets of fans in Scotland. They were always a difficult test for the ASC, even when we had good numbers. One game when Aberdeen won the League in 1984 on a Wednesday night, the Gorgie lads waited for the ASC to come out of the ground and attacked from all angles, forcing us back into our end. Eventually, we managed to get back out and there was fighting all the way back to the train station miles away.

ARE YOUR FIRM STILL DOING IT?

Week in, week out, it's become impossible to be active due to the police operations. Aberdeen can still get decent numbers for certain games now and then, especially for Rangers games at home. CCTV, prison sentences and bans from grounds have made a lot of lads think twice about going any more.

HOW WOULD YOU DESCRIBE THE SITUATION WITH THE SCENE TODAY? CAN IT COMPARE WITH WHAT HAPPENED IN THE PAST, AND DO THINGS STILL GO OFF IN THE SAME WAY?

The last row we had was with Rangers over two years, but that was more bumping into them by mistake. We were coming back from a cup game in Dumfries, Rangers were coming back from a cup game in Arbroath and we were walking to get the train; we had to walk past the bar they were in. We didn't know they were there. What happened was a couple of their lads spotted us, we spotted them, it kicked off, a fight started, even though it was in front of CCTV cameras. We knew once we were caught we were in trouble, but you couldn't help but kick it off.

Until about two years ago, there was only Aberdeen and

Rangers that were trying to have a go, and now we've got a heavy police presence, you've got other mobs like Dundee and Hibs. It can't happen like it used to, definitely. Most of the cities now have CCTV. Police intelligence, because the mobs are smaller, they know everyone on a more personal note than maybe in England and they know who to pick on. If there's trouble, they know who's caused it, they know who was there, and basically if a fight kicks off they're guaranteed five or six years and definitely getting done for it.

HOW DID YOU GET GOING WITH A FOOTBALL FIRM, DID IT HAVE A NAME AND HOW WAS THE NAME ESTABLISHED?

Aberdeen Soccer Casuals. The trouble started in the early 1980s. Obviously, the clothing that they were wearing at the time, sportswear and that, it was different from the rest of the supporters. And when the police were describing the group in the papers, they gave the name of 'soccer casuals' because of the casual dress they were wearing. And it really stuck after that. Some older lads before them had other names but they never really stuck and that's how we ended up with the 'Casual' tag. It was given by the local paper, the Evening Express.

It was made up of different areas from Aberdeen, they sort of just came together. It stopped most of the in-fighting. There used to be fighting between different Aberdeen groups from different areas in the city, and then they all sort of got together with the casual movement and basically that was it. That would have been 1980–81.

WHAT WAS THE WORST INSTANCE OF WEAPONS BEING USED?

Apart from your usual knives and stuff, I think the worst one would have been when Hibs threw a petrol bomb. We were getting escorted to the station after the game, just past the St James's Centre before you went down the big steps at Waverley. Aberdeen's mob were split in two and the last mob that were coming in, Hibs, had appeared from round the back of the centre. Hibs used to always meet there. One of them threw a petrol bomb and, although it never hurt anyone, it come in quite close and that. It still went off with the flames and everything.

There was a big thing in the papers about it. It sort of gave Hibs a name because, from then on, everyone started thinking Hibs were mad. The police came on our train going home to smell our hands for petrol as if we'd thrown it. This would be 1985–86. It was Hibs' revenge after that Raymond Morell business, their way of trying to get back at Aberdeen.

WHO WERE YOUR BIGGEST RIVALS BOTH TEAM AND FAN-WISE?

Biggest rivals team-wise, personally, from an Aberdeen point of view would be Rangers, when it came to the end of the '80s and that, after Aberdeen had been doing very well, winning leagues, European trophies and that. And then Graeme Souness came and spent big money at Ibrox, and they started winning everything and Aberdeen fans didn't take it too well. I wouldn't say it was jealousy, maybe it was a wee bit ... it was just a hatred. It's still going now between the two sets of fans.

Mob-wise, it would be the old Hibs. Always went off, every game near enough. And they were always well up for it because they knew that by doing Aberdeen then everyone would look at them and say, right, Hibs are now the top dogs and that. At the time when they were starting, Aberdeen were the biggest and best mob, and the rivalry with Hibs, it was the best rivalry because you knew that, if you went in for a fight, you weren't gonna get stabbed or slashed or a bottle stuck in your face. Even now, Hibs can give you a test.

WHO ARE THE TOP FIVE FIRMS OF ANY IMPORTANCE TODAY?

Spurs, still active and they have a solid mob. Some Aberdeen lads go down to London for the big games and are always impressed. Feyenoord – I worked in Holland for a year and went to see them quite often and they, on their day, could compete with the best in England. Dynamo Berlin, on their day, the best in Germany, and most lads over there would admit that. The old '80s Hibs mob were always a tough one for Aberdeen and also very active against other Scottish firms in the late '80s. England international away mobs are also very impressive and not to be taken lightly.

WHO ARE YOUR TOP FIVE FIRMS OF ALL TIME?

Tottenham, Old Hibs, Rangers, Dundee for about three years in the '90s, and England again for international games in Glasgow.

What is the worst ground you've ever been to and what is your favourite ground?

My favourite was Easter Road. You had to walk down the road past the Hibs pub, where it always kicked off. There was always a good atmosphere in the game. We knew afterwards there was gonna be more trouble, so you were always up for it. The worst ground would have been Hearts, Tynecastle – it was just a dump. Tynecastle ... swine castle. And there was one toilet for the whole lot. It was a dump.

WHAT IS YOUR FAVOURITE FOOTBALL FASHION-WEAR AND THE WORST YOU'VE SEEN OR WORN?

I like Paul and Shark, understated, good quality. Lacoste was nice because it was only really the football guys that wore it, whereas nowadays Stone Island, Aquascutum and Burberry and all that, it's taken over by the mainstream after a while. But Paul and Shark are still only football.

Celtic and Rangers used to wear denim jackets with cartoon characters patches on them, that was the worst fashion ever. And before that, when Aberdeen started wearing Aquascutum and Burberry the first time, Celtic's mob were wearing Nike sweatshirts four or five years after sportswear had gone out.

HAVE YOU EVER WORN A REPLICA FOOTBALL SHIRT TO A GAME AND NAME A CLUB THAT'S ALL SHIRTERS AND SCARFERS?

No, only on holiday, never to a game. Celtic and even Rangers' mob up to the late '80s used to wear scarves and mingle in with their scarfers so that if it kicked off with the mob they would hope that their scarfers would fight them off because Aberdeen had the better numbers. And Celtic are like that as well. Very rarely did you bump into them on their own away from their support. And when they did attack outside Ibrox Park, their scarfers used to get involved as well because it looked as though you were fighting scarfers.

DOES TODAY'S MODERN FOOTBALL PLAYER HAVE THE RESPECT OF THE FANS?

Very seldom. They're too detached from the support nowadays I think, with the wages they get, the lifestyle they have. It's more for money than for the love of the club. You get the odd few that genuinely love playing for the club, but nowadays no, I don't think so. And you've got players going to Qatar, fucking America, Hong Kong, just because they're getting more money. They're mercenaries now.

WHO'S THE PLAYER AND/OR MANAGER THAT WINDS YOU UP THE MOST?

Neil Lennon – plays for Celtic – and Martin O'Neill, the manager of Celtic. Also known as Zebedee, Neil Lennon's always moaning, gives it out on the pitch, but can't take it back. And Martin O'Neill is always bouncing up and down like a fool. If there's an argument on the pitch, Lennon's always in there, sticking his oar in. Martin O'Neill, after the game, he's never got respect for the team that beats him, there's always an excuse or it's always Celtic's fault, it's never the other team are better than them. Or he's never got enough money, even though he's spent 30-odd million on his team.

WORST FOREIGN PLAYER YOU'VE SEEN AND THE BEST FOREIGN IMPORT? YOUR FAVOURITE CLUB PLAYER AND YOUR FAVOURITE OTHER PLAYER?

Best foreign import is Brian Laudrup for Rangers. When he was in Scotland he was a different class. He was a very good player. He was awesome for his country (Denmark), he's done it at international level and for his club.

The worst foreign player would have to be Bert Konterman, who played for Glasgow Rangers. He was a Dutch lad who had a decent reputation for Feyenoord, but when he came to Scotland he was terrible.

Favourite club player is Neil Simpson. He played from the early '80s until he got hounded out of Scottish football by the Glasgow media after a tackle on Ian Durrant. He went to Newcastle to escape the hassles. Ian Durrant was the darling boy of Scottish football – overrated, like Paul McStay. And Neil Simpson and him had a 50–50 tackle and Neil Simpson won. He went a wee bit high and nearly ended the career of Durrant. He came back, but apparently he was never the same player, but he was never a player anyway, he was just overrated.

My favourite other player is Diego Maradona. He was different class. The skill! But he lived the lifestyle as well, he enjoyed his life.

FANS OFTEN TALK ABOUT THEIR FOOTBALL-GOING DAYS AS JUST BEING A LAUGH. ANY EPISODES YOU REMEMBER?

Too many to mention. We were at Dunfermline away one day. We had a 53-seater coach down. We were all quite pissed. Dunfermline were a newly promoted team. We knew they had a mob, and we knew they would be out to test themselves against Aberdeen. But before the game, they never came near us.

But after the game, we walked right down the town centre. We were told to go to a big park to wait for them and we would definitely meet them there. We went down into the park and it was round about December, it was really dark, quiet, just a few noises, like young kids drinking over a wall in a little public park.

So we're in the park waiting for this mob to turn up. And one guy that used to come with the mob, he was never a casual, but he came along for fights and that, liked a good drink, always out of his face, he wandered over to the wall and saw and heard the kids. So as we're all standing there psyched up ready for a fight and that, he came running back, shouting, 'Quick, quick, Dumbarton are coming.' We were playing Dunfermline! He came running back, but it wasn't a mob at all, it was just young kids. It wasn't even the same mob that were in the town.

Another time, we told this guy that the minibus door was

broken in Glasgow, so we told him he'd have to hold the door to the minibus closed or it would bust open and he'd fall out. And we told him that it was just a wind-up when we were about ten miles outside Aberdeen, so he'd actually held the handle of the door for about three hours, about 180 miles.

YOUR OPINION ABOUT ALL-SEATER STADIUMS, TICKET PRICES AND THE COMMERCIAL ASPECT OF TODAY'S FOOTBALL INDUSTRY. DO YOU STILL FEEL FOOTBALL BELONGS TO THE FANS?

No. Football now is a business. It belongs to big companies, commercial sponsorships and making their money off the executive side of things now. The fans to me are a side issue for most teams. The smaller teams might still be connected to the fans more, but the bigger teams, no.

We were the first all-seater in Britain and that was a bit of a claim to fame. We were on our way to winning in Europe and stuff. We enjoyed our away games because, when you went to away grounds, they were all terracing, segregation fences and all that. Aberdeen was always all-seater and even now it's even worse because you've got to sit in a particular seat. There are big segregation areas, and the atmosphere, it's just killed it.

RACISM AND RACE ISSUES HAVE BEEN PART OF FOOTBALL WITH CERTAIN CLUBS AND SETS OF SUPPORTERS AT BOTH CLUB AND INTERNATIONAL LEVEL. WHAT WAS YOUR EXPERIENCE OF THIS?

Up in Scotland, I think there's a few teams you may call racist, but it's more like you think they're doing it as a fashionable side; it makes them look hard. Mark Walters played for Rangers in the '80s and Hearts would throw bananas at him. Aberdeen's actually had a black Casual. There's no problem with him at all, he's a fine guy. I think it helps being twinned with Tottenham as well, because at Tottenham they've got black geezers and different races. So Aberdeen's never been a racist mob – Aberdeen's been just about football. We've always left our politics at home, we're all AFC, when it comes to Aberdeen.

HOW HAVE FANS FOLLOWING THE NATIONAL TEAM ABROAD BEEN TREATED, AND WHAT ARE YOUR EXPERIENCES FOLLOWING YOUR CLUB OR NATIONAL TEAM ABROAD?

Well, when we followed Scotland, being Aberdeen, we've always had a lot of trouble – when Aberdeen's travelled as a mob to follow the national team, because the Scotland fans, the Tartan Army as a whole, have got a good reputation, the police would concentrate on the groups of casuals that were there. So we would get the hassle, like World Cup games in Belgium and the England games we've been to. The Tartan Army, though, although they've got this great name around Europe as being friendly and all that, it's a bit different when you're actually abroad with them and you see the way they act, toileting in the street and loud and leery, and baring their arses and stuff. If it was us doing that, we'd be locked up for it. You're classed as a thug, you're a terrible disgrace, your behaviour is filthy and that. I'm sure the England fans get hassled for doing less abroad than some things that the Tartan Army do. In fact, I think that's just England's reputation going before them. Now England have got their shirts and there's the travel club and that, but they're generally well behaved, yet they still get tarred with the same brush as all the other thugs that follow England.

WOULD YOU SAY THE MEDIA 'OVER-HYPE' THE TROUBLE AND CAN YOU GIVE AN EXAMPLE OF THIS?

Yeah, definitely up here in Scotland. Every time Aberdeen play Rangers, they always seem to have Chelsea or Tottenham, and there's been Cardiff mentioned in the last few years. There was an 'assassination' attempt on Gazza when he came up, because we had some Tottenham boys up. The Evening Express said that the Tottenham boys were up to try and kill Gazza.

A couple of years ago, there was a big fight down at the train station with Rangers. Now, after this, our local newspaper reported that down in Stonehaven there were thugs from Tottenham, Chelsea and Cardiff roaming around with scarves tied round their wrists coming up to do battle with Aberdeen and Rangers Casuals. And they just over-hype it all the time. Every time there's violence up here between Aberdeen and Rangers, Chelsea always seem to get the blame, even though Rangers never had Chelsea coming up with them mob-handed for years. Chelsea get the blame for everything up here.

Even the last time we played Germany in the World Cup, they said the English thugs were coming up to get a hold of the Germans. I mean, that's just how over-hyped it is. Even a couple of weeks ago at a Dundee match, the Evening Express on Saturday, the local rag, it said that Tottenham were coming up to cause trouble with Dundee. In Aberdeen, there was a big riot planned, apparently – 'Soccer thugs planned an attack'. There was nothing planned at all, but I think the police use our local paper to build up the hype to justify the amount of police and the heavy-handedness.

SHOULD CELTIC AND RANGERS BE ALLOWED TO JOIN THE ENGLISH PREMIERSHIP OR NATIONWIDE LEAGUES?

Well, if they're gonna go to England they've got to start at the bottom as far as I'm concerned. And if they're not happy, don't let them, but I think the SFA should take a heavy hand with them. If they keep touting themselves for another league, that means they're not happy here. The SFA should turn to them and say, 'Either you want in or you want out ... make your mind up.' If they want to leave, then the SFA should let them leave and, if they cannot find another league, that's their own fault.

England don't need them. At the end of the day, they're only gonna get 3,000 tickets for away games like any other club in England and they sell them out anyway. Celtic–Rangers as testimonials prove they'll take 10,000 fans. Now, 3,000 in the ground and 7,000 outside causes trouble. There'd be a lot of trouble.

DO YOU HAVE ANY VIEW ON BANNING ORDERS? DO YOU KNOW THIS FROM YOUR OWN EXPERIENCE OR THAT OF OTHERS?

Yes, I know from experience. They work to some extent. But if someone wants to go and cause trouble, whether you're a Casual or not, you'll go and cause trouble. The thing is with banning orders, nine times out of ten you're banned from the ground because of what's happening outside. You've maybe never been arrested inside the ground or thrown out, but you get banned from it because of what's happening outside.

In my mind, they've got enough laws in place, the Section 60s and all that. You can be held for six hours without charge. They've got enough powers without the banning orders. I think the banning orders are basically to make the courts look good in the press, like they're dealing with it. I think it's victimising civil liberties, I do.

HOOLIE MOVIES AND FLICKS – DO THEY GLORIFY VIOLENCE OR CREATE A COPYCAT SYNDROME?

I think they only glorify it to the people that are already in it. You'll sit and watch it for a laugh, have a few beers and you'll laugh about it and go, 'Yeah, that's great.' But if I was sitting there and I had never been to football, it wouldn't make me turn round and think, 'Oh, I think I'll go and join a Casual gang and cause some trouble.' To me, it would make me more wary of joining a mob because, unless you're in a mob and you know your own guys about you and you trust them all, you know if something happens you're not gonna get done too bad. You don't know what it's like outside the mob, so if you see fighting like that and a couple of guys getting done in, it would scare people more, I would think. If you watch a film about the mafia or a junkie, it doesn't make you say, 'Right-oh, I might go and take smack, or I might go and kill off somebody.'

WHO'S YOUR TOP FELLOW – SOUND AS A POUND – FROM YOUR OWN SUPPORTERS, WHY HE IS NOMINATED AND WHAT DID HE DO FOR YOU?

Two of our lads who sadly passed away, who would stand against anything, do anything for you, get you out of scrapes, never leave you. When the rave scene came in, we lost a lot of older guys. Willie Thompson sort of came in and organised buses, he sort of kept everyone together a wee bit. And knowing that he was there gave you confidence. And also James Milne, who passed away last year, he was a top lad.

HOW WOULD YOU DESCRIBE YOUR FIRM/ SUPPORTERS' FAN BASE, AND HAS YOUR FAN BASE CHANGED OVER TIME?

We had a few from Glasgow and Edinburgh but the main mob's just from Aberdeen. The fan base is increasing all the time, there's more supporters' clubs now springing up all over Scotland. But most of the time I've been going it was all localised, especially with the mob. But people who supported us are moving away and working, students down in Edinburgh and stuff, guys working away from home. You get decent away support in Glasgow and Edinburgh. They go to all the southern games in Scotland as well. Our average this season at home is 12,000 and 4,000 away.

WAS YOUR LIFESTYLE WITH THE CASUALS SOLELY CONFINED TO THE FOOTBALL CONTEXT OR WOULD IT HAVE BEEN THE SAME FOR YOU IN EVERYDAY STREET LIFE?

It's just football. I wouldn't be involved in fights if it weren't for football, not the scale that I have been. Personally speaking, I've got a few convictions, all for football. For me, football is the main one. Smaller-type crimes, but nothing on the scale it is with football, and even then is a breach of the peace at football worse than a breach of the peace on a Saturday night outside a disco?

EVERY ONE OF TODAY'S KNOWN HOOLIGAN FIRMS HAS A POLICE INTELLIGENCE OFFICER DEDICATED TO IT. HOW DO THE FIRMS TODAY RESPOND TO THAT? DO YOU HAVE ANY POLICE SPOTTER STORIES?

The Grampian police spotters are very well clued up and there's more than one of them. There's no real dialogue or communication with them because we just don't get on with them, we don't trust them. We know that they say things about us that aren't true to build it up; like I said before, it justifies the treatment they dish out to us. There was a time in a bar, we were waiting for Rangers to come up and we heard they were in the city. We were waiting for them to come up into the town, so every boozer waited for a shout that they were here; they were spread out all over the town waiting to see where they were gonna come.

A door got kicked in in a bar and they said, 'Come on, we're outside.' The guy who actually kicked the door in, I'd seen him before and knew he was CID. So I grabbed my friend who was going to the door, and said, 'He's a copper.' And we looked round the door and looked up the stairs towards the street and there were the police all standing there at the door. The copper had come in and challenged us to a fight outside, so they could arrest us. It was the CID.

A couple of years ago when the Rangers came, there was a wee bit of trouble in the ground. Rangers fans were throwing coins at one of Aberdeen's players and it continued and then, eventually, there was a small group of Aberdeen who looked as if they were gonna go on the pitch and do something. And then it sort of calmed down, but then they started throwing coins again when we tried to take a corner for a second time. And then two casual-dressed Grampian CIDs were down at the front. They jumped over the wall out of the area where the Casuals used to congregate in the ground, but before they could put their hats on to identify them as police, other Casuals see these two guys going on, so they all jumped over the wall as well and started running up towards the Rangers fans. It was all caught on Sky. And that was quite funny when the police turned round and saw a group of Aberdeen Casuals following them. So, really, they started it and should be jailed. They should have banning orders.

IS THERE, IN YOUR OPINION, A NEXT GENERATION OF HOOLIGAN APPRENTICES COMING THROUGH AND WILL THEY BE ANYTHING LIKE THEIR PREDECESSORS?

There was a good crop of youngsters coming through just after

Euro '96. But at that time, because a lot of other Scottish mobs were losing numbers, Aberdeen started picking up again. And when we were travelling to games all over Scotland, a lot of the time nothing was ever happening; we were getting a lot of police hassles and that and it put a lot of the youngsters off because they just thought it wasn't worth the hassle, what with police intelligence, the hassles, the arrests, the CCTV, the jail sentences. It can never be what it was, but the memories will live on.

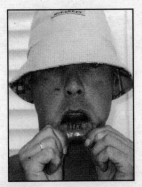

NAME: Onno
CLUB: AFC Ajax
FIRM: F-Side

**'The feeling is still
in me, the hate is
still there.'**

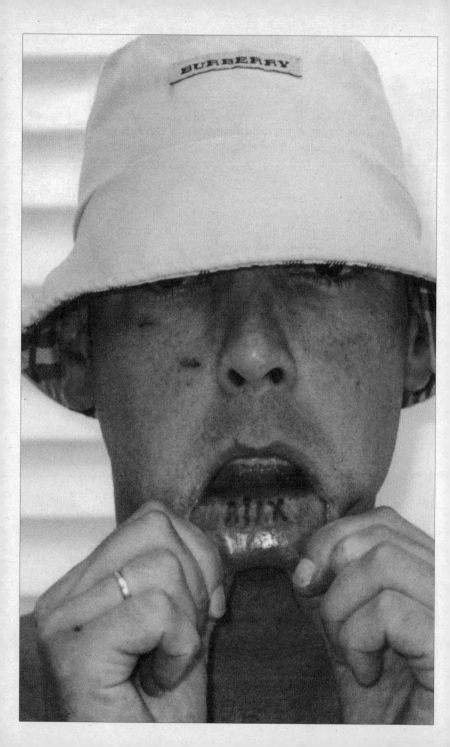

BACKGROUND AND MEET

I was picked up from Amsterdam Airport by Onno and a trusted friend and was immediately whisked away in a speeding car to a rendezvous with the F-Side, Ajax's fanatical followers – all the time watched overhead by a police helicopter. Onno warned that they would have all their firm out today. Feyenoord are their most hated rivals and it was the big game their team must not lose. They could lose every other game this season, but not this one. It runs a bit deeper than that because, off the pitch and nowhere near a football ground, they once lost their respected leader and mentor in a pre-arranged gang battle between the supporters of Ajax and Feyenoord. The outcome of this was the death of one Carlo Picornie, an event that opened Dutch people's eyes to the extent of the hooligan situation revolving around its football-loving culture.

It was in this volatile atmosphere I met the F-Siders, who are awesome in their passion to defend the honour of their football team, AFC Ajax. Onno was always going to be my first choice to give me an Ajax perspective. He was there with Carlo on that fateful day.

Born in 1969 and living in Amsterdam, he is engaged to his partner who is expecting his child. He also runs his own business and is well known and well liked by the F-Side.

WHAT HAS BEEN THE MOST LEGENDARY FIGHT OR RIOT YOUR TEAM'S SUPPORTERS HAVE BEEN INVOLVED IN?

That was against Feyenoord at Beverwijk, not in the ground, though; we met and one of our top boys was killed. It was all arranged by telephone. They were 300 … we were 150 maybe. We met just on a field. And we were stupid, we said no weapons, but they turned up with loads of weapons. They came with cars first. They were going to an away game so all their top guys were there and a lot of our top boys weren't. They knew it; it was our own stupid fault. Another fault of ours was that we weren't all together but in groups, so the first ones were fighting without the rest behind them; normally, we go together side by side. And Feyenoord had weapons like knives, machetes and things, everything you can think of.

There were police but they were so afraid, they stood and just looked, it was like Braveheart. In the beginning, the fighting was 50–50, but we had to turn back and Carlo Picornie, our best friend, was killed. He was on his knees and his last words were, 'OK, you won,' and then he was hit with a hammer on his head and, while he was on his knees, he was stabbed in the back with a knife. That's how Feyenoord fight. They knew who he was. He was a guy who doesn't walk away. It was the worst hooligan episode in Holland, ever. The newspapers called it the 'black day of football'.

There was one riot years before that, but no killings. This was like in America with the gangs, the Crips and the Bloods, this was like that. This was 1997. Even today, the memory is not forgotten. Six guys went to court for that. The authorities didn't know how to react and justice was never done.

HOW IMPORTANT WAS THE ROLE OF ALCOHOL AND DRUGS? WAS THERE ANY TIME IN YOUR EXPERIENCE EITHER HAD PARTICULAR INFLUENCE?

Everybody's drunk. There's a lot of sniffing cocaine, a lot of everything today. Every firm in Holland uses a lot of drugs, particularly because of Holland's relaxed laws. When you take it, you want to fight the world, it gives you courage.

WHO WAS THE MOST VIOLENT, CRAZY SET OF SUPPORTERS YOU EVER CAME ACROSS?

We are the craziest. Other than us, Ado Den Haag, if you're talking about drugs, they are crazy. Feyenoord in numbers, they've got more, but I can tell you we've met them and kicked their arses for the last 10–15 years, fucking kicked their arses everywhere until Beverwijk when Carlo was killed, but our firm has now fallen apart. Before that, for ten years we kicked their fucking arses up and down the country.

On one occasion at the A10 highway, we had an appointment with Feyenoord and they came. And some guys saw them and shit themselves. We had numbers but they also had more with them, samurai swords and everything. We had to run, I have to admit, we had to run. It was mental.

Before that, with Den Haag, they took drugs, like in America, PCP, they use that a lot, and were fucking mental.

ARE YOUR FIRM STILL DOING IT?

It's the younger boys now and I'm proud of them. The feeling is still in me, the hate is still there against Feyenoord, Den Haag and everything, going to the games in other countries and everything. But the youngsters are doing it now for us and my wife's pregnant and everything ... we all grow up. Our youth are fucking mental; they use weapons, they all use weapons now. It wasn't like that in my time. I can tell you I had the nicest time of my life, they fucking kicked my arse, but I kicked their arses also, but it was fighting. And now it's killing each other. For me, it was the fight. Maybe I've grown up.

HOW WOULD YOU DESCRIBE THE SITUATION WITH THE SCENE TODAY? CAN IT COMPARE WITH WHAT HAPPENED IN THE PAST, AND DO THINGS STILL GO OFF IN THE SAME WAY?

The fighting is still the same but not at the football grounds any more. There are too many police when you watch the football so in Holland we do it at raves and everything. You're not allowed to wear a football shirt, as they'll know you're a football supporter. We've taken to wearing tattoos and dressing down, but we fight each other at raves and everything. Dance Valley is the biggest open rave in Europe and we fight Den Haag, Feyenoord, everybody goes there, and we fight each other there.

HOW DID YOU GET GOING WITH A FOOTBALL FIRM, DID IT HAVE A NAME AND HOW WAS THE NAME ESTABLISHED?

Ajax's firm is the F-Side. It started when we were in Block F in the stadium and so we said we'd call it the F-Side. It was where all the hardcore guys would go every game. We just brought out a book by the F-Side which started 25 years ago, in 1979/80. We now have merchandise, which we do ourselves, we've got sweaters and shirts. We've got a big name. F-Side is Ajax's hooligan top boys.

WHAT WAS THE WORST INSTANCE OF WEAPONS BEING USED?

The night when Carlo was killed at an arranged battle that was fought on the motorway verge just outside Beverwijk. There were 300 Feyenoord there, we were half that, and they had big knives, baseball bats and hammers. Beverwijk is outside Amsterdam, about an hour by car. They went there that day to an away game so they were all together.

WHAT IS THE MOST IMPORTANT LESSON YOU LEARNED PERSONALLY DURING YOUR TIME WITH YOUR FIRM AND WOULD YOU HAVE DONE ANYTHING DIFFERENTLY?

No, it was the best time of my life. What I learned from it was stick together. I've still got all those friends. In Holland, especially Ajax, we don't call it the firm, we call it the family. We are a family. I don't have brothers or sisters or whatever, but this is my family and it was the best time of my life.

WHO WERE YOUR BIGGEST RIVALS BOTH TEAM AND FAN-WISE?

Feyenoord is the biggest rival, especially after our friend was killed, and other than that Den Haag as well. It's always been like that. We say they've got the 'second city' syndrome, because Amsterdam is the best city in the world. Feyenoord come from Rotterdam and they suck. They are about an hour from Amsterdam. There's other clubs nearer but they're the biggest rivals. And it's not only football. Even my mum, she's 70 years old, she doesn't like people from Rotterdam. They are jealous of our city; their attitude is bad ... fuck them.

WHO ARE THE TOP FIVE FIRMS OF ANY IMPORTANCE TODAY?

Feyenoord, Den Haag, FC Utrecht, PSV Eindhoven.

WHO ARE YOUR TOP FIVE FIRMS OF ALL TIME?

There's top firms everywhere. I think Poland is very strong and English firms also. In Holland, it's Den Haag and Feyenoord. As for the rest of Europe, I wouldn't know.

WHAT IS THE WORST GROUND YOU'VE EVER BEEN TO AND WHAT IS YOUR FAVOURITE GROUND?

When I was at Wembley, I think that for me was the most beautiful stadium, it was impressive, it was great to be there. And the worst is De Kuip, Feyenoord's stadium. When I was young, Wembley and the Bernabeu stadium at Real Madrid were very nice.

WHAT IS YOUR FAVOURITE FOOTBALL FASHIONWEAR AND THE WORST YOU'VE SEEN OR WORN?

Same as in England, it's Burberry and Stone Island. And the worst is Kappa because Feyenoord play in Kappa. You won't see that in Amsterdam. The F-Side is all Nike, Stone Island and Umbro.

DOES TODAY'S MODERN FOOTBALL PLAYER HAVE THE RESPECT OF THE FANS?

They're spoilt, they get too much money. Nineteen years old and no loyalty – fuck them. When they get a million more with another team, they go to another team, and there's no respect.

WHO'S THE PLAYER AND/OR MANAGER THAT WINDS YOU UP THE MOST?

Well, for a few years it was Styn Vreven, who played for FC Utrecht. He wound up all the rest of Holland because he was a mean player.

The manager is a difficult question, there are lots. At the moment it's Dick Advocaat; he was the manager of Holland and I fucking hated him and the rest of Holland did also. He messed up the national team.

WORST FOREIGN PLAYER YOU'VE SEEN AND THE BEST FOREIGN IMPORT? YOUR FAVOURITE CLUB PLAYER AND YOUR FAVOURITE OTHER PLAYER?

The worst was Nicos Machlas, he played for Vitessa, and he was a top scorer for them, then we bought him and he did nothing any more.

The best for the last few years is Christian Chivu; at the moment he's playing for AS Roma. My favourite player for Ajax? That's a difficult question because we're not doing well now. My favourite ever is Marco Van Basten and Johann Cruyff. The best player in the world ever is Johann Cruyff and Pele, of course.

FANS OFTEN TALK ABOUT THEIR FOOTBALL-GOING DAYS AS JUST BEING A LAUGH. ANY EPISODES YOU REMEMBER?

The funniest thing is that we always win in Rotterdam, at their place, always. I don't know how come but we always win there when we play Feyenoord. It fucks them up because we always win there and we make songs about it and everything.

Once, we went to Rotterdam with two buses. We all got off the buses, sent them away and we kicked their fucking arses in the square in front of their stadium and then the police came and they kicked us into the stadium to get rid of us. Not one of us had a ticket. It was fucking great. They were bleeding on the ground and we were in the stadium without a ticket.

Another time, we went to Rotterdam, about 200 of us, by train. We pulled the emergency brake maybe a kilometre or something before we got to the station and just walked into Rotterdam. The police couldn't do anything because they were waiting for us at the station. We just walked into Rotterdam and kicked everybody's arses.

YOUR OPINION ABOUT ALL-SEATER STADIUMS, TICKET PRICES AND THE COMMERCIAL ASPECT OF TODAY'S FOOTBALL INDUSTRY. DO YOU STILL FEEL FOOTBALL BELONGS TO THE FANS?

We had to move to a new stadium because the old stadium was too small. With all the seats, it sucks. You have to stand when you go to football. And I think everything's too commercial. It doesn't belong to the supporters, it's too commercial, it's not for the working-class any more.

RACISM AND RACE ISSUES HAVE BEEN PART OF FOOTBALL WITH CERTAIN CLUBS AND SETS OF SUPPORTERS AT BOTH CLUB AND INTERNATIONAL LEVEL. WHAT WAS YOUR EXPERIENCE OF THIS?

Ajax historically is a Jewish club and today we've got guys from Suriname. Carlo Picornie was from Suriname, and we've got the local guys, too. We're multicultural and Feyenoord is all Nazis. Feyenoord also sings things like, 'Hamas, Hamas, Jews on the gas ...' and they're fucking Nazis. Rotterdam was flattened in the Second World War by the Nazis and now all Nazis come from Rotterdam – how stupid can you be? They are so stupid shouting Ajax are Jews. They don't think about what they are saying and doing, that's how stupid they are.

HOW HAVE FANS FOLLOWING THE NATIONAL TEAM ABROAD BEEN TREATED, AND WHAT ARE YOUR EXPERIENCES FOLLOWING YOUR CLUB OR NATIONAL TEAM ABROAD?

As a Holland supporter, they treat you well, because there's no riots, it's a carnival spirit. But when we go with Ajax to another country it's different, because Ajax has got a name for hooliganism; the F-Side is known. But with Holland, then you're treated well.

I was arrested 18 times for fighting. When we went to Dusseldorf, I was there for 20 minutes and I was arrested. There were some Nazi skinheads from Germany and it was only shouting and they arrested all of us, just Ajax.

WOULD YOU SAY THE MEDIA 'OVER-HYPE' THE TROUBLE AND CAN YOU GIVE AN EXAMPLE OF THIS?

In Holland, they keep it quiet because, as a hooligan, you like to see the stories in the paper. They know that we like it when it's in the paper, so they try to keep it quiet. They can't sometimes, though.

SHOULD THERE BE A EUROPEAN LEAGUE?

No, because it's not fair. Real Madrid, for example, fabulous wealth. In Spain and Italy, clubs can buy bank accounts and secure wealthy loans. This is not allowed in Holland. Clubs have to show they have the money to do business in the transfer market. We would not be able to compete and wealthy clubs like Real Madrid would dominate.

DO YOU HAVE ANY VIEW ON BANNING ORDERS? DO YOU KNOW THIS FROM YOUR OWN EXPERIENCE OR THAT OF OTHERS?

I've never been banned from a stadium, but lots of friends of mine are banned from stadiums, but they get in anyway, so it doesn't work. There are lots of ways to get in, another passport or another ticket or something. They've not perfected it. You can go to every game if you want. They're totally ineffective. Both the club and the court give the ban. First, you get banned for a year or more, and the Dutch authorities, like the FA, ban you from the stadium and you go to court and they give you a fine and maybe jail or something.

HOOLIE MOVIES AND FLICKS – DO THEY GLORIFY VIOLENCE OR CREATE A COPYCAT SYNDROME?

Yeah. It's nice to see and especially the young guys, it fucks them up. I like to see those movies and documentaries and everything, but especially the youngsters they look up to you and they're going to copy it and they go for the violence then. They love it and they want to do the same. Also, they look up to the older guys and they see the movies, it winds them up, it's a combination of those things.

HOW WOULD YOU DESCRIBE YOUR FIRM/SUPPORTERS' FAN BASE, AND HAS YOUR FAN BASE CHANGED OVER TIME?

Ajax's F-Side come from all over the country. We've got a big group in Wezep, a small town far away, maybe 100km. And Ajax supporters come from everywhere because it's a big club. It's more now because it's successful. The hard core is mostly from Amsterdam.

WAS YOUR LIFESTYLE WITH F-SIDE SOLELY CONFINED TO THE FOOTBALL CONTEXT OR WOULD IT HAVE BEEN THE SAME FOR YOU IN EVERYDAY STREET LIFE?

I think I would be involved less. I think football is a perfect excuse to fight the other cities. Being at football affected my life, and it still does. I've got my own business now but two times I lost a job because I was in jail for riots and shit. I drink a lot; I've always been a happy drinker.

EVERY ONE OF TODAY'S KNOWN HOOLIGAN FIRMS HAS A POLICE INTELLIGENCE OFFICER DEDICATED TO IT. HOW DO THE FIRMS TODAY RESPOND TO THAT? DO YOU HAVE ANY POLICE SPOTTER STORIES?

There's one cop and he's specially for the F-Side and he knows us, he knows all the top boys, and we know him, and he's OK I have to admit. Sometimes he even rescues us, but he's still a cop, and we don't like them. He's OK, but there's only one and he can't help us all. And we've got a big name outside so they fuck us up anyway.

They go with us to other countries also; for example, when

Ajax plays in Germany, the Dutch Police come with us because they know the top boys. When England was playing against Holland, we were in the centre of Amsterdam and the police came, we were all in the pub drinking. The police were smashed away by England. They came in our pub and they said, 'Do something,' and then we attacked England. They asked us to help and, this is a true story, we fucking kicked their arses. England was fucking scared. This was the night before the match. I have to admit it was the only time we kicked the English because normally they kick our arses. Also, we knew we weren't going to be arrested.

IS THERE, IN YOUR OPINION, A NEXT GENERATION OF HOOLIGAN APPRENTICES COMING THROUGH AND WILL THEY BE ANYTHING LIKE THEIR PREDECESSORS?

The next generation I think are worse because they all have weapons now. It's a matter of kill or be killed now, and I think it's not nice any more. They're called F-Side Youth. It's the F-Side, but it's the next generation, and I don't agree because I don't want to stab people. But now it goes that way. All my scars and shit. OK, I've been hit and I hit people. But now it's all knives and weapons and shit and I don't like it. I had the best time of my life because it was fists and, OK, they kicked my arse sometimes. But now you have to look for knives and shit and it's not nice any more. I'm not a killer, I'm not a murderer, but it's gone too far now; that's my personal opinion.

NAME: Spenna
CLUB: Aston Villa
FIRM: Villa Youth

**'The hatred
is blues.'**

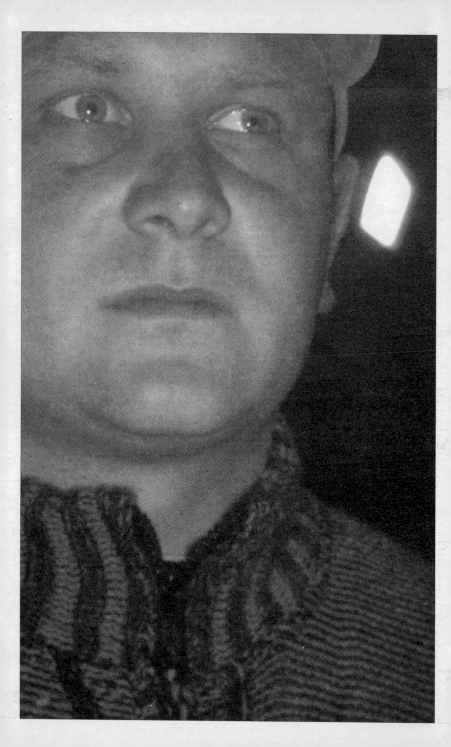

BACKGROUND AND MEET

Villa held an interest for me, not just because they play in claret and blue, but because there were that many Midland clubs with active firms. What was Villa's say and shout? Once again, I used the 2004 European Championships as a point of contact. I'd heard Villa had a firm that went to all England games. I made a connection and, when I got back, was given the name 'Spenna'.

The day I chose to do the interview was dodgy. During the morning, upon arriving at Birmingham's Bullring, my Zulu contact hinted that some of their youth weren't travelling to the Newcastle game and would remain in town that day. My afternoon destination was on to the Baggies and Section Five Squad, who, in turn, informed me of the delightful result they had with the Villa mob recently. By the time I made my way back to New Street Station to meet the Villa contact, the traffic was at gridlock due to police attempting to contain fighting Wolves and Cardiff fans.

I eventually met up with Spenna and went with him to a deliberately chosen quiet pub to do this interview. All of a sudden, around 30 Villa youth burst in, adrenalin up, stating that it had nearly gone off after a game of cat and mouse with their most hated rivals, the Blues, who were apparently at one point in a pub across the road – only CCTV was holding both parties back. So apologies if this chapter appears rushed!

Spenna was born in 1972 and has a City & Guilds in Bricklaying and Tarmacing, is married and remembers his first game, when the Villa beat Ipswich in the League in 1981.

WHAT HAS BEEN THE MOST LEGENDARY FIGHT OR RIOT YOUR TEAM'S SUPPORTERS HAVE BEEN INVOLVED IN?

That's got to be West Brom early in the season or Rocky Lane with Birmingham. In that row with West Brom, people were on the phones all day to our firm. They were slating us at first sight, saying that we weren't turning up, it being a one o'clock kick-off. And we said we were gonna be there, but were covered in by the Old Bill in Handsworth, but then we left and went our way to different pubs. We then phoned West Brom up and they were covered in, too. We didn't think they'd come; I've never known them to turn up before. But they did come this time ... with bats, sticks, knives, everything. I've never seen so many tools in my life.

Villa ran out of the pub on to the central reservation, chasing them at first, but then we clocked the Old Bill with cameras and, just like Rocky Lane, the camera was facing Villa again. As we chased them, they came back with bats and everything, about 30–35 of them. They caught us on the back foot a bit to be fair. None of our lads had bats and blades and poles and stuff.

Then we all clubbed together and we all ran them off in the end. And then the police steamed in. They just came walking down the hill, so I think the Old Bill followed them. Fair play, I've never seen them before, they were proper game but I wasn't happy about all the sticks and bars and bats and everything like that. It went on for about eight to ten minutes. We weren't happy because we could have come out with those things ourselves, but we didn't because a lot of lads said 'no tools' on the phone. We phoned them up after and said, 'What's with all the tools then?' And they blamed it on some lads who had just followed them down with tools.

Rocky Lane was in 2002, the first season Birmingham were up in the Premiership. We were in the pub and they kept phoning and saying they were coming and then they didn't. And in the end, a few of our lads went out of the pub and said, 'They're here,' and they just came up the road shouting, 'Zulus!' As they stormed into us we just stood firm and had it toe-to-toe all day long. It was more of a stand-off than anything, but it was a bit naughty because they were tooled up again. A few of the Villa were tooled up as well, to be fair. Six of one, really.

WHO WAS THE MOST VIOLENT, CRAZY SET OF SUPPORTERS YOU EVER CAME ACROSS?

Probably one of them is Hibs – I came across them in the late '80s when I was 16 when we played Hibernian in a friendly. They were nuts. Hibs are a load of headcases, to be fair. And probably Man U in the Cup – just nuts. They beat us 3–2 and Van Nistelrooy scored and they were all on the pitch. About four years ago in the FA Cup, their fans had 10,000 tickets. Leicester as well, that can be quite heavy.

ARE YOUR FIRM STILL DOING IT?

I wouldn't say it's over ... would you? A lot of the lads are all banned and they can't get in the grounds, but they're still active. There's a lot of young up-and-coming kids now. Villa has got an active firm but they pick the games, occasional ones; they're not there all the time. If the off is guaranteed, we will show; if not, we'll probably get lashed instead.

HOW WOULD YOU DESCRIBE THE SITUATION WITH THE SCENE TODAY? CAN IT COMPARE WITH WHAT HAPPENED IN THE PAST, AND DO THINGS STILL GO OFF IN THE SAME WAY?

It's more organised, it's offside, it's in pubs, stuff like that. The perfect incident recently was Birmingham and West Brom. It's more organised. But I suppose in the '80s–'90s it was more round the grounds, but you don't really get that now, except the other week with QPR, where we had a big row at the ground on a Wednesday night after playing in the Carling Cup. Fair play to them, it was a bigger game for them than us.

HOW DID YOU GET GOING WITH A FOOTBALL FIRM, DID IT HAVE A NAME AND HOW WAS THE NAME ESTABLISHED?

I'm not sure how it was established to be honest. They don't really call themselves anything. In the '70s it used to be called the Steamers, then it was called the C-Crew in the early '80s, then Villa Youth from the mid-'80s to the early '90s, and then Villa Hard Core, that's what they call themselves now. God knows how they got their names. The police called them the 'hard core', like 30–40, usually 60–80 on a good day, and I think that's how the name come around – Hard Core. But you've still got bits and bobs of the others who still show now and again, i.e. a Cup Final, semi-final, or if we go to Europe. If you're playing a big firm, they'll show now and again.

WHAT WAS THE WORST INSTANCE OF WEAPONS BEING USED?

West Brom, without a doubt. Poles, bats, knives, everything. Rocky Lane as well. Manifold tools, anything, wheel trims spinning at our heads. There was a serious injury at West Brom. One lad got hit over the head with a pole, split his head virtually clean in two. I think it was one of them little telescopic ones and his head just went – it was all over for him.

WHAT IS THE MOST IMPORTANT LESSON YOU LEARNED PERSONALLY DURING YOUR TIME WITH YOUR FIRM AND WOULD YOU DO ANYTHING DIFFERENTLY?

I suppose it makes you not scared. But if I've learned anything about it, I've probably been lucky – lucky I ain't been cut or anything. I mean the bottles have been thrown, but if I could do it again, I suppose Villa need to be a bit more organised. Sometimes they're not the most organised firm. But they just love the piss. But I think I've learned that I've been lucky.

WHO WERE YOUR BIGGEST RIVALS BOTH TEAM AND FAN-WISE?

Blues, innit. It's gotta be Blues without a doubt. We live in South Birmingham, only two junctions from the motorway, which is more a Birmingham City fans area. Villa's is north Birmingham. And, without a doubt, the banter goes on even not on match days. There's fighting in Birmingham city centre when they don't even play each other, or even out of season, all the time. It is Blues.

The biggest Midland derby's always been classed as Villa and Albion, at least it was, because they are the two closest grounds. They hate Villa, there's no question. You get pre-season friendlies, you'd get 30,000 fans there and you could feel the hatred in the ground. Villa and West Brom are the two closest. The closest ground to where we live is West Brom. My granddad always classed Villa and West Brom as the big derby and my dad does still – but the hatred? There's not really that much hatred with Villa and West Brom, the hatred is Blues, especially for us because we live in a Blues area really.

WHO ARE THE TOP FIVE FIRMS OF ANY IMPORTANCE TODAY?

Man U without a doubt. Leicester, half decent, a few dabbles with Leicester. I've got to admit after the Albion, all right I know they were tooled up, but fucking hell, you've got to give them the credit. I actually haven't come in contact with them, but the lads told me one time when we played Spurs, they were good. I'd have to go for Spurs, to be honest. So – Man U, Leicester, Cardiff, Millwall and Spurs.

WHO ARE YOUR TOP FIVE FIRMS OF ALL TIME?

Again, we ain't had much contact, but I think your lot, to be fair – West Ham, Cardiff, Millwall, I'd have to put Leeds there. I've got to go for Man U. So top five – Man U, West Ham, Millwall, Leeds and Cardiff.

WHAT IS THE WORST GROUND YOU'VE EVER BEEN TO AND WHAT IS YOUR FAVOURITE GROUND?

The worst ground me personally was Barnsley and also Plough Lane, Wimbledon's former ground.

My favourite ground? I always liked going to Hillsborough, Sheffield Wednesday. Old Trafford's up there, but my favourite's Hillsborough. San Siro – went there, that's my favourite ground abroad. Inter Milan and AC Milan play there.

WHAT IS YOUR FAVOURITE FOOTBALL FASHIONWEAR AND THE WORST YOU'VE SEEN OR WORN?

Stone Island, without a doubt. I've got a brown Stone Island jacket and they all take the piss, calling it a Paddington Bear — bastards. I love Stone Island. The worst I've ever seen is my mate's fucking stupid cord coat he used to wear down the football with two buttons missing, just one done up all the time. That's the worst I've ever seen.

WHAT IS THE WORST KIT YOU'VE SEEN A TEAM IN AND WHAT WOULD BE YOUR OWN CLUB'S BEST EVER STRIP?

The worst kit I've ever seen is Villa in the green and black. It's green-and-black stripes with a red pinstripe. This would be '94, our away kit. Black shorts, green socks. Horrible. Fucking nowhere near Villa's colours. And my favourite kit is when we won the European Cup Final, all white with a claret pinstripe and the badge in the middle, 1982. That's my favourite kit; nice kit that was.

DOES TODAY'S MODERN FOOTBALL PLAYER HAVE THE RESPECT OF THE FANS?

I view the footballer of today as a complete and utter fucking poser. To be honest, I think a lot of them are in it for the money. Some of them have got the respect of the fans if they're working hard, but a lot of them haven't to be honest, because we just think they're in for the money. One of them's got to be Stan Collymore. I don't think he tried hard at all for us. Other players, you see them with their socks right above their knees like they're a bleeding pair of tights. We just think it's a posing game now.

WHO'S THE PLAYER AND/OR MANAGER THAT WINDS YOU UP THE MOST?

Robbie Savage, who played for Blues. He called me a prick when we played them. The ball landed in the crowd when we played them last season and it landed on me lap and I tried to throw it over him but my mates say I threw it back to him and from that

Blues scored and got the equaliser in the fourth minute of injury time. And Alex Ferguson – just don't like him.

WORST FOREIGN PLAYER YOU'VE SEEN AND THE BEST FOREIGN IMPORT? YOUR FAVOURITE CLUB PLAYER AND YOUR FAVOURITE OTHER PLAYER?

Worst foreign player plays for us – Ulises de la Cruz; he's crap. He's at Villa at the minute. We call him Useless de la Cruz.

The best foreign import nowadays I'd say Van Nistelrooy or Henry, one of them two. Cantona's another one. I'd have to go with Henry now and Cantona in the past.

Favourite club player of all time for Villa, Tony Morley, for me.

Favourite player of any other club in the world, of all time, it's gotta be Maradona for me.

FANS OFTEN TALK ABOUT THEIR FOOTBALL-GOING DAYS AS JUST BEING A LAUGH. ANY EPISODES YOU REMEMBER?

We all went to Munich when England beat them 5–1 and we got the one train and then we had to change over trains on the way back from Munich to the Czech Republic. As we got off the first train to swap trains, we were walking round to the other train and our mate said, 'I've forgot my cap.' So he's gone back down the platform and back up to get his cap. With that, the train we're now on is pulling away and they're not like the stations here. So he came back down and all of us are in the train pulling off, speeding away, and he was running up the track after us and he still never got his cap, and he never got the train. That's the funniest thing I've ever seen. Running up the track in the middle of Munich. It was a Lacoste cap, he'd only just bought it. And he never got it back.

Another time, we went to Madrid in the Cup and a couple of these Spanish louts started on this young Villa lad, he was only about 18 or 19 – Athletico Madrid. So my mate's gone over there and there's this one big Spanish guy and he's run over to the biggest bloke and whacked him. There must have been about 100 Spanish and they're all chasing him down the road trying to kick him down and he's running like fuck. And me and him were just in bits because – you ever see David Pleat when his team won the Cup Final? He was running like that. These blokes were kicking him and he's running down the road with his legs flaying in the air. Me and him just couldn't do anything, we were just rolling on the floor, it was so funny. You had to be there.

YOUR OPINION ABOUT ALL-SEATER STADIUMS, TICKET PRICES AND THE COMMERCIAL ASPECT OF TODAY'S FOOTBALL INDUSTRY. DO YOU STILL FEEL FOOTBALL BELONGS TO THE FANS?

It's just changed. The stadiums I think took a lot of the atmosphere out of it. Most people try and stand up and the stewards are always bollocking you for standing up; you've got to sit down. I don't like all-seater stadiums. I think we'd all have the terracing back tomorrow.

No, I don't think football belongs to the fans. There's too much money involved, to be honest.

RACISM AND RACE ISSUES HAVE BEEN PART OF FOOTBALL WITH CERTAIN CLUBS AND SETS OF SUPPORTERS AT BOTH CLUB AND INTERNATIONAL LEVEL. WHAT WAS YOUR EXPERIENCE OF THIS?

I never really experienced any racism. Sometimes Villa fans get accused of it, but that's mainly coming from Blues fans who tend to be more black. But there's no racism that I know about. I don't know much about Combat 18. We get accused by the Blues, they say we're Combat 18 because their firm's predominantly black. But the people I know and the people I talk to, whether there's other elements I don't know, but certainly none of the firm or the lads are Combat 18.

Birmingham's crew were the apex in the '70s when it was a predominantly white firm they had. And then the early '80s when the Zulus come into it and a lot of the black lads started following Blues. We're sick of these accusations because there's black lads that run with us. We don't know where they get it from. And there's Asians that run with us. It might be because a lot of Villa supporters follow England, but, like I said, the people I know, certainly none of this lot are Combat 18. One of my best mates is a Zúlu for a start.

HOW HAVE FANS FOLLOWING THE NATIONAL TEAM ABROAD BEEN TREATED, AND WHAT ARE YOUR EXPERIENCES FOLLOWING YOUR CLUB OR NATIONAL TEAM ABROAD?

When the Villa are abroad there's a heavy police presence because we're English, I suppose. We're not one of the most notorious fans in England, but it's just one of them things.

WOULD YOU SAY THE MEDIA 'OVER-HYPE' THE TROUBLE AND CAN YOU GIVE AN EXAMPLE OF THIS?

Yeah, definitely, without a doubt. They just give England bad press and that, that's all it is. It's just my opinion.

SHOULD CELTIC AND RANGERS BE ALLOWED TO JOIN THE ENGLISH PREMIERSHIP OR NATIONWIDE LEAGUES?

I don't know. I think it would be good for the game because they're both massive clubs. I think it'd kick off definitely with the fans they bring and the numbers. I think they should go straight in the Premier.

DO YOU HAVE ANY VIEW ON BANNING ORDERS? DO YOU KNOW THIS FROM YOUR OWN EXPERIENCE OR THAT OF OTHERS?

With the banning orders, they ban them a couple of hours before the game, and they ban them a couple of hours after. I suppose they're effective and fair if they think they're gonna cause something in the ground.

I don't know that from my own experience, no, but I know others who have been banned, yeah.

HOOLIE MOVIES AND FLICKS – DO THEY GLORIFY VIOLENCE OR CREATE A COPYCAT SYNDROME?

Again, I don't think any of it's realistic, except for Football Factory, to be honest. That was half-decent, but I don't think it was anything like the proper stuff. I've seen Football Factory, watched The Firm and all that sort of stuff. I think they glorify violence, I think sometimes it's a bit too heavy because nine times out of ten it's just a stand-off more than anything to be fair, and the average rows last probably about 30 seconds. So, yeah, I think it's glorified.

HOW WOULD YOU DESCRIBE YOUR FIRM/SUPPORTERS' FAN BASE, AND HAS YOUR FAN BASE CHANGED OVER TIME?

No, I don't think it's changed. The Villa fan base is obviously a lot from Birmingham. But you've got another big club in Birmingham City. In Birmingham itself, the main Villa areas are Kingstanding, Erdington, Castle Vale, places like that. And just on the outskirts there's a lot of Villa, i.e. Tamworth, Sutton Coldfield, places like that which are more Villa. The Birmingham areas tend to be like Northfield, King's Norton, King's Heath. Erdington is probably the main Villa area. I would say it's still the same today. North Birmingham tends to be more Villa fans on the whole and South Birmingham tends to be City. It's very much a Midlands club.

WAS YOUR LIFESTYLE WITH THE VILLA SOLELY CONFINED TO THE FOOTBALL CONTEXT OR WOULD IT HAVE BEEN THE SAME FOR YOU IN EVERYDAY STREET LIFE?

No, I don't think I would be part of it if it weren't for football. Like I said, I'm not there week in, week out. I know all the lads and I've been in my fair share of scrapes, but if it weren't for football I don't think I'd be in any trouble, no, to be fair. There's something that happens down the football that just triggers it off, not just me personally, but I think a lot of supporters. I think I speak for a lot of supporters. To tell the truth, I am glad I'm out of it now.

EVERY ONE OF TODAY'S KNOWN HOOLIGAN FIRMS HAS A POLICE INTELLIGENCE OFFICER DEDICATED TO IT. HOW DO THE FIRMS TODAY RESPOND TO THAT? DO YOU HAVE ANY POLICE SPOTTER STORIES?

I don't know about all the other spotters, but we talk to them. When they come in the pubs and that, we talk to them. I know their faces, but I don't know their names. There's three or four that come in the pub. We know we're followed, yeah. I think every firm does. Not really got any stories. They just come in the pub, that's all really.

IS THERE, IN YOUR OPINION, A NEXT GENERATION OF HOOLIGAN APPRENTICES COMING THROUGH AND WILL THEY BE ANYTHING LIKE THEIR PREDECESSORS?

The young lads coming through are game as fuck, they're really – I've never known bottle like it in my life, they're unbelievable. Yeah, a lot are coming through and they're top lads. Whether they measure up or not, that's a different story. Because when you had the old days of scrapping round the grounds, in the grounds and stuff, you can't do that now, there's too many cameras and that. It's not dying off, we have a young, active firm, but like I say they have to go off-site and do it. They haven't really got a name, but probably would call themselves Hard Core.

NAME: 'Brains'
CLUB: Birmingham City
FIRM: The Zulus

'They just want me off the streets.'

BACKGROUND AND MEET

'Keep right on to the end of the road ...' the Blues fans all sing. They surely don't mean the road and roundabout where it all kicked off once when my team, West Ham, got relegated at their place last game of the season. So maybe I picked the wrong time to return to Birmingham so soon after what was a real toe-to-toe. Nevertheless, I had met a southern-based Brummie exile who was proper 'Old Skool'. Brendon more than knew all the right players and fixed me up a meet at a Blues home game.

I am heading up the hill to the ground with both pavements and the road full up with Brummies as the pubs empty out. I'm getting some looks and a few questions get asked. It took only the mention of a certain man's name and they walked away to check me out on their mobiles. People standing on corners of roads would nod me on. It appeared obvious to me I was being invited to the heart of Zulu country. None more evident than when entering D-section with all the right faces; they all got searched apart from me.

I enjoyed the company of the particular people I met that day. Showed me a lot of respect, introducing me and pointing out certain things to me. Fine, but I was here for a reason. But their main man, a name everyone knows in football, explained he had plans for his own book and decided to decline mine. Instead, they said they'd nominate a real character to do the Blues chapter. I said who? Then they just all looked at Brains.

Brains's real name is Darren McCormick. Born in World Cup-winning year, 1966, left school at 16 with GCSEs to become a bricklayer. Works for himself now and has a girlfriend of 15 years' standing, plus two kids. He remembers his first game was with his father, at home to Leeds, 1975.

WHAT HAS BEEN THE MOST LEGENDARY FIGHT OR RIOT YOUR TEAM'S SUPPORTERS HAVE BEEN INVOLVED IN?

It's got to be Leeds. The time on the pitch with the Old Bill. That's got to be the most legendary one, but there's been numerous ones. That's when the wall went down, yeah, when a young kid died. But it was mainly with the Old Bill that was.

But there's been other occasions. West Ham on the pitch in the Cup. I can remember when they came in our seats. Stoke, when we came on the pitch in order to attack their end. Loads.

The one that sticks in me mind is Leeds, 1985. It was all day long. From ten o'clock in the morning 'til eight o'clock at night. It was just one of those games. Last game of the season. The year the Bradford fire overshadowed it, I remember. It was bad, terrible.

In the morning, Birmingham done a boozer full of Leeds, the Australian Bar. The actual trouble on the pitch was mainly Birmingham with the Old Bill, and Leeds with the Old Bill. On the pitch, we never actually got at each other. Leeds started pulling the canteen down and then Birmingham come on the pitch to try and get at them and the Old Bill walked the line. Leeds were in the away end, the Tilton Road. Birmingham's mob was all over, the Kop, the Tilton, the seats.

Another one – although, personally, I don't think it was one of our better ones, but it is talked about by other firms – was at an England game. We were in a boozer in some part of Scotland and we found out Villa was in this other pub, so about 70–80 of us marched up there and got through the doors and got straight into them. And there weren't enough exits for them to get out of. But the fans who'd gone upstairs they copped it, as well as the ones downstairs. Just chaos, up, down, everywhere. Tables, chairs, windows, glass – the lot. A packed pub and everyone all England, but it was Villa we wanted and there was nowhere for them to go. Then it was all over – as fast as it started. Yeah, it was OK, but we've had better ones than that.

HOW IMPORTANT WAS THE ROLE OF ALCOHOL AND DRUGS? WAS THERE ANY TIME IN YOUR EXPERIENCE EITHER HAD PARTICULAR INFLUENCE?

Drink's really not affected me personally, because if I'm gonna do something I'll do it with drink or without. There was an incident a few years ago, our first time back playing Millwall at the old Den. There was a lot of drinking going down there on the train and plenty more consumed when we all met up at Victoria.

We all made our way over to Millwall. There was a good 700 of us. A few of the lads who were well pissed decided to bring a few chair legs from the pub we were drinking in, pool balls, bottles, etc. We got to a tunnel by Millwall, where the Old Bill had us and took us to the ground. Once in the ground, the game got under way and a couple of the lads who were pissed decided to go round collecting newspapers. Everyone was wondering what they were for. Anyway, a short while later, smoke came billowing from the back of the stand – they'd only set the canteen and refreshments bar on fire.

WHO WAS THE MOST VIOLENT, CRAZY SET OF SUPPORTERS YOU EVER CAME ACROSS?

The maddest were a team called Perugia in Italy. Yeah, I went there in the Anglo-Italian Cup a few years ago with Birmingham and that was pretty mad. It wasn't just them, we had it with the fairground workers, the Old Bill – it was pretty good. They was going round the ground on a moped, one of them was on the back of a moped picking Birmingham fans off.

We had a firm out there of about 40 and the lads had obviously been on the drink. They would come in behind you and be lumping you one. So, after the game, we'd got it together – 30 or 40 – of us, and it went proper. There was a thing called the Lunar Park which is like a fairground. Suddenly, it emptied of all these fairground workers and we were faced with this mob of about 60–70 Perugians; it was pretty mad, it did get a bit scary at times. But we got the Old Bill as well to contend with. It must have gone off for a good 20 minutes after the game. They started to come at us from all angles and they was proper game.

One of our lads, Jimmy S, crashed a dustbin off one of their boys' heads and took him straight out the game. The Old Bill came and got in between us all, but it still didn't stop. In the end, they all turned on us, attacking us. They backed us off up the road. The Old Bill started nicking some of us and handcuffing us behind these little trees. The poor cunts who got handcuffed got battered by the Perugia mob. Once the Old Bill had contained it all and got back to the boys they'd cuffed and seen the state they were in, they couldn't really nick them, could they? Anyway, we got an armed escort back to the hotel and got the fuck out of there in the early hours of the morning.

ARE YOUR FIRM STILL DOING IT?

I'd say we're not as active as we were. Obviously for the big games, you know, a few of the old faces turn out and what not, but it'll never be on the scale that it was years ago. I wouldn't have thought there'd be a resurgence. But for certain games, it's still a pretty serious firm, though. All the old faces are back out. A few games in the last few years that have stuck out – Villa obviously – first game back in the Premiership. Tottenham away last season.

When the fixtures come out at the start of the season, you pick your fixture up and you think right we'll have that one, that one and that one. There's usually about three or four games out of the season you say, 'Right, that's what we'll do.' For the Villa game, our first meeting in the league for years, all our lads had met up in various pubs around the city. We had about four different mobs out that day. But there was about 30 Blues lads who had been drinking in a pub in Nechells over Villa way. When about 150 Villa started to come to the pub, the 30 Blues lads came outside and had it with them. No one got done and no one run. The Old Bill just stood back and filmed it all. I can't really say much more about this incident as there are still court cases pending. But for me, personally, I've thrown the towel in now after my last prison sentence for attacking the Old Bill against Barnsley in the play-offs. They were good old days, never to be replaced, but I'm not going down there to get involved, to be a target for the Old Bill.

HOW WOULD YOU DESCRIBE THE SITUATION WITH THE SCENE TODAY? CAN IT COMPARE WITH WHAT HAPPENED IN THE PAST, AND DO THINGS STILL GO OFF IN THE SAME WAY?

I think today it's got to be extra special to be able to go and have a bit. The police have proper got it sewn up I think, with cameras, the intelligence what they've got, the football intelligence. Me, personally, the football intelligence came from my local Old Bill station. So I'm pretty well known. West Midlands Police, Stechford football intelligence. Mainly, the organisation part of it goes out the window a bit these days. It's just more chance. Because the Old Bill have got it pretty that much sewn up that if you don't know what you're doing, they don't. You know, when you're making plans, there's always somebody that can let the cat out the bag. Also, for the Old Bill, it seems easy for them to know where you are and where you're meeting and that these days, we make their job easier for them, you know, hanging round outside the boozers instead of getting everybody in there and police are standing on the corners and all that. I think we don't help ourselves. You've got people standing outside on mobile phones and all that. Keep it simple – I think that's the best way.

HOW DID YOU GET GOING WITH A FOOTBALL FIRM, DID IT HAVE A NAME AND HOW WAS THE NAME ESTABLISHED?

I grew up on a tough housing estate, Chelmsley Wood, and they had their own firm there – well, it was a boozer called The Happy Trooper. They were known as the Trooper Mob and it was in the old days of the skinheads and I used to tag along with them being from Chelmsley Wood and they were a pretty naughty firm in their day. It's round about 1978–79, that era.

Birmingham had its own firm, but nothing as an organised firm on the football scale. They were too busy fighting each other in the matches in them days. It was in-house fighting. And then, one day, it all stopped and everybody all joined up together. They didn't join up as the Zulus. There was a young firm at the time called the Apex in the earlier days. They weren't that good. Apex was just a name. Came from one of the lads in the building game, it was his building firm. It got established and then the next thing you know the name Zulus come after that.

Zulus got their name at the Man City game; it started off as a rugby song, believe it or not. We was at Maine Road one year and there was all singing in the ground, you know. I think we was getting beat 4 or 5–0 like we always used to do, and a couple of lads started singing this rugby song: 'Get them down, you Zulu warriors ...' which was just started off as a crack like. Then, after the game, when you used to come out at Man City, you've got all the back streets and whatever as you're in what is Moss Side. We've all come out the ground and somebody among the mob we was with shouted 'Zulu' and it echoed all down the entries and it sounded as though there was hundreds and hundreds of us coming and everyone shouting 'Zulu'. And that's how it took off, the name Zulu Warriors, from a rugby song.

WHAT WAS THE WORST INSTANCE OF WEAPONS BEING USED?

I can't really say myself that we've ever used weapons or people I've mixed with at football matches. There were a couple of young lads a couple of years ago in the '80s had a habit of carrying Stanley knives and I think there were one or two people who got cut up in them days. I think you've got to go back to the '80s with the Scousers with the old Stanley knives. That's my worst memory.

There was a time when Birmingham went to Millwall, I think, and they hung around 'til half-six, seven o'clock on the night for Millwall to get the meet up. But when they finally come through the tunnel at London Bridge, I think Millwall had everything – hammers, axes. The word was there was a shooter involved. I don't know how true it is as I wasn't there myself so I can't comment on it.

WHO WERE YOUR BIGGEST RIVALS BOTH TEAM AND FAN-WISE?

Team-wise, I'd say Villa and, possibly, fan-wise as well because of the local rivalry.

WHO ARE THE TOP FIVE FIRMS OF ANY IMPORTANCE TODAY?

I can only go by my own experience with Birmingham in the big games for us, i.e. like Tottenham, Man United ... and Middlesbrough seem to be getting excited with themselves lately. Cardiff and Hull – I was pretty impressed with Hull. I went to Hull recently.

WHO ARE YOUR TOP FIVE FIRMS OF ALL TIME?

Millwall, West Ham, Leeds, Cardiff, Portsmouth are the five, but Forest and Stoke were pretty good in their day.

WHAT IS THE WORST GROUND YOU'VE EVER BEEN TO AND WHAT IS YOUR FAVOURITE GROUND?

Them lower divisions, there are absolutely loads of them, like Macclesfield and Chester, when it was the old stadium, you know proper shit-holes. Newcastle has got to be one of the best grounds I've been to in recent years. You get up there and you're up in the air. I like Newcastle stadium. The atmosphere, you know, and all that at Newcastle – they've always had the atmosphere. And true supporters, you know, they're all Geordies. They don't come from here, there and everywhere. They're all from Newcastle. Hardy supporters.

Thinking of another shit-hole, I must add Huddersfield's old ground. And what used to stick out in my mind at Huddersfield, you used to get all their fans who used to sing at one end, they'd be behind the goal. For the first half they'd be behind the one goal, and then they'd go along and they'd start cheering behind the other goal in the second half.

WHAT IS YOUR FAVOURITE FOOTBALL FASHIONWEAR AND THE WORST YOU'VE SEEN OR WORN?

My favourite one was the old green flying jackets with the old Lonsdale T-shirts underneath and a pair of old Adidas suede trainers. The old Nike, Wimbledons.

The worst I've seen is probably the old drainpipe jeans. I think

Birmingham had a mad craze of leg-warmers. It brought it back to me, reminded me what a lot of cunts we must have looked then. The strap-over trainers, leg-warmers and tight jeans. And Slazenger jumpers. That's got to be one of the worst.

WHAT IS THE WORST KIT YOU'VE SEEN A TEAM IN AND WHAT WOULD BE YOUR OWN CLUB'S BEST EVER STRIP?

The worst football kit I've ever seen has gotta be the old Coventry away kit, the old chocolate brown one. That's got to be the worst kit I've ever seen. It was in the early '70s.

Favourite of me own club's gotta be the old Birmingham penguin strip – blue with the big white stripe down the middle, 1976/77. They brought it back out a few years ago, but I don't think it really took off. It was all jazzed up a bit.

DOES TODAY'S MODERN FOOTBALL PLAYER HAVE THE RESPECT OF THE FANS?

I don't think they've got the respect of the fans at all today. I wouldn't go as far as to say it's the footballers themselves, I just think it's football in general, you know. With the advertising and sponsorships and all that that's involved now. I remember the old days end of season, you know, you used to be able to run on the pitch and try and grab a shirt off one of the old players. And now all seats go to the sponsors. You know, the shirts, you can't get near them. You know, if you ask a player for his top these days for your kid or something, it always seems to be saved for the sponsor.

WHO'S THE PLAYER AND/OR MANAGER THAT WINDS YOU UP THE MOST?

Probably Lee Hendrie of the Villa. He gets under my skin a bit. You know, every time there's a fracas on the pitch he always seems to be getting involved as though he's the Mr Big Man or something, you know. All the pushing and shoving and that. And, on a couple of occasions, I've seen him out and he's very arrogant.

Manager? It used to be Mark McGee when he was at Wolves. Just a horrible man – I hate him. Horrible.

WORST FOREIGN PLAYER YOU'VE SEEN AND THE BEST FOREIGN IMPORT? YOUR FAVOURITE CLUB PLAYER AND YOUR FAVOURITE OTHER PLAYER?

Eric Cantona was pretty good. We had a player called Alberto Tarrentino at Birmingham. He was absolutely awful. He come from Argentina. He was an Argentina cup-winner from '78. He was awful. He just couldn't adapt to English football. I don't think he was a bad player, but he just couldn't adapt. Mind you, we've had a couple as well from Holland, a player called Bud Brochen, signed from Willem. I think he goes up there alongside. He was pretty awful.

Favourite club player – I've got one or two. I've got a personal friend who played for Birmingham – Paul Tait. He scored the Golden Goal at Wembley in the Auto Windscreens Final and revealed that famous 'Shit on the Villa' T-shirt when he took his football top off. I've still got the top. Football-wise, I'd say Trevor Francis and Mark Dennis are my favourites.

FANS OFTEN TALK ABOUT THEIR FOOTBALL-GOING DAYS AS JUST BEING A LAUGH. ANY EPISODES YOU REMEMBER?

Funny story? There's one years ago. Birmingham and West Ham were in Scotland. There was a mob of Birmingham in the boozer but Birmingham and West Ham had the two biggest mobs up there. It was an international.

It all surrounds a kid called Avril. Birmingham was in one boozer, West Ham was in another boozer. Obviously, West Ham had come up to have a go at Birmingham. There must have been about 200 either side. And this kid Avril, one of the lads, was outside on a wall having a drink and, as I've looked into the distance, and seen West Ham come up the road, Avril went into the middle of the road, pulled his trousers down and just sat in the middle of the road having a shit.

As the two firms have come out the boozer, they've all cracked up laughing and, honest to God, nothing ever kicked off. That incident of him having a shit in the middle of the road – a Birmingham lad. I ain't got a clue why he's having a shit. No one knows why. He had a habit of doing it everywhere.

I can remember we went to Bournemouth in a pre-season friendly and playing on jukebox at the time – it was Number 1 in the charts I think – Chris de Burgh's 'Lady in Red'. And we were all in this boozer called the Lansdowne in Bournemouth and Avril had this habit of shitting everywhere. It was just his way of having a crack, I suppose. And we were in this boozer and every time the birds kept putting this record on, 'Lady in Red', it was drowned out by a loud rendition of 'Keep Right on 'til the End of the Road' from all us lot. So all the money they was putting in the jukebox was obviously getting wasted.

Then these Scouse birds came in. Anyway, as the night's gone along, same kid again, Avril, was obviously chatting up these birds with his mates and one of them was sick and he'd been sick in her handbag and, what's happened, the bird's said, 'You've ruined me handbag.' And then she emptied all the contents out, the lipstick and whatever, and threw her handbag away. About half-an-hour later, I was up the bar, gone up to get a pint. I see this lipstick on the bar with a turd on the end of it. Avril up to his old tricks again. He doesn't get involved in the football lark any more.

YOUR OPINION ABOUT ALL-SEATER STADIUMS, TICKET PRICES AND THE COMMERCIAL ASPECT OF TODAY'S FOOTBALL INDUSTRY. DO YOU STILL FEEL FOOTBALL BELONGS TO THE FANS?
It's gone all commercialised now. It's down to all the money people and you know if you've got money – it's like at Old Trafford. When I was there the other season, all the corporates and the shirt-and-tie brigade seem to get all the tickets and the ones who go week in and week out had lost out on tickets, you know, to these people. The state-of-the-art football stadiums, there's no atmosphere, I don't think, not like the old days.

Obviously, with Heysel and one or two others, a lot of people suffered for it. A lot of people keep beating on about the atmosphere we've got there and you pick the paper up and they say the fans are worth a goal start. For me, personally, going back over the years, the atmosphere that they've got there now is nothing compared to what it's been over the years.

RACISM AND RACE ISSUES HAVE BEEN PART OF FOOTBALL WITH CERTAIN CLUBS AND SETS OF SUPPORTERS AT BOTH CLUB AND INTERNATIONAL LEVEL. WHAT WAS YOUR EXPERIENCE OF THIS?

I don't think we've ever really had any problem in Birmingham with racism. I know in the earlier years I think there was a magazine being sold called the Bulldog. As everybody knows, Birmingham's got a predominantly black fan base so that wouldn't last too long. But it was in the earlier years, but I think it was in most clubs. If there was no away fans it was somebody else to bash at the football. If you were home, Norwich, or, you know, somebody where there's no one to look for, you could always end up giving it to the right-wingers. That used to go on definitely at Birmingham.

In the early years, round about the late '70s, some people were trying to bring politics into football; this didn't split fans, not at all, Birmingham was a firm, everybody was one. It's never been an issue at Birmingham.

There used to be a kid down there called Nicky, the same year when we were the Zulus, we went to Man City and he's never come back since, this Nicky. He was from Chelmsley as well, as it goes. No, he's never come back since. He got slapped and what not for airing his unwanted views and that was the last issue I can remember of any racism within Birmingham's main firm.

HOW HAVE FANS FOLLOWING THE NATIONAL TEAM ABROAD BEEN TREATED, AND WHAT ARE YOUR EXPERIENCES FOLLOWING YOUR CLUB OR NATIONAL TEAM ABROAD?

I'm not a great goer of England any more. I've been to one or two games abroad with England. But when you say treatment – because of the reputation English fans have, I think the treatment is over the top, yeah. Personally, I've never had no bovver like when I've gone with England abroad, I've always been locked up. When it last occurred, I lasted no longer than five minutes before I got nicked in Marseilles, that was the last time I followed England as well. I went to Poland and got me leg broke. I've only ever been abroad once with Birmingham in the Anglo-Italian Cup on a pre-season friendly. Hopefully, Europe beckons for the Blues this season.

WOULD YOU SAY THE MEDIA 'OVER-HYPE' THE TROUBLE AND CAN YOU GIVE AN EXAMPLE OF THIS?

Yeah, I think they do over-hype it. What I'd say is they do over-hype the trouble because we've got a local paper and any time there's a big game, either the Blues or the Villa, the week before in this particular paper you always find an article in there relating to what's going to happen; it's over-exaggerating it all and obviously people get stirred up a bit. So I think sometimes it's provoked, getting a few more people on the bandwagon that maybe wouldn't have been getting involved otherwise.

SHOULD CELTIC AND RANGERS BE ALLOWED TO JOIN THE ENGLISH PREMIERSHIP OR NATIONWIDE LEAGUES?

I think leave them where they are. They're up north. Sort it out between themselves, the two of them. Four big games a season. I have actually been up to see a couple of Rangers games and they have some game lads. If they did come in our Premiership, I don't think it would do them any good. I think they'd end up both mid-table sides. Start out probably in the First Division or something, if they did do it. But as Scottish teams, I think they should stay in Scotland.

DO YOU HAVE ANY VIEW ON BANNING ORDERS? DO YOU KNOW THIS FROM YOUR OWN EXPERIENCE OR THAT OF OTHERS?

I've had three banning orders now at Birmingham and I don't think they're very effective because if you want to get involved, it's always there. On the other hand, I don't think they're fair either. I mean, the last banning order which I've just received, Old Bill brought a civil action against me where I've already served the time in jail and served the punishment for it in the past. And with this other banning order, I think it's an infringement of my human rights, basically, so I wouldn't go as far as to say it's fair at all. If you take the last occasion, I'd finished my banning order. I came out of jail a couple of years ago, served my banning order and I tried to get out to Portugal during the European Championships. I was stopped at the airport which give the Old Bill leeway to bring a civil action against me. My banning order had expired at the time. Obviously, if I was under a banning order, I wouldn't have attempted to go over there. They stopped me at the airport, it was the local Old Bill, football intelligence, and asked me if I had any football convictions, knowing full well that I had. And they took my passport off me and put me in court on the Monday morning. They held my passport. I was eventually put on trial where the Old Bill brought a civil action against me and they just gave me another two-year banning order for crimes I'd committed in the past, but I've already served my penalty for it. Basically, I've been punished twice.

The reason they gave was if I was allowed to travel to Faro, they believed I was going to be involved in major disturbances. It's just the injustice of it, I think they make the rules up as they go along with these new charges and what not. It's not a fair trial when you get to court, not at all. I was booked in at Solihull which is a well-known police court anyway, so I never had a leg to stand on. Basically, with this new charge now, if you've committed offences in the past, i.e. anything football related or have had banning orders, the police take it to court, put you in front of the magistrates or judge and it's down to you to prove why you shouldn't have the banning order. They can already prove that you've committed offences in the past, and why you should have it. So you haven't got a leg to stand on.

EVERY ONE OF TODAY'S KNOWN HOOLIGAN FIRMS HAS A POLICE INTELLIGENCE OFFICER DEDICATED TO IT. HOW DO THE FIRMS TODAY RESPOND TO THAT? DO YOU HAVE ANY POLICE SPOTTER STORIES?

You try to evade them as much as possible. But me, personally, well, I think I've been set up terribly by the police spotters at

Birmingham. They just want me off the streets and out the game, basically. As you've seen, they've got together and just took me out, it's a conspiracy. I think that's what they're doing now with all the major players; they're building up a case on them. The football intelligence don't miss a thing. They know where you work, what car you drive, where you live, where your missus works, what school your kids go to. I know this for a fact, from my own experience. I have been followed from time to time and basically they try not to give you any rest at all. I can remember going to certain games and you'd have a bit of a punch-up and they'd let a little bit go without getting nicked. These days, any little thing will land you in trouble. Basically, if they haven't got it on camera, you've got half a chance of walking, but they rely a lot on this video evidence. That's what they're doing now.

IS THERE, IN YOUR OPINION, A NEXT GENERATION OF HOOLIGAN APPRENTICES COMING THROUGH AND WILL THEY BE ANYTHING LIKE THEIR PREDECESSORS?

There's a few young lads at Birmingham what have come through. There's one or two decent lads, but they'll never be as good as us in our day. I think they've got their work cut out a bit now with the police intelligence. You used to be able to get away with a little bit more at one time, whereas the Old Bill now just clamp right on it. If they see more than three or four of you walking in a group, they're pulling you over and slamming Section 60s on you.

But they'll never be as good as we were in our day. There's a few coming through, but in our day it was the 'in' thing, the football lark. I think kids now, the young lads, they've got more to do themselves. The Zulu Juniors as they're known, they've got a little firm, there's a small mob, there's a few tasty lads there amongst them. But as I say, I think it's been dying out now, this football lark, and basically it'll never be how it was.

**NAME: Les Muranyi –
'The General'
CLUB: Cambridge
United
FIRM: Main Firm**

**'You can't just join
the firm 'cos you
saw a film.'**

BACKGROUND AND MEET

Back in the old days, if someone said to me 'Cambridge', I would have honestly said, 'You're having a laugh ... who the fuck are Cambridge?' But then you think about it and it's true what someone said to me on writing the ICF book – it don't matter how big the firm is, it's always the same 30-40 doing the work. Now there's something to be said for that and, if using that rule of thumb with the likes of Cambridge, who would be lucky to muster up 40, then that would make them workaholics, I guess.

So I took my mind properly back to the heydays. Didn't little Cambridge make all the news headlines once? Well, yes, they did, and it was a riot with the notorious Chelsea Headhunters. Such was the savagery that day, 25 young men got jailed for the total of 28 years. Chelsea's travelling army were awesome in bringing violence with them, but that day against Chelsea the spotlight fell on one man they simply called The General. His real name was Les Muranyi and he was the mastermind behind the riot. The attack had been planned for months and he had led his gang for at least ten years.

My good friend, Terry Smith, now an author, was once Britain's most wanted armed robber and I knew he had acquaintances up in Cambridge. One came through for me in the name of Paul and very soon I was in touch with The General. Found him to be not long out of prison and living a quiet life writing his memoirs. The publishers were showing an interest, so I said, did it have a title? Yeah – The General.

Well, The General was born in 1959, picked up a few GCEs, is single, and once worked for an Irish construction firm before becoming an author. Here's what he had to say.

WHAT HAS BEEN THE MOST LEGENDARY FIGHT OR RIOT YOUR TEAM'S SUPPORTERS HAVE BEEN INVOLVED IN?

The Chelsea match is, without a doubt, the nearest thing to a riot that our fans have been involved in. Basically, we had a continuous history of four years of violence with Chelsea which had built up each time they came down. The last time they came down we mobbed up, they were being promoted that season, and we looked good for relegation so we knew that would be the last time they came down, so we decided to have one last big pop at them. This was February 1984.

We finally left the pub at about two o'clock and, within one minute, we walked into a mob of them coming round the corner and it kicked off from there. Quite spontaneously we've ended up chasing them in two groups and cutting their retreat off. This was later claimed to be a pincer movement that I'd planned deliberately before the game, but it wasn't planned. It was totally spontaneous. They were all armed, they all had bottles, they had two or three bottles apiece, there was a lot of bottles being used and we were taking weapons out the pub, you know, coshes, beer glasses, bottles, few knives, ashtrays, that sort of thing. And so because they were armed and because we'd just come out of a pub there was a lot of that type of weaponry used.

One of their lads got caught when they all jumped over a traffic barrier; he got dragged back, he got bashed up and got his throat cut with a broken bottle. After that, there was running battles right to the ground and we ended up chasing them. So it was a good victory for us. It certainly wasn't the whole Chelsea firm in that trouble, this was shown by photographs that appear in my book. You can see just how many Chelsea we were dealing with when they all come down. I mean, we had a firm of about 100, maybe 150, all together in one spot. We would actually stand and have it with them. But as I say, it was unprecedented scenes. There were a lot of police trying to break it up, and there were a lot of motorcycle police down on the scene straight away. You had a lad nearly died. They tried to attack us twice, and we run them off twice, and there was a lot of people going down on the floor, a lot of people getting badly hurt.

HOW IMPORTANT WAS THE ROLE OF ALCOHOL AND DRUGS? WAS THERE ANY TIME IN YOUR EXPERIENCE EITHER HAD PARTICULAR INFLUENCE?

I can remember one occasion when drink definitely played a part, more than usual. I ran a coach for an evening match at Northampton. We left Cambridge at about four o'clock and there always used to be a few lads from Royston in Hertfordshire used to turn up to Cambridge matches. And one of these lads, his dad kept a pub and he turned up with a sports bag full of spirits – we'd all been drinking since lunch and drinking cans in the car park waiting for the coach. And then the spirits got passed round on the coach. At one point, we laid down in the road, in the middle of the motorway and stopped all the traffic, all doing a dying fly, we was that drunk.

And when we got to the ground I stepped off the coach and, as soon as I stepped off, the air just hit me and my head went completely and the whole lot of us rampaged off round the ground and we damaged a bit of property and then we tried to attack Northampton's pub outside their end. I led the charge across the road. I kicked a bus shelter window out, cut my foot quite badly, although I didn't know it at the time. I ran across the road, into a pub. The police chased in after me, dragged me out, had a massive tug of war with my mates. I ended up getting nicked and I ended up getting six months for that, first prison sentence. So drink definitely played a major part – actually getting me jailed for the very first time. That was 1978.

WHO WAS THE MOST VIOLENT, CRAZY SET OF SUPPORTERS YOU EVER CAME ACROSS?

I'm struggling to think of a good interpretation of crazy, but without a doubt the firm that frightened me most – and there's only really been one team that frightened me down through the years –

and that was an evening game at home to West Ham. They've all turned up. You've got to remember it's only 50 miles down the road, it's an evening game. The police were fucking bricking it.

Just before the end of the game, they've come round, they've made an attempt on our end, so it's trouble kicking off, and it's spilled out as the game's finished. And when we came out of the ground, West Ham were everywhere, they were waiting out in the road and I actually got chased into the ground. I'd been thrown out by the police and they were waiting outside the gate, they recognised me, and I had to run back in the ground with five or six West Ham hot on my heels. And I've had to jump on the pitch to escape. Then I run into the same copper again who threw me straight back out.

When I came out there, West Ham were waiting on both sides of the road, both sides of the entrance to the car park, and it was scary. And I knew there was a very good chance of getting a knife in my ribs then. And that's the only time I've ever been concerned for myself at a football match. West Ham, I think, had that reputation of being knife happy.

The second time I bumped into the policeman who threw me out, when I thought I'd escaped out of danger, I really had a go at him as we were going out into the car park. I said, 'Listen, you saw what happened here. These guys, they want me real bad ... you can't throw me out there again.'

And he said, 'Listen, if we're gonna get it tonight, so are you.'

That shocked me and surprised me, that comment. I've never heard a copper speaking in terms like that before, or since in fact.

ARE YOUR FIRM STILL DOING IT?

This season, we've just had a very, very hot encounter with Oxford, which we consider is an old score going back to the '70s which has finally been settled, and we're basically thrilled to bits with the result. And the details of this are quite simple: 25 of our lot, top lads, had gone down on the train, they bussed in from Paddington to Oxford bus station and then immediately were spotted by one of Oxford's boys and they've swapped numbers and said, 'Ring this number if you want it.' So an hour later, there's been phone calls exchanged and they've been saying, 'Where are you … where are you … we're here in the Blackbird on the Leys Estate.'

So, basically, our lot have known the score that they're gonna go and they're expecting a warm reception. Nevertheless, they've gone over there, not knowing what they're walking into, it could have been anything. They've gone over on the bus. As they've got off the bus, they've got a final call and the guy is standing outside in the road, he's saying, 'Where are you?' So our lads said, 'We're behind you.' So he's put his phone down quickly. They've turned the corner and there they are, standing in the car park about 30-handed with bottles, pool cues, glasses. All the girls have scurried in the pub real quick. Our lot have gone into them and that has started off a ten-minute battle, serious, with people getting ribs broken with chairs. It's gone inside and outside the pub two or three times. Windows have gone through. But all the while it's happening, this pub is the sort of heartbeat of the estate if you like, and there's locals turning up in carloads and coming out of shops and coming running down from flats and all sorts. And the last five minutes of it our lot got bombarded with stones, glasses, bottles, ashtrays, bits of wood; anything they could pick up, it's come raining down on us. Everyone's been struck with something and it looks like it's coming on top because more and more locals are turning up.

Eventually, the police arrived and broke it up and one of the locals who was watching turned round to our lot and said, 'You done them, you done them.' And the police have decided to put our boys straight on the bus and take them straight to Paddington. The next thing, they're on the train celebrating on the way home. You know, job done.

HOW WOULD YOU DESCRIBE THE SITUATION WITH THE SCENE TODAY? CAN IT COMPARE WITH WHAT HAPPENED IN THE PAST, AND DO THINGS STILL GO OFF IN THE SAME WAY?

I'm totally inactive these days. I've been in prison from 2001 to 2004 and am still on licence so it's out of the question for me. But from what I know about these things, if two firms seriously want to get it on, it can be done. You'll never get it in and around the grounds like before, but with a bit of leadership, planning and guile, you can get a result away from the ground.

HOW DID YOU GET GOING WITH A FOOTBALL FIRM, DID IT HAVE A NAME AND HOW WAS THE NAME ESTABLISHED?

We came together in schooldays at the Abbey and grew into a decent mob. West Ham created a massive impression on me with ICF in 1979. I'd heard of Millwall's F Troop, Treatment and Halfway Line on the 1977 Panorama documentary. I chose the name Main Firm for our crew in 1979. It was a Chelsea schoolboy who gave me the idea when he used the phrase to large himself and his mates up. It had a very authentic ring to it.

WHAT WAS THE WORST INSTANCE OF WEAPONS BEING USED?

The near-fatal stabbing of a Chelsea fan on Newmarket Road with a broken bottle was the worst thing I've seen. It was an appalling spectacle. Blood shooting out of his neck. You can't seriously intend to take it that far.

WHAT IS THE MOST IMPORTANT LESSON YOU LEARNED PERSONALLY DURING YOUR TIME WITH YOUR FIRM AND WOULD YOU DO ANYTHING DIFFERENTLY?

Motivation. I was one of a few who made it happen. If I had the chance again, I'd put even more planning into it.

WHO WERE YOUR BIGGEST RIVALS BOTH TEAM AND FAN-WISE?

The Cambridgeshire derby is with Peterborough. It's deadly. It never ceases to shock me just how much hate there is in the air when we come together. We didn't play them very often in the '80s though. We always made a big effort for Chelsea when they came to the Abbey. That was like Christmas and birthday rolled into one. A real festival of football violence.

WHO ARE THE TOP FIVE FIRMS OF ANY IMPORTANCE TODAY?

Tottenham are strong at the moment. One of our boys is high up in the Yids. Also Nobby my co-defendant in the Chelsea case was very close with Trevor 'T' Tanner in the early '90s. I heard about what the Yids were doing back then from him. Those stories would make a bestseller. It galls me to read the way they have been mugged off in certain books. They are a serious firm and that's that. You can't ignore what you hear about Cardiff just because they're Welsh. Mind you, they ought to be tasty having all the thugs in one club. Millwall, the original football nutters with an enviable reputation. Years ago, going to the Den was like signing your own death warrant. They will always warrant utmost respect.

Birmingham have always got a dangerous crew. I took a coach to St Andrew's in the early '90s and it was a rough hooligans' paradise with waste ground on one side of it, streets full of derelict houses with caravans in the road. I hear they are still as lethal as ever. I know Stoke are fairly lively. I met one of their boys, David, on my recent sentence. He is a credit to them as football is totally about respect in my opinion and he knew the score.

WHO ARE YOUR TOP FIVE FIRMS OF ALL TIME?

West Ham ICF, Millwall Bushwackers, Chelsea Headhunters, Spurs Yids, Scousers (Liverpool or Everton). There are many more great firms, of course, but these are the big legends for me.

WHAT IS THE WORST GROUND YOU'VE EVER BEEN TO AND WHAT IS YOUR FAVOURITE GROUND?

Worst ground, Stamford Bridge in the '80s, stuck on the open North Stand. Not many options for away fans at Chelsea in those days.

Best ground for occasion and atmosphere was Wembley, winning the 1990 Fourth Division play-off against Chesterfield. Every team should know what that feels like.

WHAT ARE YOUR TOP HOOLIE BOOKS, AND WHAT IS YOUR OPINION ON THESE BOOKS?

Steve Cowen's Blades Business Crew – I thoroughly enjoyed that one. Steve's stories made me nostalgic for the early '80s heyday when you could travel in a group of 100 undetected, pack out a pub and wait for joy to happen. I also enjoyed Rob Silvester and Cass Pennant's Rolling with the 6.57. Well written and structured with some great battles. Once I got into it, I was rarely bored. Hull's City Psychos. Loved the author's blunt Yorkshire outlook.

Not all the books (mine included) are up to date but you can tell the Hull boys have matured and still love it. That's my top three but I read a lot of football titles during my recent stay with the Queen and enjoyed them all.

WHAT IS YOUR FAVOURITE FOOTBALL FASHIONWEAR AND THE WORST YOU'VE SEEN OR WORN?

The original casual labels firstly because I'd never worn expensive clothes until then. You felt a million dollars. The casual 'look' was a thing that only football lads knew. Other people couldn't work out why you looked so smart. I also rate the green flight jacket, Adidas T or Lonsdale sweatshirt, Levi's and Adidas trainers worn in the 1979 skinhead phase. That was a very thuggish but casual look. The worst I've ever worn was high waistband trousers and Brutus pointed collars with silly prints on them like some pratt on a penny farthing 1975/76.

WHAT IS THE WORST KIT YOU'VE SEEN A TEAM IN AND WHAT WOULD BE YOUR OWN CLUB'S BEST EVER STRIP?

The best Cambridge kit in my opinion is the '76/77 season, that was when Ron Atkinson was manager and we won the Fourth Division title. That was the vertical thick black-and-amber stripe, with black shorts, and amber-and-black socks. The worst football kit I've ever seen has to be in the early '90s, Brighton & Hove Albion came down and they were wearing blue-and-white-striped shirts, with blue-and-white-striped shorts, and you had to think of Andy Pandy looking at that.

YOUR FAVOURITE BAND OR MUSIC DURING YOUR FOOTBALL-GOING DAYS?

The first record I ever bought was David Bowie's Ziggy Stardust and the Spiders from Mars album in 1972 when I was a second-year at school. I used to lay on the front room floor at nights listening to it on my mum's Pye record player. My favourite band of football-going days was Simple Minds. I got into them in 1981 after hearing them on the John Peel show while I was in prison. I saw them at Hammersmith Odeon in 1984 with my mate Muzzy. At the end of the concert, Jim Kerr stood staring at me and Muzz for about a minute. It was uncanny.

DOES TODAY'S MODERN FOOTBALL PLAYER HAVE THE RESPECT OF THE FANS?

Premiership wages are a joke. How can you respect a guy who gets paid so highly and then doesn't give 110 per cent commitment? When you see top players out abusing their bodies with alcohol and drugs it makes you question the integrity of the whole sport. They're treating it as a joke. This surely doesn't happen so much abroad. Football today isn't the same game I used to watch from the terraces. You hero-worshiped players in those days.

FANS OFTEN TALK ABOUT THEIR FOOTBALL-GOING DAYS AS JUST BEING A LAUGH. ANY EPISODES YOU REMEMBER?

At Wembley, I ran into a guy I hadn't seen for years (that was my first game back since 1984). We were talking about life philosophically and he said, 'It's all in the Good Book, Les.' I thought, 'What the fuck?' About five minutes later, I saw him being wrestled across the road by the Metropolitan Police with his arm up his back. I thought that was quite amusing.

YOUR OPINION ABOUT ALL-SEATER STADIUMS, TICKET PRICES AND THE COMMERCIAL ASPECT OF TODAY'S FOOTBALL INDUSTRY. DO YOU STILL FEEL FOOTBALL BELONGS TO THE FANS?

I've never been to a state-of-the-art football stadium; missed our trip to the Millennium Stadium in February 2002. It's nice to sit down when I go away (never go to home games 'cos I'm banned for life). After traipsing round train stations and boozers all morning, the last thing you want is to stand for 90 minutes. I'm getting too old for that. You shouldn't have to pay more than a tenner entrance for smaller grounds. A neighbour was complaining to me today that she paid £35 to see West Ham on Saturday. Fuck me, is that what it costs these days?

RACISM AND RACE ISSUES HAVE BEEN PART OF FOOTBALL WITH CERTAIN CLUBS AND SETS OF SUPPORTERS AT BOTH CLUB AND INTERNATIONAL LEVEL. WHAT WAS YOUR EXPERIENCE OF THIS?

As far as I know, at Cambridge we've never had racial issues. Most of our black players were well liked. Brendon Batson was captain '76/77. Dion was magic. We had Devon White as well.

HOW HAVE FANS FOLLOWING THE NATIONAL TEAM ABROAD BEEN TREATED, AND WHAT ARE YOUR EXPERIENCES FOLLOWING YOUR CLUB OR NATIONAL TEAM ABROAD?

As Euro 2004 proved, the authorities are obviously determined to eradicate violence from England games abroad. Foreign fans never seem to kick off when they come here. But I dare say they get similar treatment to English fans when visiting other countries in Europe. The Turks have had a reputation since Copenhagen. I don't really know enough to say whether they get a hard time off Old Bill now, but you'd think in these times of intelligence that the local law force has weighed up who's coming to town and will act accordingly. The way English fans have behaved over the years, I can't see what there is to complain about. It was refreshing to see very little trouble at the England games this year.

WOULD YOU SAY THE MEDIA 'OVER-HYPE' THE TROUBLE AND CAN YOU GIVE AN EXAMPLE OF THIS?

The papers printed all sorts of outrageous bollocks about me when I got sentenced at the Old Bailey. They made wild claims that were nothing to do with the evidence. You can read all about that in my book. I should have sued them.

SHOULD CELTIC AND RANGERS BE ALLOWED TO JOIN THE ENGLISH PREMIERSHIP OR NATIONWIDE LEAGUES?

I don't see why not. They are too big for the Scottish league. I think it would create healthy competition to have the two Jock giants in with the best of ours. It would probably ruin the Scottish league, though.

DO YOU HAVE ANY VIEW ON BANNING ORDERS? DO YOU KNOW THIS FROM YOUR OWN EXPERIENCE OR THAT OF OTHERS?

I got a life ban from the Abbey in 1983 and I haven't been up there since. It didn't stop me going away or from being involved in the firm, though. I think these two-year banning orders they dish out now are outrageous. How is it fair to stop someone watching their club for that length of time just for being a little drunk? The police have way too much say in these matters.

HOOLIE MOVIES AND FLICKS – DO THEY GLORIFY VIOLENCE OR CREATE A COPYCAT SYNDROME?

So far there hasn't been a hoolie movie that's come anywhere near capturing the essence of football. I love The Firm, that is a classic. Who was in charge of the wardrobe on ID? All those brand-new scarves in the crowd ruined some promising scenes. I thought The Football Factory was thrown together, though it was good to see some of the faces taking part. I don't think these films really encourage anyone. To be a proper thug, you have to do years of background. You can't just join a firm 'cos you saw a film.

HOW WOULD YOU DESCRIBE YOUR FIRM/SUPPORTERS' FAN BASE, AND HAS YOUR FAN BASE CHANGED OVER TIME?

Our fan base is fairly localised, obviously, but they have always come in from towns within about a 20-mile radius, which doesn't say a lot for the support we get in the city. Everyone seems to be wearing replica shirts of Premiership clubs in Cambridge pubs these days. And then there's hordes of young people in England shirts for the internationals. But where the fuck are they on Saturdays during the season? It's sad for small clubs like us. I was brought up to view the Abbey as my second home and I can't understand why young people won't get behind their home team. The completion of ground improvements at the Abbey would undoubtedly help.

WAS YOUR LIFESTYLE WITH THE MAIN FIRM SOLELY CONFINED TO THE FOOTBALL CONTEXT OR WOULD IT HAVE BEEN THE SAME FOR YOU IN EVERYDAY STREET LIFE?

If you mean would I have been a thug and then a crook if not for football, then probably not. I'm a quiet bloke really. Ask anyone. Football definitely led me into the direction my life has taken.

EVERY ONE OF TODAY'S KNOWN HOOLIGAN FIRMS HAS A POLICE INTELLIGENCE OFFICER DEDICATED TO IT. HOW DO THE FIRMS TODAY RESPOND TO THAT? DO YOU HAVE ANY POLICE SPOTTER STORIES?

The thing is about your spotter he knows you almost intimately. He's almost part of the firm. Our chappy has been going to the Abbey for decades. He's a local boy. You just accept that he's got his ear to the ground and will be there waiting to greet you at the away fixture. In a way, this close scrutiny from the police helps keep the lid on the violence which would otherwise just get everyone locked up for life. During '90/91, I was involved with a big Cambridge fanzine called The Globe. For the cover of one issue, we used a photo from my collection, of United and their fans celebrating winning the 1969 Southern League Championship. Our police spotter once was a ball boy at the Abbey and he was in the picture that we chose. I didn't notice it until it had been printed. He weren't happy; he thought we were taking the piss.

IS THERE, IN YOUR OPINION, A NEXT GENERATION OF HOOLIGAN APPRENTICES COMING THROUGH AND WILL THEY BE ANYTHING LIKE THEIR PREDECESSORS?

You have to give these new lads the respect they deserve. They haven't the freedom we had back then but they are eager to keep the traditions alive and seem just as enthusiastic. Mind you, the test comes when they start banging you away for it. I kept going despite that.

NAME: Jason Marriner
CLUB: Chelsea
FIRM: Headhunters

**'I don't think you'll
ever get rid of the
so-called disease,
the real love.'**

BACKGROUND AND MEET

Many folk will recall the now famous investigative journalist John Macintyre's BBC documentary on the Chelsea Headhunters, which was edited to highlight a world of football violence with some racial undertones. The focus fell on Jason Marriner. As a result, a court case ensued, resulting in a prison term of six years. This was the backdrop to my meet, so you can understand slight apprehension as to what might be the motive here. The ICF book, if I'm honest, is scathing on the Chelsea boys as a mob, but personally speaking I am not so one-eyed that I wouldn't put them down in my own top five. They've taken a firm everywhere and proved awesome on the day. Sunderland, Brighton, Leicester, Portsmouth and Cambridge were just a token of the headlines made by a Chelsea mob on the rampage.

So the meet was on and off I went to interview my Headhunter face-to-face, convinced we may have already met. When I did meet Jason, he was a man with a different story to tell, far bigger than a chapter in my book. Jason was a man who had suffered as a direct result of trial by TV, but he refuses to let the system break him. Now at liberty to offer a counter-argument, he is putting his past behind him to write a book of his experiences. The stage he was at when I met him, he was already actively seeking a publisher, and maybe there's even a reverse documentary there – Macintyre Uncovered ... who knows?

Born in 1967, Jason started as a carpet-fitter and is currently

now a market trader. He is currently engaged, and breaking off
from his busy life he gave me this interview.

WHAT HAS BEEN THE MOST LEGENDARY FIGHT OR RIOT YOUR TEAM'S SUPPORTERS HAVE BEEN INVOLVED IN?

Well, I'd say Sheffield United at Camden Town, but that's been
very well documented. The one I would really like to talk about
was Bruges '95. Chelsea played Bruges in the quarter-final of a
European Cup Winners' Cup and you're talking about everyone,
not just the firm, everyone went over there because it's only
across the water remember. It was the most fans ever deported at
any game, ever, in the history. But I mean Joe Public was getting
deported; you couldn't have taken your fucking mum with you
or she would have been deported with you. I mean they were
just nicking absolutely anyone.

We was all walking down a street. Now, someone had done
about 400 snide tickets, it was only a bit of blue paper, so they was
the easiest ticket to forge in the world – they had done them a
week before and we all had them over there. Obviously, the Old
Bill got wind of this. So anyone with a ticket or without a ticket
was just getting lifted and marched – they were either marched
back or put into vans. They put us all in these vans, put handcuffs
on us and they took us to a warehouse. And in this warehouse
they had a water cannon, they had little fences all around the
place and that. And at the time there was only a few of us that had
got nicked and they was bringing us in little by little, slowly but
surely. And then fucking three to four hours later, there must have
been 500–600 of us in there. Not all thugs, not all herberts. Like I
was saying, fucking anyone and everyone. But then they brought
an old boy in and they was treating him really quite bad.

In the meantime, a few of the boys had blades on them, so
we'd cut the plastic handcuffs off. People had been burning the
handcuffs off and what have you. And everyone just said, 'Right,
we've had enough now.' And then a big scream went up and we
started singing, 'We are the famous, the famous Chelsea ...' and
everyone lifted their hands and started clapping. And the Old
Bill looked absolutely gobsmacked. And before they knew it, we

just fucking absolutely steamed into them, smashed the living daylights out the Old Bill. They put the water cannon on us all. But people ran round the back trying to turn the water cannon off and everything. It makes me chuckle to this day, it was fucking so funny. I mean the Old Bill really bollocked themselves, they pulled their truncheons, but Chelsea are just not fucking interested, they're just steaming into the Old Bill. I mean we had a proper, proper off with them. We was picking up fences, running at the Old Bill. We'd backed the Old Bill off.

What you've got to remember is it wasn't only the hardcore element, we was all leading the firm, even your average supporter, it doesn't mean he can't have a fight, he has got the fucking hump because he's been treated like a dog. He must have thought, 'Well, fuck me, we can have some of this and all,' and we've steamed in and we just backed the Old Bill off and they just fucking retreated and we really, really gave it them. So as we've got outside, I said, 'Look, if we're all together, they'll fucking round us up all together ... all split up, it's every man for himself.' It was like *The Great Escape*.

Camden Town v Sheffield United. They was good, they brought some good numbers. It was Camden High Road before the game. They had good numbers and we had good numbers, but you know when you just look at your mob, when you look, and you think, 'I don't give a fuck who we're having today, no one's going through us.' And I take me hat off to them, they was there and they was firm, but we had fucking flare guns, tear gas, everything. This is documented in the Blades Business Crew book and it's also in the Naughty Nineties. The book states that United had to go to everyone that season. We was in Camden and so were they. Apparently, their biggest mistake was coming to the pub we were in. Enough said!

HOW IMPORTANT WAS THE ROLE OF ALCOHOL AND DRUGS? WAS THERE ANY TIME IN YOUR EXPERIENCE EITHER HAD PARTICULAR INFLUENCE?

Drugs ain't my scene, so none of that. But I was one of the silly 27 that walked into Leicester's town centre for the last game of the season when they went down, and that's just fucking drink for you ... I don't care who you are, you just fucking would not do this if you was in the right state of mind. The other lads had gone to the game, they done this, they done that, everyone's gone their own ways. We're 27-handed. Leicester's just gone down. I mean, fuck me, they can pull a firm when they want to, to be fair to them.

We walked into their town centre, bearing in mind these people love their team like I love my team. They've just gone down, they're gutted. We've got a fierce reputation and a fierce name and we don't underestimate anyone, but we must have been very foolish to go into their town centre 27-handed. They came round the corner, a good 100 of them, no exaggeration. And we went, 'OK, this is it.' And all of a sudden you just heard this almighty roar. We turned round, and there must have been another 150 behind us. We was now sandwiched. I thought, 'Fuck this.' But, as luck would have it, the Old Bill turned up – a few of them and us got away from the Old Bill who had come from everywhere. We wound up on the station platform, me, the twins and a few others, and a few of their boys come over the bridge and come on to the platform and we had it toe-to-toe on the platform. But, I mean, that to me is drink.

WHO WAS THE MOST VIOLENT, CRAZY SET OF SUPPORTERS YOU EVER CAME ACROSS?

I've really got to say the Poles. I mean, all these people in Eastern Bloc countries, they are a good 10–15 years behind us. But as much as they hate the English, they look up to us so much because we invented the football violence. Now, it is their life. They go and fucking queue for a loaf of bread or they do whatever they do.

This was an England international match in Poznan, 1993. I remember being in the hotel; it was half-past eight in the morning. My pal's knocked on the door and went, 'They're here.'

'Who?' I said, 'Fuck off, I've just gone to bed ... I don't know about "they're here".'

'No,' he said, 'the Poles are here, the Poles are here.'

I've looked at me watch; it's half-past eight. I thought,

'Fuck me, no, this is upside down.' I went, 'What are you talking about?'

'Look, they're here, they're 300-handed,' he said.

'They ain't fucking 300-handed ...' I went, and, as it happened, they weren't, but they were 150-handed and it was half-past fucking eight in the morning! I thought, 'These cunts have been sitting up all night, drinking their mad vodka. It's half-past eight in the morning.'

But there was some English that hadn't been to bed, still sitting there drinking, talking bollocks, other people having breakfast and, like I say, I was in bed. But to be fair, everyone just knocked on everyone's doors, we got our act together, which weren't bad for that time of the morning and gone out and absolutely run them all round the gaff.

ARE YOUR FIRM STILL DOING IT?

I can't honestly answer whether the firm's still doing it due to the fact that I got fucked by that BBC documentary which resulted in six years' bird for me – which you will be able to read the truth about when my book comes out – but I know that there are new recruits, although I don't think you'll ever see what it was before. I think, especially us older lot, we should remember our good times and fucking dust yourself down and put it in the past and we all like to reminisce, don't we?

Going back to your first question, is the firm still doing it? Leeds–Chelsea, last game of the season. Chelsea was everywhere. Leeds had a mob, made their show at half-past ten in the morning, got surrounded. Listen, and this is not just Chelsea, but I'm talking all clubs, all round the country – I don't think you'll ever get rid of the so-called disease, the real love.

HOW WOULD YOU DESCRIBE THE SITUATION WITH THE SCENE TODAY? CAN IT COMPARE WITH WHAT HAPPENED IN THE PAST, AND DO THINGS STILL GO OFF IN THE SAME WAY?

To me it will never be the same. Nowadays, you've got cameras, the video footage that's gonna nick you six months after the fucking event. You think you're home and dry. With all the CCTV tapes. You've got the mobile phones, you've got the Internet. In the '80s, I've actually come face to face with you, but I couldn't phone you up and say, 'Listen, Cass, we're gonna meet you down the Barking Road or whatever.' But nowadays, these things happen. Everyone bangs on about their phones and this and that, but it's also a known fact that the Old Bill scan your fucking phones and they do this and they do that. They've got the Internet. I mean, who the fuck wants to get on the Internet, arrange a row on the Internet – don't the Old Bill look at the Internet?

HOW DID YOU GET GOING WITH A FOOTBALL FIRM, DID IT HAVE A NAME AND HOW WAS THE NAME ESTABLISHED?

We used to have a coach going locally and we used to take our own little herberts on there and then, after a fashion, it used to be the same faces. A prime example – we got tickets once to go into Southampton's end, and it was the whole of our coach, and we went into Southampton's end. And people might go, 'Oh, it's only fucking Southampton.' Let me tell you, we fucking had a good row with them.

Then we walked across the pitch at half-time, as it's all kicked off and all the Chelsea were singing, 'We're proud of you, Chelsea ...' and people, they recognise you and it escalates.

I don't really know how the firm got its name, the Headhunters. This was the early '80s when everyone was giving themselves a name, and Chelsea – I could never tell you, because I'd be totally lying, who give Chelsea the name Headhunters, and it's stuck with us ever since. Off the top of me head, it's got to be something like 1984, it was early '80s. Listen, no one over at Chelsea says, 'Oh, I belong to the Headhunters,' no one uses the name, it's only the media and the people from the outside would saying, 'Are you part of the Headhunters?' And it's not like a yes or no, it's more, I suppose, when you think about it, you are.

WHO ARE THE TOP FIVE FIRMS OF ANY IMPORTANCE TODAY?

I couldn't tell you because I'm banned so I ain't up with the times and, to be honest, I couldn't give a fuck because I ain't a part of it.

But at the same time, I seriously, seriously believe anyone can have a fucking good day, anyone can pull a firm. You hear so-and-so turned over so-and-so. I mean, let's put it this way – I heard that Cardiff had a 1,000 mob out for Wolves the other week. So that's great numbers, that's early '80s stuff, that's tremendous. But then when England played Wales in the World Cup qualifier recently, where was Taffy? We was told they was in Liverpool. I don't know if they actually knew that the game was in Manchester.

Listen, in our day, we was guaranteed to go and pull a 500–600 mob, same faces, same people, talking the same bollocks week in and week out. Now, you only get 30 a head and they want to be top dog. But the truth of it is, on anyone's day they can all pull a firm. I do not underestimate anyone.

WHO ARE YOUR TOP FIVE FIRMS OF ALL TIME?

Tottenham and West Ham in the '80s; I think that goes without saying. Millwall, they've always been there, they always will be there. Fucking hell, when they played Birmingham, the video footage shows there's a 56-year-old man kicking a fucking horse and you got kids out there from 14 years old. The best northern firm I've ever seen is Middlesbrough. And, my personal opinion, another one would be Wolverhampton Wanderers.

WHAT IS THE WORST GROUND YOU'VE EVER BEEN TO AND WHAT IS YOUR FAVOURITE GROUND?

I've got a few, to be honest with you. Carlisle, I'll never forget. Took us fucking nine hours to get there. Took us 38 hours to get back and we drew 0–0. They were the good old days. Another one would be Grimsby, just because I remember going into the town and, as we entered the town, I know it's an odd thing, but you could physically smell the fish as we entered the town. We had absolute thousands there. Last game of the season and we won the League. But the gaff absolutely stunk of fish. And also a little place like Grimsby, there was trouble in all quarters of the grounds and it was a really memorable day. I used to love going to Wembley, I used to love it. But just a bit biased, I'd have to say Chelsea because I call it the centre of the universe.

WHAT IS YOUR FAVOURITE FOOTBALL FASHIONWEAR AND THE WORST YOU'VE SEEN OR WORN?

Well, I like the smart clothes – Boss, Prada, Armani, etc., but the best has to be things like Levi Sta Prest, the college shoes, brogue shoes, Fred Perrys, Harrington jackets. It brings back happy memories. And the worst fashion is Hickie's (Steven Hickmott, a well-known notorious Chelsea character and author) – he's a very good mate of mine, but I mean, fuck me, he ain't been anywhere without his Dr Marten's. He's had them for fucking 338 years; he's still got the same old flying jacket. Listen, for someone who's got a few quid, nine times out of ten when I used to go away with England he'd stay on my fucking floor and sleep there. He'd go to sleep with his arms crossed and wake up with his arms crossed. I told him, he's got to spend a few quid. I must admit, I did like the Lyle & Scott, Tacchini, the Fila and Lacoste, I thought they was classics. The '80s casual, I thought, was very smart.

DOES TODAY'S MODERN FOOTBALL PLAYER HAVE THE RESPECT OF THE FANS?

Well, I personally don't think that the players, those fucking pricks in suits and whoever else is behind the stands, understands and appreciates the lengths that the supporters go to. Geezers lose their wives, they lose their family household. My personal opinion is a lot of them do come for the fucking money nowadays. I can't say all of them, because if you looked at someone like Zola, he was passionate about his football; someone like Vieira even, and Di Canio, always wear their hearts on their sleeves. I think there's too many foreign players because I tell you what it does, to be truthful with you, it holds back our own talented youth players. Give these kids a chance, man; where are they going?

WHO'S THE PLAYER AND/OR MANAGER THAT WINDS YOU UP THE MOST?

The player's easy – Diego Maradona, he ain't got the arsehole to put his hands up and say, 'All right, I did cheat but we won the

World Cup.' He was an out-and-out, world-class quality player, you could never take that away from him. That fucking deprived us once again of winning the World Cup and that's a very sore point with me.

Manager? Jack Charlton. He managed the Republic of Ireland. Don't get me wrong, I don't agree with Sven Göran Erickson being England manager, don't worry about that, I don't agree with any of that bollocks. But Jack Charlton played for England in 1966, and was a fucking national hero for young boys to old men. Then, all of a sudden, he manages the Republic of Ireland and talks about them and then you see him on an interview and now, all of a sudden, it's 'we' as in English, but it wasn't fucking 'we' when he was Ireland's manager. And I just think it's disgusting. I think he should be hung for treason.

FANS OFTEN TALK ABOUT THEIR FOOTBALL-GOING DAYS AS JUST BEING A LAUGH. ANY EPISODES YOU REMEMBER?

I remember the judge giving me six years for football violence, which I thought was fucking hilarious. But I also remember Sunderland away. It was a Wednesday night, a semi-final of the Milk Cup. Do you remember that two-bob Milk Cup? Awesome! I tell you something, we took thousands, we must have took 8,000–10,000 up there. We met up at Gateshead and, obviously, it's a long journey from London. Everyone was just boozing. You might stop off at a little town halfway up there, so you had a booze. Then you get to the pub and you're just drinking all day. And we got to this place where everyone's meeting and we was going to get the Metro from the station to take us to a place called Seaburn which is the old Sunderland's ground. But as we're all meeting and we're all getting everyone together, one of the lads that was on our coach – Oddball, we used to call him – he's fallen over and hit his head and he's just knocked himself out. He's so fucking drunk, he's absolutely lagging. Hickey looked at me and said, 'Who is that man?' And I went, 'Oh, it's all right, it's just a lagging bloke.' He said, 'I don't care, get him on the coach, we haven't come here to get drunk, we've come here for a war.'

So we lay him down and we've left him on the coach. We've

gone back, got on the Metro, come out at Seaburn and had a fucking awesome row. It's kicked off fucking absolutely everywhere. We've got in the ground, there's fucking more trouble, the ground's got smashed to fucking bits, Chelsea were just being lunatics, being nuisances. Sunderland were hard cunts, they was up for it, and it's gone absolutely fucking berserk. Chelsea lost 2–0.

We're coming back down the motorway home and got to somewhere like Leicester. Oddball's woken up and gone to me, 'All right, Jas.'

'All right, Soppy,' I went, 'How are you?'

'Oh we should be there soon, shouldn't we?'

And we'd just had the biggest fucking row ever. I said, 'Listen, you silly cunt, we're nearly home, we've lost 2–0, and there's been 132 arrests.'

'Don't keep winding me up,' he said.

I mean, don't get me wrong, he weren't the sharpest tool in the box. You wouldn't want him playing for Chelsea; you wouldn't want him in the 18-yard box, but he's just come round.

YOUR OPINION ABOUT ALL-SEATER STADIUMS, TICKET PRICES AND THE COMMERCIAL ASPECT OF TODAY'S FOOTBALL INDUSTRY. DO YOU STILL FEEL FOOTBALL BELONGS TO THE FANS?

Listen, the grounds are at the park, they're very nice, that's all very well. But what about your working-class man that is fucking born and bred blue? I mean, if you cut me, my blood's fucking blue, it ain't red. Now, all of a sudden, these fucking people cannot go to football and smoke. They give £1,000 to sit on the fucking seat and they get told by some cunt that's on £3 an hour, that he can eat as many hamburgers as he can and is allowed to take a programme home, but he cannot smoke. There's just no atmosphere these days.

You go back, there was plenty of atmosphere, there was plenty of hatred. The tradition has gone. It's fucking ridiculous. I remember before I got banned, I remember a steward coming up to me and he asked me to sit down. I said, 'Listen, mate,' I said, 'I paid fucking 1,200 quid for this ticket … if I want to stand on me fucking head, I'll stand on me poxy head.'

I just think it's all gone, the atmosphere's gone, the working-class man's gone. All of a sudden, you've got a tourist day-tripper next-door to you and someone else that's had his camera out more times than fucking David Bailey, it's a joke. I think it's bollocks. I think it's a shame and it's a sorry state of affairs; you go there to voice your opinion and to let a bit of steam off and you're not allowed to do that nowadays. You've got to get up, you've got to clap like Mary Whitehouse has just walked past you or something. What's all that about?

RACISM AND RACE ISSUES HAVE BEEN PART OF FOOTBALL WITH CERTAIN CLUBS AND SETS OF SUPPORTERS AT BOTH CLUB AND INTERNATIONAL LEVEL. WHAT WAS YOUR EXPERIENCE OF THIS?

One thing about this country is it really does seem to me about all they go on about is fucking race issues. I'm not a racist, I've got mates of mine who are black, they fucking laugh at it. They're sick to death, I'm sick to death of hearing about all these white people keep going on about fucking race issues. They go on about Combat 18 are going to Chelsea. That's the biggest bag of bollocks you've ever heard. There might be some people that support the Combat 18 who go to Chelsea, I don't know. But as a whole, at Chelsea, if you want to call us the Headhunters, fine, do that, but stop saying that because you have a gin and tonic or a vodka and coke that you've got to have a line of Charlie because that's not the way. It's not Chelsea Headhunters and Combat 18. Just because you've got one doesn't mean you've got to have the other. You see what I'm saying?

These football people who keep bringing up these race fucking things, what they really really want to do is go to some of these Eastern Bloc football grounds and see what racism is all about because I've been there. I've never seen Commies turned to Fascists so fucking quick in all my life. It's a fucking joke. You come to our ground, half of the fucking ground's full up with foreigners nowadays. Where do you get the racism bit from? People are bored of it.

One thing that does really dishearten me is the national

anthem. Going back to the rugby, they sing the national anthem with fucking pride. England fans sing it with pride. The fucking English footballer players want to learn the fucking words because they don't even sing it and I think it's disgusting. They don't even sing the national anthem. It really amazes me. I mean, what I say is, be proud of who you are and where you came from, that's the fucking bottom line.

WOULD YOU SAY THE MEDIA 'OVER-HYPE' THE TROUBLE AND CAN YOU GIVE AN EXAMPLE OF THIS?

Yeah, without a doubt, yeah. For me, to be really truthful with you, it would be Republic of Ireland at Lansdown Road. It was shocking, but the first thing they want to do is take a picture of some little girl crying at a football match. Listen, I understand you should be allowed to take any one of your family to football. But there's such hatred between the English and the Irish when it comes to football.

Listen, that was the first time ever the national anthem had been played at Lansdown Road, the first time ever in history. But it was all right for them to play the national anthem and to boo it and hiss it all the way through, that's fine. But as soon as it's the other way round, we're not allowed to do it because we're English, because we're fucking dogs, because we're this, because we're that. But you know what? We're dogs that fucking like to attack, we can't have all that fucking bollocks. You could hear clearly they were singing Republican songs. What's all that about? They go and report it one way, so it went the other way and there was an awful lot of trouble outside the ground to be honest with you. Every single corner I turned there was just mobs of English, they wasn't geezers wearing Stone Islands thinking they could have a row, there was proper, proper mobs. And everyone that wanted to be out there was out there. I've seen so much worse trouble, why do they keep going on about it? They've abandoned the game after 18 or 21 minutes – pathetic.

DO YOU HAVE ANY VIEW ON BANNING ORDERS? DO YOU KNOW THIS FROM YOUR OWN EXPERIENCE OR THAT OF OTHERS?

Right, when I got sentenced, I got a 20-year ban from football – a 20-year ban, the most ever which has even been handed down. The maximum is ten years and that's how much the judge wanted to sentence me. I've now got it down to eight years. Now that means, for eight years, every time Chelsea or England play abroad, I have to go to the police station five days beforehand and hand in my passport. On the day of the game, I have to sign on at the police station. So I've served the time, but what I'm saying is, I am a market trader, I could work at any market at any town, anywhere. But on that day, I can't – although they give me four hours' grace between certain times … well, thank you very much. But what my biggest hang-up about this is, I've done my fucking time, that's it, let me get on with it.

I'll give you an example. I walked into a police station and went to sign on and the copper went, 'Oh, here he is, the famous Jason Marriner.'

So I went, 'Oh, that's funny.'

He said, 'You follow Chelsea, don't you?'

'I don't follow anyone because I'm banned … that's why I'm in here signing this poxy one-eyed bit of paper.'

'There's no need to be like that, is there?' he said.

'I tell you what,' I said, 'there's every fucking reason to be like that and I'm gonna tell you why now. Last week, the school holidays were on.'

'What's that got to do with it?' he asked.

'I'll tell you what it's got to do with it … I saw a man sitting over the park, but I don't know him, he might have been a bacon, he might have been a paedophile or a nonce as far as I'm concerned. But when the school holidays are on, you don't make them fucking sign on. They're put on a sex offenders list, right, and that is it. They don't have to go to the police station and sign a bit of paper to say "I've served my time".'

Listen, I would personally like to go the Human Rights and fight it all the way, but no one's got the bollocks, no one wants to do it. They think they're fucking clever. But what does annoy me is, like I say, we are treated worse than sex offenders.

WHO'S YOUR TOP FELLOW – SOUND AS A POUND – FROM YOUR OWN SUPPORTERS, WHY HE IS NOMINATED AND WHAT DID HE DO FOR YOU?

To be honest, there's too many to mention. I mean, when I was away, going back to the old school, to the Chelsea lot, they was doing whip rounds for me and Andy quite often, once every three months or whatever. And it came to quite a few quid. All of a sudden, you'd get a monkey from the lads, keep your spirits up. And you think, 'You know what, I'm in here and they're fucking out there. They ain't just standing in a pub, just talking about you, they're walking about.' But I'll be honest – I do know deep down that was Ian and David, the twins, that would always sort the whip rounds out for me.

HOW WOULD YOU DESCRIBE YOUR FIRM/SUPPORTERS' FAN BASE, AND HAS YOUR FAN BASE CHANGED OVER TIME?

Changed? It cost you £8,500 to watch a game? You've got to come from China? Ruddy joke, change! All our fans have always, from what I've ever ever known, from day dot that I've gone, have always come from different suburbs. You got the odd geezers or whatever, the odd family that comes out of Fulham or Chelsea or whatever. Kent has always been an area. Crystal Palace, that sort of area. To be honest, in the early '80s or in the mid-'80s should I say, we had a pretty strong northern contingent, very strong. But you know what, they go far and wide, Chelsea, they are far and wide. It's the location, that's basically it.

WAS YOUR LIFESTYLE WITH THE HEADHUNTERS SOLELY CONFINED TO THE FOOTBALL CONTEXT OR WOULD IT HAVE BEEN THE SAME FOR YOU IN EVERYDAY STREET LIFE?

I know an awful lot of geezers that can have a proper fucking tear-up, they can have a proper row, and they don't go to football, but they're just fucking pub fighters or street fighters, and if it's in you, it's in you; if it ain't, it ain't. Me, I've got convictions outside football. I suppose at an early age you sort of climb the ladder without realising, and next thing you know you're in the fucking heart of it and you're enjoying it and you don't live on a housing estate that's fighting another housing estate or you're not at school any more where you're fighting another school, so you're now at football and you've got a bigger aspect of it and you're doing it for something you passionately, passionately believe in.

I mean, they can play the worst fucking football ever. When you was younger, you would swear black and blue that they fucking should have won, that they played really well. Today, you wouldn't because you're grown up, you can see the bigger aspect, but back then you was like, fucking hell, what you talking about? And you want to fight over it. And, really, you was wrong.

Your lifestyle at football depends on your age. You get older, you get wiser, you've got a missus, you've got a family, you've got so much that goes on the back burner. Your lifestyle depends on who you are and how you are.

EVERY ONE OF TODAY'S KNOWN HOOLIGAN FIRMS HAS A POLICE INTELLIGENCE OFFICER DEDICATED TO IT. HOW DO THE FIRMS TODAY RESPOND TO THAT? DO YOU HAVE ANY POLICE SPOTTER STORIES?

The Old Bill, they can be very two-faced towards you. Five years ago, we was fucking mobbing up against some team and they walked in and they said, 'Hello, lads,' and they put a card on the bar, it was Christmas time – 'To all the lads, the Chelsea Headhunters, Happy Christmas, Fulham Old Bill'. They knew wherever we used to go we used to send them cards, postcards. If I was out in Sweden or Spain or wherever I would be, I'd send a postcard, 'Wish you were here ... it's nice having a rest from you ... see you soon, etc.', it was a jolly up. But they always knew where we was anyway or whatever.

When I come out of prison not too long ago, I come out of

Chelsea's ground because I was at a wedding reception there. And this cozzer went, 'Oh, hello, Jason,' showing off in front of this other copper. 'How are you since you been out of prison?'

'Well, you're meant to have broken the mould when I went away,' I said.

'I really think you got stitched up,' he said.

'Woah, let me stop you there. If you thought I got stitched up that much, you should have gone and defended me at court about how much I got stitched up and all this old bollocks. Don't tell me, go and tell the judge.' And that was that.

And I saw him again at Leeds' last game of the season. I was just having a drink with the lads, and he tried to fucking chat with me again. 'Hello, Jason, what's happening today?' Well, my response to that is, hopefully, we'll get three points. Well, what did he want me to say? What I normally say to them is, 'You tell me, you've got all the Berties.'

NAMES: Mowgli, Yauza, Doc and Cashpoint (the interpreter)
CLUB: CSKA Moscow
FIRM: Yaroslavka, Kids, Gallant Steeds

BACKGROUND AND MEET

CSKA Moscow are one of five Russian football teams in Moscow. On the hooligan front, they are one of the main firms, with their fiercest rivals being Spartak Moscow. They can pull a firm of up to 300-strong. They are mostly younger than their British counterparts, 18–25 being the age group. Their leaders are all of high education and have practised as doctors, lawyers, teachers and managers. There are four main firms within CSKA Moscow – Red-Blue Warriors, Yaroslavka, KIDS, Gallant Steeds, and they all mean business. I interviewed three of their main boys after a chance encounter at Portugal's Euro Championships. Further meetings followed when they visited London en route to Champions League fixtures. That's when I met a fourth main lad, Cashpoint, top boy of the Gallant Steeds, who could translate the Russian chapters for me.

So there is Sergei 'Mowgli' (as in Rudyard Kipling's The Jungle Book), the leader of Yaroslavka, aged 24, university educated; Yauza is Yaroslavka, too, one of the Generals, aged 24, university educated; Doc, the innovator of KIDS – Kick-Insult-Destroy-Suppress – aged 24, university educated; and Cashpoint is Gallant Steeds, aged 20, a university student working in London.

I have got to know all of them, and all carry that same look in their eyes. It's a look I recall us having 20 years ago – that same look that said, 'We're living this, 24/7.'

NAME: Sergey 'Mowgli'
CLUB: CSKA Moscow
FIRM: Yaroslavka

'We are not dandies,
we are football
hooligans.'

WHAT HAS BEEN THE MOST LEGENDARY FIGHT OR RIOT YOUR TEAM'S SUPPORTERS HAVE BEEN INVOLVED IN?

The most legendary was the fight Yaroslavka versus The Union, 17 February 2000, on a railroad station. There were 17 of us, 44 of them. And in spite of all, we won that fight. We had been fighting for more than five or six minutes, so it was the most cruel and violent fight. No weapons, just bare knuckles. We arranged to come across with an equal mob on the railway station, but they cheated us and 44 of them arrived. So it took us more than five or six minutes to win that fight.

The biggest fight and the biggest riot was the fight in the park near Metro station Kitay Gorod: 300 CSKA hoolies versus 400–500 Spartak Ultras. We came out the subway each for himself, not organised at all. The Spartak lads were waiting for us. They used a lot of weapons, such as rods, bottles and iron bars. Most of the scars on my head are from that fight. They put nails into oranges and threw them at us. Lots of iron bars, lots of different types of shit.

The biggest riot with the police we had was during a Russia–Switzerland match broadcast. There was a big screen at the Dynamo Stadium in Moscow and we were watching the qualifications for World Cup 2002, so there was some trouble with the riot police and we fought and, for the first time, crushed them.

HOW IMPORTANT WAS THE ROLE OF ALCOHOL AND DRUGS? WAS THERE ANY TIME IN YOUR EXPERIENCE EITHER HAD PARTICULAR INFLUENCE?

I have some experience, like everybody in Russia! When we were young, we used to drink loads! But it was so long ago. I was a young boy trying to prove that I was a hard man. Now, I do not drink at all. I've already drunk my barrel of vodka.

If we are talking about drugs, most of our boys do not use drugs at all. Maybe grass sometimes – just to relax. We're strictly against it and, if we're talking about Yaroslavka, it is prohibited to drink or use drugs before action. You can do whatever you like after the fight, but before it you should have clear conscience, sober mind and good reactions. Most of our boys go in for sport, boxing mainly. As far as I know, all other firms and Spartak's ones drink, and sometimes a lot, but it is not a common practice in Russia to use drugs. As far as I know, nobody in Russia uses drugs before a fight. We prefer to fight with a clear conscience, so you can control yourself without killing anyone in a fit of passion. We don't go fighting stoned or under the influence of anything else.

WHO WAS THE MOST VIOLENT, CRAZY SET OF SUPPORTERS YOU EVER CAME ACROSS?

Spartak are the most violent and they are our main enemies; some of their firms are really crazy, really violent supporters. In 1998, there was some trouble near the Hockey Centre in Sokolniki. There were about 100 of us, and we met there when our opponents had a hockey match that day. There were about 250 of them, they came out from the hockey centre and action was on. The fight lasted for more than ten minutes, nobody wanted to lose, no one wanted to quit. That was a really good fight. I had my head smashed. We had a lot of problems because of different kinds of weapons, such as bottles, big pieces of ice, rocks and even a huge can of gasoline. It was a really good fight and CSKA won it.

ARE YOUR FIRM STILL DOING IT?

Yaroslavka is one of the top firms of CSKA, and we're still doing it and we are aiming for the top. Right now, we are progressing because there are around 80 of our real hard men. Maybe young, but really active. We are considered to be one of the top firms in Russia and we do our best to keep our reputation.

HOW WOULD YOU DESCRIBE THE SITUATION WITH THE SCENE TODAY? CAN IT COMPARE WITH WHAT HAPPENED IN THE PAST, AND DO THINGS STILL GO OFF IN THE SAME WAY?

It doesn't matter what the authorities try to do to stop us – all their efforts to restrict and control us are just a waste of their time. We always look for ways of avoiding attracting their attention to us and our actions. We are one step ahead. For example, if you're in 'Category C' and you have a stamp in your passport, some people – for some reward, of course – will erase it for you. It's not a problem. It's possible to solve most problems by money; almost any problem can be solved like this.

HOW DID YOU GET GOING WITH A FOOTBALL FIRM, DID IT HAVE A NAME AND HOW WAS THE NAME ESTABLISHED?

When I started going to football, the only CSKA firm was the Red-Blue Warriors. They are all old hooligans; everybody wanted to go with this firm, because it had a brand name already. But a little bit later, our firm was formed and Yaroslavka was born. I recruited lads who went to football on the railway and some time later we became a firm. I started my football career when I was 14, and when I was 16, I started my own firm. Now I'm 24 and I cannot imagine my life without it.

WHAT WAS THE WORST INSTANCE OF WEAPONS BEING USED?

The muffler from a car, nailed oranges and iron rods, of course. I've got a dent in my head from such a rod used by Spartak hooligans. We arrived to help our allies from Dynamo Moscow; there were about 30 of us but somehow our opponents found us and brought more than 150 hoolies. Some of them appeared with wooden poles in their hands, walking down the street towards us beating the pavement with this shit. Of our 30 men, only three stayed in that park. The others left us and ran away. That left me, and two lads from our firm. Traditionally, Yaroslavka doesn't run. And it would never run. We stayed there, three against 150. They crushed us, and our injuries were really serious. We understood that it would happen that way, but we didn't run away. The others did. That's why we made a decision not to go together with Dynamo any more. It happened in 2001.

The situation has changed a lot since then. People try to avoid using any sort of weapon now. We fight with bare fists. It's a matter of your personal honour. If you consider yourself to be a real man, fight with bare hands, prove it honestly.

WHAT IS THE MOST IMPORTANT LESSON YOU LEARNED PERSONALLY DURING YOUR TIME WITH YOUR FIRM AND WOULD YOU DO ANYTHING DIFFERENTLY?

First of all, it's friendship among members of the firm. You always know that your lads will always help you, not just in a fight, but in everyday life with all its problems. We are a brotherhood!

WHO WERE YOUR BIGGEST RIVALS BOTH TEAM AND FAN-WISE?

Spartak Moscow is the most hated team and fans.

WHO ARE THE TOP FIVE FIRMS OF ANY IMPORTANCE TODAY?

The Union – Spartak Moscow (we admit it); Yaroslavka; Gallant Steeds; Red-Blue Warriors – CSKA Moscow; the Gladiators Firm – Spartak Moscow.

WHO ARE YOUR TOP FIVE FIRMS OF ALL TIME?

Red-Blue Warriors – early '80s; Yaroslavka; the Union; Steeds; the Gladiators Firm.

WHAT IS THE WORST GROUND YOU'VE EVER BEEN TO AND WHAT IS YOUR FAVOURITE GROUND?

Stopendon, South Russia, is the worst because of its construction and location of the stadium. We sat there with the riot police sitting among us – one fan, one cop … one fan, one cop. The best stadium is Stade de France in Paris. In Russia, the best stadium is Saturn in the town of Ramenskoe.

WHAT ARE YOUR TOP HOOLIE BOOKS, AND WHAT IS YOUR OPINION ON THESE BOOKS?

City Psychos – Hull City; The Guvnors – Man City; and Football Factory. I like them, 'cos the process of fighting is naturally described. Such books let me know how people in other countries do the thing that I do. I get some experience while reading such books, some ideas which I try to put into life in Russia. It's experience and it relates to my own.

WHAT IS YOUR FAVOURITE FOOTBALL FASHIONWEAR AND THE WORST YOU'VE SEEN OR WORN?

I don't care about football fashion. I'm interested in not standing out from other people. It's a question of style in Russia. I don't care about brands, about names and so on. I just don't want to be recognisable to the police. Puma, Adidas and other sport brands are popular among Yaroslavka. The main idea is that we're trying to avoid the attention of the police so that's why we try to look like normal people. We do not care about brands. The more you show outside the less you have inside. We are not dandies, we are football hooligans.

EVER MADE A SPORTS BET? IF SO, WHAT WAS YOUR WORST AND BEST BET EVER MADE?

I always put a lot of money on it. It's a kind of a drug for me. I know all the statistics, I know all the emblems of all the clubs all over the world. The best bet brought me $300 and I bought a TV and music centre. At the same time, I bet on football, basketball and other games. The name of this bet is Express. Once I lost all my salary of $500 in one day on one bet; it was the game between Real Madrid and Marseilles.

YOUR FAVOURITE BAND OR MUSIC DURING YOUR FOOTBALL-GOING DAYS?

When I was 14 it was a record of The Exploited and different sorts of fast and hard 'Oi!' music. Now I prefer Drum 'n' Bass.

DOES TODAY'S MODERN FOOTBALL PLAYER HAVE THE RESPECT OF THE FANS?

Every football player should respect his fans and notwithstanding the result of the game he should come to the stands and express his respect to his fans, his supporters. Sometimes they don't, but sometimes they do, especially CSKA. Once, they did not show respect to the fans and CSKA supporters ambushed the players' coach near the stadium and threw eggs at it. Now they think twice after the match before leaving the ground without greeting their fans.

WHO'S THE PLAYER AND/OR MANAGER THAT WINDS YOU UP THE MOST?

Roland Gusev, a current player for CSKA. He's a stupid player, useless. And, of course, Egor Titov (Spartak Moscow). He failed a drug test in 2003. We have flags saying 'Go and fuck yourself'.

Worst manager – Oleg Romantsev, an ex-manager and a coach of Spartak Moscow. He was fired and then became a coach of the Russian World Cup team. I felt that he ruined the team, he crushed all the spirit. Now he is not working, fortunately.

WORST FOREIGN PLAYER YOU'VE SEEN AND THE BEST FOREIGN IMPORT? YOUR FAVOURITE CLUB PLAYER AND YOUR FAVOURITE OTHER PLAYER?

The best one is Rahimich, he's Bosnian, playing for CSKA. The worst one was Robson, who used to play for Spartak. My favourite CSKA player is Sergey Semak, the captain. He's been playing for CSKA for more than ten years. He always helps the others, gives money to supporters, a good player and a really good man.

FANS OFTEN TALK ABOUT THEIR FOOTBALL-GOING DAYS AS JUST BEING A LAUGH. ANY EPISODES YOU REMEMBER?

One of our lads went to Tomsk in Siberia, the furthest away trip; it's more than 33,500km from Moscow and he bought a ticket only to the nearest station and he went all the rest of the way for free. Russia is quite a big country – the closest trip from Moscow is 1,500km.

There was one funny story concerning a fight. Once we found out the place where the Torpedo Moscow lads gather and there were 18 of us and more than 40 of them near one subway station in Moscow. We steamed in screaming, 'Union, Union,' to make them think that we were Spartak hooligans, because there is an alliance between Torpedo and Spartak Moscow. They were confused. We started beating them and they couldn't understand what was happening, what the fuck was going on. Only when half of them ran away and another half were lying on the ground, we told them who we were.

Once, on a trip to Belgrade, Serbia, we were travelling from Hungary to Serbia and on the train there was a Hungarian girl standing near us. We were extremely drunk and invited her to join us. We bought a bottle of vodka and gave her a glass of vodka saying, 'OK, drink it.' The girl drank it. Then I suggested having sex with her doggy-style. She refused so, to impress her, I started masturbating, lying back so she could see it. I told her, 'Oh, honey! You see … I can't control myself, do you see what I'm doing?' She was shocked. We gave her one more glass of vodka. She drank it and then showed us her police identification badge. She turned out to be a policewoman from Budapest, from the Illegal Drugs Department. We said, 'No problem, honey, let's drink some more vodka.' She drank it, and, after two or three bottles of vodka, she started telling us where we could buy some grass in Budapest.

When we were in Budapest, two of our drunk lads went to the railway station when local hoolies were returning from their away game. There were more than 200 of them and only two drunk Russian lads in CSKA T-shirts standing on the railway station and screaming, 'Come on, you dirty wankers, let's fight!'

Two drunk guys against 200 local hooligans. The most interesting thing is that nobody beat them.

DO YOU FOLLOW OTHER NATIONAL SIDES?

In Russia, it's kind of a tradition to support not only a football club but also basketball CSKA, and we support hockey CSKA. We support everything connected with the name CSKA, but also other teams. Three weeks ago we travelled to the Ukraine to support the Russian gymnastics team and fought against Ukrainian guys. Basketball, hockey, volleyball, football … it doesn't matter, WE SUPPORT CSKA!

RACISM AND RACE ISSUES HAVE BEEN PART OF FOOTBALL WITH CERTAIN CLUBS AND SETS OF SUPPORTERS AT BOTH CLUB AND INTERNATIONAL LEVEL. WHAT WAS YOUR EXPERIENCE OF THIS?

The problem is that in Russia there is no racism, because there are very few black people in our country. It's much better to raise a question of nationalism, illegal immigrants from southern ex-USSR countries. That's the real problem in Russia. But if we are talking about hooliganism, I believe nationalism adversely affects it. You shouldn't mix politics and football hooligans. We separate ourselves from all this shit. We are football hooligans and we have our own enemies (other football clubs) and we are indifferent about politics – just the club in our heart and nothing else. In Yaroslavka, there are no racists or skinheads, we are totally indifferent towards politics.

The only thing is that we would prefer all FC CSKA Moscow football players to be Russians, not because we do not like foreigners, but because we think we have our own talents who can strengthen our team.

HOW HAVE FANS FOLLOWING THE NATIONAL TEAM ABROAD BEEN TREATED, AND WHAT ARE YOUR EXPERIENCES FOLLOWING YOUR CLUB OR NATIONAL TEAM ABROAD?

You see it wherever you go – fans from different clubs, little bit of Spartak Moscow, CSKA and some other clubs, when we support the Russian national team, sometimes we can make a kind of a truce. We really do care about our reputation not only in Russia but also abroad.

We do not want to be the second Poland, we do not want to be the second Turkey, we do not want them to think about us as hooligans who use knives, we just want to tell everybody that we care. OK, guys, there's Russia and this country and these hooligans are really good and they have honour and they have their own history and they are real guys and you should think twice before messing with them. And we want everybody to know that if they come to Russia, if they come across Russian hooligans, they must be absolutely aware that they will have an honest fight without any weapons, without any knives. It's an honest fight with real men.

WOULD YOU SAY THE MEDIA 'OVER-HYPE' THE TROUBLE AND CAN YOU GIVE AN EXAMPLE OF THIS?

Our newspapers are corrupt – they're just to make news, they want to make a kind of sensation and that's why they are almost always lying. They're telling fucking bullshit about what happened, what was going to happen. They do real harm to hooligans' culture and to real supporters because they feed society with lies, and society pays us back by regarding us as fucking bastards, Fascists, etc. But we don't care! They do not know anything about our culture, they do not know anything about the real life of hooligans. So fuck them! Nobody likes us – we don't care!

WHAT DO YOU THINK OF ENGLISH HOOLIGANS?

I consider English hooligans to be a kind of brand. At the present moment, they are not the best. You should admit it! There have been lots of incidents and fights which prove it: Poland, Turkey, France, etc. They are playing on their reputation from the '90s. It's a bad reputation and all their problems with the police and other hooligans are because of it. Everybody wants to try to test how good English hooligans are.

WHAT IS THE ENGLISH INFLUENCE?

First of all, it's in the gang's name; 90 per cent of gangs' names are in English. The exception is Yaroslavka. Then, the fashion, of course; Burberry, Stone Island, etc. It's not Russian fashion, it's a fashion which came from England. There's also a different kind of slang. The reason? England is the motherland of hooliganism.

HAVE THERE BEEN ANY FIGHTS AGAINST ENGLISH CLUBS?

We couldn't wait for Wales to come to Moscow to play Russia in the European qualifiers back in November 2003. We had heard a lot about this Soul Crew (Cardiff City) and other firms from Great Britain.

We arranged with a contact to have a fair fight, but they didn't come and they shouted abuse at us, so we attacked their hotel. In our fight with your own famous Soul Crew, we'd say things like, 'OK, guys, you are Soul Crew, the best in Great Britain, come on, let's fight.' They remained inside the hotel screaming stuff back at us, and we were shocked because this is your real Soul Crew. One of them was their leader we had been fighting with earlier by the buses, so we threw him one of the sleeves of his expensive coat we had ripped off him in the fight.

We also fought against Liverpool when they played in Moscow and took their banner in a fight.

This season in Moscow, the day after a Champions League match with Chelsea, the fucking Headhunters decided to give us a marvellous opportunity to fight against them; 30–35 real hardcore lads – so they said – met with 40–50 mostly youngsters, 19–20 years old from CSKA, who came to their hotel very late in the evening. No weapons were involved, it was a fair fight that lasted for about five minutes and was stopped by the Moscow Riot Police. I heard they considered it to be a draw! SHIT-HEADS!

NAME: Yauza
CLUB: CSKA Moscow
FIRM: Yaroslavka

'Yaroslavka doesn't run. And it would never run.'

DO YOU HAVE ANY VIEW ON BANNING ORDERS? DO YOU KNOW THIS FROM YOUR OWN EXPERIENCE OR THAT OF OTHERS?

Well, in Russia we do not have any kind of banning orders, so the government and officials cannot forbid you to enter the stadium. We do not have any kind of legislation specially oriented towards football hooligans. Of course, we have criminal legislation, and officials can put us in jail only based on criminal legislation. But that's only if you assault another person and he complains to the police.

You can fight with someone and the cops will just stop it, break it up. Then, if the other person doesn't make a complaint (you can solve that problem simply by giving him some money) they will let you go in a few hours. No claim – no crime.

Besides, it's not part of Russian tradition to inform against your enemies, it is unfair, and that's why the most common charges against hooligans are 'hooliganism', 'inciting mass disorder' or 'disturbing the peace', usually only when there are civilians involved.

HOOLIE MOVIES AND FLICKS – DO THEY GLORIFY VIOLENCE OR CREATE A COPYCAT SYNDROME?

Absolutely. Hoolie movies promote football violence and they clone hooligans. There are too many wannabes these days. Lots of people want to be like that lad they've seen in the film. Many people simply want to belong to some sub-culture, to be a member of some group. It's a matter of human psychology. A feeling of belonging.

Besides, I think every man is a warrior at heart, a hunter. These are primeval features of every man's character. And all mass media today do their best to kill these pure instincts in you. By seeing modern TV or films, you would rather become a gay or pervert than a real man. Fuck it! I would rather prefer to see thousands of wannabes fighting tooth and nail than one gay teaching me about life on a TV screen. So ... Hail to hoolie movies! Hail to flicks! I welcome them!

I started my hooligan career by seeing quite an old film – ID. I still believe it was one of the best films about hooligans I've ever seen. When I saw it for the first time, I was young and naïve and it was something fucking crazy for me seeing people who fight about football. A year later, I was involved in violence in football.

In Russia, when we invade other teams' terraces and start some trouble, then we call that action 'Shadwell' after that film.

WHO'S YOUR TOP FELLOW – SOUND AS A POUND – FROM YOUR OWN SUPPORTERS, WHY HE IS NOMINATED AND WHAT DID HE DO FOR YOU?

I think it's Michael – 'Gnus', we call him – the King of Hooligans. He's 38 years old now, and has got two children. He's been in jail three or four times. He is our living legend. He is the best, he's our soul. He's 'the King'.

In spite of his age, he's involved in everything. And I remember there was one incident when we got leathered by the Union. We had about 50 guys but most of them were wannabes. The Union spotted us. They came well organised, prepared and ready to fight and took us by surprise. And we had a few top boys and a lot of wannabes. Most of our wannabes ran away, and finally we got fucked – I remember I had long hair at that time. All my hair was caked in blood like dreadlocks, and my shirt got covered with blood, and even my body was covered in blood through my T-shirt, too.

I was taken to hospital where there were about ten CSKA boys, who also fought there against the numbers. I was sitting there waiting for my treatment and, after some time, I saw two lads bringing Gnus – at least, I thought it was Gnus – to hospital. He was bleeding in their arms; one lad was all covered with bandages. We were trashed, just trashed. Gnus, me and all those lads who were there with us. I couldn't recognise Gnus at first, he looked like a big bloody piece of meat. Then we took him home because he couldn't walk on his own. Spartak lads hate Gnus and it simply wasn't his day. They recognised him in the fight. They were beating him, screaming, 'Look here! It's Gnus! Kill him!' But he stood and fought, tooth and nail. Lion heart. Real top boy.

HOW WOULD YOU DESCRIBE YOUR FIRM/SUPPORTERS' FAN BASE, AND HAS YOUR FAN BASE CHANGED OVER TIME?

CSKA Ultras and fans come not only from different parts of Moscow, but mainly from the suburbs of Moscow. It's the same situation with Spartak lads. We used to go to the same schools, and share the same district – we are local. Sometimes you may be living next door to your enemy. We've got everything mixed.

WAS YOUR LIFESTYLE WITH YAROSLAVKA SOLELY CONFINED TO THE FOOTBALL CONTEXT OR WOULD IT HAVE BEEN THE SAME FOR YOU IN EVERYDAY STREET LIFE?

I started going to football at the age of 17. Now I'm 24. When I started going to football, I didn't know or care about the game or about the club; I just wanted to fight. I went in for some martial arts and wanted to test myself in a real fight. Then, step by step, fight after fight, now you see the result. I do not imagine football without football violence.

If there is no football at all, I will fight anyway because, in Russia, it's in your nature, it's an old tradition to fight. Russians fought all through their history. There is an interesting historical fact – in the eighteenth century in Russia, there was special legislation introduced by Queen Katherine II, focusing on bare-knuckle fighters, regulating the procedure of bare-knuckle fights in Russia.

I like violence, but I'm not an animal. I'm a typical Russian man trying to follow his instincts, trying to be real.

Some people consider football hooligans to be blockheaded idiots without any education or a career, following football hooliganism because they have nothing else to do. It's not true. You can hardly put me in that category. I finished school with a silver medal for my good results, and then graduated from one of the best Russian universities with a Master's degree in Economics. Now I'm working as a manager for a big company. And I've also been a football hooligan.

EVERY ONE OF TODAY'S KNOWN HOOLIGAN FIRMS IN THE UK HAS A POLICE INTELLIGENCE OFFICER DEDICATED TO IT. HOW DO THE FIRMS TODAY RESPOND TO THAT? DO YOU HAVE ANY POLICE SPOTTER STORIES?

In Russia, we have one main policeman whose activity is specially dedicated to football hooligans. I heard he used to be a physiognomist (an expert in studying facial features) before he took the position. He created portraits of criminals for the police. That's why he's got a marvellous memory for faces and he became the main chief of this special department dedicated specially to football hooligans. His name is Uryi Evgenievich Homutsky. He knows everything. He has got all the video tapes with all the fights. He's got a special dossier on every top player. He knows every top player by sight and his most favourite phrase is, 'Haven't seen your face in ages, mate. Haven't I put you in jail yet? I think I should. It's a great mistake … I have to correct it.' Something like that. He's the only person who is not afraid to charge into our area of the stands when there's trouble. He knows everybody. Everybody is afraid of him.

But sometimes he helps. He has been responsible for football hooliganism for more than five years and that's why our relations with him have become almost informal. Of course, he's a cop but he understands us and we respect him for that.

IS THERE, IN YOUR OPINION, A NEXT GENERATION OF HOOLIGAN APPRENTICES COMING THROUGH AND WILL THEY BE ANYTHING LIKE THEIR PREDECESSORS?

It's quite a difficult question. Every old lad, who has been in the firm for more than five or six years, looking at youngsters says, 'When I was your age ...' Then you can choose one of the following: '... I was more cool'; '... I fought much better'; '... I sang better on the terrace'; and so on.

It's not true most of the time, but still ... I think it's common practice. I will never treat a novice as an experienced old lad. I would rather have ten old lads than 50 wannabes in a fight. I'll do my best to treat them as equal, but I can hardly do it. I believe they do not have enough motivation, enough heart. We fight for our team, we don't care who's the manager, or who the players are. The majority of novices fight just to fight, that's the problem. We have made a reputation for ourselves as football hooligans, we fight for our club. They fight just to fight. They want to call themselves football hooligans, to be involved in it, but there's no CSKA in their heart.

Some of them may really be cool, some of them are really tough, but they have to earn their reputation, they have to prove to everybody that they can be named Yaroslavka. Very few people can do it.

NAME: 'Doc'
CLUB: CSKA Moscow
FIRM: Kids

'The Amon are the most violent, crazy fans we have ever met.'

WHAT HAS BEEN THE MOST LEGENDARY FIGHT OR RIOT YOUR TEAM'S SUPPORTERS HAVE BEEN INVOLVED IN?

The most legendary fight and the most violent riots were when CSKA played a football club called Eiets. We went to the south of Russia. We had lots of trouble with the police and a lot of locals. Firemen tried to stop the riots with a water cannon showering us with cold water. The fight continued for the second time for more than 40 minutes. The match was stopped several times because of the fight. But it was a really great fight.

After the game, lots of local citizens came to punish the CSKA hooligans. We also had fights with those guys. Almost half of the city came to fight; there were about 50 or 60 CSKA guys and about 200–250 local citizens and it was a really great fight. They had knives, bats, cables, rocks, bricks – everything they could throw at us, they did.

HOW IMPORTANT WAS THE ROLE OF ALCOHOL AND DRUGS? WAS THERE ANY TIME IN YOUR EXPERIENCE EITHER HAD PARTICULAR INFLUENCE?

We do not do drugs at all, especially during fights. We do not consider marijuana or hashish as drugs, but at CSKA we do not do drugs at all. And if you're speaking about alcohol, when we're not in our own country and you've got a chance to try it, you drink alcohol; we drink a lot. We believe the current law on alcohol is the reason for all our misfortunes.

The guys remembered one thing when they drank too much and went to fight – they lost. So usually everybody tries to avoid drinking alcohol before a fight. After the fight, it's your personal business. Well, they drink a little just to feel more comfortable, just to get the feeling of some power. So a little alcohol before a fight helps you to be the best you can be.

WHO WAS THE MOST VIOLENT, CRAZY SET OF SUPPORTERS YOU EVER CAME ACROSS?

The most violent fans are the Moscow Rail Police. The Moscow Rail Police are the most violent, crazy fans we've ever met. The name of the rail police is Amon, a special team of Russian militia, and they believe that they are the most crazy and violent mob who will never lose. When CSKA played in Ramenskoe, one of the biggest fights against the police kicked off. It caused an increase in hooligan behaviour, even disobedience towards cops, who up to then had always been in control of the fans inside the football stadiums.

ARE YOUR FIRM STILL DOING IT?

CSKA is one of the top hooligan firms in Russia; it is still doing it, and is a great firm. Still very active. Not long ago, they fought against Spartak hooligans. But they have lots of problems with the police, lots of problems.

HOW WOULD YOU DESCRIBE THE SITUATION WITH THE SCENE TODAY? CAN IT COMPARE WITH WHAT HAPPENED IN THE PAST, AND DO THINGS STILL GO OFF IN THE SAME WAY?

The profile of hooligans is raised a lot. We reckon most CSKA people would say being a hooligan is a great thing, it's an honour. The problem is that it's much more difficult to control too many people. In the past, we had small groups and when we organised different kinds of actions we could control all the participants and entire groups. And right now there are too many people, too many firms – we don't even know the names of some of them – and it's too fucking difficult to control them.

And if you're speaking about the police, they are following us, they've become much more clever than they used to be. They've got loads of information on us. We're trying to avoid their attention, we're trying to avoid the control, but it's more difficult because in Russia they have organised a special department to deal with more hooligans and the control has become much stronger. They also film us.

HOW DID YOU GET GOING WITH A FOOTBALL FIRM, DID IT HAVE A NAME AND HOW WAS THE NAME ESTABLISHED?

Well, it started in 1998. First, there was just the one big CSKA firm which controlled all the guys. It was very good. But in 1998, a group of guys, hooligans with a reputation, decided to organise their own firm, and form a new strand of hooliganism, because they had their own ideas. Doc came up with the rules of that firm and the first name was KIDS – Killing Idiots Demolition Squad. And then, after some time, they decided to rename it Kick-Insult-Destroy-Suppress. And since that time they have been one of the top firms of CSKA.

WHAT WAS THE WORST INSTANCE OF WEAPONS BEING USED?

I remembered that once, in the middle of the '90s, when they were fighting against Spartak hooligans, they were throwing hammers at us, small hammers.

I remember when they were on trip to Samara, they had to face machetes. When we stopped at a service station, we went to buy some meat or some beer and we fought with the Asian store owners; knives and machetes were involved. They threw manhole covers at us, too. But sometimes fake gangsters in Russia use guns with gas.

WHO ARE THE TOP FIVE FIRMS OF ANY IMPORTANCE TODAY?

The first firm is CSKA, Yaroslavka, but they do not like their hooligans because they're Communists. We don't like

Communists in Russia. Shalka 04, Stoke City, Serbian, Red Star (Servena Sersna). They have their own place. So Yaroslavka, then Shalka 04, then Red Star, Serbia – Ultras Boys, and then Leeds United, then Lekh Poznan in Poland.

WHO ARE YOUR TOP FIVE FIRMS OF ALL TIME?

CSKA hooligans – Red and Blue Warriors. Then Chelsea Headhunters, Millwall, Barcelona Borchas Noise and Riverplate Argentina.

WHAT ARE YOUR TOP HOOLIE BOOKS, AND WHAT IS YOUR OPINION ON THESE BOOKS?

City Psychos – Hull City; Hicky Hickmott, Armed for the Match; Paul Dodd, England's No. 1.

WHAT IS YOUR FAVOURITE FOOTBALL FASHIONWEAR AND THE WORST YOU'VE SEEN OR WORN?

Fashion victims pay a lot of attention to their look; our lads change their clothes so they can't be tagged by CCTV, and be recognised by the police. The clothes must be comfortable and relatively smart so you can go to a club after the football if necessary or sit on a bus or go on foot. The lads told me that they hate it when in the stadium they see people with painted faces and with big wigs and hats like clowns, it's not good.

WHAT IS THE WORST KIT YOU'VE SEEN A TEAM IN AND WHAT WOULD BE YOUR OWN CLUB'S BEST EVER STRIP?

They believe that the worst kit they've seen on a team is when the football players have got shirts that are too big and when the colour of those shirts don't match the original colours of your club. We want our football players to wear well-designed shirts that reflect the history of our team, one of the main features being the colours of the club.

HAVE YOU EVER MADE A SPORTS BET AND, IF SO, WHAT WAS YOUR WORST AND BEST BET?

I am a bad addict. And for half a year I tried to kick it, but I earn lots of money and started betting once again. My best bet was when Russia was playing against France when they were the World Cup holders; nobody here could ever imagine Russia winning that match, but I put a bet on even though I knew I wouldn't win. The odds were extremely high and I won $3,000!

YOUR FAVOURITE MUSIC DURING YOUR FOOTBALL-GOING DAYS?

Madness from London – Suggs, 'One Step Beyond'; that was my first single when I first joined CSKA Moscow. We have a special dance and when we go away everyone does the dance, about 100 of us. Now we like Audio Bullies. I think they are from Liverpool. They have a CD named Hooligan House. It's their first album and they're probably my favourite band.

DOES TODAY'S MODERN FOOTBALL PLAYER HAVE THE RESPECT OF THE FANS?

The team respects our fans. When they won the Russian Championship, they wore shirts with the logos of all CSKA's major firms. The message to the fans was: 'OK, guys, this is for you.' It was really great that they respect fans loyal to the club, not only those who just come to see the game.

FANS OFTEN TALK ABOUT THEIR FOOTBALL-GOING DAYS AS JUST BEING A LAUGH. ANY EPISODES YOU REMEMBER?

CSKA had a trip to St Petersburg to play Zenith and our men conquered the city; for more than five hours the city was under the control of CSKA.

When we were playing away, one of our guys decided to travel for free so he hid in a box under the seat and he was lying there waiting for the conductor to pass by. Suddenly, his mobile rang just as the conductor was standing near the seat, so he asked him for his ticket. As he was lying under the seat, he said into his mobile, 'OK, you guys, I cannot speak right now because the conductor is standing here and I'm hiding.' And the conductor heard everything.

Another time, some of our guys were travelling from Moscow to St Petersburg, but didn't have any money – they had money to pay for some vodka, but they had no money to buy something to eat. They were going to Niguyinovgorod. Two miles away they stole a goat, killed it with their Dr Marten's boots, and they cooked it. They cut off its head and ate it. They were near the railway station, and while they were waiting for the next train, everybody watched the guys playing football with the head of the goat.

One lad is a CSKA hooligan called Winter. CSKA played away and some of our guys wanted to go on the trip, but as usual they didn't have enough money for it, so they decided to travel for free. They had to get on the train somehow, but because of the conductors they decided to board it through the rubber couplings between two carriages. In order to travel for free by train, you have to peel the two sides of the rubber away and push your way through. So Winter went through the rubber seal quite late in the evening, it was nearly night, and then he reached out back through the seal to pull one of his friends through from outside.

While this was happening, one of the railway workers was walking along the outside of the train checking the wheels, so Winter's friends went to stand a little further away. It was then that Winter put out his hands and grabbed what he thought was one of his friends by the throat, and started pulling him into the train. The railway worker was terrified – all of a sudden, a hand had appeared and grabbed him. All the other lads standing nearby were laughing their heads off.

YOUR OPINION ABOUT ALL-SEATER STADIUMS, TICKET PRICES AND THE COMMERCIAL ASPECT OF TODAY'S FOOTBALL INDUSTRY. DO YOU STILL FEEL FOOTBALL BELONGS TO THE FANS?

If you're speaking about prices of tickets, of course they rise. Of course, we do not like it but it's not a critical situation. If you speak about all-seaters, we are glad that more and more people visit the stadium but the level of noise and any real atmosphere by our fans is extremely low. We are trying to raise this somehow. For example, not long ago we made a kind of a disc with CSKA football chants a week or two before we came to Europe, and we think it'll help a lot because we're extremely annoyed with all-seaters. Usually, the fans are screaming some fucking chants with no sense.

But we have to admit that we have problems. And if we speak about football, it does not belong to the fans; it's a money-making business. Among the priorities of the clubs, football fans come extremely low down.

RACISM AND RACE ISSUES HAVE BEEN PART OF FOOTBALL WITH CERTAIN CLUBS AND SETS OF SUPPORTERS AT BOTH CLUB AND INTERNATIONAL LEVEL. WHAT WAS YOUR EXPERIENCE OF THIS?

There's a close connection in Russia between nationalist organisations and football hooligans. It's a really close connection. But if we are speaking about me personally, of course we have organisations similar to Blood & Honour (a right-wing group affiliated to Combat 18), and they're trying to influence football hooliganism. But if we speak about football hooligans, we believe that it doesn't matter what colour of skin you have, if you were born in that country, if you are a patriot of that country, it doesn't matter the colour of your skin. But if you're a fucking immigrant, we don't like it. We do not like the immigrants from the former republics of Russia.

HOW HAVE FANS FOLLOWING THE NATIONAL TEAM ABROAD BEEN TREATED, AND WHAT ARE YOUR EXPERIENCES FOLLOWING YOUR CLUB OR NATIONAL TEAM ABROAD?

When we follow and support the national team, all supporters of football clubs gather together and end any differences or any problems they had before. But the situation in Russia changes a lot. If we support the national team or our own club, of course we'll fight for that, and our club is superior to our national team.

WOULD YOU SAY THE MEDIA 'OVER-HYPE' THE TROUBLE AND CAN YOU GIVE AN EXAMPLE OF THIS?

Of course they over-hype the situation with hooligans to exaggerate 100 per cent the impression they give. We get pressure from politicians because they want to gain control of the hooligans. An example of this is this situation with the fight in Red Square which happened around the match with Japan. In the World Cup, there were no hooligans at home but it was hyped by the mass media. This was generated by politicians to force through a new law against hooligans and that is why we see it as extremely bad for us. People who don't know anything about hooligans or football supporters consider us to be stupid and ludicrous. When people find out who we really are, of course they are shocked because all of us have got a good education and are in good jobs and have money; when they find out what we're really like then they understand that it's not true.

NAME: Jim 'Jinks' McTaggot
CLUB: Glasgow Rangers
FIRM: The ICF

'I'm banned for life.'

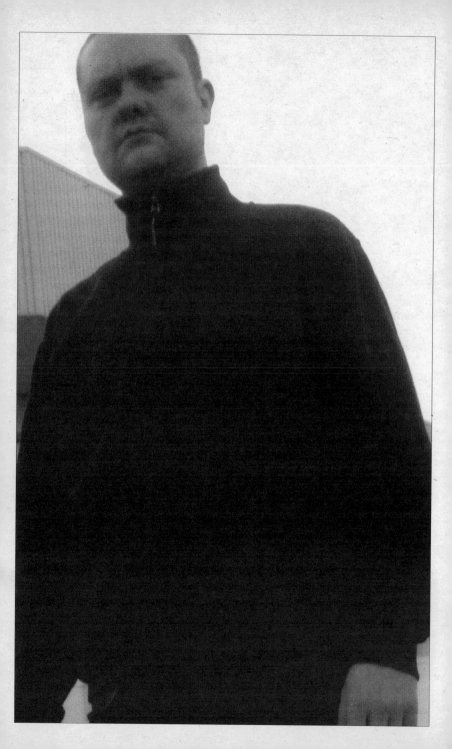

BACKGROUND AND MEET

My search for a Rangers representative had been on since the first book. I've heard about them having a firm called Her Majesty's Service, then it was this ICF, which confused me, as I thought we were ICF and didn't the 'Gers have links with Chelsea? Another reason holding me back was the heavy politics, the sectarian side of things; it's serious stuff and – I'll be straight with you – I am not political when it comes to my football. I've always wanted to go to an Old Firm derby purely from the perspective of seeing how it rates with a Millwall–West Ham derby. I get the offer of that opportunity every year and it comes from both sides, usually from some proper serious faces and, in order to remain neutral, I have never taken up that opportunity out of respect to both sets of fans. Even so, I have a good idea what they want to show me from others who have been up Old Firm derbies.

My first glimpse of a Rangers viewpoint came when 6.57 co-author, Rob Silvester, took me to a pre-season friendly at Fulham. The Rangers team were down and they could have been playing up in Scotland, such was their support. Every 'Ger residing in England made the pilgrimage to Fulham's new ground. With the Rangers supporters that day must have been representatives from every single one of England's hooligan mobs. The whole game was a real education for me regarding the supporters. I saw Scots flying the St George and Union Jacks, and English lads stood in Rangers hats and the Scottish club colours. Later, after the game, on the word of the English loyalists I was to meet the top man. I received a warm, friendly handshake and his gruff Glaswegian voice was short, welcoming and straight to the point. On learning the purpose of my visit, he simply said, 'Don't worry, we have entertained others and we have no problem with yourself. You are welcome to be our guest for the day and we will put you in touch with someone for the book.' Then he was gone to take a private call on the mobile. Couldn't help noticing the police standing outside, their eyes following his every move.

Many weeks later, I took a call; it was Big Kirky, a mate of Rob's who travels all over following Rangers. They had a man for me and I was to come to Glasgow where Big Kirky would be my chaperone. I was driven here and there, but the meet was to take place in the most famous pub in Scotland, The Louden Tavern, right by Celtic's ground, the one that on match days would have Celtic fans walking by in droves. The same pub once featured in a TV series called Britain's Hardest Pubs.

Well, upon entering the pub, I near stopped in my tracks as a customer who was leaving muttered, 'I'm going to stab him.' Someone had pissed him off inside the pub. I looked to Big Kirky who laughed. He had heard his comment, but as we went in, everything was intact, and the place was spotless, with all the Rangers memorabilia on the walls. I think the regulars saw me as a bit of a novelty and one of them, on being told I was the author, simply shouted over, 'Wrap the books and get back to fighting.' Then my fighter walked in – Jim McTaggot.

'You can call me Jinks.'

Born in 1973, his first job was a trainee welder, and his first game was Rangers v Clyde. He is single.

WHAT HAS BEEN THE MOST LEGENDARY FIGHT OR RIOT YOUR TEAM'S SUPPORTERS HAVE BEEN INVOLVED IN?

I don't know if it was a riot, but the papers said so – Sunderland away 1993, Gary Bennett's testimonial. Rangers fans took the biggest away support ever to the old Roker Park, they just took it over. We were in a pub with a lot of Rangers scarfers and in came a few guys from Sunderland who started to take the piss, mouthing off, offering people outside. And then it all kicked off.

Some of them were slashed. One of my mates was responsible for the slashing, he's now sadly passed away. Rangers had about 100 down there; Sunderland's mob never really fancied it so it was merely these guys in the pub. The coppers were really heavy-handed. A few people got pulled in, but they pulled the wrong people in; as I say, the person responsible is dead now.

That game was really fucking bad, really bad, especially up here in the papers. It ran for about a month at least in the papers. We had the top man of the Scottish Police saying, 'What is this ICF? What does ICF stand for?' Well, he should know what he's saying. He came out with things like 'Ibrox Casual Firm' and things like that and saying that was what the mob was called. It was really fucking bad that day.

The worst riot I've ever seen was the 1980 Scottish Cup Final, Rangers and Celtic. Celtic scored the last-minute winner. Rangers–Celtic fans ran on the pitch at the same time. After that, they banned alcohol in Scottish football grounds. Fighting all round the park, it went on for maybe half-an-hour until they cleared the pitch with police horses. And then, afterwards, it was the usual Rangers–Celtic evening. The hatred's been there for maybe 100 years or more. That was at Hampden Park. I was with my brother in the traditional Rangers end. A frightening experience. The police were there on horses, baton-charging everyone. There was bottles, every fucking thing going on; easily the worst I've ever seen.

HOW IMPORTANT WAS THE ROLE OF ALCOHOL AND DRUGS? WAS THERE ANY TIME IN YOUR EXPERIENCE EITHER HAD PARTICULAR INFLUENCE?

Once the rave scene appeared, it seemed to kill it at football for a few years, late '80s to early '90s. The Ecstasy period if you like. It definitely killed it for a few years, it seemed especially down south as well as up here.

Alcohol, I don't think it's an important part. You meet in the pub, you don't want to meet in the streets, so we meet in pubs and drink's part of it, but not a major part. A lot of people I know go to football but don't drink at all.

WHO WAS THE MOST VIOLENT, CRAZY SET OF SUPPORTERS YOU EVER CAME ACROSS?

In Scotland I would have to say Hibs; any time they showed, especially late '80s, early '90s. In 1990, after we had been through the previous game early in the season, we took the piss and turned Hibs over, they admitted that. But at the next game, we only appeared with about fucking 40 lads and Hibs come out of the Tube at St Enoch 200-handed. We were in Jamaica Street, escorted to the ground, but Hibs casuals mingled in with us and the coppers thought it was one mob. They were slapping us all the way up the street.

I was arrested. Easily 25 Rangers lads got arrested. I was in the cells with Hibs. But that day, Hibs, after the previous game when we took the piss, they returned the favour. But Hibs, any time, any time.

Others? I'd have to say Feyenoord as well in Rotterdam, very intimidating. Many Feyenoord fans lined the route for the escorted Rangers fans coming in, throwing fucking everything at all the buses, banging windows, fucking all sorts, really nasty atmosphere, terrible, terrible. It was a fucking awful day. Loads of them had bottles and bricks aimed at all the fans, but apparently that happens every week there. The worst atmosphere in an away ground, definitely.

And they come over here and they was just as bad. That was the return match. There was about maybe 80 Rangers there. That would be 2002. We were parked up in Sauchiehall Street in Glasgow, early afternoon. Feyenoord were dotted all over the place. There must have been, I would say, good numbers, maybe 200, but they were never all together. And a lot of them were in the famous pub in Glasgow, the Horseshoe Bar. Someone spoke to them, tried to sort something out for later, meet over a pub called The Lauders.

Eleven o'clock at night, we was walking down to meet them and they fucking bolted which I was very surprised at considering what I'd seen. Then they regrouped, there was only fucking five or six of us left, and they tried to give us a fucking big slap, but the coppers intervened. That was us off the mark. But Feyenoord were definitely game.

ARE YOUR FIRM STILL DOING IT?

The situation now with Rangers is they're still definitely going; the past couple of seasons they've had run-ins with Hibs and Aberdeen and a few guys from either side have been given at least two years' sentences. But people are still going to the matches. Myself, though, I don't go with the firm any more. Just probably because of the sentences that they're dishing out now.

As I say, three seasons ago, if you hit someone at a football match you were looking at a £250 fine. Now, they're dishing out a year or two years and they're really clamping down, not just down south, but up here as well. Because there's no big numbers any more in Scotland, it's easy to eradicate the problem people.

I've got a life ban for being arrested in Eindhoven in 1999 at a European Cup match. Seven of us went over to Eindhoven. Outside the ground before the game, we had it with them. Coppers let them off the leash; 200–300 of them, 40 of us. We had to stand and fight, there was nowhere else to go, we had to stand and fight. But the coppers let them go. Until then, we didn't realise we were guinea pigs leading up to Euro 2000. England were playing Portugal at the same stadium, so the particular night Rangers played was the biggest police presence ever for a football match, about 500-odd coppers. Three times they went for it, three times we backed them off. That was an absolute ding-donger. There must have been 18 or 20 of us got between three and four weeks' imprisonment.

I was on an indefinite ban after I got arrested at Ibrox at a testimonial with 'Boro. After the Eindhoven game, I got a life ban along with everybody else who was arrested.

HOW WOULD YOU DESCRIBE THE SITUATION WITH THE SCENE TODAY? CAN IT COMPARE WITH WHAT HAPPENED IN THE PAST, AND DO THINGS STILL GO OFF IN THE SAME WAY?

Yeah. The scene today is smaller numbers up in Scotland which means more violent clashes between rival firms, despite the heavy police presence and spotters, football intelligence. It's smaller numbers but, I would say, the trouble's more severe at times, but there's still definitely ways of getting round it. Mobile phones are a fucking godsend for the casuals and they can meet anywhere. So I never see it stopping completely, although it's looking that way at the minute.

HOW DID YOU GET GOING WITH A FOOTBALL FIRM, DID IT HAVE A NAME AND HOW WAS THE NAME ESTABLISHED?

Well, I got going with the firm basically through my mates. We were all at school; some were a couple of years older and had been going for a few years. I just got on board that way. The first name Rangers' mob had was HMS, Her Majesty's Service. After that, we changed to ICF, which was probably taken from West Ham. There was no organised mob in the '70s, but after that it was HMS and then the ICF – Inter-City Firm.

WHAT WAS THE WORST INSTANCE OF WEAPONS BEING USED?

I've seen a few, especially involving Motherwell fans; Motherwell's mob were nasty bastards. In the early days, they'd have Stanley knives, this would be the '80s. But a few lads for Rangers were pretty handy themselves. After a 1987 Rangers–Celtic match in Duke Street, Glasgow, a mob of Rangers, maybe about 80 out of a mob of about 500, they were split up. Then Celtic's mob appeared. I saw a guy with a machete. A Rangers boy got a Celtic boy in the face, his face was pretty bad. Passers-by tried to cover it to try and stem the flow of blood.

The Sunderland fight I've already mentioned. I'm not saying it's right what they got, but you should never fucking walk into a pub filled with another mob and try to take the piss like they did.

Motherwell – nasty bastards in the early days, late '80s. Never the biggest mob, numbers were maybe 200–300, travelling 100-odd, but they were Stanley knife users and I've seen them cutting a few boys.

WHO WERE YOUR BIGGEST RIVALS BOTH TEAM AND FAN-WISE?

Team-wise, Celtic, both, definitely. It's because people have called it bigotry. I don't, that's above us. It's just a hatred between two teams since the '30s because of the legend and the ties. Celtic are basically a Catholic team, Rangers is a protestant club. This is dating back to when they started and it's always been there. I mean, 1909, the Scottish Cup Final between them had to be abandoned because of riots. They say there was a conspiracy with the SFA at the time to make the first match a draw so they could get gate revenue for a replay and, in 1909, a riot took place. It's always there, and it always will be there for 100 years.

WHO ARE THE TOP FIVE FIRMS OF ANY IMPORTANCE TODAY?

In Scotland it would be Hibs, Aberdeen, Rangers. Others, I would say Birmingham, Cardiff.

WHO ARE YOUR TOP FIVE FIRMS OF ALL TIME?

Hibs, Birmingham, Red Star Belgrade, Cardiff and England, 1989 at Hampden.

WHAT IS THE WORST GROUND YOU'VE EVER BEEN TO AND WHAT IS YOUR FAVOURITE GROUND?

I would say Celtic Park before it was modernised. The Rangers fans used to take 18,000 on at one end up to the early '90s. To this day, I still don't know where the toilets were. You used to go outside, not actually outside the stadium, but outside the sort of periphery, and they'd be pissing – everybody. And it was never uncommon to be standing beside a copper, or a load of coppers, pissing themselves and piss was all over the fucking gangway. But that was Celtic Park before it was modernised, it was a fucking disgrace.

My favourite ground I'd say is Amsterdam Arena, Ajax's stadium. Went there in 1996 for Rangers playing Ajax in the Champions' League. Rangers were beaten 4–1 but Rangers had a fucking huge support as usual. But that was a nice ground, probably the best I've been in.

WHAT IS YOUR FAVOURITE FOOTBALL FASHIONWEAR AND THE WORST YOU'VE SEEN OR WORN?

No particular brand name but shirt, jumper, jeans and trainers for myself. It's just what I've always worn, just simple, no particular brand name.

The worst fashion I've ever worn was a few years ago; I had a multi-coloured Lacoste T-shirt, it was fucking awful. I wore it to the boozer. I got fucking caned, it was that bad. I think my sister got it. But the other worst fashion I've seen – it seems to be mainly a northern English thing, late '80s–early '90s, sort of Happy Mondays era – are the flares, paisley-patterned shirts and the long hair. They were a fucking disgrace, a fucking shambles. That's easily the worst I've seen.

WHO'S THE PLAYER AND/OR MANAGER THAT WINDS YOU UP THE MOST?

Easily, it would have to be Neil Lennon because he plays for Celtic. He came from Leicester. There's been all sorts about him in the media up here. He's alleged to have been in scrapes, been involved in fights. He was involved in a fight up the West End; two young guys got fined for attacking him. But Lennon said he couldn't give a fuck, 'I'll still be a millionaire in the morning,' so the papers said. People say it's because he's a Northern Irish Catholic playing for Celtic, that's what they're saying, but it's more because he's ignorant basically. And his manager, Martin O'Neill, of Celtic as well. They're always trying to manipulate the media for the benefit of the Celtic fans up here, and anything they say is the gospel, according to the papers. Anything any Rangers player gets up to is front-page news. Even a small thing gets in the papers, while Celtic players fight in the street or at the players' Christmas night out in Newcastle and fuck all really happens to them. It's the way it is up here.

FANS OFTEN TALK ABOUT THEIR FOOTBALL-GOING DAYS AS JUST BEING A LAUGH. ANY EPISODES YOU REMEMBER?

Two years ago we played Hibs away in a cup tie. So it was pissing with rain, midweek. We were in the pubs after the game; a no-show from Hibs. The Edinburgh coppers batoned us down towards the railway station. I'm standing beside my mate. His phone goes. It turns out it was the Glasgow coppers asking him about his car being broken into a couple of days previously, while we're being baton-charged by the fucking coppers on the railway station. He said, 'It's quite inconvenient at the minute.' The copper said, 'Well, it's fucking inconvenient for me as well. We need your fucking details right now.'

So he's trying to fucking give this Glasgow copper details while the Edinburgh copper is cracking him one in his attempts to get him to the station. That was easily the funniest.

Leverkusen, 1998 European match. We were all well pissed. I went into the game and was choking for a beer. So I went to the bar, bought about fucking 18 pints of lager. A fellow Rangers fan said they're fucking useless, non-alcoholic. So I had to leave them in a fucking pile at the bottom of the steps. I couldn't give them away. I never heard the last of that one.

YOUR OPINION ABOUT ALL-SEATER STADIUMS, TICKET PRICES AND THE COMMERCIAL ASPECT OF TODAY'S FOOTBALL INDUSTRY. DO YOU STILL FEEL FOOTBALL BELONGS TO THE FANS?

Well, Ibrox Park is a state-of-the-art stadium which I'm banned from for life. It severely lacks atmosphere. You ask any Rangers fan; Ibrox is like a fucking morgue unless they play Celtic or maybe European ties. The real Rangers fan is seen in their travelling support, especially recently, because if you stand up at Ibrox now you'll get half-a-dozen stewards telling you to sit on your arse. You can't sing, you can't shout, you can't do fuck all. A lot of people don't go and, in a way, I'm glad I'm banned now because it's really fucking bad.

In the old days, we used to stand in the West Enclosure, all terracing. Years ago, before they introduced the seating after

Hillsborough, they tried to campaign for Rangers Football Club to keep that enclosure just standing, but they said by law they had to change it anyway.

Ibrox is severely lacking in atmosphere but, obviously, it's safer and reduces any potential fighting inside the ground. I would say ticket prices are a fucking disgrace. Football is just about screwing money out of the fans now.

RACISM AND RACE ISSUES HAVE BEEN PART OF FOOTBALL WITH CERTAIN CLUBS AND SETS OF SUPPORTERS AT BOTH CLUB AND INTERNATIONAL LEVEL. WHAT WAS YOUR EXPERIENCE OF THIS?

Well, I was in Rangers mob and we always had a few of our boys who had loose ties with the BNP. Personally, I was never involved in all that. The worst incidence of racism I've ever seen was when Mark Walters signed for Rangers in the late '80s. He signed the night before the Celtic match at Parkhead. Celtic fans all turned up in monkey suits throwing bananas. The following week, they played Hearts at Tynecastle away and they did exactly the same again. That was easily the worst incidence of racism. He was a fantastic player.

I think it's changed now. A lot of people, especially the media, if there's any outbreak of violence involved with Rangers, they always kick back to this Rangers–Chelsea thing and the National Front lot. It was well over the top. Me personally, though, I've never been involved with it.

HOW HAVE FANS FOLLOWING THE NATIONAL TEAM ABROAD BEEN TREATED, AND WHAT ARE YOUR EXPERIENCES FOLLOWING YOUR CLUB OR NATIONAL TEAM ABROAD?

Scotland – never been a fan of Scotland's, never will be. The reason, for a start the team's a fucking disgrace, well, it has been for a number of years now, but also what the SFA, the Scottish Football Association, dish out to Rangers players. For example, Duncan Ferguson, who's at Everton now. I was at a match ten years ago and he was deemed to headbutt a Raith Rovers player and he was only yellow-carded, but the SFA pushed and pushed and got the police involved and the guy ended up doing three months in Barlinnie Prison, things like that, that shouldn't have happened. The SFA pushed and pushed it. I think that fucked off a lot of Rangers fans from watching Scotland. They'd rather see England doing well. Celtic fans would rather see the Republic of Ireland doing well. It comes back to the sectarian type thing, if you like.

Coppers abroad are generally OK. Amsterdam coppers in 1996, they were bastards. We had running battles with them outside the ground. I can say I've always been treated quite fairly abroad.

I don't think the English lads when they follow their club or England abroad are treated fairly. If you're an England fan, from the foreign copper's point of view, everybody thinks you're English and a fucking animal. To me, that's wrong. I don't think they deserve a lot of what they get, because a lot of times there seems to be nothing much happening at a game, the coppers simply want to have a fucking fight with the English. I think foreign coppers definitely go over the top when dealing with the England fans.

SHOULD CELTIC AND RANGERS BE ALLOWED TO JOIN THE ENGLISH PREMIERSHIP OR NATIONWIDE LEAGUES?

I would say so, yes. Some team manager said that, for the benefit of Scottish football, why not Rangers and Celtic go elsewhere? But I think there'll be a resurgence in trouble mob-wise for Rangers and Celtic. I think you'll start to see decent numbers again because Rangers fans will go anywhere. Celtic fans are the same. They have fucking 20,000 at European away games and they'll go anywhere. From a football point of view, I think it would benefit both clubs and it would benefit the fan bases of other clubs up here. Financially, for Rangers and Celtic definitely, but trouble-wise, I think it will fucking really increase. Because at every away game there will be thousands.

The rest of the Scottish teams? Fuck them. I think it would benefit them as well because there's Aberdeen, Hibs, Hearts, they'll all be vying to win the league and then the winner gets into the Champions' League, so from their point of view it would be better. But Rangers and Celtic carry the majority of fans. If you look at any, say for instance, a Motherwell–Livingstone game, you'll be lucky to have fucking 5,000 there. But when Rangers and Celtic play at Livingstone Stadium, it's a 10,000 capacity, and 80 per cent will be Rangers and Celtic fans. So it cuts both ways.

DO YOU HAVE ANY VIEW ON BANNING ORDERS? DO YOU KNOW THIS FROM YOUR OWN EXPERIENCE OR THAT OF OTHERS?

I've got a life ban from Ibrox after I got involved in Eindhoven. I don't think the banning orders have any effect whatsoever. I think the banning orders are ineffective. Scottish and English laws are different. Certainly the 20 that were arrested at Eindhoven got club bans. I've not got one from the courts, but I was under a club ban before. I was arrested outside Ibrox, a Rangers–Middlesbrough match in 1999, where I got an indefinite ban and six months later at Eindhoven I was arrested and that's where I got the life ban. But they'll never stop me from going and watching my team.

HOOLIE MOVIES AND FLICKS – DO THEY GLORIFY VIOLENCE OR CREATE A COPYCAT SYNDROME?

I don't think they glorify violence, I just think they get across why people do it and are there, as opposed to these sociologists who get money for fuck all in my opinion. They say you come from broken homes and unemployment – what shite. I'm a Rangers fan, and I don't know anyone in the firm who's unemployed. But sociologists, as far as I'm concerned, are a waste of fucking time, they get money for nothing.

The best one was the hooligan documentary on West Ham. I don't see how anybody can take the point of view from watching that these people are fucking animals or because they come from a broken background and all that sort of stuff. I'd like to see more reaction and get these sociologists to speak directly to the lads because they are talking a lot of shite. But at the first instance of violence anywhere, the papers will always go to these people for their view for such and such a reason. Their reasons are different to the people who are actually doing it.

WHO'S YOUR TOP FELLOW – SOUND AS A POUND – FROM YOUR OWN SUPPORTERS, WHY HE IS NOMINATED AND WHAT DID HE DO FOR YOU?

One of my best mates who sadly died a few weeks ago, Barry Johnstone. He was regarded as the main boy at Rangers' firm. A good loyal friend. I'd have liked you to have talked to him.

IS THERE, IN YOUR OPINION, A NEXT GENERATION OF HOOLIGAN APPRENTICES COMING THROUGH AND WILL THEY BE ANYTHING LIKE THEIR PREDECESSORS?

I'm 31 now; there's not many people younger than me coming through. There is a few, but very few. I certainly don't know any 15- or 16-year-olds coming through. Basically, it's all the same faces that are involved that have been going for the past 15–20 years, so certainly not at Rangers. Aberdeen possibly; they seem to have a lot of younger guys coming through, but certainly not at Rangers. I don't know why. Probably because Aberdeen is on its own, there's no Rangers–Celtic, there's no rivals, there's no team to rival them. Their closest rivals are Dundee, basically.

A lot of people in Glasgow still think that the Casuals are long gone, that the Casuals doesn't exist any more. It was a big, big thing, certainly in the mid-'80s.

NAME: Woody
CLUB: Halifax Town
FIRM: OMD

'I don't think I'd ever change anything'

BACKGROUND AND MEET

Six months before Euro 2004, there was a press release saying £5 million was to be invested in the war on hooliganism in this country. Now that money gets distributed in many different ways, but I don't think the lower leagues are seeing much of the impact that kind of investment would have. Apparently, proper serious disorder is centred around one or two Conference League sides. It only involves small numbers – it has to when the crowd is around 1,500 – but has been growing to the point there is definitely a scene going on at this level. I've met and spoken to guys who have given up following big clubs to get involved in the lower league scene. Now I think about it, 30–40 lads counts as a full-on mob. Hardly any Old Bill, unmanned stations, no pub watch and the clubs can't afford enough stewards.

Take a town like Halifax. Surrounding Halifax is a multitude of football teams within striking distance – Bradford, Huddersfield, Leeds, Darlington, York, Scarborough, Barnsley, Scunthorpe, Sheffield, Stockport, Oldham, Manchester, Burnley. Now Halifax haven't got to be playing any of these teams to get a row because they will be bumping into them en route near enough any game they travel to or, more likely, rival fans will be using Halifax as a port of call. So now you see my reasoning for a Halifax chapter; they must have had more rows than the Slater family. So who would I find? I had no knowledge of a proper contact linked to any Halifax lad, firm-wise.

As luck would have it, I'm out following England during the

Euros and hanging about the main square in the centre of Lisbon. I meet the funniest character who just kept me entertained with his stories. I also clocked he knew plenty of the right people from other English firms. I learned he'd travelled on most of England's ventures, everyone knew him just as Woody, and I bumped into him several times during my weeks out there.

The second time I met him, a Leeds firm had given him or his pals a bit of a slap because they couldn't find the person they were really after. Was he a top boy? I half knew what his answer would be. He said, 'Cass, I was never top lad of our firm, I was a lad in a firm. Our top lads, they really were top lads and big respect to all of them, they know who they are. But I am a lad who's been there; sometimes I've been battered to fuck, and sometimes we've dished it out. It's just like I was there, had a good laugh, still having a good laugh. So what do you wanna ask me?'

His name is David Woodward, born in 1968. Qualifications are eight O-levels and served fitter apprenticeship. Divorced and works self-employed in the plant construction industry.

WHAT HAS BEEN THE MOST LEGENDARY FIGHT OR RIOT YOUR TEAM'S SUPPORTERS HAVE BEEN INVOLVED IN?

Everybody's got different views of different rows that they've been in. For me and the lads, our firm, ours has got to be against Burnley, and I'd say that's the biggest row with stabbings. That would have been '84/85. Had it in the town centre, during the game, after the game, everything. Dragging them off the buses.

At the start of weekend, Friday, everybody was out on the piss, everybody getting it planned where to meet. Saturday, we met in our main pub then which was Bailey's Bar. Good turn out; all the lads were there. Some young lot came down and told us Burnley had just got off the bus at the top of George's Square. They were walking down, and we walked up to meet them. Had it in the centre of the square, no Old Bill, going back and forth, having it with each other. Total numbers of our firm were about 80, their firm a bit more.

Our main firm in those days, back to the OMD thing, was off the biggest estate where all the lads used to live, called

Ovenden. We had lads from other towns, from different estates, but we all used to come together for the big ones. It's always been bad, Halifax–Burnley. We may have Bradford and Huddersfield dead close to us, but in the '80s in the old Fourth Division it was always Burnley because the main thing is the Yorkshire–Lancashire thing. We just fucking hate each other. It's always been like that. My old man was saying it's always been like that. We just do not get on.

This was the Casual era – you'd call us Perry Boys, Casuals, Smoothies, whatever they were called then – the bleached jeans, diamond Pringles. In 1985, Armani had come in by then, everybody had Armani on. There were a lot of lads who followed Leeds out of it, and there were a lot of lads who were Man U. Halifax were split down the middle, either Leeds or Man U, and then Halifax, the actual lads who went to the Halifax games.

In those days, Burnley, when the syringes were in use, a lot of lads were carrying syringes to chiv you with, which were pretty evil, to say the least. And I've been slashed twice in my life. I got done with a syringe full of ammonia. That were late on at night, because, after the game, all Burnley just stayed about trying to drink in Halifax and it was on all night. We'd go into a pub – some of the bouncers were our lads anyway, so they'd tell us where they were and we'd go round there. We was fighting all night long.

I remember one of our other pubs, it's called Griss, we met them on the corner there, had a good row with them, about 20 each side. Proper toe-to-toe, no arsing about. As I say, in those days it was syringes that were in fashion weapon-wise, and that was it, end of story. I didn't even know I'd got done 'til I went down. I felt really weird. And I was just out of it, out of the game, that was it.

For a good couple of days, I was totally fucked. I didn't really worry about AIDS, because in those days it was different. I didn't have any stitches because I didn't even know I'd got done until I went to hospital and got informed what it most probably was. Something just came over me, and I just collapsed. There was no pain, just a dull ache. Not a pain like if you get a right-hander, it's just there, you can't get shot of it.

HOW IMPORTANT WAS THE ROLE OF ALCOHOL AND DRUGS? WAS THERE ANY TIME IN YOUR EXPERIENCE EITHER HAD PARTICULAR INFLUENCE?

Of course, with all lads it's always coming back to the drugs thing. After all us lot in the '80s, as soon as the evening came in, everybody was either too busy earning out of it or getting pilled out of their heads, and there were no lads who come through after our firm then, everybody was too busy having a good time or making a stack load of cash out of it. I think, if you talk to any proper lad, they'll all agree that that's what really killed a lot of the firms. A couple of our lads, influential lads, there were just too busy – in those days you'd travel anywhere and everywhere in a car to meet in a field before these big proper rave pubs came about. There was a load of us Halifax lads who went to the Hacienda all the time, I'd say from '83 onwards, all going down to Manchester because they were right next door.

Alcohol, I wouldn't say it played any part or doesn't play any part. We could be stone-cold sober and have a major row, people pulling blades, or you could be pissed out of your head and you could do it.

WHO WAS THE MOST VIOLENT, CRAZY SET OF SUPPORTERS YOU EVER CAME ACROSS?

It's probably a mob who we haven't even been playing. Halifax is a well-known drinking town so we've had everybody from Spurs stop off here. The maddest were probably Wrexham; we played them a long, long time ago, and they were just fucking lunatics. They had a particular well-up mob of about 10-handed and we battered the fuck out of them a good few times that day, but they just kept coming back, they just wouldn't leave it alone. I'd say it was about 20 years ago, it could be '85/86, but they just kept coming back and back.

One lad sticks out in all our memories – Derby shirt, golfing umbrella. He just wouldn't leave it alone. He was about 5ft 8in, pretty tubby lad, but he must have either been as thick as fuck or as game as fuck, one of the two, because we battered him about four times individually.

ARE YOUR FIRM STILL DOING IT?

I'd say our firm that we had in the '80s, all the old lads, it doesn't happen, we're not active any more, as in pursuing it all the time. There's a young lot who've come through, they're about 23–24 now, the average age. They're trying to get it started again. We've been to quite a few games this season, like Chester with the Old Bill all over us.

Chester came to Halifax, fair play to them, they brought about 50–60 lads and it was like being back in the 1980s. We had it on the streets with them before the police got there.

At the start of this season, we had it with Huddersfield lads. I remember when they steamed into our main pub, the Bass House. That was a good 'un. Again, no Old Bill. Everybody turned out from work, everybody was expecting it. That was start of last season. The Huddersfield lads were saying they gave us a bit of respect, they said 'fair play' to us on the old Internet. I mean, I don't do that computer bollocks lot; the young lads do. It went down as evens that day, really. There were about 40 of them, about 40 of us. Later on in the day, about 20 of their old lads came back to our pub again, had it with a couple of us lot. So yeah, it was a good day. It's the best one we've had all season.

As I say, there's some new young lads, they're out, they're going out every week and they're trying to get a mob interested in it again, they're trying to get people to do it. But as with all firms, people grow up, get married, go to jail, whatever, or they don't want to know any more. There's quite a lot of lads who, through other things, have gone to jail for quite a long time; one, I think, has just got a nine-year sentence. That's outside of football. I think everybody was a bit criminal-minded, that's the only way to make cash in Halifax. It's a really big drugs town, everybody knows that.

HOW WOULD YOU DESCRIBE THE SITUATION WITH THE SCENE TODAY? CAN IT COMPARE WITH WHAT HAPPENED IN THE PAST, AND DO THINGS STILL GO OFF IN THE SAME WAY?

Oh, definitely. I don't think it's ever going to go back to what it was because nowadays you go to any town and there's CCTV, and the pubs have got two-way radios to tell each other when there's a firm. I don't think it's ever going to go back to what it was in the '80s, but our firm then, if you were dressed up in the fashion of the day, your Pringles and your Ellesses and your bleached jeans, your Puma GVs, if you went to somebody else's town and you were dressed, it meant one thing – you were there to have a row. Now, there's too many lads who can buy this designer clothing and they may wear it all but they haven't got a clue about it. Now you can't have the rows like you did, there's too many Old Bill, too many cameras, everybody's always concerned about getting a tug. You may not get tugged on the day of a row, but you could get tugged two to three months down the line.

The police know me personally. Our Intelligence Officer comes up to us, he tries to call you by your nickname to crack on that he knows us; maybe he thinks if he knows our names we're going to stop doing what we're doing. Every time they see us they come up to us, either calling you by your nickname or your full name: 'Hello, Mr Woodward, are you going to get into trouble today?' 'Yes officer ... no officer.'

HOW DID YOU GET GOING WITH A FOOTBALL FIRM, DID IT HAVE A NAME AND HOW WAS THE NAME ESTABLISHED?

It's not a place where I grew up, which is outside of Halifax. We had a firm then called the HBF, the Hebden Bridge Firm. Then when we started going into Halifax and we started drinking when we were about 15–16. Halifax had a firm then but it didn't have a name. The lads all my age range now, they had a name; it may sound silly but we were called OMD, Ovenden Mad Dogs, after the estate where the main lads grew up and after the group at that time, the '80s group OMD. That was our name. That was any time from '83 onwards. It lasted about four to five years, did that. We were well known, everywhere around our place, they knew us and they knew where to find us in our main pub and that was the name of our mob there, OMD.

WHAT WAS THE WORST INSTANCE OF WEAPONS BEING USED?

The first time I ever saw a knife being used was when Huddersfield came over. And I suppose if some firms used a knife, then some other firm will start carrying them. One of our lads was a really well-known lad in Halifax when Huddersfield came over. We were having a row, but they definitely had the numbers, so this lad – he knows who he is – he stabbed some lad down his back. He got jailed for it, he got a bit of time for it. But he fucked this lad up big time. I think it was about a 2ft job on his back. Opened him all the way up.

As we were rowing, it was just like everybody was having their own battle, none of us knew he had a knife. He just went like that, and that's the first ever time I've ever heard of or seen anybody use a knife. He's known as a lad who can have a row; he can definitely put his hands up to it.

WHAT IS THE MOST IMPORTANT LESSON YOU LEARNED PERSONALLY DURING YOUR TIME WITH YOUR FIRM AND WOULD YOU DO ANYTHING DIFFERENTLY?

I don't think I'd ever change anything I've done. I mean, I've been arrested a load of times and had the occasional little spells away, but I wouldn't change anything. I mean, it's part of growing up. The most important thing is you must always stay together. I've got one lad, he's my best friend out of it, he went to prison because of it. It's friendship, it's staying together, it's that bond. I mean everybody goes on about when you did the National Service or you got friends from the Army, we just stuck together. I mean, we still stay together now. We're just like late thirties and going into forties now, but we may be married and have kids, but yeah, it was staying together, friendship.

WHO WERE YOUR BIGGEST RIVALS BOTH TEAM AND FAN-WISE?

Being where Halifax is, we had everybody – Huddersfield, Bradford. Me personally, and I reckon most of our lads would agree, it had to be Burnley, our biggest game, our biggest row and our biggest rivals were always Burnley. On the field, off the field, the hate's still there, the rivalry's definitely still there.

WHO ARE THE TOP FIVE FIRMS OF ANY IMPORTANCE TODAY?

Stoke, I would rate them as one of the firms now in England, definitely. Pompey, another set of good lads. Yourselves on your day when you turn out. I went to West Ham–Stoke the other week; that was a good turnout. Definitely got to be the 'Boro; they've got a good firm there, still really active. Firms I've met on my travels, especially with the England team, probably Birmingham, they've always got a good firm, always go everywhere.

WHO ARE YOUR TOP FIVE FIRMS OF ALL TIME?

Well, now you're talking old school, old First Division. And it's got to be what everybody knows and it's got to be Chelsea, it's got to be West Ham, it's got to be Leeds in the '80s, the Leeds Service Crew. Again, first-hand experience, definitely 'Boro again because they always turn up everywhere. Fifth, I'd say Tottenham, because on the days they do turn out … we played Tottenham in a Cup game, I think it was 1981, and even then in those days they brought a good lot up to Halifax. But I think they came a bit unstuck because they were thinking we were going to be a dozy set of northern bastards and I think they came a bit unstuck when they walked into our square because, to us, that was like our game of the decade. We've got Spurs coming up, we're going to have to put up a big mob. And if any Spurs lads are reading, I think you'll put your hand up to that, especially when we shot them with a flare gun. It was as funny as fuck.

We turned round, Spurs come at us. One of our lads had a flare gun, we always used to carry flare guns then, a little pin flare gun, size of a fucking big marker pen. Shot it, bounced all over and this lad tried to put it out, but flares just don't go out. He set his trainer on fire – Puma GV, the big white trainers that all lads had in the '80s. Even his firm were laughing their bollocks off at him. It were one of those things where fighting just stopped and everyone was laughing their bollocks off. It were fucking classic, mate, know what I mean? It was one of those things.

WHAT IS THE WORST GROUND YOU'VE EVER BEEN TO AND WHAT IS YOUR FAVOURITE GROUND?

Worst ground I've ever been to is Hartlepool on a wet Tuesday night. It was shit. Had a good laugh at Torquay once because they'd banned away supporters then, but we all got in and we sat in their end. We all said we were down there doing a bit of work on site. And they must have known who we was, about 20 lads all traipsing in, full of Lacoste and Tacchini, and the away fans are banned, and we walked straight into their end. It didn't take long for their fucking lads to suss us and come round, no introductions were needed, it were smash, smash, smash. But I don't really know about grounds. I mean, I didn't take a lot of notice or interest in them.

WHAT IS YOUR FAVOURITE FOOTBALL FASHIONWEAR AND THE WORST YOU'VE SEEN OR WORN?

Well, I'll start with worst first. It had to be when the dungarees were in in the early '80s because me being a fat bastard couldn't really wear them. And if I had anything, my abiding memory's got to be Adidas New Yorkers, the hooded top, the bleached jeans, and the Puma GVs or the old Borg Elite. Blinding fashion.

WHAT IS THE WORST KIT YOU'VE SEEN A TEAM IN AND WHAT WOULD BE YOUR OWN CLUB'S BEST EVER STRIP?

The worst kit I've ever seen has got to be that Arsenal one late '80s/early '90s, that thing where somebody on acid has designed it. Fucking awful. Whoever did that is a right cunt. And, of course, my best one's got to be the old Halifax Town one, the old blue-and-white one, about 1986. Again, I keep on harking back to the '80s. Nice white top, bit crisper, Halifax Town, nice. I think we had a local firm sponsor then. Some building site or something. Now we're sponsored by the Nationwide, been sponsored by them for years, but then in the '80s it was like your home town firm and sponsor.

DOES TODAY'S MODERN FOOTBALL PLAYER HAVE THE RESPECT OF THE FANS?

I view them all as money-grabbing bastards who'd jump ship as soon as piss on your face. Halifax Town, I always keep going back to the old days, but there were a couple of our lads who even played for Halifax Town. They'd come out on the piss with you on a Friday night, but on Saturday they'd be playing. I don't know how they played sometimes, because we were all doing stuff we shouldn't.

When we went to Torquay once, we lost the keys to our Ford Trannie. We couldn't get in the Ford Trannie so the manager at the time, Billy Ayr, who's unfortunately dead now, he allowed our lot on the team coach to come back home. That's what kind of a club it was. You knew the players; if they played shit, you'd slag them off, and they'd still show their face in the pub after the game because they all used to come out on the piss with us.

I hate it at other clubs like Leeds, because anybody who they get always goes to one club over the border which just happens to be the most hated club by Leeds and by just about anybody in England – Man U. I mean, you've got Smithy kissing that club badge all year long, and he fucks straight off to Man U. Happened with Cantona, and it happened with Ferdinand. It just seems that anybody who believes they are any good, they're going across on the M62 straight over to bloody Manchester and that's it.

WORST FOREIGN PLAYER YOU'VE SEEN AND THE BEST FOREIGN IMPORT? YOUR FAVOURITE CLUB PLAYER AND YOUR FAVOURITE OTHER PLAYER?

Best foreign import I'd definitely say was Zola for the old Chelsea. And the worst foreign import, again it's Chelsea. They had that Dutch lad, Winston Bogarde, there for about two-and-a-half years and he ain't even started a first-team game, and he's on 40 grand a week. I wish I could get a job like that.

FANS OFTEN TALK ABOUT THEIR FOOTBALL-GOING DAYS AS JUST BEING A LAUGH. ANY EPISODES YOU REMEMBER?

I think the best one I've ever seen was when a couple of Halifax lads were in Marseilles in '98; a couple of your lads will back me up because they were there an' all. We're outside Marseilles train station the day after we played Tunisia. We were all waiting for our train to go back to wherever it were. Two lads ambled over, all Stone Islanded up. We just thought they were English. They walked over. They went, 'You English?' We went, 'Yeah, we are, lads, obviously.' The two lads had come from Spartak Moscow. Come all the way from there.

He went, 'We like to fight like you English hooligans.'

They had on all the gear, all Stone Island, Armanied up. 'We Spartak Moscow, we come, we like to fight.'

'All right then, lads.'

Argentina were playing in Marseille after England and there were all scarves and hats coming out of the train station. So one of our lads said for a laugh, 'Just go over there and batter them.'

So these two Spartak lads are off like they've got an Excocet up their arses and I have an abiding memory of these two headcases from Moscow kicking fuck out of these Argentinians. We just sent them over. Bosh, straight there. And we were like, 'What the fuck is happening here?' We couldn't get our heads round it. It was absolutely mental and the lads who were there that day still remember it, because we still talk about it. Absolute fucking headcases.

YOUR OPINION ABOUT ALL-SEATER STADIUMS, TICKET PRICES AND THE COMMERCIAL ASPECT OF TODAY'S FOOTBALL INDUSTRY. DO YOU STILL FEEL FOOTBALL BELONGS TO THE FANS?

It's not like being on the terraces. I hate sitting down. Half of these grounds that you go to, you can't sit down because they're designed for 5ft 5in people. I hate sitting down. Even though when every ground had a seating area, your old lads in the early days always went and sat in the seats because it showed a bit more class. No, you'll never get the terraces back. I wish we could, but we won't. It's all commercialised as you know, it's all money, money, money. As a northern town, it's always been a Rugby League town, and it's always been known for rugby more than Halifax Town FC. When we tried to ground share with them in the '80s, they turned round and went, 'No, we're the big club of Halifax, you're the little club, basically fuck off.' Now, unfortunately, we share a ground with them and I can't abide them, but they own it and we're the poor bloody comparison to them. It's all Halifax Rugby League or Rugby Union, that's how much interest I don't take in it. I don't even know what code's playing there.

RACISM AND RACE ISSUES HAVE BEEN PART OF FOOTBALL WITH CERTAIN CLUBS AND SETS OF SUPPORTERS AT BOTH CLUB AND INTERNATIONAL LEVEL. WHAT WAS YOUR EXPERIENCE OF THIS?

It hasn't really affected us because, when we were very active, when we had a firm, we had a black lad with us, a good lad. Sadly gone now, Zeko. And it didn't matter to us at all. No, it didn't mean anything to us. They could be black, white, Chinese, anything. If you're part of our firm, you're part of our firm. And if nobody liked that, well, fuck them. Like we've always said, one go, we all go.

Don't get me wrong, I like the BNP. Halifax has got the most BNP counsellors in England, but a lot of people, they think the BNP's just a racist mob. It isn't. I mean, it's the only party that's sticking up for the English. I mean, if you've ever been to Halifax, it's a bit like Bradford. And they all feel they daren't do anything to the Asians in Halifax. So every time they attack people, it'll give a description but it will never say what colour they were. If it's a white person who attacks them, you're on the front page of paper and you're bollocksed.

So, no, race hasn't been an issue for us, as I say. We've had black lads in our firm and we've got black lads now. Don't mean nowt.

HOW HAVE FANS FOLLOWING THE NATIONAL TEAM ABROAD BEEN TREATED, AND WHAT ARE YOUR EXPERIENCES FOLLOWING YOUR CLUB OR NATIONAL TEAM ABROAD?

On the club level, I wouldn't have a clue because it's Halifax, and we've never been anywhere, but on the international level I can definitely say something because I've been here, there and everywhere with England and we get treated like shit basically everywhere.

The best respect that we've had and the best places I've ever been to have got to be your Dutch countries and your Scandinavian countries. They treat you with respect, so you're going to give them respect back. You start going to places like Spain and Italy, and it's as soon as you step off the plane, it's like, yeah, we're there for one thing only and batter the fuck out of you all the time.

For instance, in Turkey, there've been a couple of abandonments – they've even shot a goalkeeper with a flare gun – but were they kicked out of the Euros and were they kicked out of UEFA? No. As soon as England do something, it's always like everybody's always on England's case, just waiting for us to cock up.

I went to Sunderland, and ended up having an extended stay up there. I mean, OTT weren't the word up there, it were like unreal. In Marseilles, there were that many English Old Bill they were running about trying to tell the French Old Bill, 'He's a hooligan, go and arrest him.' We got treated like shit. A couple of our lads got arrested out there, especially Flapper. He got the biggest sentence of any English lad over there. I think he stayed in nick three months, a 14 grand fine and banned from France for two years. He got stitched up and he ended up staying there for three months. But you don't hear that when he came out of prison, because he was in the RAF and everybody was calling for him to be chucked out. It was on the front page of every paper. The headline said: From hero to zero. And I was personally standing with that lad and he was doing nowt, he was just pissed out of his head. He couldn't run when the Old Bill did a baton charge, he was just an easy body. Pissed-up Englishman, you'll do, and the papers vilified him.

WOULD YOU SAY THE MEDIA 'OVER-HYPE' THE TROUBLE AND CAN YOU GIVE AN EXAMPLE OF THIS?

Yeah. It's their job to write, but we never get it right. At some of these major rows, well, I've been there, I've been in these squares where it's all supposed to have gone off, and I was there and I didn't see it. Basically, they're liars. The biggest instance is when a TV crew came up to us and asked us to play up – they actually said to us, 'If you play up, lads, you're all right for a beer.' So we played up for them and just chucked all the beer on them.

In Charleroi in 2000, just before the Germany game, TV crews were coming up to us, 'All right, lads, you act the goat … blah, blah, blah … you all right for beer.' It was a major network; it weren't any little TV station.

HOW WOULD YOU DESCRIBE YOUR FIRM/ SUPPORTERS' FAN BASE, AND HAS YOUR FAN BASE CHANGED OVER TIME?

The general support it's Halifax. We get around from 1,000 to 1,400 people every week and after you've been going for a number of years you just get to know everybody because 1,000 people may sound a lot, but it ain't and then when you're going to away games and you're taking anything from 40 people to 300, you just get to know everybody. Support is very localised and it's very Halifax. It's always been like that with Halifax.

IS THERE, IN YOUR OPINION, A NEXT GENERATION OF HOOLIGAN APPRENTICES COMING THROUGH AND WILL THEY BE ANYTHING LIKE THEIR PREDECESSORS?

I think there are some lads who are definitely coming through and definitely trying to keep it going. These lads still wear the gear, they do go, and they do have it if we meet anybody. More often than not, we are outnumbered. Some of the people, they're 21–25. Always up for it. They're not gonna be like us because our time was, quite simply, our time. There'll never be another time like it in my opinion. Do they measure up? Well, nothing's gonna be like it was in the late '70s/early '80s, nothing. They can only but try.

NAMES: Philly & Ian Bailey
CLUB: Hartlepool United
FIRM: Blue Order

'If we met anyone from Darlington there would be riots.'

BACKGROUND AND MEET

Standing in Charlie Breaker's pub in a half-decent part of South London, I got talking to reformed hard man Richy Horsley and, like every other hard man and gangster in the place, they'd all become bestselling authors. So you make yourself sociable as it's all in aid of charity and I'm trying to hold a conversation with Richy Horsley's North-East accent, which is a Hartlepool one. I stuck with it because I was up that way when doing the Newcastle and Sunderland chapters in *Terrace Legends*, and my man from Peterlee said Hartlepool are as game as fuck. Now, coming from a man that has been in that many scraps, I took note.

The interest increased when people kept telling me about some serious stuff going on between Hartlepool and Darlington; no quarter, no inch given whenever these two meet. Richy said he'd give me the mobile of Philly Bailey. 'He is your man up there. Believe me, that is a name that is very well known in Hartlepool.'

So I drove up in the middle of the autumn and met this Philly Bailey and thought I'd been hit on the chin because there was two Baileys, the other unrelated but Phil's mate, who had been just as involved. Double trouble to any rivals for sure. Both assured me for the book that they had knocked it all on the head, banned from every football ground, banned from every nightclub. 'We've just got one more court case to sort out, Cass, and that's it. Our names are getting put down to everything that goes on in this town.' One tape recorder and two voices later, I left Hartlepool wondering does that mean retired with the Darlington game or without?

Phil was born in1962, is single and a window-fitter by trade. Ian was born in 1978, also single, and a qualified roofer, now self-employed. The first game he went to was Hartlepool v Darlington.

WHAT HAS BEEN THE MOST LEGENDARY FIGHT OR RIOT YOUR TEAM'S SUPPORTERS HAVE BEEN INVOLVED IN?

Phil: I would probably say the Darlington match about five to six years ago. I'd had a phone call in the morning telling me that they were turning up. So I got in the car, went round everybody's houses, phoned loads of people up, and told them that they were definitely coming. So we all met in a pub called Oscar's back then. You're talking 150–200 lads.

Anyway it got to half-past two and everybody was saying, 'I thought you said they were coming.' I said, 'They're definitely … believe me, they're coming,' and as I said that I've seen this dozen lads start walking to the main entrance and I recognised them straight away. I said, 'Here they are now.'

So they stopped at the door and looked in, obviously thought better of it, and did a U-turn. So we followed them out and they were running down York Road. There were only about 12 of them at this stage, it was the first numbers that turned up. So we chased them down York Road and all their other minibuses turned up; there were seven to eight minibuses, all full. They all got out, they could see their lads and us chasing them down the road until they stopped at a certain point. Well, actually, either they couldn't go much further or they were knackered, because they'd run that far, and they turned round and everybody just tore into each other.

I don't know where they got them from, but they had big bags of milk bottles. They were throwing them at us. Everybody got toed in. It was a massacre, but once Old Bill turned up everybody got separated.

We came back towards the town centre because the Old Bill were chasing us up there and Darlington were actually being pushed through the town centre. So as they were coming through the centre, we were coming out the other way, basically ending up in a head-on collision.

As we came round the corner, we could see all their lads coming down; there must have been about 100 of them and one of our lads was actually in front of them. When the police had separated them, he'd actually got pushed into their lines, and he was pretending to be a Darlington fan. And it was quite funny actually, he was coming towards the Hartlepool fans with these Darlington fans saying, 'Let's get into the Hartlepool bastards.' And we all just stood there and said, 'What's going on here?'

So all of a sudden, they got within about 20 yards of us. Our lad with them then went, 'Woah, stop,' and they all stopped. And then he just turned round, smacked one of them in the face, and walked over slowly to be with the Hartlepool lads. There was just a fucking mass battle again. But it went on for ages. Darlington was up for it, they always are, they're always pretty game.

WHO WAS THE MOST VIOLENT, CRAZY SET OF SUPPORTERS YOU EVER CAME ACROSS?

Phil: Personally, it was a one-off – and people don't believe me when I say this – but it was actually Rochdale. We'd got an old Transit van with about 20 people squashed into the back of it, and got to Rochdale about opening time. We found this pub, went in, and it was full of Rochdale fans, and they never said a word, they all left. So we'd had a few pints, and then we thought we'd go down to the next pub. As we came out the pub, there must have been about 50 Rochdale fans outside this other pub on the opposite side of the road. And they all just started pelting us with glasses. There were three of us at the front – myself, a lad called The Mauler and a lad called Hewy. We were all pretty good boxers; I'd had about 20 fights at the time, The Mauler had had about 120 fights in about two years, and Hewy had just won the junior middleweight ABA championship. So as they were coming across the road, us three were basically knocking down anybody who came towards us.

It was just chaos. There were no police in sight. It went on for about 20 minutes. There were only 20 of us, and about 50 Rochdale. Anyway, they broke up and basically ran down the road. There were a couple of lads mouthing off on the corner, so me and The Mauler ran down and just fought with these two lads. The one that The Mauler hit, he hit the deck and he didn't look very clever at all. He looked in a very bad way. The rest of the lads went back and got the van. They jumped in the van, came down the road, and saw this lad on the road. The lad who was driving got out of the van to make sure he was OK. He was trying to resuscitate this lad and the Old Bill came and put two and two together, obviously got five and thought that he'd attacked this lad and they arrested him for it.

The lad was in a bad way; he'd got a cracked skull in the middle of all this. So obviously word must have got round that this lad was in a bad way in hospital, so I think half of Rochdale had come out at the end of the match. Meanwhile, we drove round to find out what was happening to our lad that had been arrested at the police station, and myself and another lad entered the police station and we heard this shouting. And we looked out and I could see 200–300 lads surrounding our van, just kicking and booting it, trying to get the doors open, because our lads inside were obviously not going to come out.

So we ran down towards the van; they saw us, turned their attention away from the van and chased us. So we ran back into the police station. Then the police came out of the police station, all batons, the full carry-on. But these Rochdale lads weren't having it, they decided to target the police really big style, so the police had to back off. They locked the police station doors and they were just going mental, they were kicking the police station doors trying to get into it. And the police were shitting themselves. Actually, so was I. There's nothing you can do because you're talking about 200–300 lads outside.

They had to phone for assistance from Greater Manchester or somewhere. About another 20 police vans came eventually but they still took time dispersing these lads. It was very scary. We found out that the lad did have a fractured skull. One of our lads actually got charged with it.

HOW WOULD YOU DESCRIBE THE SITUATION WITH THE SCENE TODAY? CAN IT COMPARE WITH WHAT HAPPENED IN THE PAST, AND DO THINGS STILL GO OFF IN THE SAME WAY?

PHIL: The thing about it is everybody has got everybody else's phone number.

IAN: The Internet plays a big part in it these days. We do get numbers or addresses or whatever – you get talking and you start from there. What we do is we send part of the messages to people. We don't actually put it on the website, we just send somebody an e-mail. If we have contacts with another club, they'll give us a number or have a number for one other club, another number for such and such a club. If we can't get in touch with them, we have spotters out, we'll have people all over the town just ready for a phone call.

HOW DID YOU GET GOING WITH A FOOTBALL FIRM, DID IT HAVE A NAME AND HOW WAS THE NAME ESTABLISHED?

PHIL: Well, for me it's been a long road. I've been going since the '70s. We had lots of little individual groups, but nobody really had a name, it wasn't like a firm. Our first named group was called the Moosemen.

IAN: There's quite a few stories, but you had your squad of lads who were not as good as the Blue Order these days, but they were still a nasty firm, the Moosemen. Blue Order's been going since about 1997. We started off as a vanful of us, there was 15 of us. We went everywhere and from there it's just got bigger and bigger, more and more.

As we'd just got formed, we needed a name. the Moosemen were like years before us. We were gonna take over the Moosemen, keep the Moosemen name going. But being a new firm, new songs, we thought we'd rename it and we came up with Blue Moose, like Hartlepool play in blue, and keep the Moosemen running. Blue Army was another one. Someone come up with Blue Order, because there was a group called New

Order – that's how we finally got our name Blue Order seven to eight years ago.

WHAT WAS THE WORST INSTANCE OF WEAPONS BEING USED?

Something that comes to mind is when we played Birmingham at home, it would have been about '96/97 I think. Obviously, you know Birmingham's firm is called the Zulus. We had a bit of trouble with them at one club. We chased them down the road and when we got to the bottom, it's actually now a car park, but at the time it was wasteland.

A few black lads, big lads and all, they just pulled these knives out. But they weren't small; you're talking blades of about 8–9in long and that was quite scary. These Birmingham lads, eventually they bottled it, they actually put the knives away, and we allowed them to go.

Another one was Burnley, late '80s; we had a carry on with them and they came from all over the place. Every one of them had a baseball bat or big wooden sticks or something to hit you with. We got in our van and we were away.

WHAT IS THE MOST IMPORTANT LESSON YOU LEARNED PERSONALLY DURING YOUR TIME WITH YOUR FIRM AND WOULD YOU DO ANYTHING DIFFERENTLY?

PHIL: Well, I've learned not to trust anybody because I know for a fact that there's a grass amongst us. Before you get to where we're playing, I've even tried in the past not telling people 'til the last minute about what we're gonna do and, for some reason, the police know exactly what we're gonna do. There's a police escort just waiting outside the pub we're going to, things like that.

Last season, we went to Sheffield Wednesday and we didn't tell anybody where we were going. We actually went to a little village just outside Barnsley. And that game, we did try to find out who the grass was because we knew someone was informing. So we sent the word about to certain lads that we were taking CS gas, air bombs, smoke canisters, even though we weren't, just to find out who the grass was.

Anyway, it turned out that we were two miles away from Barnsley and passed a lay-by teeming with police – 50–60 of them, vans, motorbikes, you name it. They searched that bus and I mean they searched the bus, down the seats, everyone's socks, their shoes, round your belt, every part they searched. Even in the bins in the bus and everywhere.

It was a back road leading up to Barnsley, it wasn't a main road, but they were waiting for us. They knew exactly which road we were coming on and everything, so somebody was informing the police. Well, we actually got rid of a couple of lads that we didn't trust.

For me, I would go back to when we started. When we first had that 15, we knew who to trust, we knew everyone that was anyone. Now, there's that many people coming and they bring their friends, half the time we don't know who to trust.

WHO WERE YOUR BIGGEST RIVALS BOTH TEAM AND FAN-WISE?
PHIL: Darlington – team-wise and fan-wise.

IAN: And Carlisle, we always have a good run-in with them because they're like Darlington, everybody hates them. We hate Darlo with a passion. It's been going on for years and years, before my time. I think it's a bit of both football and a community thing. It's the same in the nightclubs. If we met anyone from Darlington, there would be riots.

WHO ARE THE TOP FIVE FIRMS OF ANY IMPORTANCE TODAY?
PHIL: I'd say Millwall, Cardiff, and Man United have put up a hell of a squad. They don't get the reputation they deserve, Manchester United. So I'll put them up. I would personally say Stoke, and Birmingham have a hell of a squad. So Millwall, Cardiff, Man United, Stoke and Birmingham.

WHO ARE YOUR TOP FIVE FIRMS OF ALL TIME?

PHIL: Leeds, West Ham, Chelsea, and I've got to put Millwall in again.

IAN: Man City.

WHO'S THE PLAYER AND/OR MANAGER THAT WINDS YOU UP THE MOST?

PHIL: It's going back a while, it's a personal thing – Carlton Palmer. Hartlepool were playing – it was a big cup match with Sheffield Wednesday. One of our players at Hartlepool was a lad called Brian Honour and he was like your bread and butter footballer. He'd have played for Hartlepool for nothing. They were getting peanuts at the time, basically, when you compare it to what they're all on at Wednesday. And Carlton Palmer, all he was doing all the way through the match was trying to wind him up: 'How do you manage on £200 a week? ... I'm getting £2,000 for this match.' And this wind-up went on the whole time. Brian went public about this, saying Palmer was a disgrace to football.

IAN: And another one in later years was Marco Gabiadini. He went from Darlington to Hartlepool and, a few years ago, he played at our Victoria Park ground and I think he scored and one of the Hartlepool fans actually smacked him a few times in the face and then the Darlington manager, Dave Hodgson, got assaulted. A few years later, Gabiadini came to sign for us. Hartlepool fans were against him. He got taunted. I think he stayed a season. He said he was injured and had to retire but I think he couldn't hack it.

I would say the manager has to be David Hodgson. He was at Darlington and he always used to go on about Hartlepool fans. When he used to come down here with Darlington, we used to throw missiles and things at him.

FANS OFTEN TALK ABOUT THEIR FOOTBALL-GOING DAYS AS JUST BEING A LAUGH. ANY EPISODES YOU REMEMBER?

Phil: One was just last season. We'd been to Scunthorpe and we had a 75-seater double-decker bus; obviously, it was full. The police were waiting for us and, as soon as we got off, they put our coach firm into the ground.

After the match, we were coming back. We always stop off at the service station; it's one of those things where the service station must lose thousands of pounds because everybody steals as much as they can get under their coats. So 75 of us went in and we came out – it was Easter, actually – and there must have been 30–40 Easter eggs, bottles and sandwiches. Somebody even stole shampoo, everything you could get your hands on – sweets, bottles of pop, things like that, stuffed down everybody's coat, they could hardly walk. And as we came out the service station doors, a busload of Grimsby fans pulled up and so we still had all this gear in our coats and, obviously, when you see another coach of fans ... so we said to Grimsby, 'Do you fancy it?' And they said, 'No, we don't want no trouble, there's far too many of you.' So we said, 'OK, no problem.'

So we go back to the coach, but clearly somebody had seen us at the service station. They'd phoned the police and, all of a sudden, we see all these blue-and-white flashing lights. About 15 cars pulled on to the forecourt. The coach was loaded, so I said pass everything upstairs and we'll put it all on the roof through the skylight. So as this inspector came on the coach, everything was going out the skylights.

He said, 'We've been told that you've stolen all the gear from the service station.' We asked what he was on about.

He said, 'I'll get the officers to search the bus.'

'Fine,' we said, 'please yourself.'

So all the police came on the bus, they searched the entire coach, under the seats and everywhere. So they went back outside and the inspector came back again. He said to me, 'Was there only you that was in that service station?'

We said, 'No, there was a coachload of Grimsby fans.'

I said, 'I saw some of them pinching all sorts.'

'Where are they?' he asked.

'Just pulling on to the motorway,' I said, 'there they are.'

He went, 'Oh, thanks very much.'

So all the Old Bill cars started chasing this Grimsby coach.

And they left one car near our bus. So the policeman said we could go. So the bus driver pulled away and everything fell off the roof. There were Easter eggs going down the M1 and everything else that had been on the roof of the coach. The policeman was just shaking his head.

On another occasion, we were playing Sheffield Wednesday in the Cup. We went to the match, came out, and stayed on to drink round Sheffield. And we saw this brewery, called Castle Eden. We used to have a Castle Eden brewery just outside Hartlepool. It was like a pub attached to the brewery. So we knocked on the door and this bloke came out, shirt and tie. He said, 'I'm sorry, sir, this is for brewery reps only.'

We said, 'Oh, we are brewery reps from the Castle Eden brewery at Hartlepool.'

He went, 'Oh, OK then. Please come in.'

We went in and, because it was for brewery reps, it was something like 30p a pint. We thought, 'This is OK.' And there was only us in there, about a dozen of us. We were drinking all day. We started playing pool and the lads who were playing pool took it upon themselves for some reason to take all their clothes off, so they were playing naked pool. This bloke from behind the bar came out and he said, 'Are you sure those are brewery reps?'

And we went, 'Yeah, we're on our day out.'

'Oh, OK.' So he went behind the bar. This went on for ages, until one of the lads went over and asked, 'Excuse me, do you mind if I take some pictures?'

'No, feel free,' the barman said.

'OK.' So one of our lads went behind the bar and took all the pictures off the wall. He then stole all the pictures from the pub.

IAN: When we were playing Peterborough away, and we took a squad of 40–50 lads and we stopped at the services on the M1. Just before you go in, there is a sign for the Little Chef and it was Alec Gilroy, a life-size cardboard cut-out – Alec Gilroy off Coronation Street. So I picked it up and I ran to the coach with it. So I went to all the lads, 'This is Alec, he's coming to the game for the day.'

I sat him in the seat there, this cardboard cut-out. And there's people driving down the motorway pointing and waving – 'There's Alec Gilroy ...' So we get to Peterorough and I take it with me through the town. I was stopping cars and everyone's shouting, 'Alec, Alec ...' It wasn't even him, it was a cardboard cut-out.

I was in the pub and people were going up to talk to him, and he was a cardboard cut-out. I couldn't believe how people could be so stupid and believe that he was real. So we stuck around.

We used to have these calling cards and stickers saying you've been visited by Blue Order. And we stuck Blue Order on his head and just left him in the pub. So God knows what happened to him.

PHIL: Another one that was quite funny was Scunthorpe in the mid-'80s. For some reason, they always give us Scunthorpe on a Boxing Day – away to Scunthorpe. And we always used to go in fancy dress. This year, we went dressed in a Hawaiian theme – we all had Hawaiian shorts, shirts on, sandals, sunglasses. And another squad of lads, there was about 20 of them, all went dressed as nuns. They had the full habits on, the lot.

So when we went, nothing happened and we went in our end. Apparently, when the nuns came out of the pub, they walked past one end of the ground and didn't realise it was the away end. So from where we were looking, we could see the away end and all these nuns coming down. And they all attacked the Scunthorpe fans. And all you could see was 20 nuns having it off – bang, bang, bang – with the Scunthorpe fans. What a sight it was.

YOUR OPINION ABOUT ALL-SEATER STADIUMS, TICKET PRICES AND THE COMMERCIAL ASPECT OF TODAY'S FOOTBALL INDUSTRY. DO YOU STILL FEEL FOOTBALL BELONGS TO THE FANS?

PHIL: It's a business now, isn't it? I can't believe some of the prices you pay. I think I paid £54 at Newcastle last season.

IAN: It's not on, especially if you take a couple of kids; you're talking a week's wages. Most families can't afford it these days. Then you've got to buy the shirts and everything that goes with it.

Years ago, people used to go because they loved the team, whereas football now they go because maybe a certain player's signed for them, or they've got a new ground or that type of thing. People don't go any more because they like it. You get a lot of women and kids going now. Years ago, it wasn't that type of thing, was it? I suppose it's for anyone, but at one time it used to be lads at football, didn't it?

PHIL: I've had it myself. Somebody might do a bad tackle and you go, 'Oh, you fucking dirty bastard.' And this woman next to you will complain. And, basically, they shouldn't be there; it's football – it's where you go to get out of the way of women on a Saturday.

RACISM AND RACE ISSUES HAVE BEEN PART OF FOOTBALL WITH CERTAIN CLUBS AND SETS OF SUPPORTERS AT BOTH CLUB AND INTERNATIONAL LEVEL. WHAT WAS YOUR EXPERIENCE OF THIS?

PHIL: Well, it's affected me. I actually got charged with racial chanting – the police had been after me for years and we were playing Oldham. There was an atmosphere. The Oldham fans started singing, 'Town full of monkeys ...' They do like to torture you. This was just after the race riots in Oldham. The monkey-hanging legend is the most famous story connected with the town of Hartlepool.

So some of the Hartlepool fans – we're not racist – started singing, 'You're just a town full of Pakis ...' It wasn't meant as a racist thing, it was just because of the monkey abuse aimed at us, and I actually joined in with it for about three seconds. But the lad I go to matches with, Wayne, he's black. I was standing next to him and they charged me with racial chanting. I said, 'How can I be done for racial chanting? I've stood next to a black lad. I go to matches with a black lad.' I didn't even know the word Paki was classed as racist. The black lad was singing it as well.

Spenna of The Villains.

'If you can't fight with your fists then don't bother turning up.' – The Forest Executive Crew

'You're nicked!' Boatsy in action.

The Bailey Boys, Hartlepool's men of The Blue Order (*top*)
The legend that is Eddie Beef: 'To pay is to fail.' (*bottom left*)
(*Bottom right*) 'They like to use the words Men In Gear, they love to do all that shit,' says MIG Man Tommy.

KIDS – Kick Insult Destroy Suppress. The men of CSKA (*top*)
In Moscow every man is a warrior at heart – 'Yaroslavka' (*bottom*)

'I'll say one thing, it was a bloody good day out.' Tony Cronshaw reflects on his years on the terraces.

'It's still a pretty serious firm' – The Zulu's main man 'Brains' and (*inset*) pictured with the infamous 'shit on the villa' Paul Tait.

Coalville DAZ: 'We will always maintain a firm at Leicester.
We always have done.'

Rolling with ex-657 crew's Eddie Crispin.

Apparently, if you look in the dictionary under the word 'Paki', it says 'short for Pakistani'. Apparently, this judge had made this new order – it was a load of crap.

DO YOU HAVE ANY VIEW ON BANNING ORDERS? DO YOU KNOW THIS FROM YOUR OWN EXPERIENCE OR THAT OF OTHERS?

PHIL: I think the police make a lot of work for themselves, actually, with these banning orders because half of the world is banned now and obviously half aren't, so they've got to keep an eye on the half that aren't who are around the ground during the match and half the lads who are banned obviously around the town, so they've got to split themselves up. If you weren't banned, you're all in one place; they can just keep an eye on you, can't they? Whereas now, we're all over the place during the match. They're stretching their own resources, aren't they?

IAN: They've reinforced the bans now, haven't they? They've put these travel bans on so, when you're playing away, you can't visit that town within a five-mile radius, where before we could. And that's why they put that in because police were on a wild goose chase, back then anyway. There weren't enough of them, they didn't know where we'd gone.

Most Hartlepool fans on away matches don't go out the night before, keeping themselves fresh for the next day in case there's a firm waiting! I'm on my third ban now. I've served seven years out of nine. I got banned in March 2000 for three years for violent disorder with Darlington's mob. Basically, we were coming from Barnet and Darlington were playing Leyton Orient at the same time. We clashed on the trains, fighting all the way from London to Darlington. The police thought they had it all in hand at Darlington Station, but there weren't enough police officers. They actually got us off first, Darlo kicked the doors open and there was about a 50-man battle. Those police officers didn't do anything.

I think banning orders are so unfair because I've done my time and I've been banned again at Halifax and I've served two years of that so they put another three years on me. They keep coming in with more laws. They're actually banning me out of me own town centre within five miles for three years. Just because of me past.

I don't mind being banned, I've been banned for that many years. It's the little ones they're throwing in now, the travel bans, which mean you can't go anywhere, you can't leave your house. There's a map where you can walk along certain allowed streets and not others. This is in your own town. Plus it's the hours – it starts four hours before the match.

When I got my banning order, which was a town centre ban, it was from eleven o'clock in the morning to eleven o'clock at night, so I couldn't leave my house because I only live across the road from the ground. It's breaking all civil liberties, really.

HOOLIE MOVIES AND FLICKS – DO THEY GLORIFY VIOLENCE OR CREATE A COPYCAT SYNDROME?

PHIL: I don't think they glorify violence. I think they're quite funny, actually. Well, I thought that Football Factory was more of a comedy than anything else. It had me in stitches. It's more reality of what goes on. It's got the point across of what actually goes on with the white powder. But it gives you that buzz ... some people will obviously think, 'Let's go to football.'

There's just more to it – it's the clothes, the way it's organised, the way you have to know the right people. I have actually had people come to me and say, 'Is that what goes on? Can I come with Blue Order? Is that what really happens?' And it's more exciting for people when they want to come along, but when it actually comes down to it, they would get frightened and shit themselves when it actually goes off in front of you, because it does. People do want to join because they see it on the film and think it's great. It's got to be in you, you've got to be in a firm to really know or understand what it's like and the buzz you get, it's like a drug.

HOW WOULD YOU DESCRIBE YOUR FIRM/SUPPORTERS' FAN BASE, AND HAS YOUR FAN BASE CHANGED OVER TIME?

PHIL: It's everybody from Hartlepool. Hartlepool is for Hartlepool. Within 20–30 miles you've got three big teams –

Middlesbrough, Newcastle and Sunderland. And everybody is either a Newcastle or a 'Boro or a Sunderland fan. Hartlepool is Hartlepool. Anyone outside of Hartlepool either comes under Middlesbrough, Newcastle or Sunderland, there's no one else. They'd rather see a big team like them. Go down the road, and there's a place called Blackwell and Easington where everybody walks about with a Sunderland shirt or a Newcastle shirt on. I've always supported Hartlepool, it's always been a part of me. We all stick together in Hartlepool.

IS THERE, IN YOUR OPINION, A NEXT GENERATION OF HOOLIGAN APPRENTICES COMING THROUGH AND WILL THEY BE ANYTHING LIKE THEIR PREDECESSORS?

PHIL: We have, yeah. Two Little Boys they're called – TLB. That came from the Rolf Harris song. There's a squad called the TLB, but it's only young lads and they're probably going to get stamped out. They've just started coming through now, just the last couple of years. Only 15 to 17-year-olds and they just started following us and getting a foot on the ladder, they've started coming through the ranks. I mean, we're banned. Blue Order's more or less on its way out, so these ones are gonna have to come in and do what we've done in the past. I don't think it'll ever be like it used to be, especially with today's technology and CCTV.

**NAME: Cockney Jacko
CLUB: Hull City
FIRM: City Psychos**

**'Banning orders
are an absolute
infringement of
civil liberties,
in my opinion.'**

BACKGROUND AND MEET

Personally, I am curious about Hull as a mob. Over the years, I have been aware that they have a reputation. A big city fishing port way up north and rather remote, it's always been in the news for rugby more than the football team. So it tells me a lot that their fans have a bigger name than the team and who better to select a character for the Hull chapter than City Psychos author, Shaun Tordoff? He introduced me to Cockney Jacko, part of the old school that's been around for three decades. Top boy? I wouldn't know, but he's got a CV to match.

I found him quietly spoken, but as passionate about his club as he is for the fight, as we reminisced about the good old bad days stood outside the Silver Cod just down the road from Boothferry Park, Hull City's old, overgrown ground. It's still intact, and I remember West Ham being beaten here 1–0, fourth round of the FA Cup, in 1973. Clockwork Orange-dressed boys were in evidence on the terraces, as half-a-dozen West Ham went on the Hull end to do well before getting absolutely hammered. There was trouble near the station as the Londoners arrived on football specials, and one hard man, when pushed for his recollections, simply said, 'Good firm, Hull. Good firm.'

Simply known as Cockney Jacko – real name Mark Jackson – he was brought up in North London and says he has early recollections of watching Tottenham. He remembers his first game was 1967, West Ham v Tottenham, went with his dad. Moved to Hull aged 11 and is a long-time follower of England games. His qualifications are listed as a clean driving licence, though he worked in an office as his first job. Says he's a child of the '60s, is separated and has a son aged 18.

WHAT HAS BEEN THE MOST LEGENDARY FIGHT OR RIOT YOUR TEAM'S SUPPORTERS HAVE BEEN INVOLVED IN?

The Hull City v Bradford City game from the back end of the '96 season always sticks in the memory; not for size, scale or ferocity, but because this one was the proverbial accident waiting to happen. Between the club's owners and the police, they came up with the brilliant idea of giving the south stand end (Hull City's home terracing) to Bradford on the grounds that they would make more money that way. This was not a popular decision with the Tiger Nation; it wasn't just the Silver Cod Saturday clientéle that were enraged, it was everybody – everybody from the ten-year-old lad to his lifelong season ticket-holding granddad.

The inevitable pitch invasion occurred just before kick-off. The whole scene was videoed and the commentary was provided by a 12-year-old who had won a competition and had the mike wired up as it started. 'We were afraid this was going to happen, and it has, and I'm sorry to say the fans at this club have a bit of a reputation for this sort of thing.' This sounded quite funny coming from a person so young, obviously in the know. Stills from the video were run in the local paper for a few nights running and approximately 60 people ended up being convicted. Some went to jail and at least 90 per cent had banning orders placed on them. The club included these scenes in their end of season video.

I think this one sticks out above others for the way it was allowed to happen. Everyone arrested for those events half-expected it when they left their houses in the morning. Not one person I know who was banned gave up watching Hull City and one lad I know claims the four months he got was well worth it.

WHO WAS THE MOST VIOLENT, CRAZY SET OF SUPPORTERS YOU EVER CAME ACROSS?

Millwall – they have visited us on promotion party day and,

when they fully turn out, they are a pretty unstoppable force. The thing with Millwall is the fact that it is such a small club with no record of football achievement, yet somehow they managed to band together a complete set of nutters and maniacs that were prepared to die for that team. These people made the old Den a terrifying, hostile, bleak place to visit and it's been the same there for as long as I can remember. I think many people went to one away game at Millwall to say they had been and then never went there again. That sort of says it all about the place, really. There are exceptions to this based on London rivalries, but for lads from up north on an away day in the capital, Millwall was not top of your 'places to visit' list.

ARE YOUR FIRM STILL DOING IT?

As recently as the back end of last season ('03/04). As usual, this is a third-hand telling based on local gossip or myth, whichever you choose to believe. Nobody knows the name of anyone who was actually involved and on either side it could be any 50 of a few hundred regular suspects.

Hull City played Huddersfield Town in a sell-out game, the outcome having a major bearing on who would be going up. At the end of this game in the bright sunshine of the car park, a group of approximately 60 Huddersfield fans came across a group of 30 or so Hull fans and set about them. The Hull lads struggled for a while but, as reinforcements arrived in dribs and drabs, things began to turn round. By the time the police arrived on the scene, all dancers have stopped dancing and fled and all that's left are the injured.

The Huddersfield policeman then appears on the scene and proceeds to slate the Huddersfield fans for getting done over by a smaller number. It came across as if he had been involved in a bet and lost. He didn't have an enamel team badge on so his own football loyalties could lie with any team. So, if two groups of like-minded individuals come across each other in the right circumstances, it can still happen, but it is getting rarer due to tighter policing controls.

HOW WOULD YOU DESCRIBE THE SITUATION WITH THE SCENE TODAY? CAN IT COMPARE WITH WHAT HAPPENED IN THE PAST, AND DO THINGS STILL GO OFF IN THE SAME WAY?

There's a bigger interest than there ever was; the spate of books and films didn't create the interest, the interest was always there for such material to thrive. It has now become pretty mainstream and easily available in any good book shop. The police are much better at dealing with matters off the pitch than they ever were. It's cost them an awful lot of money, but they are starting to get the hang of it. On top of which, they are getting the backing of the magistrates in the courts.

I don't think the problem will ever be beaten as it is now ingrained into football globally. In Eastern Europe, where people have only had their freedom for a limited number of years, it seems every male of a certain age wants a piece of this action. Scenes of major disturbances on news channels are just re-enacted all over the globe, sometimes not long afterwards.

HOW DID YOU GET GOING WITH A FOOTBALL FIRM, DID IT HAVE A NAME AND HOW WAS THE NAME ESTABLISHED?

I started using the Albemarle Youth Club in Hull City centre when I was about 13; this was a well-known meeting place of the older Hull City skinhead gang. I moved to Bransholme and became part of the Selworthy mob about the same time as leaving school. By the time the Psychos came around, it was the time of punk rock. The lads who did the organising for these buses did wear donkey jackets and were punk rockers. The clientéle was pretty mixed as we were not a well-supported team around that time. However, the Psycho buses would always get you to matches one way or another when no other transport was available. The Psychos, via their organisers, were in attendance at all Hull City matches during this period and many of them never missed a match.

It was during this period that some people started to move away from the beer belly and donkey jacket look; such people wouldn't hear of being described as Psychos. As a side-issue, the terrace chant 'Hello, hello … City Psychos … City Psychos …'

was heard every time there was a disturbance in the ground and rapidly gained popularity in all parts of the ground. It was such a singalong name it just stuck down the years to the point that Shaun Tordoff's book was titled City Psychos. The chant just seemed to encompass everyone at the time.

WHAT WAS THE WORST INSTANCE OF WEAPONS BEING USED?

It is the guys in the uniforms who have all the weapons these days – long shields, short shields, helmets, scarves, CS gas, etc. The English Police are no angels; as they say themselves, 'We're not paid to be nice.' But in comparison to their foreign counterparts, they are a shining example of discipline. Over-reaction by police in other countries during the visit of English football fans is legendary and has gone on for years.

So, the worst instance of weapons being used in football that comes to mind was when the Turin Police fired off an unlimited amount of tear gas into the crowd during the Belgium versus England match. There were only just over 6,000 people in the stadium that used to host Juventus and Torino games. This led to the players being taken off the pitch due to the effects of the gas. This was all because a small number of people were having a minor disagreement in an empty stadium. I'm sure there was a better way of dealing with the problem. The police made it their business to leather everyone in sight and then do the same again straight after the game, with the taunt, 'See you on Sunday.' England were due to play in the same stadium on the Sunday night against Italy.

This same scenario has been played out over and over again down the years. Those tear gas scenes were seen all over the world and helped to promote the myth that the English football supporters abroad are a pack of animals. Based on the facts of what had happened before the tear gas canisters started flying about, there is hardly a case to answer. This was minor handbags stuff being indulged in by people who had spent the day in the sun drinking. If this had happened on the Costa Brava, the incident would never have been mentioned in the first place. If it was mentioned at all, it would certainly have been forgotten about by the following morning by all involved.

WHO WERE YOUR BIGGEST RIVALS BOTH TEAM AND FAN-WISE?

Team-wise for me it would have to be Leeds United, based on the usual reasons of jealousy and envy. Growing up in the '70s, Leeds United were very big and at one time were the boss team of all football. We were bombarded with these facts by our local television stations who plainly ignored the goings on of Hull City. Leeds is 70 miles from Hull but there is no other major team in this radius. The Leeds United decline has only recently started and long may it continue. Nothing would give me greater pleasure than to see Hull City above Leeds United on a regular basis.

Fan-wise, it would probably be Sheffield United who seemed to follow us about the leagues all through the '80s. We bumped into them on many occasions and, as is the way, there were good days and bad. Lumps and bruises, no excuses. Sheffield United? Game as pheasants.

WHO ARE THE TOP FIVE FIRMS OF ANY IMPORTANCE TODAY?

The top three in any order you like has always been Manchester United, Millwall and West Ham. This has never really changed all the time I've been watching football. There are some good candidates for two others, but at a push Tottenham and Birmingham. The other candidates would be all the usual suspects and they all know who they are and who all the others are of any relevance.

WHO ARE YOUR TOP FIVE FIRMS OF ALL TIME?

Same three as above. Add Rangers and Celtic, two more examples of an unstoppable force.

WHAT IS YOUR FAVOURITE FOOTBALL FASHIONWEAR AND THE WORST YOU'VE SEEN OR WORN?

Favourite football fashionwear would include Three Star jumpers, Prince of Wales check Harrington jackets, red tag Levi jackets, Fila Borg tops, early Armani jumpers with the leather crown badge on the sleeve, Adidas Samba trainers, Timberland boots, plain Lacoste polo shirts and sheepskin flying jackets.

My personal fashion disaster would be permed curly hair. Fashion disasters clothing-wise would include Arrow stretch pinstripe jeans, the tartan-trimmed denim clothing as worn by Doc's Red Army in the mid-'70s. Kio's shoes were a cheap copy of similar shoes by Pod and Kickers. They came in loud colours and didn't last long. The other item that came in loud colours was the leather box jacket. One of the lads had a yellow one – he looked a complete twat in it.

WHO'S THE PLAYER AND/OR MANAGER THAT WINDS YOU UP THE MOST?

I've thought about this one and come to the conclusion it's probably none. I don't even begrudge Sol Campbell his move from Tottenham to Arsenal. They are just blokes making as much as they can, while they can, to support their families in future times. There will always be some you dislike, but not to that extent. They are too separate from us to dislike them that much. It's like wanting to beat Tom Cruise up for not being good in his latest movie – I don't think so.

Manager? Kevin Keegan. And there are several good reasons for this. As a player, Kevin had the habit of sounding off about events off the pitch of which he had no knowledge. This made him quite unpopular with older England fans. He walked out on England when he thought qualification unlikely. His breakdown on television when he was the manager of Newcastle United. Best of all, though, was when the Manchester United fans were singing 'Keegan for England' – he genuinely thought they were being complimentary. What a twat! Need I go on?

WORST FOREIGN PLAYER YOU'VE SEEN AND THE BEST FOREIGN IMPORT? YOUR FAVOURITE CLUB PLAYER AND YOUR FAVOURITE OTHER PLAYER?

Best foreign import is far easier than worst, and I have this one – a tie between Ossie Ardiles and Eric Cantona. Eric for the way he turned his game round after the Crystal Palace incident and went on to become one of the all-time greats. Ossie was one of the all-time greats from the first day he kicked a ball in English football.

At club level, I think Jermaine Defoe has a special talent for scoring goals and my favourite other player? Wayne Rooney. People say he's a white Pele; they're probably right.

The worst foreign import is harder to fathom. The really poor ones came and went before you had noticed. Some stayed for a while, took the money and disappeared. One that puzzled me – how did Mauricco Tarricho spend six years at Tottenham, through various managers, masquerading as a footballer?

FANS OFTEN TALK ABOUT THEIR FOOTBALL-GOING DAYS AS JUST BEING A LAUGH. ANY EPISODES YOU REMEMBER?

During the '84–'85 season, there were a regular group of us who never missed a match for any reason. The same dozen travelled by minibus every week. However, when we were drawn away at Brighton for an FA Cup third round fixture in January, someone decided to run an overnight coach. This coach was to pick up outside two local nightclubs at 2.30am (Tiffany's and Henry's). People fell out of these nightclubs, bought a burger, kissed their girlfriends goodbye and we were off. The coach was oversubscribed and there were far more people than seats. Money was collected as we went and the financial matters were to be sorted out at Trowell Service Station on the M1 – our first scheduled stop.

It was at Trowell Services things started to go wrong. After the usual tomfoolery, a few police cars turned up and arrested the full coach. They informed us we would be going to Nottingham to sort the matter out. There were 40 copies of the Sun newspaper missing and the Nottinghamshire Constabulary was determined to solve this heinous crime.

When we arrived in Nottingham, we parked directly outside the main door of the police station. The driver and two lads who were a bit more sober than some others went into the station to see what could be done. For some reason, they left me with an invoice in the name of a Mr Robinson and a bundle of tenners to match the figure on the invoice.

It was freezing cold and still dark, and the more experienced settled down for a long wait. The opening bid from the police was £100 to be handed over towards damage/loss, and one person would have to be prepared to admit to causing criminal damage and on that basis we could be on our way within a few hours. A whip round for the money was no problem, but finding a volunteer to miss the match and be left behind was not so easy. This message was passed back to those in the station.

There was then a lull in activity and the few policemen stood guarding the coach on the pavement were getting pretty cold. Out of nowhere, a police traffic car appears and parks about ten yards in front of us. There are other police vehicles parked in the same street and that street has quite a steep gradient. The driver of the car gets out and proceeds to stare at everyone as he heads uphill towards the station entrance. It was as he was heading past the halfway point of the coach, I began to feel movement. Someone had released the handbrake. The policeman realised at about the same time. We then witnessed one of those Toyota Corolla moments – 'My car ... that's my car!' It is slippery underfoot and he starts to give chase. He is unable to stop the coach rolling into his car and his car is now being pushed toward the next one. He slips as he runs round in front of his own vehicle but manages to get back in his car and apply the foot brake. Downward momentum ceases, but it didn't do much for the shape of his car. At the same time the coach hits the police car, it dawns on those still awake that going to Brighton on this vehicle and watching football are no longer on the agenda.

Everyone decides to run. The front and rear emergency doors are flung open and, despite the best efforts of the handful of policemen on the scene, people are fleeing in all directions. Out of the station races a large number of the local constabulary. It is hilly and there is black ice underfoot. It is just turning daylight, there are no people about and the whole district is like a skating rink. This was definitely the Keystone Kops, live and direct. I was lucky enough to get clean away and seemed to be quite well off money-wise. I continued to the match and thought we were unlucky to lose 1–0.

Not everyone found this incident funny in the same way. At football training on the Wednesday, some of the lads took the view that the organisers should award refunds for this shambles. I told them they were part-time bastards who hardly went to away matches these days and the Jackson 100 per cent guaranteed no-refunds policy was in effect.

Whether the coach company ever managed to get in touch with Mr Heath Robinson to send him a duplicate invoice for the coach travel is unclear. I do know this, though; two weeks later, I was arrested and then taken to Nottingham to be charged with criminal damage. The following morning, I appeared in court and was remanded in custody for a week to Lincoln Prison. At my bail hearing a week later, I was released on conditional bail, the main condition being not to enter the County of Nottinghamshire. When the case came up for trial, I was cleared of any wrongdoing and left the court building without a blemish on my character.

YOUR OPINION ABOUT ALL-SEATER STADIUMS, TICKET PRICES AND THE COMMERCIAL ASPECT OF TODAY'S FOOTBALL INDUSTRY. DO YOU STILL FEEL FOOTBALL BELONGS TO THE FANS?

There's a lack of atmosphere definitely in the new modern grounds. As for commercial interests, it's like football's been Americanised. Everybody's got to bring their aunties or uncles, you have to promise not to swear and, if you do anything outrageous such as stand up and show passion for your team, then it will not only be the stewards who will give you disdainful looks, it will be those around you as well. You will probably be with a small group of friends surrounded by people you have never seen before. Conversations with mates four or five rows away are dealt with by mobile phone.

I much preferred the freedom and space of the terraces. I think the product is overpriced these days but it is market forces that dictate. So clubs will charge what they can get away with. This gate money, however, is not the main income for clubs these days and the thought that the fans are the ones paying the players' wages has gone right out of the window. So I don't feel that football belongs to the fans in the same way I used to.

RACISM AND RACE ISSUES HAVE BEEN PART OF FOOTBALL WITH CERTAIN CLUBS AND SETS OF SUPPORTERS AT BOTH CLUB AND INTERNATIONAL LEVEL. WHAT WAS YOUR EXPERIENCE OF THIS?

When the first black England footballer, Viv Anderson, played his début game at Wembley, the booing started when his name was announced on the team sheet, never mind when he got the ball. Nobody made issue of this and the FA seemed to take the view that 100,000 people at ten quid each can express whatever views they want. No one wanted to kill this golden goose or rock any boats.

With Hull being remote from other places, everyone knowing everyone else, it would not have been unusual in times long gone by to see supporters known for either being Commies or Fascists to be sat next to each other discussing the finer points of the game. Politics was never an issue and it certainly never stopped anyone from going to matches. The black lads amongst us would not stand up with the Eidelweiss choir and sing 'Tomorrow Belongs To Me', of course.

However, there were some people who would have joined in such songs because they had learned the words on scraps of paper. They became one-day-a-week Fascists, probably without realising. There were not and are not many non-white Hull City supporters; this is a reflection of the area we live in, nothing more. When it comes to the Tiger Nation, black, white or Martian, male or female, young or old, all welcome and bring a friend.

The football authorities have quite rightly changed their attitude dramatically on this front. You do still get examples of racism as Dwight Yorke found out on his return to Blackburn recently. These rare outbursts are dealt with swiftly and severely. If you do behave in this manner, you are likely to end up with a criminal conviction, fined a lot of money, and banned from all football grounds for a number of years, unless, of course, you're a famous television pundit.

HOW HAVE FANS FOLLOWING THE NATIONAL TEAM ABROAD BEEN TREATED, AND WHAT ARE YOUR EXPERIENCES FOLLOWING YOUR CLUB OR NATIONAL TEAM ABROAD?

The treatment of the fans of the national team over the years is nothing short of a disgrace. We have been treated differently over the years; the most obvious example being the way Scottish and Irish fans can turn up anywhere en masse with no tickets. For such behaviour, they are given UEFA awards. When the English fans do this, they cancel all police leave, put the Army on standby and close all ports and airports.

I have not spent too much time following Hull City around Europe so I have no personal experience of this. Mates who follow other teams and have been abroad to watch them tell me it's pretty much the same as watching England. The same level of suspicion and hostility is there. It's always great to go on these trips, but you're always glad to get back home.

WOULD YOU SAY THE MEDIA 'OVER-HYPE' THE TROUBLE AND CAN YOU GIVE AN EXAMPLE OF THIS?

At the 2000 Euro Championships when England played Germany in Charleroi, the Belgian authorities took it upon themselves to start using their water cannons in the main square. Later on, while the match was being played, they surrounded a bar filled with Germans and handcuffed and arrested all of them, for no reason that was apparent. The same vehicles that had been used earlier arrived back on the scene later on and the same procedure was duplicated with what seemed to be a bar picked at random full of English fans.

The following day's headlines: '900 arrested. Police have to resort to using water cannon to restore order'. They just happened to have all those resources available and obviously decided they were going to make full use of them, no matter what. Those arrests justified the cost of the operation, but the amount of people arrested for the small amount of disturbance there was (hardly any) did not tally up at all.

What they didn't tell you in the media, of the 900 arrested, over 800 had done nothing other than be in the wrong bar at the wrong time. Seventy were drunk and arrested for their own safety, to be released later without charge. Ten were litter louts. Of the remainder, two were for assault, three for ticket touting and seven people from the North Lincolnshire area, a mixture of Scunthorpe and Grimsby fans, were arrested for vagrancy, same as always.

SHOULD CELTIC AND RANGERS BE ALLOWED TO JOIN THE ENGLISH PREMIERSHIP OR NATIONWIDE LEAGUES?

Definitely not. And while we are on this subject, if we play in an English league, is it necessary to have Welsh teams involved? If the Scottish teams became involved in our league, it would become a UK league and nobody wants that.

Goalposts are at their best at either end of a football pitch and then left alone. So, in order to keep our pitch furniture safe, Rangers and Celtic can stay north of the border and keep their sectarian bickering to themselves. They are not welcome in our league and they never will be.

DO YOU HAVE ANY VIEW ON BANNING ORDERS? DO YOU KNOW THIS FROM YOUR OWN EXPERIENCE OR THAT OF OTHERS?

Banning orders are an absolute infringement of civil liberties in my opinion. But in these post-9/11 times, I do accept that they are here to stay and unlikely ever to be rescinded. It seems wrong in principle that you can get a banning order without committing an offence.

Myself, I have twice been arrested and cleared of breaching banning orders. The restrictions are tightened up as the years go by to prevent this. The terms of modern-day exclusion orders are quite draconian. The original banning orders were for all football league grounds. I received such a ban at the same time as myself and some friends were stewarding at Wembley on a regular basis. Despite being banned from football grounds, I continued with this. It was during the England v Ireland game on an occasion when we were not stewarding the event that I ended up being arrested by the local Hull spotter for breaching my banning order and placed in a large cage inside Wembley, along with many others. We were ferried to West Hendon Police Station many hours later. I was bailed in the early hours of the morning and never heard another thing. Wembley was never a football league ground; it was a greyhound track with a football pitch in the middle – I loved the place.

The next occasion comes from the time when the bans only applied inside the grounds unless intent to breach the ban could be proved. At the all-ticket match between Hull City and Scunthorpe United, I was arrested at just gone three o'clock for being involved in an altercation on the car park of the ground. One of the three charges for these matters was for breaching my banning order. Because I did not have a match ticket, or enough money to purchase one, and the club couldn't even let me in the ground for free – not even as an act of charity could they let someone in for free and not breach their safety certificate – it was decided that on this basis I had nothing to do with the football match whatsoever. I was cleared of breaching my banning order and no others could be imposed for the other two offences, one of which I was cleared of. I pleaded guilty to the third and received three months' imprisonment. I told you no good ever comes of it.

HOOLIE MOVIES AND FLICKS – DO THEY GLORIFY VIOLENCE OR CREATE A COPYCAT SYNDROME?

I don't think it glorifies violence or brings out any copycat syndrome, but I'm a certain age and have lived through plenty for real. It seems to me that Football Factory is to football violence what Trainspotting is to heroin. It sort of does give you an insight, but unless you actually do it, you don't really know. It's a good outline sketch for those that don't know the subject, but anyone who does knows it's far, far different to what is on the film and, as you know yourself, violence isn't funny. For some people, it's all right, but others would never take to it.

So those kind of films don't have a big effect on me. Some people regard the current spate of books and films as 'Harry

Potter for disturbed young men', but I don't subscribe to this view. If I was young and impressionable, I may feel differently.

WAS YOUR LIFESTYLE WITH THE CITY PSYCHOS SOLELY CONFINED TO THE FOOTBALL CONTEXT OR WOULD IT HAVE BEEN THE SAME FOR YOU IN EVERYDAY STREET LIFE?

Just about all my convictions are for football-related matters, an example of the one-day-a-week criminal. However, during periods of unemployment, you would obtain money by whatever means in order to attend matches. This was just northern life on the dole during the '80s. In this country, people aspire to be 18 and start drinking in pubs. I was no different. Hull has a very lively town centre and, through drinking and fighting in pubs, I have ended up with two life-threatening injuries – one punctured lung (knife wound); one severed artery (beer glass) – and many others less serious. So if drinking and fighting in pubs with other people who wish to fight is criminal behaviour, then yes, I suppose so. However, there is no stigma attached to this behaviour, not in the way there is if football is involved.

EVERY ONE OF TODAY'S KNOWN HOOLIGAN FIRMS HAS A POLICE INTELLIGENCE OFFICER DEDICATED TO IT. HOW DO THE FIRMS TODAY RESPOND TO THAT? DO YOU HAVE ANY POLICE SPOTTER STORIES?

There have been many spotters down the years and, at the beginning, it was a plain-clothes affair. Then they went back to uniforms. There have been good and bad. Dialogue and communication is out of the question for the bad ones because they take it personally. Not all spotters are like this, though. One in particular was, and still is, a football coach of some repute and deals with a lot of junior football teams. Everybody is delighted to see him on a Sunday morning, far happier than seeing him on a Saturday following you about with his video camera shouting witty remarks.

Another of the spotters was at least as big a Hull City fan than anyone on earth. He wasn't in it for the overtime, he got to see the team he loved for free. He was a good bloke and a die-hard fan. The others, though, have mostly been weasels.

When any two plain-clothes spotters are following 20 of their own supporters from a short distance in a strange town, there is the possibility that the locals will appear from nowhere and attack them with everything they have got in their hands. On such an occasion they do not reach for warrant cards and shout, 'Everyone stop fighting.' They do not have time to nick people; they have to start looking after themselves and start knocking people out. And to all intents and purposes, for that few minutes only, they are part of the gang. When it's over, everyone goes their separate ways and it's business as usual. These things happen.

IS THERE, IN YOUR OPINION, A NEXT GENERATION OF HOOLIGAN APPRENTICES COMING THROUGH AND WILL THEY BE ANYTHING LIKE THEIR PREDECESSORS?

There definitely is a next generation and most youngsters who involve themselves have a dad, an uncle or an older cousin, or something along those lines. They will have seen it all their lives, know the faces, heard the stories and know all about it. They will be on the edge of it from the start. They, like all young lads, knock about in groups. So it may not necessarily be that nephew or that lad, but it will be that nephew's mate or his other mate. Over and over again, young people will be drawn to this. It does seem to have a certain glamour or kudos for some. Only time will tell if they will be anything like their predecessors. Sometimes, the authorities have a good run and keep the lid on things for a few years, sometimes they don't.

One thing is for sure, though – the police will have to be ready every week 'til the end of time – just in case. On the hooligan side, they can pick and choose; it's always there for those that want it. How much the next generation wants it remains to be seen. I think the best days may have been and gone, but also I don't see these activities ever coming to a total stop. They have become ingrained into football all over the globe. English disease? Don't make me laugh!

NAME: Coalville Daz
CLUB: Leicester City
FIRM: Baby Squad

**'We always go
to Pompey and
they know why.'**

BACKGROUND AND MEET

I travelled to Leicester to meet Coalville Daz after doing the interview for the Forest chapters. The Forest lads' words were still ringing in my ears: 'Don't trust 'em, Cass, they're moody … Watch yourself … You know they even joined up with Derby to have a pop at us, don't trust 'em.'

Well, quite the contrary, I was looking forward to catching up with Leicester as my memory was all about the '70s – I remember being in their end when Tottenham tried to take it. Proper boot boys were Leicester back then and the big four – Arsenal, Tottenham, Chelsea, West Ham – always took numbers.

Leicester, being the nearest of the Midland clubs, the London fans always had a tale about going to Leicester, so their pedigree is there, even then. A different Leicester firm reappeared in the Casual era of the '80s. Leicester got dressed up and their calling cards declared they were now the Baby Squad. As the ICF talked of leaving before the end of the game to have a pop at their end, the Baby Squad became more than just a name – every firm had to have one at the time – the Leicester mob started to travel and the National Criminal Intelligence Service chalked up the words 'Baby Squad' after every reported incident. They were getting a nice profile.

So, for the book, I ended up getting one of the Baby Squad, known as Coalville Daz. He came through my England source contact. I met this clean-cut casual dresser on the outskirts of his home town one early midweek morning. A chirpy, honest-talking character, who says he was never the main man but has done his bit for the cause and will do the chapter for the lads. Then he let slip he's bang into the Cockney Rejects. Enough said!

He was born in 1965; real name Darren Smith. Left school without qualifications to work as an underground miner at Ellistown Colliery until it shut down. Married with one son. Saw his first game with his father when Leicester played Queen's Park Rangers.

WHAT HAS BEEN THE MOST LEGENDARY FIGHT OR RIOT YOUR TEAM'S SUPPORTERS HAVE BEEN INVOLVED IN?

I've going to have to say Chelsea at home in 1989. In fact, it was the same day as the Hillsborough disaster, so I remember it well, really. They had a massive mob, Chelsea, to be fair, a proper mob. They were good in those days, weren't they? In fact, some came and had it with some of our lads on Friday night, so it started Friday night, really. So word got round. It was before the mobile phones, obviously, so people were ringing each other up at home … 'Fucking Chelsea are here … they're here.' 'What, Chelsea are here? Now? You're joking!'

So, obviously, people got into town, had the row. All day long it was going off. I mean, Chelsea were fucking massive that day, they really was. I hold me hands up to them. There were seven or eight stabbed/slashed that day. It was really naughty, it was a naughty day, it really was.

I remember after the game, they was coming out the ground and there were fucking hundreds of them, there really was. And we'd be about 150–200-handed ourselves, we turned out a good mob that day. But we did in them days, as you know. And we smashed this fence down and behind the fence was a pallet of brand-new bricks and we just threw the bricks at Chelsea and they threw them back at us, and it was going on for 40 minutes, which is a long time without the Old Bill being there. And even when the Old Bill came, to be fair, they couldn't control it. Chelsea had more numbers than us, but we held our own, I'd like to think. There were cars damaged and houses – it were just a riot basically. That's the one that sticks out in my mind more than any.

There's another reason I am unable to forget that day. Unbeknown to me, my fiancée was at home and her mum had come round and said there's been some people killed at a football match. And my wife, who was my fiancée at the time, she heard all the talk of trouble before the Chelsea game. So when her mum warned her of trouble, she naturally thought that it was the game I was at. So when I walked in at half-nine–ten o'clock, she wasn't too impressed that I hadn't been in touch. But I didn't know anything about the Hillsborough disaster, you see. I've walked in the door and she's very upset.

'What's going on ... what's going on?' she says.

'How do you know?' I asked.

'It's on the telly ... it's been on the telly,' she ranted, 'there's people been killed ...' and I still didn't realise.

We put the old telly on then, obviously, it become clear what had happened at Hillsborough and, obviously, it did put it into perspective, it was absolutely dreadful.

It was strange. I remember I shot off and had a shower after it, and I felt so knackered – me legs, me arms, everything were aching. Got a few bumps and bruises as well. And I got dry and lay on the bed and I were thinking, 'What's this all about?' As soon as I walked through that door, when my missus said there's people dead, I thought 'What are you talking about?' Obviously, I knew that people had been slashed and stabbed. But then it become clear what had happened. And then when I saw the pictures on the telly, well, we all felt the same, I think, didn't we? But having gone through what I'd been through all that weekend, the Friday and the Saturday, it did bring it home to me a little bit. It did really bring it crashing home to me. I thought, 'What the hell ... it's not worth it ... it's not worth it.'

But then, the following day, you get back in the boozer with the lads and you're talking about the next game. There's nothing will ever change that.

HOW IMPORTANT WAS THE ROLE OF ALCOHOL AND DRUGS? WAS THERE ANY TIME IN YOUR EXPERIENCE EITHER HAD PARTICULAR INFLUENCE?

Personally speaking, it's not made any difference to me. I mean, I love a drink, as most of the lads do. But I've actually been arrested at a home game once for fighting with Leeds. I'd had one pint that day, I'd been working 'til one o'clock and I shot straight into town, I was still in me work clothes. And I'd had one pint. And then again I went to Bournemouth one Wednesday night and got arrested there for having a bit of a row and I was absolutely blind drunk. So, it doesn't matter.

As for drugs – not me personally, but some of the lads on the firm just gave it up during the rave scene period; it makes you wonder, really. Everybody did, didn't they? We will always maintain a firm at Leicester, we always have done, and drugs are bigger now aren't they, especially coke, it's bigger now than it was then at football. It's more open now. It's everywhere these days. I've noticed for two or three years it's been as open as it is because people now are just snorting off tables, ain't they? It doesn't seem taboo any longer for some reason. Again, like going back to the rave scene, it never bothered me, I was never into any of them.

WHO WAS THE MOST VIOLENT, CRAZY SET OF SUPPORTERS YOU EVER CAME ACROSS?

I'd have to say it's West Ham or Middlesbrough, from my own personal experience. Twice when West Ham come up to Leicester – you were probably with them – they were fucking mental. I've also had an experience down at Upton Park as well.

There was one incident at Leicester. We heard a rumour ten minutes before the game finished, we were going out, West Ham were outside, they were waiting for us. And we went outside and they ran us back up into the ground. It was all standing then, and we had nowhere to run. Before you knew it, you could have had another Hillsborough on your hands if you weren't careful, but obviously the Old Bill sorted that out. And then as we all got together, I remember I went hiding up an entry, got caught out on me own because they were carrying fucking coshes and it went mental, absolutely mental. They were proper tooled up, they really was.

At the time, Leicester were known for it, as well as for blades and everything. Although, to be perfectly honest, I never see too much of that with Leicester, although there were incidents like at that Chelsea game as I said earlier. But that's one incident with West Ham and every time I've been to Middlesbrough or Middlesbrough have come to us, they've been fucking game lads, they really are, proper game lads. The one that sticks out in me mind with Middlesbrough was the last game of the season. It was up their place, Ayresome Park; if Middlesbrough won they went up and would be promoted, but we beat them 2-1. Gary McAllister scored two, I remember, and obviously they were a little bit upset, to say the least. So the Old Bill said to all the away supporters, 'We're keeping you in the ground,' which is normal procedure.

I remember lifting meself up on this wall at Ayresome Park and looking over and they were tipping cars up, they was literally tipping fucking cars up. All right, we've seen it before, but it's not the norm is it, in football, it never has been. And they was going absolutely mental. Bear in mind, I think, we only had 500 tickets, that's all we had at that game. So out of that 500, we'd got about 60 lads up there, and most of them have come on the train, except for us on a minibus. So when the Old Bill escorted everybody to the train station and the coaches, it left us on our own, really, to fend for ourselves.

Well, you've never seen anything like it. I mean, I don't think any of us got back without a good hiding. We were lucky that's all we got, really.

Another instance at Middlesbrough some years later, it was at Ayresome Park again. We got chased and if you turned right at Ayresome Park, there's a big green and we got done over on that green. Fucking beasts. I got kicked all round the floor. So I got up and legged it into this shop and the shopkeeper locked the door. But I'm scared of dogs, I'm fucking petrified of dogs, and the shop owner got his dog out and said, 'They won't come in here.' So I looked at the dog, and thought I'd sooner go and fight them.

And I remember a bloke, he'd got a yellow Lacoste jumper on, he was the one who'd been kicking me in the head on this green. I looked out the window and I thought, 'What do I do here? Do I stay in here with this dog, this big Alsatian, or go back out and have a bit of that with them?' But I chose to stay in with the dog, fortunately.

ARE YOUR FIRM STILL DOING IT?

The thing is with the Baby Squad, since '81 when it all started, we've always maintained a firm, always have done, even through the rave scene. All right, there was a few got pulled away, but we've always had a firm, especially at home, and we've been slagged off in the past because we don't travel away, and I can see where people are coming from in some respects. But we've always had a firm. And it's like people seem to hate us, people don't seem to rate us. But I found it hard to believe because most firms in the country over the last 20 or so years must have had some sort of row with us, they must have had. We've had rows right through the '70s and '80s. The '70s I can't comment too much about.

The firm now – we're by no means the best firm in the country, I wouldn't suggest that for one minute but I know for a fact we're not the worst, not by any stretch of the imagination. I'll tell you the honest truth, Cass – when it first started, obviously there's still some of them lads going today. And there's even three or four lads' dads and their kids involved in it. And now there's the young lads coming up. Mix it all together, and I think we would probably be a main firm again. We might pick our games perhaps now, just three or four a season away, because it is harder now as you know. But at home, we're always 150-handed, probably sometimes more.

This season against West Ham, there'd got to be 200 of us there. I mean, nothing went off, nothing serious. We were there still, though, and it's the same faces, a few young ones in, but we have kept pretty much the same all through it, and it's great. Some of them are now personal and family friends and they will be 'til the day I die, and that's what it's all about, really.

HOW WOULD YOU DESCRIBE THE SITUATION WITH THE SCENE TODAY? CAN IT COMPARE WITH WHAT HAPPENED IN THE PAST, AND DO THINGS STILL GO OFF IN THE SAME WAY?

It's nothing like the '80s was, or even the early '90s. The police are pretty well on top, aren't they, now? With the bans. People are banned from city centres now, whereas with the earlier bans you were only banned from the game, so you just tagged along. I mean, I've been banned twice and I've never been banned from town centres, so I've just tagged along, I even got to an away game. But now it's so difficult.

But I think, basically, nowadays it's for the diehards, if you like, the ones that are committed to it, because it's so difficult. You've got to have a little bit of luck with it as well, you've got to be a bit clever. I mean, for an example, Birmingham last season. Leicester had 120 lads in Birmingham from eleven o'clock in the morning without Birmingham knowing they were there. Digbeth High Street was where they were told to go, and they were there at eleven o'clock in the morning. All they did was instead of getting on trains and coaches, they got taxis booked from different areas of Leicester and basically nobody knew where they were going, maybe five or six knew, but the rest didn't before the taxis turned up and they got to Birmingham. They turned up and they did the business. The Birmingham lot will tell you that. Leicester had them on their toes, it was fantastic, yeah. It was one of the best for quite some time. If you can mobilise 120 lads and get them to Birmingham – all right, it's not far from Leicester, but you've still got to get over there and the lads were there and, yeah, it worked a treat. So there's your answer – if you're committed and you really want it.

HOW DID YOU GET GOING WITH A FOOTBALL FIRM, DID IT HAVE A NAME AND HOW WAS THE NAME ESTABLISHED?

The Baby Squad originally got its name in the 1981 season by a group – I wasn't part of this at this stage – of very young lads going to Leeds, Elland Road, and having a row up there and they were standing their ground, basically. And legend has it that the Leeds lot were calling them babies, a load of babies come up from Leicester. And that's how the name originally stuck 20-odd years ago now, the Baby Squad. The Baby Gang, I think the Leeds lot were calling it.

I got into it because I'm from Coalville which is ten miles out of Leicester. I just used to keep in with the lads from Coalville until I could find myself being in the right place at the right time. The Baby Squad was, by and large, a city gang, a town gang, really. The football was another string to their bow. I just kept going into town and that's what we do, be there, be there every week, and before you know where you are, without any invitation or anything, you're there, aren't you, and that's how it works. We're going to Grimsby on Saturday at eleven o'clock. I'll be there and I'll be ready at half-past ten to make sure, because I'd nothing else in me life other than the football and family.

WHAT WAS THE WORST INSTANCE OF WEAPONS BEING USED?

Again, I'm going to have to refer back to that '89 Chelsea game. Personally, I see one Chelsea lad, a big fellah, lying on the floor, his head was ripped to bits, and he was in a right state. There were seven or eight stabbed or slashed that day. I did see another Leicester lad cut down his chest and the back of his head. That was the worst I've seen. Like I said earlier, it was a good old ruck, it was a good row, it really was.

But I suppose the worst incident really was the two Leeds boys in Istanbul. That sickened me, it really did. I've got no history with Leeds as such, they're not friends or anything, but to see them two lads killed that really did upset me, and I think likewise for a lot of lads. They seemed to get a bit caught out. I do know that Leeds had a fucking massive firm out there as well, and the Old Bill kept Leeds together pretty much, I think. These lads got caught out and lost their lives. That sickened me, it really did.

WHAT IS THE MOST IMPORTANT LESSON YOU LEARNED PERSONALLY DURING YOUR TIME WITH YOUR FIRM AND WOULD YOU DO ANYTHING DIFFERENTLY?

The only thing I could say I would change is how easily I've been arrested personally in the past, which has led to bans, which has led to fines, prison and all the rest of it. Personally speaking, I would try not to get arrested as easy.

A classic example for me is '96 when we went to Chelsea. There were 32–33 of us and I think 18 of us didn't have tickets. So the lads went to the game; we were in Covent Garden and all various places in London. Two of the lads came out the ground at half time, and walked by the White Hart. They stuck their noses in and rung us back on the mobiles and said, 'Look, there's 50 Chelsea in there, it's four o'clock.' So 18 of us went to the White Hart knowing, really, we was only going to get a slap and obviously we got a slap of sorts and I got nicked along with about another four Leicester lads. And that's mental to think about doing that really, it's absolutely mental. Because you know when you leave, you're buoyed up and you're all thinking, 'Well, what have we come for, to sit in a pub in Covent Garden? If there's Chelsea there at four o'clock, let's go.'

I can understand the mentality, but it's really stupid. I got community service and a two-year ban, even England games. They took me passport from me and all the rest of it. I've been charged nine or ten times. Some of the times you get nicked, all right, hands up, it's a fair cop, but it's the silly times. Like as I said, once in Bournemouth I got nicked trying to get in the ground drunk. Things like that, it's ridiculous, it's absolutely ridiculous.

Most of it I wouldn't do different and I wouldn't change it for the world, but I wouldn't have gone on these suicide runs. You're gonna get done. And the name of the Baby Squad was down another level because you've been done and the chances are you're going to get seriously hurt or nicked, and that was always the big worry with me –getting nicked. You recover from a slap, don't you, quite easily.

WHO WERE YOUR BIGGEST RIVALS BOTH TEAM AND FAN-WISE?

Team-wise, Derby and Forest, because of the close proximity, but add Coventry to that as well. We don't like Coventry, to be honest.

As regards firms, again Forest, Derby and Coventry. Forest fancy themselves, that's for sure; not sure why. Seem to think they are the best in the East Midlands. We are all entitled to our opinion, I suppose, but I don't agree. We have had some good 'uns with Derby over the years, home and away.

As for Coventry, we just don't like them and vice versa. Now, in Leicester, we have this thing with Chelsea. They seem to hate us, but if you listen to them they don't rate us. We never travel, they say. Well, lads, that is not strictly true, is it? Been there many times, White Hart, for example, and not to forget the time at the stage door – yes, we were there. Chelsea always come to Leicester, I'll give them that, but they never have it easy, I am sure they will agree. Better stick Portsmouth in there, too, we always go to Pompey and they know why.

WHO ARE THE TOP FIVE FIRMS OF ANY IMPORTANCE TODAY?

Cardiff – whether you love them or loathe them, you've got to say Cardiff because they've got such a massive firm, they really have got a massive firm and you've got to put them up there, you've got to be honest about things. We've not had the pleasure yet of going there or them coming to us, but this year we'll see how good they really are, but I've heard from Forest they're pretty good.

I'll say Middlesbrough as well, because they're always here, they always come to Leicester and we go to them. Again, they're always there, definitely.

I'll say Millwall. We've had two or three rows with them in the past.

There's one I'm going to have to add – Leeds. I've got to add Leeds because they have been pretty active. They really opened my eyes last season, they really did. We were away at Arsenal, last game of the season. They were at Chelsea. We bumped into a few Leeds, around 250 of them then, and this geezer said to us that they had another 200 down at Chelsea. Now you've got no reason not to believe the fellah. Then we saw them later on ... fucking Jesus Christ. It was awesome. We were drinking with them in Euston, in the Euston Flyer. We was in there and, to be fair, they were pretty impressive, very impressive.

The last one, I'll go for Birmingham. Got a lot of respect for Birmingham over the years and they probably have dropped off a little bit, but that day last season when we had a right old ding-dong with them, and done them in the morning, hands up on it, after the game it would have been a totally different story. Our lads were sent back on the train without tickets, which left 30–40 of us in the ground. If we'd come out, if it weren't for the Old Bill, we would have been murdered, I tell you, there was hundreds of them, hundreds of them. Then we went back to where it all went off and they were there in every pub. So I've added them for that reason, really, because I think they are as good as most.

WHO ARE YOUR TOP FIVE FIRMS OF ALL TIME?

I've got to go for Chelsea ('80s–'90s), West Ham (because of the '80s), Millwall – you've got to throw them in. I'm going to put Leeds in there as well. I'm not going to put Cardiff in because, in the '80s, they weren't about then. In the '80s, they might not have lasted it. I'm going to have to throw Birmingham in.

DOES TODAY'S MODERN FOOTBALL PLAYER HAVE THE RESPECT OF THE FANS?

I don't think they have the respect, I really don't. On a personal thing, last season when we went down, Paul Dickov, Scimeca, Thatcher, they all left Leicester and, all right, they got clauses in their contracts that would let them go if we were relegated for a nominal fee. We stood by them, Leicester City stood by them – the manager, the director – stuck by them, especially Dickov, because he was in some shit with his wife and everything. They stuck by them and, as soon as he had the chance, he said, 'Cheerio.' So I personally feel he owed us a little bit more, but again, it probably wouldn't have happened in the '80s or '90s, I don't know. There seemed to be a bit more loyalty then. There ain't any now, there really ain't.

RACISM AND RACE ISSUES HAVE BEEN PART OF FOOTBALL WITH CERTAIN CLUBS AND SETS OF SUPPORTERS AT BOTH CLUB AND INTERNATIONAL LEVEL. WHAT WAS YOUR EXPERIENCE OF THIS?

It's never really affected us, to be honest. You see, over the years we have had black lads in our firm, fucking good lads, too, some of which are great friends of mine. I suppose in the '80s, most grounds had a bit of banana-throwing and silly monkey chants, but I never really witnessed it at Leicester, certainly no worse than anywhere else.

HOW HAVE FANS FOLLOWING THE NATIONAL TEAM ABROAD BEEN TREATED, AND WHAT ARE YOUR EXPERIENCES FOLLOWING YOUR CLUB OR NATIONAL TEAM ABROAD?

I would say that England are obviously treated different, it's so obvious now. You must be treated differently because, for want of a better word, they're scared, aren't they? You get there and they're obviously just waiting for you to kick it off because your reputation precedes you and we are treated differently. I mean, the Jocks and the Irish approach their international games a little bit differently with their outfits and the fancy dress and the club shirts, where in England games, by and large, that's not the case. It's lads in the gear having a few beers. And in some countries, that does look violent, don't it? It intimidates and, to be fair to them, they're worried and scared at the end of the day.

I've been abroad twice with Leicester; obviously, we're not big hitters in Europe, but I've been both times. You're treated pretty much the same, really, you're English and that's it at the end of the day. The police are always ready, definitely always ready for you.

SHOULD CELTIC AND RANGERS BE ALLOWED TO JOIN THE ENGLISH PREMIERSHIP OR NATIONWIDE LEAGUES?

I would personally say no because of my hatred for Celtic. I cannot be doing with Celtic under any circumstances whatsoever. We played them in a pre-season friendly. For me,

Martin O'Neill fixed it, he promised to come with Celtic to Leicester. And he come down and there were thousands and thousands of Celtic, as there always are. Our little mob met early, it was a weekday morning, about ten o'clock. The Old Bill got us, put us in two pubs and locked us in all day long 'til the kick-off. If you ain't got a ticket, you was arrested. That was how severe it was, but the Celtic hordes were allowed to do what they wanted. It wasn't quite the same afterwards, obviously, when there were some serious good hidings because we got at them.

But I like Rangers, I do like Rangers, but I hate Celtic so much, I really do. If they come down here, there's going to be trouble every single game they play and on that I'm 99.9 per cent sure. There'd be major disturbances if they played in England on a regular basis. And without Celtic, you can't have Rangers – you can't have one without the other, so I personally say no.

DO YOU HAVE ANY VIEW ON BANNING ORDERS? DO YOU KNOW THIS FROM YOUR OWN EXPERIENCE OR THAT OF OTHERS?

They do the trick, don't they? I have been banned twice in the past, but my bans were just from the grounds. The newer ones stop you going into towns when a game is on as well as the grounds, so you can't even go and meet the lads for a beer, etc. With the earlier bans, all the lads would just go about their business as usual on a match day apart from going to the game. Even at away games it would just mean you sat in a pub while most of the boys went to the game. It's not nice to admit it, but they do work.

IS THERE, IN YOUR OPINION, A NEXT GENERATION OF HOOLIGAN APPRENTICES COMING THROUGH AND WILL THEY BE ANYTHING LIKE THEIR PREDECESSORS?

Oh yes, there is a massive youth scene at Leicester and, from what I can gather, it's the same at most clubs. Like I said before, the young lads have it a lot harder than we ever had it. They hear all the stories of how it was in the '70s, '80s, '90s, hearing how we done this, done that, and they want to repeat it. But with all the restrictions, banning orders, CCTV, etc., it must be very frustrating for them, and I suppose that some of them feel that the older ones don't really have time for them.

But from what I can see, the future is in good hands at Leicester, because they are committed, that's for sure. At nearly 40, my time is done, but I look at these lads and think it will always be there. I think there will always be a Baby Squad, there will always be lads that want to do football this way.

NAME: Tommy Robinson

CLUB: Luton Town

FIRM: MIGS

'We don't get the numbers, we don't get the baggage. We're just a good, tight, handy firm.'

BACKGROUND AND MEET

I still remember those images played across our TV screens of a Millwall mob rampaging at Luton Football Club in 1985. The ground was bursting to the seams with travelling thugs who must have come from every town south. Police, fans and even local residents came under attack in scenes so horrific it brought a statement of condemnation from the outraged PM, Margaret Thatcher. If you study the football more closely, you can actually see pockets of Luton having it with Millwall both on the pitch and in the stands. That alone I thought was quite unbelievable, for I don't care who you support or who your firm is, you would have not wanted to be up against that lot on that particular night.

This was the height of the football Casual period when every firm decided to get a name. Luton took one of the most memorable from that era, calling themselves the Migs. Luton was also one of those grounds that every firm had been to, such was its easy location. Continuous trouble from the terraces saw the club Chairman impose a total ban on all visiting supporters coming to Kenilworth Road.

So what's the real story from the Migs end? For that, I needed an original Mig. Again, Euro 2004 saw me connect up with film producer Tuse and Mig Virgil who put me in touch with Tommy Robinson. I had also watched at some stage a video of CCTV footage showing a full-on attack from Luton Migs on a Watford pub in a high street. The assault was relentlessly carried out and it is interesting to see the camera zoom and freeze on one person in particular ... you guessed it, our man Tommy Robinson. We did the interview and I found him to be an intelligent, articulate and persuasive person. He says he has the whole Mig story, chapter and verse, and it's an unbiased account to the normal 'done this, done that, make a good book, Cass'. You know what, I believe him.

He was born in 1968, and has an O-level in English Literature, is single and works as an engineer. Remembers his first game as Luton v Man City back in '77.

WHAT HAS BEEN THE MOST LEGENDARY FIGHT OR RIOT YOUR TEAM'S SUPPORTERS HAVE BEEN INVOLVED IN?

Probably Chelsea, '94, FA Cup semi-final at Wembley. We hadn't done nothing for a couple of years and you know how big Chelsea's name is. We turned out with 200 including old heads, all the Migs were there. The meet was at West Hampstead. We come over the hill at West Hampstead, heading towards the Underground. We saw a good mob at the other end, but they was all Luton, too. So we turned back and went to Kilburn High Road instead. Chelsea were waiting there for us under the station. Give it to them there, laid them out in the street, all that sort of stuff. Old Bill came. One of the boys set some CS off – blamed it on Chelsea, we said they were fucking animals, the Old Bill got busy with them. We fucked off, we actually took off down Kilburn High Road, split up, got on buses to Wembley Way. Met a mob of West London boys there. Told them we'd be waiting at West Hampstead after the game. We said we'll wait as long as it takes.

Back to West Hampstead after the game. Probably 80 of us, the old Migs. Chelsea turned up, absolutely fucking fuming. One of the twins comes in the pub, sits in there, give it the big 'un, 'Is this the Migs, then?'

'Of course.'

Goes away, saying, 'You've got 200 of Chelsea's finest coming here. You won't get better than this all day, lads ...'

Everyone leaves the boozer, but no sign of Chelsea. We had an argument amongst ourselves. Half the lads say, 'Fuck it, Chelsea ain't coming,' they fuck off home, leaving about 40 of us on the platform. We look up and the sky goes black, it was like something out of Zulu, just silhouettes coming across West Hampstead bridge, coming down the stairs. We're 40-handed, they're 200-odd, we knew they couldn't all get in the station at once. This would be half-nine, ten at night.

Went straight into them, pushed them back up the stairs, made them look silly really – they bottled it. But I know what their argument is, they'll say to you, if we had come out in the road, they'd have done us. I don't know, maybe, but our front line is always our strength, it isn't numbers. It's being tight.

There was one at Watford that was called on at Bushey Station because, for as long as I can remember going to football, 15 years, they've never turned out against us and everyone knows your derby's meant to be your big day, and we feel cheated because everyone else gets a good derby, don't they? We get nothing. That lot, barking, shouting, 'We can do this, we can do that.'

So the meet was called on at Bushey to make it easier for them. Ten o'clock in the morning, 200 Migs headed to Bushey Station via Euston. We were met by Hertfordshire Old Bill who basically put the dogs on us, tried to force us back on the train, but we burst through and across the tracks. We broke out of the station, Watford nowhere to be seen. Went up to the Moon Under Water. Again, no sign of them. Spent the next two to three hours drinking in the town, then 15 of us decided to slip off and have a little drink to stay away from the main show. Don't want to get involved with the Old Bill, we're not up for that.

We get a ring later on saying Luton's just had it with Watford's mob, they're about 40–50-handed. By now, we're getting the phone calls, there's 300–400 Luton taking on Hertfordshire Old Bill up by the ground who are trying to hold them back. So we tried to walk up behind them, stayed back for a bit, walked past the Moon Under Water at the same time as 40 chaps walk out the pub. The rest is history. Whatever they say, that was their chance, 15 faces that they know, and they couldn't do it. And they had a dozen Tottenham in there with them. That's the end of the argument as far as we were concerned.

When you talk about a legendary fight, that's the one everyone knows about, but to us it's nothing, it's money for old rope and a lot of guys going to prison for nothing.

WHO WAS THE MOST VIOLENT, CRAZY SET OF SUPPORTERS YOU EVER CAME ACROSS?

There's only two that are worth talking about. I remember Millwall came down, the famous time everybody knows about when they ran riot, 1985. But that wasn't just Millwall, that's what people don't understand, that was a London night out. The whole of the south-east basically comes to us and decides to fucking tear the place to bits. It was unbelievable. And when you're a young guy there and you think you're a bit of a chap and then you see something like the Kenilworth Road end bulging, smoke coming off their bald heads and them big fucking animals staring at you, and then take liberties, just coming on the pitch, jump in your end, picking you off in small groups and that. That was intimidating, definitely. That's why we basically turned round and changed things and split ourselves off from the rest of the Luton lads.

Other than that, we went to Everton in a Cup quarter-final reply, 1985/86 season following a 2–2 draw at our place. It was the first day they installed CCTV at the football ground down at Luton. Word had it someone robbed the keys to the control room, made sure a job was done on the control room on the day so the Old Bill were pissed before the day started. And on the day, there was a massive turnout by the lads, everyone came down, game, we had good numbers. It was also the first time I'd seen a flare gun fired, they fired a flare gun into us outside the ground. We were double their numbers. A small group of them broke away, but got caught. One of them got pretty badly cut up, to be honest. The story goes that he was so terrified, he got back on their coach that moment when they picked the guy up, they wouldn't even stop at Luton Hospital, went straight up to Milton Keynes to get him treated.

The game ended up 2–2 so we had to go on a Wednesday night up to Everton with 20 lads. We went into Stanley Park, as we had been warned not to do. One of the lads got a rock on the head within five seconds of walking in the park. There's a graveyard on one side and a park the other. We was walking up the middle of that. By now there was about 15 of us, I suppose, in total. Ended up with 100 Scousers each side of us, fucking showing us blades, threatening us all the way up the road, then they come into us. Three or four Old Bill helped us, fucking survived that one. Luckily, another group of Luton came up the road and joined in, we held our own, fought our way to the ground, literally. We were lucky Old Bill saved us, we was actually petrified at that time. One of the guys got slashed just above his eye. I would say that was intimidating. But the buzz was tops.

ARE YOUR FIRM STILL DOING IT?

The Migs are still very active. But you can't compare nowadays with the '80s, you don't get turnouts of 80 lads every Saturday in the pub looking for it. Your guys don't turn out every Saturday unless you're a big club, one of the big city clubs. So, you're really looking at when you know there's a definite mob gonna turn up at Luton. If we know 100 per cent that any club's gonna turn up here mob-handed, then all of a sudden there's a bit of interest and the old faces will turn out. As for away games, we might pick one or two a season, no more than that because it's not fair to ask for the commitment. But there's also the younger guys, the MI2's as they call themselves – Migs Initiative 2, a name they basically stole off the old Mission Impossible 2 thing.

A good one involving the Migs recently was Mansfield, two years ago. We all knew Mansfield had a similar mob to us, little club, a little town near a big city. We don't get the numbers, we don't get the baggage, we just got a good tight, handy firm. We heard Mansfield were the same as us. We knew they had a lot of the old Nottingham lads going across there; when Forest are busy, they go across there and have a beer with them. We also knew they'd been building themselves up as something special.

To us, they're just northerners, so we went up there two years ago, the year we got promoted. We turned up at ten o'clock in the morning, 150-handed, straight into town, walked round, found their boozer, and then went and set up in another boozer. Half-an-hour later, we went back in there. Met their first few lads, and said, 'Have we picked the right spot for you to come to us?'

They said, 'Yeah, fucking hell, what time do you lot get up?'

Went back over to our pub, mobbed up by now, we're up close

to 200 and we hear they're gonna make a show ... nothing happens, so we take it to them. We're actually a little bit out of order because if a few of the lads go in a pub and give their word to them that there would be no trouble in here today until everyone's ready, as I turned my back on the door, a few of the lads blocked the door and went straight into them, which is uncalled for.

Then we head up to the ground. The Old Bill won't let us in the ground at Luton's end, saying it's full. We forced the turnstiles and take over a stand. Old Bill move all the home supporters out of the stand and gave the Migs basically their own stand, 200 of us in there. Ten minutes into the game, we're 3–0 down; another five minutes and it's 4–0.

We decided to leave the game. People try to make their way round to the back of the Mansfield end, but a bunch of Nottinghamshire Old Bill that had been pulled away from the Forest game come to stop us. So they decided to baton charge. There's a bit of history with Nottinghamshire Old Bill and Luton's boys, so it kicks off, spills on to the pitch, fence goes down. Old Bill go down. It's a proper tear-up and I think, at the end of the day, there were about 11 arrests, after which no one was convicted. To round off the day, we bump into the Leicester Baby Squad that night and give it to them, too.

HOW WOULD YOU DESCRIBE THE SITUATION WITH THE SCENE TODAY? CAN IT COMPARE WITH WHAT HAPPENED IN THE PAST, AND DO THINGS STILL GO OFF IN THE SAME WAY?

Yeah, there is. Definitely. For example, at Mansfield, as soon as they rounded us up from the fight in Mansfield's pub, they forced us back up towards the bulk in the other pub and penned us in this pub for close to three to four hours. So what do you do? You drink. When you are escorted to the ground, you're chaperoned, the Old Bill's kicking your heels, giving it loads of shit, 'Southern twats' and all that bollocks, 'Cockney cunts' – we're not even Cockneys. They tell you to get the other side of the turnstile. You get the other side of the turnstile and they start nicking lads for being drunk in the ground. So you just go for it and get stuck in.

The way that it really does happen these days, and it always will do, is when there is a big game. No matter what they do, i.e. Watford last year. If it is a big game, they can police it how they want to. If the guys are intent, it will happen, that's it.

HOW DID YOU GET GOING WITH A FOOTBALL FIRM, DID IT HAVE A NAME AND HOW WAS THE NAME ESTABLISHED?

The Migs got going really because of two things. One was the West Ham programme that was put on the telly, the old documentary with Animal and all those guys (a hooligan documentary featuring the ICF). A lot of the guys watched that at school and went back to school absolutely dumbstruck by it. We'd been watching a load of drunks running round the town on a Saturday, running round, laying into each other and then you see something like this, it just wakes you up a little bit. And very quickly we was buying Pringle jumpers at Scotchhouse on Marble Arch and walking round school in them, fighting the school next door like all lads do. They would all come out in their leather jackets, we'd have our Pringles on. We started getting our airs and graces then if you like.

The name Migs very quickly came about because, when you watch the documentary, you see ICF, the Inter-City Firm, and then at the same time the other famous name was Leeds Service Crew. You hear the name 'firm' and 'crew'; these were unique words at the time, we'd never heard nothing like it. So a couple of wise guys decide that we'd call ourselves the Pringle Boys, Mig Crew. It's a bit of a play on words really. There's a crew on an aircraft for example, and Migs is a Russian word for fighter. So you get Mig Crew. It's just a joke. But it very quickly became Men in Gear. The press got hold of it, the police got hold of it, other firms got hold of it. It's our joke, we simply have a laugh with that one; '82/83 it started.

WHAT WAS THE WORST INSTANCE OF WEAPONS BEING USED?

The worst I've seen, we played Arsenal in three games in '85. For a while leading up to the games, we had Arsenal's Miller and

Rossy drinking with a guy called Bailey, who was a local lad who turned out to be a right turncoat in the end. They were showing him the ropes, how the Cockneys do it. Basically, I think he was bringing out his own brand of football violence and learning off of these Gooners. We used it down at QPR and used these tactics a few times afterwards, and came off a lot better.

By the time we faced Arsenal, their 'faces' had been drinking with us up in our pub in town. They turned up on the Saturday. I don't quite know what they thought they were doing, but they walked across the town green, big numbers I'm talking, one of the biggest mobs, 400–500 lads, idiots though, they weren't 400–500 fucking good lads, they were 400–500 lads with about 20–30 good. We had 150 waiting, and got stuck straight into them, scattered them.

Went off for the rest of the day, much the same scene, scattering them, which set the scene for the replay on a Wednesday night down at their place. We went down there, we came second because we didn't turn up with the numbers we should have had; 30–40 of us got scattered at St Pancras. We then end up on the following Wednesday playing again back at Luton and they turned up with an absolutely fucking solid 200, a really good 200. They reckon it's their best 200. They said, 'This is it, this is the year of the herd,' as they called it.

After the game, they come bouncing into a park in the snow and, fair play to them, they was outnumbered. There'd been a series of incidents all day, all pretty even stuff. After the game, there was a mob of about 80–100 Luton walking through Moor Park. These lot come in behind us, 30-handed only but they were main faces. To our shame, most of the Luton lads got on their toes. Thirty to 40 of us stood, turned round, equal numbers. One of their lads we all know came bouncing through the snow – 'Who wants it then?' A lad, I'll just call him Darryl for now, stuck one straight in his face. To this day, he still has that Nike sign on his face. He went down; his mate who'd come to help him got one in the chest, then their real top boy is down on the floor, he was close, he nearly got it as well. We jumped all over him, but he managed to crawl up the fence and get away. We sent them packing and that was the night the herd got herded.

'No-one's going through us.' Chelsea Headhunter Jason Mariner.

'We had to stand and fight.' The last word from Jinks, of the Rangers' ICF

Renno: 'We never had a name, we were just City's boys.'

'They hated us, and we hated them, and we still do.' FYC Spencer

Plymouth's Mike, of The Central Element.

Little Jela, of the original Under-Fives.

Mr M of ASC, Scotland's first football casual firm.

'We've all had a go,' say The Bunters, as Bunter himself shows (*above*), it really is a question of sport.

WHO WERE YOUR BIGGEST RIVALS BOTH TEAM AND FAN-WISE?

Everybody expects us to say Watford here, but they ain't. Most of the fans would say Leicester and QPR. On the pitch, it's Watford; off the pitch, it's Leicester and QPR.

WHO ARE THE TOP FIVE FIRMS OF ANY IMPORTANCE TODAY?

First, I'll say Tottenham because they seem the only team in London that seems to be on top of their game, Tottenham still persists in London. They always get a heads up at Stoke because, as long as I've been going, they've always been around in some form or other.

We know Man United, although we haven't come up against them since '82, but everything I hear about Man United is numbers, they've got the numbers.

I'll say Millwall purely because of history, but they're mostly vandals.

I'll give a shout for Birmingham because of their numbers. I've seen them at England games up in Scotland with 300–400 lads, that's tops to me.

WHO ARE YOUR TOP FIVE FIRMS OF ALL TIME?

Millwall have obviously got to be there; Man United – pure numbers; Birmingham; West Ham in their day; and Leicester – original babies.

WHAT IS YOUR FAVOURITE FOOTBALL FASHIONWEAR AND THE WORST YOU'VE SEEN OR WORN?

The old Benetton rugby shirts with the blue stripe, because any firm stood out a fucking mile, so I liked that. The worst was them stupid deerstalker hats.

WHAT IS THE WORST KIT YOU'VE SEEN A TEAM IN AND WHAT WOULD BE YOUR OWN CLUB'S BEST EVER STRIP?

Coventry – that brown kit. Best ever strip – it's got to be the one we won the Littlewoods Cup in. Beautiful white shirt, orange and navy-blue trim on the sleeve and collar, navy-blue shorts, white socks. This would be '88.

WHO'S THE PLAYER AND/OR MANAGER THAT WINDS YOU UP THE MOST?

The player – I remember seeing Luther Blissett (Watford) once when he scored against us. They beat us 5–2 down at Vicarage Road. He scored the fourth and he came right up to our end and I think about 300 of us tried to punch him at once. I ended up in the cells. I was only 16 or so.

But I also actually had a tussle with Burnley's manager, Stan Tennant. This is going back about ten years ago. They come to Luton and it was a relegation battle. I was sitting in the stand with the lads. We needed three points. They come down and everyone behind the ball kept kicking it out the ground, falling over, all the usual stuff. I just turned to me mates and said, 'I've had enough of this.' I walked down to the dug-out, stuck me head in the dug-out and told him, as politely as I could, he's a fucking disgrace playing this sort of football down here. It all got out of hand, proper fracas and I got into the dug-out with him. Got pulled back by Luton players. I saw our old copper, the liaison officer, shaking his head, saying, 'Go back and take your seat and behave yourself.'

FANS OFTEN TALK ABOUT THEIR FOOTBALL-GOING DAYS AS JUST BEING A LAUGH. ANY EPISODES YOU REMEMBER?

Well, a lot of things we find funny first of all, as you know, ain't that funny to everyone else. But in the late '90s, we went to Peterborough, which ain't that far from here. We come off the train and we ended up in a pub, then we've made them look silly in the ground. We're behind the goal on the terrace, all bunched up behind the goal. There's about 150 of us, and we've all had far too much to drink.

At this point, a copper behind the goal, doing one of the gate duties, turns up and starts fucking winding the lads up, saying we're idiots, little boys, all this sort of stuff. The guys exchanged a bit of banter with him. It's all building up and building up, at which point our liaison officer calls me down with their head of police and says, 'Can you calm the lads down? What's going on up there?'

I said, 'It's that idiot on the gate, he's winding the boys up.'

He says, 'If they don't stop, I'll send in the fucking boys and they'll get nicked.'

I said, 'If you send them in there, they're all pissed, it will just go off, it would be stupid, you'll just make a big scene out of nothing.'

'Well, what we gonna do?'

'Move him away from the gate and I'll go back and try and calm everyone down.'

'OK,' he says, so he walks over to this copper and this copper looks like a told-off schoolboy. Luton score, everyone ran straight through the gate on to the pitch, and we're all jumping around in the goalmouth. The Old Bill came running down, and we all ran back in the stands. At which point, one of the lads called Savage makes his way to the front and asks the Old Bill if he can go on to the pitch and get his trainer as it's stuck in the mud. He comes out, makes his way into the fucking goalmouth … 'You're nicked, my beauty!'

YOUR OPINION ABOUT ALL-SEATER STADIUMS, TICKET PRICES AND THE COMMERCIAL ASPECT OF TODAY'S FOOTBALL INDUSTRY. DO YOU STILL FEEL FOOTBALL BELONGS TO THE FANS?

When I was young going to football – this is where a lot of guys of my generation are lost now – because when I went to football as a youngster you was part of it; from the moment the morning started, you'd go down, you'd go and buy your streamers, nicking toilet rolls out of toilets. You headed down to the ground, you got behind your team, you made noise for an hour before you come out. They come out, you're fucking screaming and shouting, you want that ball in the net.

Nowadays, you sit back and wait for something to happen and that's it. You're not driving it any more. And that's what they've done; OK, it's fantastic to hear 60,000 people attending, but I think the day when Chelsea went up to Old Trafford, and that song '60,000 Muppets', I think that said it all. It's great for people now who've never seen football before, but every one of them would love to be able to get a taste of some of it – and the only time you do is when there's a derby. They never get the full whack, they don't get it.

RACISM AND RACE ISSUES HAVE BEEN PART OF FOOTBALL WITH CERTAIN CLUBS AND SETS OF SUPPORTERS AT BOTH CLUB AND INTERNATIONAL LEVEL. WHAT WAS YOUR EXPERIENCE OF THIS?

Well, we think we're lucky because one thing we've got at Luton, we've always had black boys in our mob, who we call 'blackheads'. We've always had blackheads in our mobs. For that reason, we've never had the problem like other clubs with black and white, etc. Leicester, we know, they were pretty similar. We don't think we're unique. I think too much is made of it. I think we're obsessed with racism these days. In my life, I've never seen no real issues of racism and I've been going 20-odd years. I think it's best left alone and it will go away, that's my opinion.

WOULD YOU SAY THE MEDIA 'OVER-HYPE' THE TROUBLE AND CAN YOU GIVE AN EXAMPLE OF THIS?

Certain clubs suffer from it, i.e. Millwall – I think they're scrutinised every single thing they do. If incidents which happen at their club happened at most other clubs, it wouldn't even be a fucking issue. The thing we all know, I mean in our own town here, we've read all the time about this – any little thing that the Migs are involved in is banged in the paper. They like to print the words 'Men in Gear', they love to do all that shit. Basically, it gets people to read their papers. You end up doing bird for things that fucking happen every Saturday night and guys would just be let out in the morning. The bottom line of a lot of football violence is it is violence, but it's not as damaging to people's lives as paedophiles, for example. Eighteen months for what he does. Football thug throws a fist, he might get fucking more than that. It's crap.

SHOULD CELTIC AND RANGERS BE ALLOWED TO JOIN THE ENGLISH PREMIERSHIP OR NATIONWIDE LEAGUES?

Rangers should. Celtic should be put in the fucking Irish league.

DO YOU HAVE ANY VIEW ON BANNING ORDERS? DO YOU KNOW THIS FROM YOUR OWN EXPERIENCE OR THAT OF OTHERS?

I'm on a banning order. I deserved it, and it's gonna work. Mine is for seven years. My banning order is any England international away from home. I'm not allowed to travel. I have to hand my passport in a few days before, and sign on on the day of the game. Banned from any football, what they call a designated football match, which I take it is from the Conference up. Seven years.

On any Saturday when Luton are playing, we've got two maps we're not allowed to enter areas on, one in the Bury Park area, one in the town centre. We've actually got maps, exclusion zones if you like. You work all week, you can't go into town to do your shopping, so you have to go out of town. But you shouldn't be naughty boys, eh?

WAS YOUR LIFESTYLE WITH THE MIGS SOLELY CONFINED TO THE FOOTBALL CONTEXT OR WOULD IT HAVE BEEN THE SAME FOR YOU IN EVERYDAY STREET LIFE?

Our lads, all the Migs, go to work, they've all got good jobs. They don't rob, they don't thieve, they respect people. When they're babies and they come through with us, they're taught courtesy, not to misbehave in the pub, not to pick on individuals. We're only interested in one thing, and that's football. Their mums that we speak to sometimes think they're amazing, they love them. They have to work because it gives them something to aim at, doesn't it? Go to work, get your money, so you can buy the clobber. So it gets them motivated in the right direction straight away. They're clean-shaven, they care about their appearance. They learn to be punctual because if they're not at the station on time, they miss the train. There are certain aspects we think makes the guys better – they don't go mugging or any of that stuff, so there's a certain quality there. Boys will be boys, is what we say, but try to be controlled with it.

EVERY ONE OF TODAY'S KNOWN HOOLIGAN FIRMS HAS A POLICE INTELLIGENCE OFFICER DEDICATED TO IT. HOW DO THE FIRMS TODAY RESPOND TO THAT? DO YOU HAVE ANY POLICE SPOTTER STORIES?

Three years ago, the Migs and MI2 ambushed Cardiff at Paddington Station at eleven o'clock at night. They'd just come back from QPR, and we were at Orient. The only reason we were over there in the pub that they was in was because intelligence as good as told us. It happens all the time. And I say to anybody, if you could be a copper on the beat and walk around doing parking tickets, dealing with burglaries, etc., in their daily lives, or you could be paid to travel all over the country watching lads have a punch-up, which would you choose? Our officer even walks around in football gear off-duty – Burberry, though! He was actually quite hurt when a few guys went to prison. Made an effort going round apologising, saying he didn't want it this way, but had no choice … I actually believe it.

IS THERE, IN YOUR OPINION, A NEXT GENERATION OF HOOLIGAN APPRENTICES COMING THROUGH AND WILL THEY BE ANYTHING LIKE THEIR PREDECESSORS?

We've got the MI2s. They're now, they're doing it. They go from 15-year-olds right through to about mid-twenties. Some of their guys actually look right lumps, fucking hell, I wouldn't want to be in front of them in ten years. They're shaping up, but time will tell. If you want a second opinion on them, just ask QPR.

NAME: Renno
CLUB: Manchester City
FIRM: City

'A real firm member in my day was a criminal 24-7. It was a day off from the crime.'

BACKGROUND AND MEET

I was interested in meeting Renno as he was an older head and it would be interesting to compare notes. I've got my own lively West Ham memories of going to City. Before we got known as the ICF, we went on the Kippax Stand side with a small firm but the right faces and claimed a bit of a result because we held our own. That said, mind, we were made to pay after the game, but still felt good about it because we remained intact and felt we'd had it with true Manchester, and I guess City have always been known as just that with the rest of us down south, maybe because they had no Cockneys and southerners in their fans.

One of the best books around hoolie-wise for its unbiased accounts from the frontline is written by Micky Francis who was once a Man City mob leader. City as a firm have just about had it with everyone and a lot of it major league stuff, all your big boys, all your real players, right through the seasons. So when I met Renno, I knew I was in for a long day, specially when I found he'd been with his good friend Eddie Beef of their most despised rivals, United. Apparently, they are a bundle of laughs who complement each other, but the week I met them their teams were due to play each other in the weekend derby. They had started to wind each other up so much I thought they might even come to blows. My north-west contact assured me, 'Cass, whatever the result between United and City, they will not be on speaking terms for at least two weeks after.'

His real name is Colin Rennicks, born in 1961. He's single and remembers his first job as selling the football pink outside pubs. Currently unemployed; first ever game Manchester United v Everton, a reserve game that saw Sammy McElroy make his début.

WHAT HAS BEEN THE MOST LEGENDARY FIGHT OR RIOT YOUR TEAM'S SUPPORTERS HAVE BEEN INVOLVED IN?

It's got to be that one where City played Liverpool at Anfield and the same day Everton played Millwall. No chance of getting in Anfield, impossible, thousands locked out of it. Over to the Everton–Millwall at Goodison, Gilroy and Stanley Parks, the knives were out. It were mental. People were just getting slashed on each side of the park. In the middle you've got Anfield, Goodison the other side, and you have to go through this massive big park. Ambulances, helicopters, the lot. But all the Scousers joined up together then, they joined up together and it was fucking mayhem, pure mayhem. They were flying out of everywhere, you just couldn't see, everywhere you looked there were big fucking riots going down, riots over there, dogs, murders, horses. Millwall got done in that day, slashed up to pieces. It was in the paper – razor war. And the Millwall got done in, proper, proper hardcore, they got captured in Liverpool and that's bad.

You know what ... me old fella took me and our kid down and when we got to Goodison, we were young, he stuck us in what we call the kiddies' pen, it was the safest place in Liverpool that fucking day, I swear to God. But when you came out, there were fucking murders, man. And that was it. You couldn't describe it.

HOW IMPORTANT WAS THE ROLE OF ALCOHOL AND DRUGS? WAS THERE ANY TIME IN YOUR EXPERIENCE EITHER HAD PARTICULAR INFLUENCE?

Alcohol was always there.

WHO WAS THE MOST VIOLENT, CRAZY SET OF SUPPORTERS YOU EVER CAME ACROSS?

Man United, Rangers, Cardiff, all the London firms more or less. Birmingham and Fulham, semi-final of the Cup at Maine Road.

It was on a fucking Wednesday night. You'd got all of Manchester there, you'd got the Cockneys down and the Brummies, man, and fucking war, war, war. Every alleyway there was people lying there with bins on their heads, big time. They were kicking people down the street. I thought these people were dead at one point.

These Birmingham fans had got this Fulham lad and just mercilessly booted him on the floor for a good 200 yards right down fucking Prince's Road. And they've all got the same coaches from the same fucking car park. And you had the Manchester after them, big time. They were waiting for the lot of them to come out. There were murders. Very violent that night. Proper Moss Side, you know what I mean?

ARE YOUR FIRM STILL DOING IT?

City have a firm who are still at it, but our firm from the '70s and '80s have long gone, all too old. We still come out for United if there is going to be fun and games.

HOW WOULD YOU DESCRIBE THE SITUATION WITH THE SCENE TODAY? CAN IT COMPARE WITH WHAT HAPPENED IN THE PAST, AND DO THINGS STILL GO OFF IN THE SAME WAY?

No chance! The real bad times exist no more!

HOW DID YOU GET GOING WITH A FOOTBALL FIRM, DID IT HAVE A NAME AND HOW WAS THE NAME ESTABLISHED?

We never formed or joined a firm, we were all mates and went to watch City together, everywhere they played. We never had a name, we were just City's boys. This was just before The Guv'nors. I fucked off then, I went to Spain for a little bit. I've come back and the next minute Pat and all them – I was a bit older than them, Pete and all his fucking psychopaths – they're called The Guv'nors because they were the fucking guv'nors.

Our firm, it was just like we're all fucking mates and no one comes near us. So you had all this respect between us from different parts of Manchester. And then you had The Young

Guv'nors, that's when Pat joined in. We've known Pat since he was a little kid, he was always with us, Pat. They were the younger members of The Guv'nors and The Guv'nors were all our fucking mates like, but we didn't call ourselves fuck all. The Guv'nors were the older firm and these young 'uns used to come up and follow their route and they got the name Young Guv'nors rather than The Guv'nors, that's exactly how it happened.

WHAT WAS THE WORST INSTANCE OF WEAPONS BEING USED?

Steel toe-capped boots before the Dibble used to take your laces out and old sterilised milk bottles with 1in-thick glass. Get a good grip on them and they were a handy tool to have, plenty of damage done.

WHAT IS THE MOST IMPORTANT LESSON YOU LEARNED PERSONALLY DURING YOUR TIME WITH YOUR FIRM AND WOULD YOU DO ANYTHING DIFFERENTLY?

The lesson to learn was don't show fear; once you do, you're a goner. Put fear into another firm and watch them crumble. What a great feeling.

WHO WERE YOUR BIGGEST RIVALS BOTH TEAM AND FAN-WISE?

Man United – both. In the '70s – you just don't see it no more – it were just like rude boy days, weren't it, and that would be just pure fucking mayhem. Probably fucking started on the Monday of the match week. A lot of my mates are Reds and that, but come derby day in them days you were like George Bush, you're either with them or with us, simple as that. Come the fucking day, behind the Kippax Stand there used to be a massive big car park with stones and rocks. It was always very bad, very bad. There was always trouble. We've never joined up. We've always been proper rivals. A lot of Blue people won't talk to Reds, and vice versa. With the hardcore ones, it's really fucking hatred, but I think it's just more rivalry, just pure rivalry, because all them Reds we know and they're our mates on any other day.

WHO ARE THE TOP FIVE FIRMS OF ANY IMPORTANCE TODAY?

Birmingham, Cardiff, Rangers, Middlesbrough and Man United. The thing with Birmingham is, they just want to kill you. They dream about Mancunians coming down, they really dream about it, they can't wait. It's like waiting for Christmas.

Middlesborough – they're tough, they're up for it. If you go down to Middlesbrough, you're in for a hard time.

Glasgow Rangers – they're heavy, no mercy with them.

Cardiff – major lunatics. No surrender with them, is there?

WHO ARE YOUR TOP FIVE FIRMS OF ALL TIME?

Chelsea, Everton, Birmingham, Man United ... Chelsea – what can you say about them? Just hardcore lunatics, aren't they? Everton – very shifty hardcore lunatics. Man United – mobbed up.

WHAT IS THE WORST GROUND YOU'VE EVER BEEN TO AND WHAT IS YOUR FAVOURITE GROUND?

Derby – the Baseball Ground was a shit-hole.

WHAT IS YOUR FAVOURITE FOOTBALL FASHIONWEAR AND THE WORST YOU'VE SEEN OR WORN?

Best is the modern casual stuff when it's been lifted. The worst is the Eddie Beef Baker pants and butcher's coat style.

WHAT IS THE WORST KIT YOU'VE SEEN A TEAM IN AND WHAT WOULD BE YOUR OWN CLUB'S BEST EVER STRIP?

Worst I ever saw was a Coventry away kit, like a green-and-black-striped number. The best was the old City sky-blue top with a crew neck.

DOES TODAY'S MODERN FOOTBALL PLAYER HAVE THE RESPECT OF THE FANS?

Cunts. Overpaid prima donnas, mostly middle-class twats.

WHO'S THE PLAYER AND/OR MANAGER THAT WINDS YOU UP THE MOST?

Glenn Hoddle as a player and then another for being a cunt as a manager.

WORST FOREIGN PLAYER YOU'VE SEEN AND THE BEST FOREIGN IMPORT? YOUR FAVOURITE CLUB PLAYER AND YOUR FAVOURITE OTHER PLAYER?

Worst – Paddy Roach. Best – Dennis Law; in my day they were regarded as foreign. Dennis was my hero. Sent the Reds down at Old Trafford. What more can you ask for?

FANS OFTEN TALK ABOUT THEIR FOOTBALL-GOING DAYS AS JUST BEING A LAUGH. ANY EPISODES YOU REMEMBER?

The City last match awayday fancy dress parties. We were original. They were unbeatable days, top drawer. To me, it was Man City's big fancy dress party at Stoke, about '89 I think. I think there were probably about 30,000 fucking City fans dressed up as fucking coppers, Adolf Hitler, there were a big gang of Nazis walking down the road. Bus conductors, nurses, doctors, the Blues Brothers, all dressed up with bowler hats and suits on doing a mad dance down the road. It was fucking everyone that got fancy dressed up. It was City's humour, weren't it? Some people went as sunbathers, you know, the old beach gear. They're all lying outside the pub with suntan lotion on. A lot of people cottoned on to that. I think City brought the humour out of the hooliganism bit. They took it out a little bit at that time. Every cunt had an inflatable banana in their hand, shouting, 'Bananas ... bananas.'

YOUR OPINION ABOUT ALL-SEATER STADIUMS, TICKET PRICES AND THE COMMERCIAL ASPECT OF TODAY'S FOOTBALL INDUSTRY. DO YOU STILL FEEL FOOTBALL BELONGS TO THE FANS?

They are fucking shite. Rip-off prices to pay just a fraction of the overpaid bastards' wages.

RACISM AND RACE ISSUES HAVE BEEN PART OF FOOTBALL WITH CERTAIN CLUBS AND SETS OF SUPPORTERS AT BOTH CLUB AND INTERNATIONAL LEVEL. WHAT WAS YOUR EXPERIENCE OF THIS?

Everton and Liverpool were bad; the Scousers were very racist. It was a tough one to deal with when one of your best mates was black and they were being hounded all day long. You had to stick with him and when you went there it was scary.

HOW HAVE FANS FOLLOWING THE NATIONAL TEAM ABROAD BEEN TREATED, AND WHAT ARE YOUR EXPERIENCES FOLLOWING YOUR CLUB OR NATIONAL TEAM ABROAD?

The national team's fans and English club fans abroad will always be a target for the nasty foreign police and, after the shit they have put up with over the years, who can blame them? The dickheads who go abroad today get a raw deal after our wrongdoings years ago. Tough shit. I think the new-style Dibble at home are just as bad. There is a serious thug element in the police force.

WOULD YOU SAY THE MEDIA 'OVER-HYPE' THE TROUBLE AND CAN YOU GIVE AN EXAMPLE OF THIS?

The media are scum. They get snippets from bar staff and landlords and then make up stories. One fucking easy job, that is.

SHOULD CELTIC AND RANGERS BE ALLOWED TO JOIN THE ENGLISH PREMIERSHIP OR NATIONWIDE LEAGUES?

Yes, Cardiff can, so why not the Jocks? But I'd start them off in the bottom league.

DO YOU HAVE ANY VIEW ON BANNING ORDERS? DO YOU KNOW THIS FROM YOUR OWN EXPERIENCE OR THAT OF OTHERS?

I think they are effective, but at times unfair. Depends on the crime. You get banned for being pissed. Agreed, being pissed can escalate into trouble, but some people who get banned are not thugs, they just like a beer and they can't watch their team because they swore and stunk of ale. That's wank. At the end of the day, the person who is banned decides if they are effective. If you want to go and you're banned, you take the risk if you want it bad enough.

HOOLIE MOVIES AND FLICKS – DO THEY GLORIFY VIOLENCE OR CREATE A COPYCAT SYNDROME?

They are all the same old shite. Of course they glorify violence, but you will always get a copycat syndrome in mob action. It's when they get a fucking good kicking and realise it's not a game that they wonder what's going on.

WHO'S YOUR TOP FELLOW – SOUND AS A POUND – FROM YOUR OWN SUPPORTERS, WHY HE IS NOMINATED AND WHAT DID HE DO FOR YOU?

Charlie Conning at City. A top bloke who never, ever ran from anyone. He came to my rescue on countless occasions. He was the real Manc deal.

HOW WOULD YOU DESCRIBE YOUR FIRM/SUPPORTERS' FAN BASE, AND HAS YOUR FAN BASE CHANGED OVER TIME?

City have always been the same, true Mancunians with blue blood at boiling point.

WAS YOUR LIFESTYLE WITH YOUR FIRM SOLELY CONFINED TO THE FOOTBALL CONTEXT OR WOULD IT HAVE BEEN THE SAME FOR YOU IN EVERYDAY STREET LIFE?

A real firm member in my day was a criminal 24/7. It was a day off from the crime, a good day out putting the fear into some cunt who wasn't City.

EVERY ONE OF TODAY'S KNOWN HOOLIGAN FIRMS HAS A POLICE INTELLIGENCE OFFICER DEDICATED TO IT. HOW DO THE FIRMS TODAY RESPOND TO THAT? DO YOU HAVE ANY POLICE SPOTTER STORIES?

It really pisses me off to see some so-called hooligans enjoying light-hearted banter with sneaky spotters who want to nick them. What's all that about? Avoid the cunts as much as possible. The lads got one undercover pickpocket officer in Münchengladbach in 1978, he tried to blend in with our firm. What a fucking idiot. He will remember the hiding he got as long as he lives. I bet he never went firm-spotting again!

IS THERE, IN YOUR OPINION, A NEXT GENERATION OF HOOLIGAN APPRENTICES COMING THROUGH AND WILL THEY BE ANYTHING LIKE THEIR PREDECESSORS?

There are youngsters now trying to keep the ball rolling, but they don't come fucking near to the old firms. The new kids on the block are too scared to get their once-a-week fashion uniform ripped to bits. Most of them need Es and Charlie before they go into battle. They spend all their time talking into mobile phones. Quite simply, not fit to lace our boots. No, they don't measure up, but most of them do tell good porkies on a Sunday.

NAME: Eddie Beef
CLUB: Manchester United
FIRM: ICJ

'We were kings of Europe and I was king of the jibbers.'

BACKGROUND AND MEET

Man U. There's no love lost here for, back in the '70s and '80s, we West Ham used to look for them with a passion. But, really, this whole football scene started with them. They showed the country's youth what it is like to travel away all as one mob in the name of your football team and they have done this as far back as 1967 when they got on to our North Bank en masse. The papers said at the time that it was the worst ever outbreak of football violence recorded in the south, and they've never been forgiven for it down in the East End.

For the next two decades as the Red Army, they rolled into your town and everybody else's; vintage black-and-white film footage shown on Channel Four in the documentary Football Fight Club captures everything that was your Man Utd '70s bovver boy in baggy trousers, boots, long hair and scarves round necks, waists and wrists, storming off yer old football special trains.

It was classic Man U and they are still active today. They used to have this nasty chant – 'You're going home in a fucking ambulance' – and we would only laugh at that if we were the home team. But the one chant I used to find difficult to answer back, if your own team was also a United, was when they would taunt you with 'There's only one United ...' That really hurt, for you look at their support, the history, the trophies ... what could you reply? It took three decades for someone to come up with 'Stand up if you hate Man U ...' and every club in the land stood up. They are legend. We are all jealous and they do get off on our hatred because of it.

So I would need a hell of a good contact if I was to obtain a United chapter for the book. There were also loads of names in the hat for a United legend, but one kept cropping up and, luckily enough, one of our infamous north-west contacts was able to sort us with a meet with the leader of the ICJ, the Manchester United legendary gang, the Inter-City Jibbers, whose motto today is as strong as it was when Eddie formed the gang – 'To Pay Is To Fail'. Here's what Eddie 'King of the Jibbers' had to say.

He was born in 1961, and lists his qualifications as a City & Guilds in criminal activities. Currently still looking for his first job since leaving St Peter and Paul RC School, Gorton in 1976. Single at the moment, although the longest stint he had was 15 years with Mandy, mother of two of his four kids. His first game was when he wagged school with James O'Flannagen to go in the Scoreboard end at Old Trafford, watching Manchester United play Liverpool. After the game, the Scousers got chased back in when they tried to leave the ground, so nothing has changed in 35 years!

WHAT HAS BEEN THE MOST LEGENDARY FIGHT OR RIOT YOUR TEAM'S SUPPORTERS HAVE BEEN INVOLVED IN?

There's been hundreds over the years, loads that hit the headlines. The battle at Ninnian Park in the old Second Division; the battle on the ferry with West Ham; St Etienne away; Chelsea at Kensington High Steet Tube station; Everton and Liverpool away every game through the '70s and '80s; Birmingham away; Stoke away; Leeds every time we met for years.

I suppose the most legendary was the West Ham ferry one, but I missed the boat when we were getting searched for having the duty-free shop off. We were waiting for the next ferry a couple of hours later and we saw the other one coming back. I laughed and was waving on the docks saying, 'They've come back for Beef.' But then vanfuls of 'the odd lot' [the police] turned up and we saw the carnage that had gone off between us and the ICF. Loads has been written about it. I wasn't there, but it was mental by all accounts. A good mate involved in that got eight years for piracy and it wasn't the blag DVD and CD kind.

Cardiff was bad when loads of ours starting singing about Aberfan and then the fucking lot went, morning to tea-time, we never stopped fighting all day. Chelsea pulled the line at High Street Ken and it all went up. We were stuck on the train for ages and it got trashed. There were fucking hundreds of them. Some of ours were getting pulled out of the windows, we had to get off in the end, about 100-strong, and we chased them out but it was a scary fucking stop.

We went 200-handed to Anfield when just seven of us got on to the Kop. The odd lot sussed us and shut the gate with 200 United locked out behind us. To cut a long and not very pleasant story short, we got fucking leathered.

But the all-time favourite was at Birmingham. After the match at the back of the away end, we came out on to the green and there was 1,000 of them, no blagging. It took at least half-an-hour for the odd lot to get between us.

HOW IMPORTANT WAS THE ROLE OF ALCOHOL AND DRUGS? WAS THERE ANY TIME IN YOUR EXPERIENCE EITHER HAD PARTICULAR INFLUENCE?

In the '70s, it didn't matter if you were drinking tea or Bovril, all day some cunt was getting it. Drugs fucked it up with all this Ecstasy nonsense, although, over the last few years, the rice and barley [cocaine] has introduced new kids on the block to football violence. To the old school, drugs was never an issue, we had it pissed or sober, drugged or straight ... hooliganism was our drug.

WHO WAS THE MOST VIOLENT, CRAZY SET OF SUPPORTERS YOU EVER CAME ACROSS?

I've had a few ding-dongs with them all but the worst lot I ever saw was Newcastle up there once after a Cup match. We opened the gates up five minutes before the end and all our main lads piled out, but we couldn't get out the fucking place. They were seriously mob-handed and threw everything they could get their hands on at us – bricks, bottles, concrete, wood – some were charging at us with a big road sign they had pulled out of the ground. I've seen some angry mobs, but something had upset the fuckers that day. We got out in the end, but it was a tough one.

I expected Feyenoord to be mad because they have a bad reputation but when we went there they shit themselves. Big disappointment, them Dutch kids were. We didn't bother with the game, done them in town and fucked off back to the 'Dam.

The craziest individual was a bloke at Coventry. He was a fucking huge tower of a man, game as fuck and we couldn't pull him away. I had to hit him with a rock in the end. He was the craziest ever, fair play to him.

ARE YOUR FIRM STILL DOING IT?

United are still bang at it, loads of mobs of 40 and 50 who can join up and total 400–500 when we play City or fancy a big day out. We still take 200 to the likes of Everton, Chelsea, Birmingham, when we know there will be a spot of mither. Not kids either, lads who were at it in the '70s and still enjoy it; blokes in their fifties, for fuck's sake! Look at that live game on the telly a couple of seasons ago when we played Villa in the Cup and tickets were easy to get your mitts on. We were 2–0 down and came back to win. There was about 300 lads on the fucking pitch when we scored. When we can get the tickets, no one can touch the mob we can pull.

HOW DID YOU GET GOING WITH A FOOTBALL FIRM, DID IT HAVE A NAME AND HOW WAS THE NAME ESTABLISHED?

Early years, it was just association, there were loads of us young kids all used to go to the game dipping and getting what we could. Then we were all in Borstal together and stayed close. We all used to met in a boozer called Klosters on Oxford Road from about '76 'til it got shut down in about '81. Then it had snowballed and we had a massive mob.

United were always called the Red Army from the late '60s–'70s, but that included all the bar scarf brigade so we formed our own mob called the ICJ. Our motto was 'To Pay Is To Fail' and it still counts today. We could go all over Europe jibbing and on blag tickets, robbing what we could, doing the tills, grafting, it was the best years of our lives. The Scousers claim they were the best at it, but we had hundreds at it at the same time. We were kings of Europe and I was King of the Jibbers.

WHAT WAS THE WORST INSTANCE OF WEAPONS BEING USED?

The Scousers, blue or red, they started that Stanley knife craze and were fuckers for it. Everton done one of ours at Old Trafford, a well-known coloured kid, cut him head to toe. After that, it went tit for tat and quite a few of ours were at it. I always found the Cockney mobs were blade men as well, and the black firm in Birmingham. At one stage, it took off everywhere. If you went down, you used to check your arse for a stripe. Nasty times, very nasty indeed.

Overall, I found that in a pub brawl anyone would use whatever they could get their hands on if it tilted a barney in your favour. It was a survival sketch, not a fucking arm wrestle or a game of conkers. My own personal favourite was a bottle and brick and an aggro stick.

WHAT IS THE MOST IMPORTANT LESSON YOU LEARNED PERSONALLY DURING YOUR TIME WITH YOUR FIRM AND WOULD YOU DO ANYTHING DIFFERENTLY?

Don't get fucking caught! That's all I'd do different. The late '70s to late '80s were the best and will never come back. We had a fucking ball. Apart from the jail, they were the best days of my life and, unless I win the lottery, will always be.

WHO WERE YOUR BIGGEST RIVALS BOTH TEAM AND FAN-WISE?

Fans – Leeds, fucking scum cunts. Team – Man City.

We have pure hatred with Leeds. They do have a go every year and stand their ground, give them that, but we have the upper hand and it hurts them. As well as all their players coming to us over the years, that pains them, too – Joe Jordan, McQueen, King Eric, Rio and now Smith, it makes them hate us more, silly twats.

On the pitch, MCFC, the bitter, bitter blues, all you get off them is 'We beat you 5–1 ...' 'We beat you in 1923 ...' 'We got a better chippy ...' They choose not to say, 'We never won fuck all ...' though. They even rent a ground off the council, the sad bastards, bitter and sad. Yeah, that makes me laugh. Them and Leeds deserve each other.

WHO ARE THE TOP FIVE FIRMS OF ANY IMPORTANCE TODAY?

These aren't all against us, but recently I'd go for:

1. 'Boro – they walked through Manchester the other season as if they owned it. They were playing City but it was a massive show that I ain't seen for years.
2. Huddersfield Town – I saw them with over 200 last year stop off in Leeds. I think they had been to Hull and they wrecked the joint.
3. Birmingham – that city centre is on top if you're not serious-handed.
4. Everton – always come looking for it at Old Trafford and, a few seasons ago, they came and walked all the way from Oxford Road unchallenged. Only about 100 of them, but all old lads like myself.
5. Spurs – they have got it together again and turned up for the past couple of seasons looking for it, fair play to them.

WHO ARE YOUR TOP FIVE FIRMS OF ALL TIME?

1. West Ham – we had some great times there but they always gave as good as they got, home and away.
2. 'Boro – don't budge an inch and always stick together.
3. Everton – always came to Old Trafford mobbed up and still do and that place in the '70s and '80s was nasty.
4. Sunderland – at their place it could be frightening years ago.
5. Leeds – give them some credit, they have earned it over the years.

WHAT IS THE WORST GROUND YOU'VE EVER BEEN TO AND WHAT IS YOUR FAVOURITE GROUND?

Worst ground – Halifax. Years ago, we went there and got piss-wet through. Then a big gang of blokes in sheepskin coats had it with us after the match. And the pies were shit.

Best – Old Trafford. Even when we were shit the atmosphere was awesome.

WHAT ARE YOUR TOP HOOLIE BOOKS, AND WHAT IS YOUR OPINION ON THESE BOOKS?

I only read a few and they are mostly bollocks. Will have to say Scally, 'cos I know the lad, but that's a good read and honest and at least he has done a bit. Most of them are written by fringe players. ICF was OK but a bit one-sided; suppose they all are, though.

Some are fucking rubbish. That West Ham Want Some Aggro?, the Boro one and that Liverpool one are pony. That Scouse cunt in Boys from the Mersey calls me a 'rough-arse Manc'. You see the state of him and his mates? Reckons they were the boys. Well, it's fucking news to me. I know a load of the main Scouse firm and no one has ever heard of the stupid cunt. Scum Airways was the worst, not a fan book, but it's on the shelves with them. Fucking grasses, ruined good dough for the lads and the kids responsible are not welcome at Old Trafford if you get what I'm saying.

WHAT IS YOUR FAVOURITE FOOTBALL FASHIONWEAR AND THE WORST YOU'VE SEEN OR WORN?

My butcher's coat in the '70s, it's legendary, with white skinners jeans and monkey boots, fucking mint. Last year we had a '70s reunion in Blackburn. I was in my fucking element. I robbed a butcher's coat but could I fuck get my hands on some monkey boots? There was a good few hundred of us, what a top day. Those kids at Leeds take some beating with fashion, lamb dressed as mutton.

HAVE YOU EVER WORN A REPLICA FOOTBALL SHIRT TO A GAME AND NAME A CLUB THAT'S ALL SHIRTERS AND SCARFERS?

Never ever worn one to a match. I've had them bought me for Christmas by the kids and I wear it around the house for a few days to keep them happy, but I'd be happier if they gave me the money instead. Leeds or City are the worst. Forget the Geordies, those pair always come to Old Trafford in their shirts. They fucking never had them on show in the '70s though, they were all fucking hidden under their coats.

WORST FOREIGN PLAYER YOU'VE SEEN AND THE BEST FOREIGN IMPORT? YOUR FAVOURITE CLUB PLAYER AND YOUR FAVOURITE OTHER PLAYER?

Worst – Maradona, for the hand of God. What a twat he was, a good player, but a twat. You look at him now, though, he's fucked, too many visits to his mate's gaff in Columbia, the lucky bastard.

The best ever was Eric Cantona, no need to even explain, easiest question I have ever been asked. King Eric, what a fucking footballer he was.

My favourite club player ever was Mark Hughes; he was my hero, another United legend. I hate to admit it, but that Scouser Gerrard is quality. I'd love him in a United shirt.

FANS OFTEN TALK ABOUT THEIR FOOTBALL-GOING DAYS AS JUST BEING A LAUGH. ANY EPISODES YOU REMEMBER?

I'd be all day if I went through just a few of them. The crack was better than the fighting. I love a laugh and I love making people laugh. If you can't have a crack, there's no point in getting up in the morning. I hate all these serious cunts you see walking around trying to look important. Smile, you cunts!

The best ever was when we nicked a Government Minister's trousers off the train. We used to jib the midnight train to Euston as there were no hectors on it and they had a load of sleeper cars we used to try and dip from. Well, this night we were going to Chelsea and we went in one cabin and this bloke was lying there with not a stitch on and I swear he had the smallest nob you've ever seen. Anyway, his briefcase and trousers were lifted and when the lads opened the case it was full of House of Commons papers, so they flapped and slung them out at Dunstable. His trousers went out at Luton after £150 was lifted from his wallet and, when we got to Euston, the odd lot were swarming and he was led off the train with a British Rail towel around him, it was fucking hilarious.

Next few days, the doors were going in, MI5 and the like – boom. Loads on that train who could be traced were nicked and it was in all the papers that this Government bigwig had been robbed and loads of important papers had gone AWOL. I still have one paper with the headline '100mph sneak thief has government minister's trousers'. It was bang on in case the IRA had robbed them and loads of Government meetings had to be rearranged for security. But the ICJ had them, not the fucking IRA!

YOUR OPINION ABOUT ALL-SEATER STADIUMS, TICKET PRICES AND THE COMMERCIAL ASPECT OF TODAY'S FOOTBALL INDUSTRY. DO YOU STILL FEEL FOOTBALL BELONGS TO THE FANS?

It's shit, no singing, no standing, and you're not allowed to fucking swear. Everything that your working-class fan likes doing is fucking banned. All-seater grounds might look the bollocks, but they're shite. There should be a bit of standing, a regulated area for a set amount, a controlled number. I know Hillsborough was bad, but I think it would never happen again if the areas were controlled.

Ticket prices don't bother me, I never buy them. Commercially, it's one big fucking rip-off. They will be sorry when the Sky bubble goes pop. They will be coming around to our houses, picking us up in a big yellow bus, saying, 'Please come to the match, you can stand and swear as much as you want, lads, we're fucking skint.'

RACISM AND RACE ISSUES HAVE BEEN PART OF FOOTBALL WITH CERTAIN CLUBS AND SETS OF SUPPORTERS AT BOTH CLUB AND INTERNATIONAL LEVEL. WHAT WAS YOUR EXPERIENCE OF THIS?

Truthfully, I never heard it at Old Trafford, ever, and not much away. Everton was the worst. We could go there and we had black lads with us and we'd say, 'You watch your fucking backs.'

Once, me and a mate, a black kid, hitched it to Everton and this fucking daft lorry driver pulls over by that Las Vegas arcade and drops us. We clocked about 200 of the cunts, all Evertonians, waiting for the Manchester train to come in. We got out and tried to do a quiet one and the soft twat hoots his horn and waves at us. That was it. All you could hear was, 'Get the nigger,' and they came piling off the station. My pal runs off and I just stood there waiting to get killed. The lot goes flying past and he gets chased for miles. I never got a single glance.

With England, we went together, black and white, all Mancs, no one gave a fuck. We stood and fought them all; as long as you had a go, it didn't matter.

WOULD YOU SAY THE MEDIA 'OVER-HYPE' THE TROUBLE AND CAN YOU GIVE AN EXAMPLE OF THIS?

They not only over-hype it, they instigate it. Days before the game's kick-off, they stir it up. In the old days, they had a point, it was a battlefield and there were some very bad incidents that deserved reporting, but today they put stuff in the papers that is not worth a column in the fucking Beano or Dandy. My worst instance of the press was after the terrible murder of the England fan, Steve Smith, in Portugal during the European championships. I had had a drink with him and this fucking wino tramp was bothering everyone and the poor kid from Wolverhampton got stabbed by him. Later, before a flower had been laid on the spot, the press were offering people ale for a story with a hooligan slant to it. There was no fucking slant – the lad was a true fan and a top bloke enjoying himself and this junkie tramp killed him for nothing. But that's no good for the gutter press and they tried everything to turn it around to a hooligan story.

SHOULD CELTIC AND RANGERS BE ALLOWED TO JOIN THE ENGLISH PREMIERSHIP OR NATIONWIDE LEAGUES?

Yes, right at the bottom of the Nationwide. Fuck 'em, have them playing the likes of Stockport County for a year and see how they like it.

DO YOU HAVE ANY VIEW ON BANNING ORDERS? DO YOU KNOW THIS FROM YOUR OWN EXPERIENCE OR THAT OF OTHERS?

I had a little swig of brandy one night at a European game at Old Trafford, I got spotted on CCTV, nicked, fined £500 and a three-year ban. If that's fair, I'm from fucking Jupiter. It was very effective but very fucking unfair. If you're a known face, you're bollocksed; a dickhead who gets banned for running on the pitch can still go and not get clocked, but if you're a known hooligan you may as well call it a day 'til the ban's up.

HOOLIE MOVIES AND FLICKS – DO THEY GLORIFY VIOLENCE OR CREATE A COPYCAT SYNDROME?

They might encourage a few wannabe clowns to be a hooligan, but, if it's in you, you don't need a film to kick-start it. I enjoyed Forrest Gump, but I didn't go running around Manchester for two fucking years.

WHO'S YOUR TOP FELLOW – SOUND AS A POUND – FROM YOUR OWN SUPPORTERS, WHY HE IS NOMINATED AND WHAT DID HE DO FOR YOU?

Tony, a top United man. He put a pool cue across a fellow's head when I was going to get done in bad. It was outside Jim Holton's pub in Coventry. They used to sing, 'Six foot two, eyes of blue, big Jim Holton's after you …' I remember looking at him before it went off, and his eyes were fucking brown.

Anyway, only eight of us were left and I went out by the door and a big mob of them pulled me down and I was in for it until he saved my arse, big time. Will always remember him for that, a top man, fearless.

Jim Holton was a top fellow, too. They reckon when it was going off at Cardiff, he was warming up near the fence shouting for us lot to give it them. He's dead now, so you can put that in.

HOW WOULD YOU DESCRIBE YOUR FIRM/SUPPORTERS' FAN BASE, AND HAS YOUR FAN BASE CHANGED OVER TIME?

We have a load of fans worldwide ever since Munich. That makes us the biggest club in the world. But loads of dickheads call us 'rent-a-mob'. Apart from the Cockney Reds, 95 per cent of our firm are Manchester, Gorton, Salford, Ancoats, Wythenshawe, Newton Heath, Stretford, Swinton, Collyhurst. They say it's a rent-a-mob, but that's one fucking top Manchester mob. When that lot get together, believe me, it is a pure Manchester firm and it's fucking frightening.

WAS YOUR LIFESTYLE WITH THE ICJ SOLELY CONFINED TO THE FOOTBALL CONTEXT OR WOULD IT HAVE BEEN THE SAME FOR YOU IN EVERYDAY STREET LIFE?

The jibbing, fighting and pinching has been my lifestyle since I was old enough to understand right from wrong. I understood it, I just didn't take any notice of it! I first went to Borstal when I was 15. Soon escaped and since then have done a total of 13 years worldwide jail. Longest was a five handed out at Preston Crown for robbery.

EVERY ONE OF TODAY'S KNOWN HOOLIGAN FIRMS HAS A POLICE INTELLIGENCE OFFICER DEDICATED TO IT. HOW DO THE FIRMS TODAY RESPOND TO THAT? DO YOU HAVE ANY POLICE SPOTTER STORIES?

They have got one fucking tidy job looking after us. They get more trips abroad than Judith Chalmers. It's a piss-take, they take the piss out of the taxpayers' money and we take the piss out of them. They try and get on with us and turn a blind eye for something. If we weren't at it, they would be on the beat getting shot at in Moss Side, so they leave us alone most of the time. The minglers are more danger than the known spotters, CID latching on, and then the grasses; believe me, all firms have got them.

My best spotter story was when we had one called Tash. He was a bit of a twat, but got kicked in the head by a police horse and had to give the job up, so the lads had a whip round and sent a bag of carrots to the police stables. Quality.

IS THERE, IN YOUR OPINION, A NEXT GENERATION OF HOOLIGAN APPRENTICES COMING THROUGH AND WILL THEY BE ANYTHING LIKE THEIR PREDECESSORS?

There is not a dog in hell's chance they could measure up. They will never get the chance to do what we did. You would need to build a new prison every week to fit us all in if it went back to the good old days. The kids today may have all the gear, better grounds, posh trains and coaches with bogs on, but we had fuck all but the crack and the crack at the football was all we needed. It was brilliant, fucking fantastic, and it will never be bettered and only a fucking idiot would argue the toss.

NAME: Boatsy
CLUB: Nottingham Forest
FIRM: Forest Executive Crew

'I've had some great times and my life certainly hasn't been boring.'

BACKGROUND AND MEET

Gary Clarke – although everyone calls him Boatsy – was the original Forest lad we first headhunted when the *Terrace Legends* book was put together, but a stay with Her Majesty's Service prevented that. So when I learned of his availability for a Forest chapter in Top Boys, I was on my way to Nottingham after being reminded to get there early as he was on a tag as a result of the England–Turkey game incidents.

I was eager to meet up with the Forest man and get up to date as I was still stuck in my '70s time-warp when every end would chant out the song that began with 'We hate Nottingham Forest ...' Every fan that ever stood on an end sung or chanted out those words, then adapted the rest to suit. I must say, it's probably more to do with the words rhyming than there being any real hatred.

Forest, they were respected as a firm right back to the original bovver-boy years because it was no myth that rival fans who came unstuck got punched and kicked into the River Trent that ran behind the Trent end. Forest have maintained a firm with a decent rep right throughout, even today. And as the drink flowed, and a few more lads came out, we went right through all the clashes in the '80s up to the present day. They wanted to put right a few things, like they really resent the scab taunts coming from the various Yorkshire clubs. 'None of our firm ever worked the mines. Ones that did stayed out on strike.'

When I eventually left, I realised Boatsy and his boys are a real handy crew, so maybe the word 'Nottingham Forest' put into that famous chant from the terraces, is not without justification after all.

His real name is Gary Clarke, born in 1965. His listed qualifications are seven CSEs. First job was on the YTS in the City Council housing works. Divorced and went to his first game when Forest played Norwich in 1974.

WHAT HAS BEEN THE MOST LEGENDARY FIGHT OR RIOT YOUR TEAM'S SUPPORTERS HAVE BEEN INVOLVED IN?

One of my most favourite games for pure violence was Anderlecht away in 1984. It was mental from day one, the first night we left on the ferry at Dover. Man United were on the same boat going to Juventus in Italy. It was a Saturday night and there were about 40 of them, mostly Cockney Reds and their famous one; there was only eight of us, but we were all steaming, it didn't matter. The boat went up with about 20 minutes before docking in Ostend with the riot police steaming on when we'd docked. They nicked three of us and about 20 Mancs. It came on top but it was great. It's mentioned in Bill Bufford's book Among the Thugs; it said the ferry was turned back to England, but that wasn't true.

They let me out the cells the day after, blaming the Man U fans. For the next two to three days, loads and loads of our boys arrived, then we moved on to Brussels. We heard that their firm were called The 'O' Side Boys or something, so before the game we went round their end where we were told they drank before the game and we had a running battle outside their boozer. They were all in green flying jackets with the riot police eventually splitting the two groups apart.

We were escorted to the Forest section which was vastly overcrowded with over 4,000 squeezed into one tiny section. So most of our boys jumped over the fencing into their end behind the goal. As soon as they scored, that was it, mayhem, we cleared their end three times. We lost that night 3–0 and went out 3–2 on aggregate. If you have seen or watched the goals on replays, you see big gaps open on the terracing every time they score.

I arrived back in Dover on the Thursday morning expecting it to be all over the papers. We got about five lines in the Sun. If that was Man United, Chelsea or Leeds it would have been front page. I was gutted.

Birmingham away in the fifth round of the FA Cup in '88 was also a good one: 87 arrests headlined one national Sunday paper.

Middlesbrough away around 1995/96 season was a good day out; we hadn't been there for a while as a firm. Forest had a few battles there in the early '80s. In one unfortunate incident, one of their lads died in a street battle with one of our top boys getting four years for manslaughter and a lot more getting locked up, too. So I decided to hire a battle bus with some of our finest on board. We met at Darlington around 80-strong with the 'Boro knowing we would be coming. We got the train in and every pub near the station emptying and the Old Bill separating what would have been a pretty good one. They put us in the ground at 1.00pm. We told the 'Boro we would be getting the train back to Darlo; they said they would be waiting.

After the game, we were escorted and put back on the train to Darlo with only three transport police for company. Anyway, first stop down the line, Thornaby, and there was a mob waiting on the platform. I don't think they thought we'd get off. The lot went with three Old Bill running around in circles trying to hit people. We ran them up the hill three times under a railway viaduct. There was bodies everywhere. It seemed to last around ten minutes until the riot police arrived and everyone just seemed to slip back on the train as if nothing had happened. It's funny, it's never mentioned in their book, but I have the utmost respect for the frontline firm.

HOW IMPORTANT WAS THE ROLE OF ALCOHOL AND DRUGS? WAS THERE ANY TIME IN YOUR EXPERIENCE EITHER HAD PARTICULAR INFLUENCE?

Not much, really, with the proper boys. There used to be two hooligans' coaches regularly going in the late '70s/early '80s. One was called The Battle Bus and the other The Pisshead Bus. The proper loons didn't drink before the game, they just wanted to fight.

WHO WAS THE MOST VIOLENT, CRAZY SET OF SUPPORTERS YOU EVER CAME ACROSS?

Turkey has been an experience. I've been there twice with England, and also Yugoslavia was not for the faint-hearted. I ended up in hospital there with my mouth smashed open in '87 with England. West Ham in the early '80s were a very naughty, intimidating firm – pure evil.

Man U, that fucking '92 League Cup Final at Wembley. The only time they've ever won it. There were fucking millions of them. And they arranged at QPR away about two weeks before the Cup Final, that's before the mobiles were in. They're all down King's Cross. Five of our lot, a bunch of lads come up to them and said, 'Hey, tell Gary from Nottingham, Kilburn half-twelve. Kilburn High Street, half-twelve.'

So he come back and told me. We went the night before the final. Anyway, all the old 'uns weren't bothered, but all those my age said, 'Fuck it … Kilburn High Street, half-twelve.'

We went down about 100-strong. We didn't realise all their scouts were on the train station at Kilburn and they all went running off to tell the Mancs and they filled every pub in Kilburn High Street. And as soon as we come off the train down the road, every pub emptied. There must have been 500. I looked down the road; it was like the start of the Olympic fucking games. The lot went, the lot. All this was later shown in World in Action. They showed you on video all the violence down that road. Somebody had a portable camera in a shop and filmed it all.

I was throwing fucking tins out through a veg shop. We got proper battered, we got proper hammered. Half our lot legged it into a pub, the little Irish pub under the bridge. Our lot legged it in there. But Man U smashed it, proper smashed it to bits. We were still in the street, they left us with it. That was mental.

ARE YOUR FIRM STILL DOING IT?

It's died a bit over the last season with all the banning order shite. There's over 90 of us on it now. That didn't matter before, but now they've started putting the radius bans on. But I think over the last few years it's one of the biggest firms Forest have had. We took around 300 down to Cardiff last January and 250 to West Ham the year before, but I think a lot of it's just show nowadays. I mean, what started it was we never played them. And then we played them down here first, didn't we? And they phoned up and said, 'Right, we're here.' But they got rounded up. Anyway, there were about 60 of them out at Nottingham and they rung up. We said, 'Right, where are you? We'll make our own way. There's 200 of us. '

And 60 of them came. Fair dos to them, they came. It went off a bit but the cops got in there, fucking blah, blah, blah, nicked a load of us. And that was it. And so Cardiff says, 'Right, you've got to come to Wales.'

We say, 'Don't you worry, we're coming, make no mistake in that.'

Now, 50 were there on the Friday night. There was 400 of us in Cardiff by eleven o'clock. The biggest police operation, the fucking lot. And on the day, we never saw Cardiff, did we? We never fucking saw them. They turned round, Cardiff did, and said, 'That is the best firm that's ever been to Cardiff.' Nowt went on. We said, 'We're not claiming nothing, we ain't claiming fuck all.' We turned up.

There was also a massive turnout of over 400 for Derby at home last year for a night game – blokes I haven't seen for five years.

HOW WOULD YOU DESCRIBE THE SITUATION WITH THE SCENE TODAY? CAN IT COMPARE WITH WHAT HAPPENED IN THE PAST, AND DO THINGS STILL GO OFF IN THE SAME WAY?

Things have been tried over the last couple of years but it's usually only one side that seems up for it or the Old Bill get wind. It's obvious someone's getting paid and, with the penalties you get today, is it really worth all the hassle just for a bit of a punch-up? We get treated worse than sex offenders.

HOW DID YOU GET GOING WITH A FOOTBALL FIRM, DID IT HAVE A NAME AND HOW WAS THE NAME ESTABLISHED?

I've always been fascinated by the flare-ups at football since an early age and when I first started drinking in the City at 16, I met some of the Forest boys and started drinking with them. I was bang into the clothes from leaving school and all us young ones got into the Casual scene. The older ones were called The Forest Mad Squad in the '70s so we thought we needed a name, too, with most firms around the country adopting one. So a few of us had a meet one Saturday afternoon and, as we used to sit in the lower tier of the Executive stand next to the away section, for reasons you can guess, we came up with the Forest Executive Crew.

WHAT WAS THE WORST INSTANCE OF WEAPONS BEING USED?

Stanley knives were bad – if you can't fight with your fists, then don't bother turning up. The Scousers were bad for it. CS gas became a handy tool when discovered in the '80s and could get you out of some tight situations. I can remember Leeds fans skimming sliced-up cans into the Forest section, around '78. Loads got took out on stretchers. That was a bit of a disgrace, but that was the '70s for you.

That time England played the Poles, we drew 0–0. I've been twice to Poland. We all went to Champions' Bar, about 90-strong, and they weren't all major players. We had 15 Forest, and there were a few Huddersfield. Anyway, the call went up. This German man said, 'Right, we're meeting at the park, it's all been arranged,' and we all went, fuck them, we'll all go together. We stood behind and left two minutes later, about five minutes behind, walking behind. And then we saw England being run towards us. We thought it must be the Old Bill chasing them. It wasn't, it was the Poles. And we got there and we got the back end of England being legged. We said, 'What are you doing? It's the Poles.' They had it off with the Poles in the park. It was all arranged.

We got there when England got to the gateways and we're turning round, 15 of us. They were massive these Poles were, all leather jackets on, and the fucking lot went. Bins, fighting – we turned it round, and legged the Poles back into the park. We didn't realise when England first got legged off the park two or three lads had got stabbed, left in the park, stabbed and cut up. A lad from Sheffield got an axe in his head. A Millwall lad got stabbed in the leg. It was all in the national press. It was proper mental, running battles, I was there, got a bin round the fucking back of me head.

WHAT IS THE MOST IMPORTANT LESSON YOU LEARNED PERSONALLY DURING YOUR TIME WITH YOUR FIRM AND WOULD YOU DO ANYTHING DIFFERENTLY?

You meet some top lads following football and they stick together through thick and thin, and I can trust a hell of a lot of them, more than can be said in other walks of life. I wouldn't change anything. I've had some great times and my life certainly hasn't been boring.

WHO WERE YOUR BIGGEST RIVALS BOTH TEAM AND FAN-WISE?

Derby always have been and always will be, but I also have a dislike for the Mackems (Sunderland).

WHO ARE THE TOP FIVE FIRMS OF ANY IMPORTANCE TODAY?

Man United – huge numbers and still doing it; Middlesbrough – always been handy; Birmingham – best in the Midlands besides ourselves; Chelsea – can still turn it on when required; Cardiff – been going everywhere for the last few years and brought a decent firm to Forest last year.

WHO ARE YOUR TOP FIVE FIRMS OF ALL TIME?

West Ham – best organisers ever and pure evil in their day; Man United – always have had the biggest firm and you'll always get a fight; Chelsea – their firm always seemed to be huge man mountains; Brum – like I said, best in the Midlands; Newcastle or 'Boro, both had good firms but the Geordies were the Chelsea of the north, especially in the '70s.

WHAT IS YOUR FAVOURITE FOOTBALL FASHION-WEAR AND THE WORST YOU'VE SEEN OR WORN?

I did like Burberry the first time around, early '80s, and the diamond Pringle jumpers first off. The Casual scene. The worst has got to be the '70s flares, daft haircuts and scarves round their wrists.

WHAT IS THE WORST KIT YOU'VE SEEN A TEAM IN AND WHAT WOULD BE YOUR OWN CLUB'S BEST EVER STRIP?

All Derby kits with that horrible ram badge. I like the new Forest kit of today with the two stars representing our two European Cup triumphs – back-to-back, I might add.

WHO'S THE PLAYER AND/OR MANAGER THAT WINDS YOU UP THE MOST?

David Platt and David Platt for what he done to Forest. If ever I bump into him …

FANS OFTEN TALK ABOUT THEIR FOOTBALL-GOING DAYS AS JUST BEING A LAUGH. ANY EPISODES YOU REMEMBER?

Paul Scarrett turning up in Glasgow's Barrowlands before a Scotland–England game with a First World War helmet on draped in an England flag ready for battle, the complete nutcase.

DO YOU FOLLOW THE RUGBY AND CRICKET NATIONAL SIDES?

I watched the Rugby World Cup Final in Glasgow and they switched the TV off when we was going to collect the Cup. I might start going to a few cricket aways soon, seeing I'll be a total of nine years without watching the football side when I've finished the ban. Just completing a three-year civil ban and just got another six at the England–Turkey game.

RACISM AND RACE ISSUES HAVE BEEN PART OF FOOTBALL WITH CERTAIN CLUBS AND SETS OF SUPPORTERS AT BOTH CLUB AND INTERNATIONAL LEVEL. WHAT WAS YOUR EXPERIENCE OF THIS?

It was pretty bad at some clubs in the '70s and early '80s, but I think it's near enough gone nowadays. Personally, I've never been into that sort of thing and have a lot of good friends who are of different races.

HOW HAVE FANS FOLLOWING THE NATIONAL TEAM ABROAD BEEN TREATED, AND WHAT ARE YOUR EXPERIENCES FOLLOWING YOUR CLUB OR NATIONAL TEAM ABROAD?

It has been a disgrace the way England fans have been treated over the years in some countries. I've seen it with my own eyes. One example was in Santander around '92 in a friendly. There were only around 300 fans made the trip and I saw women hit with truncheons just because people were trying to lay their St George flags over empty seats. The Spanish police were well out of order and I got a right kicking off them for voicing my opinions. Half the time the foreign police just stand there and let their own fans throw stuff, spit, do what they want, and when we retaliate it's our fault as usual and the media in this country are just as bad. It hasn't been as bad following Forest abroad, but there have been a few problems. I got deported from Bruges, Belgium, and locked up for two days for absolutely nothing in '84.

WOULD YOU SAY THE MEDIA 'OVER-HYPE' THE TROUBLE AND CAN YOU GIVE AN EXAMPLE OF THIS?

They are just as bad hyping everything up. For example, I got in trouble at the England–Turkey game in Sunderland last year and my local paper was saying I beat a Turk up. I only wished I had because I hate them, but I never saw one all day. It just shows what bollocks they are allowed to print and get away with.

SHOULD CELTIC AND RANGERS BE ALLOWED TO JOIN THE ENGLISH PREMIERSHIP OR NATIONWIDE LEAGUES?

I'm a bit of a Rangers fan anyway, so I'd love them to join the English league. I go up now and again and I am very good friends with one of their ex-boys, Davie White, who's a top bloke who used to run with the Rangers ICF. He's been down to watch Forest a few times, too.

DO YOU HAVE ANY VIEW ON BANNING ORDERS? DO YOU KNOW THIS FROM YOUR OWN EXPERIENCE OR THAT OF OTHERS?

Yep. I got my first football ban in '89 and then again in '95, but they didn't have a clue in them days. But their recent ones are not very nice, especially when you get served with a civil one like I did in 2001. I'll be a total of nine years without watching the football side when I've finished the ban, as they gave me another six at the England–Turkey game.

There's also all the hassle of handing in your passport and reporting to your local police station on the day of the game. Hopefully, some rich hooligan will take it to the European Court of Human Rights and get it sorted for everyone sooner rather than later. They just done my mate for it who's only 19 and he's never thrown a punch at football – bang out of order.

HOOLIE MOVIES AND FLICKS – DO THEY GLORIFY VIOLENCE OR CREATE A COPYCAT SYNDROME?

Not really. I did enjoy The Football Factory; it was funny, and the nearest thing yet to the real thing. I think it will become a cult British film like Scum in years to come.

HOW WOULD YOU DESCRIBE YOUR FIRM/SUPPORTERS' FAN BASE, AND HAS YOUR FAN BASE CHANGED OVER TIME?

It's mainly localised around Nottinghamshire with the main lads coming from within the city, but we have a good few come from Mansfield who we drink with, they have a tidy little firm. There's a good mob from the Newark-on-Trent and Grantham areas.

WAS YOUR LIFESTYLE WITH THE FOREST EXECUTIVE CREW SOLELY CONFINED TO THE FOOTBALL CONTEXT OR WOULD IT HAVE BEEN THE SAME FOR YOU IN EVERYDAY STREET LIFE?

No, it's purely the football that's the buzz; nothing else could have gave me that outside of football.

EVERY ONE OF TODAY'S KNOWN HOOLIGAN FIRMS HAS A POLICE INTELLIGENCE OFFICER DEDICATED TO IT. HOW DO THE FIRMS TODAY RESPOND TO THAT? DO YOU HAVE ANY POLICE SPOTTER STORIES?

They always try and talk to you with their tape recorders in their pockets. Some of our lot talk to them now and again. I think we try and use each other sometimes for information. I wouldn't trust them but one or two have been OK over the years as far as Old Bill go.

There was a time at Sunderland's Roker Park; after the game there was only 25 of us. We'd run them around before the game, even numbers, outside the turnstiles. So afterwards, everyone got together but some were parked in cars on the seafront and some the opposite way at the station. So we came out together and turned right towards the centre. There were loads of them waiting and we just steamed in and scattered them until the police got control. Then it was, 'Right, how have you lot got here?' Half were sent back to near the ground and eight of us were sent to the station, but as soon as we got up this alleyway, we were told that the station is that way along a road they called The Gauntlet where all those pubs are, unescorted, but for our two faithful spotters in the distance.

The first pub emptied as soon as we walked past, about 20 of them. It was a bit of a stand-off until our truncheon-wielding finest got in between and told us to carry on walking with them; it was getting a bit nervy. Our Old Bill asked a vanload of Mackem plod for assistance. They looked at their watches and said they were off duty in ten minutes.

Then the next pub emptied, The Wheatsheaf, and our Old Bill said to us lot, 'No one run, stand your ground,' and then, 'Come on then, you bastards,' truncheons drawn. Thank fuck the Mackems bottled it and then the Mackem Old Bill finally got their act together.

Our main spotter, who we used to nickname Gap Tooth for some reason or other, said I owed him a few pints. Later, I heard the lads on the seafront had a torrid time.

IS THERE, IN YOUR OPINION, A NEXT GENERATION OF HOOLIGAN APPRENTICES COMING THROUGH AND WILL THEY BE ANYTHING LIKE THEIR PREDECESSORS?

We have about 50 young lads just recently come through over the last couple of years ageing from 17 to 21. They're game as fuck but I do feel sorry for them. They'll never have what we had with all the Old Bill and banning orders, CCTV and so on today, and I think a lot will pack it in sooner rather than later with all the tough sentences handed out today, just for a bit of fun at the match. We had it every other game. Nowadays, you're lucky to have a couple of days to remember a season.

**NAME: Spencer
CLUB: Oldham Athletic
FIRM: Fine Young
Casuals**

'You're going for
the violence,
and everybody
knows that.'

BACKGROUND AND MEET

When I think of Oldham as a firm of note, I think of them as a late '80s/90s sort of firm, that Football Factory look of baseball caps and Stone Island. I also think of race riots and football mob politics. I don't think of Oldham as one of your major Premier League firms and how can they be when there are some very close bigger attractions nearby, such as your two big Manchester clubs? But you do hear some amazing accounts from lower league clubs with small tight firms that have come across Oldham and know the true story with Oldham's lads, and they'll tell you they've not just had it with them, but they've gone in with some major firms on their day.

If this was going to be the right sort of book I would have to take a look at Oldham and I particularly wanted someone from when I first heard of them as a proper mob, when they were known as the FYC. A couple of England lads told me, 'Spence is your man ... He's Man U, but he's Oldham.' They said he was a top boy when he went and at Man U he's respected enough to be with their firm. It was also firmly stated that he knew a lot of people and got a lot of respect off a lot of people on the England scene. Now this was not third-hand but from a couple of right faces that are top boys themselves.

Mr Lee Spence was someone I had to travel up to Oldham and interview and learn about for myself, which I did, and I came away knowing I'd met a serious player who would happily share some of his experiences of having been there.

His real name is Lee William Spence, born in 1968. He lists his qualifications as three O-levels. His first job was a carpet-fitter, he's single and his first game was Blackpool v Oldham, 1975.

WHAT HAS BEEN THE MOST LEGENDARY FIGHT OR RIOT YOUR TEAM'S SUPPORTERS HAVE BEEN INVOLVED IN?

Leeds United away, FA Cup fourth round tie. This was in the '90s. We were a very active firm, prepared to meet anyone in arranged battles. But thinking Leeds might have been a bit out of our league, we was going to go in through the back door on the train and not let them know we were coming.

We didn't have mobile phones in our firm at this time, but I had a phone call when I was living at me grandma's off a guy called Griff from Leeds, asking me, 'Where do you want it?' So it was like, 'Shit, we're going to have to face up to them now here.'

And so we met; we only had 40 turn out. We met at a Metro station called Mills Hill, then went to a pub called The Old Cock. No one was really interested in going to the match, we were just going for the row. So we decided to turn in late without any police escort at ten past three. So we phoned Griff up – he had a mobile – and we said our train arrives in at ten past three, and we'll go on a Metro train, one of them trains that stops absolutely everywhere, with two carriages.

On the train it was the first time I'd seen cocaine being used by the lads, the first ever game I remember at which all the lads were in the toilets in the train. Maybe it's a confidence thing, I don't know. But it was being used for the first time. So when the train pulled in at Leeds, we pulled off out of the station, we were bouncing about, really, expecting just to run into Leeds. There's no police and there's no one about, it's quiet because the football game's on. So we just walked into the city centre and just gone drinking in various pubs. We started phoning him up. We didn't have one mobile between us. So we're phoning him up off the pub phone.

'We're here,' he said, 'we're in the match.'

'We're not here for football, we're here for fucking violence, get your boys out, we're here, we're in city centre now with no police, they don't even know we're here ...' So we kept phoning him up. We're like, 'Fucking hell, have they got any boys these or what?'

Anyway, we found a pub called The Viaduct. Perfect. Loads and loads of pool tables. So we tooled up, pool balls in socks and all that, loads of pool cues. At about six o'clock, he asked where where we were. And I said, 'We're in The Viaduct,' and he just hung up. So I knew, right, that's it.

I've gone outside and I'm actually having a fucking piss against the wall and to me right the fucking street's filled with Leeds; they've come roaring round, fucking hell, maybe 150 of them at least. So I'm like, fucking hell, I'm pissing myself getting me dick in. As I run in the pub, Leeds are basically outside and they're putting all the windows through, fucking loads of them. And we wanted to come out and we couldn't get out because they were throwing things at us. We're like, 'We want to come out.'

So they all walked back to let us all come out the pub, which was a big mistake for them. We all just ran out the pub tooled up. We're into them, proper into them. So once the front line was getting pulled down and dragged on the floor, you're getting the toes in. And we started running a big pack of them. And they done a right up this road and it's got them bollards where the cars can't drive up and there's that many of them they're running into the bollards, aren't they, they're all falling over, tripping over each other, the rest of us are running the front and just keep running them, splitting them up, and the people who are on the floor, you know what people are like, just jumping all over their heads.

Eventually, we ran them into the police, and so we doubled back and got off then. And we've gone back in the pub, the police come in and got us out, and so we're heading up the back roads towards the station and we're sort of trying to break away again. We're running like this because we can hear Leeds have come down another side street but it's sort of on top at this stage. But we still fronted them up again and we were just laughing at them saying, 'Fucking hell, you're meant to be a big club, you've just been done by 40 fucking lads.'

Our football intelligence officer told us after we put four of them in hospital. You get battered, you don't go hospital; actually going to hospital means they've been well and truly fucked. But Leeds knew we were coming, and you're turning up on a train that's going to arrive at Leeds Station. There's no wannabes, you're going for violence, and everybody knows that. You're not going to watch a game of football. They know you're coming, so if you've turned up for the train, you know you're getting involved in a proper battle.

For Oldham to go Leeds it's a big scalp, isn't it? We played Ireland shortly after in Dublin and, coincidentally, when we got to Manchester Airport, Oldham and Leeds were booked on the same plane. And, obviously, the intelligence has found its way beforehand and the police are waiting. They refused to let us on. The pilot says, 'There's no way you're getting on the same plane together.' It was in the national press all that.

HOW IMPORTANT WAS THE ROLE OF ALCOHOL AND DRUGS? WAS THERE ANY TIME IN YOUR EXPERIENCE EITHER HAD PARTICULAR INFLUENCE?

Well, when I first started going to football, there weren't a drug thing going. And you've got to remember a lot of violence in the '80s was kicking off at twelve o'clock in the afternoon. You go up to a town centre, and it'd be going off, so you weren't pissed or nothing then. So I wouldn't say alcohol is to blame for the violence.

But there's a big cocaine culture now in football violence and I think Oldham are as bad as anybody at the height of it. Not me personally, but I think now at football it's very widespread to say the least, but I don't think it affects the violence; you're going to have it anyway, aren't you?

WHO WAS THE MOST VIOLENT, CRAZY SET OF SUPPORTERS YOU EVER CAME ACROSS?

The Poles. Ask anybody who's been to Poland. I've been three times. They fucking fight each other and they fight you. Hard bastards. In Poland, I remember the police had us quite boxed off, but in the ground the Poles were just kicking fuck out of each other, all the different mobs, all the way through the match. They're fucking mad. This was I think 1992.

But the next time was, I think, in Katowice. It was just going off everywhere, loads of toe-to-toe street fighting. They just probably had a hard upbringing, they're just probably tough lads, aren't they? They haven't had it as bloody easy as the English have, with the Commie rule, hard upbringing, just hard bloody lives. They'll attack you, all over.

When we went to the ground, we come off this tram, there must have been 25–30 of us. There was a forecourt and there was hundreds of them and we just come off the tram and bounced and I thought, 'This is silly.' It went fucking right off, proper boxing, you was fighting for your fucking life. Mad. But, really, the police, they did a good job there, the police. The police like a fight themselves. Wrap them truncheons right round your back, they don't give a fuck.

ARE YOUR FIRM STILL DOING IT?

Well, there's a new young firm coming through now. Apparently, they're all right. They dress the part, but I don't really know a lot of them, I don't know where they come from. It's just one minute they weren't there, the next minute this new firm's come through 12–18 months ago, and I think nearly half of them are banned already, but the older lads will pick a game.

Last season, they took 150 to QPR which I thought was an amazing turnout all the way down there. But 23 were arrested, apparently, by the police at Euston. Oldham was also involved in mass disorder at the England v Wales game in Manchester after a clash with West Brom's Section Five.

HOW WOULD YOU DESCRIBE THE SITUATION WITH THE SCENE TODAY? CAN IT COMPARE WITH WHAT HAPPENED IN THE PAST, AND DO THINGS STILL GO OFF IN THE SAME WAY?

No, not at all now. It's murder now, isn't it, it's murder to get a kick-off. It doesn't matter where you seem to meet, the police will find you these days. I mean, it's obviously informers. It's a rarity now to get a proper row. There'll always be occasions when it kicks off, but I think the best way now to get it is maybe going in the ground and coming out the ground and just steam in the other end, but you're just going to get arrested, aren't you? I know the United–Arsenal FA Cup semi-final went bananas, didn't it, but that was all near the stadium after the game when they both come out.

HOW DID YOU GET GOING WITH A FOOTBALL FIRM, DID IT HAVE A NAME AND HOW WAS THE NAME ESTABLISHED?

It's just a development of growing up. But I remember when I was around 16, there was 15 of us similar-aged lads who just started to follow the older lads and it was when everyone was getting names coming out and our rival firm, Man City, come out with the Young Governors and so we called ourselves the Fine Young Casuals. And I think that was formed in 1985, the FYC.

WHAT WAS THE WORST INSTANCE OF WEAPONS BEING USED?

That would be Tottenham away. We'd been to Tottenham two years on the bounce on the High Road and we'd had it with them. Obviously, Oldham weren't a big name for them so we're not taken seriously. But the next game, the mobile phones were going, a bit of organisation. So we knew we was having it, so the firm we turned up with numbered 25 on the train down from Manchester Piccadilly.

Once there, we plotted up in the Holloway Pub on Holloway Road. One of our boys was a Chelsea kid from Oldham and he brought four faces with him. Tottenham drove up to the pub, they come right up. We went, 'Look, we've got 30 lads here, that's it, you want us, you come and get us. We ain't moving for nobody, we've only got 30.'

Now, even though they looked a bit moody, these four Chelsea faces, all famous faces, one of them pulled a big fucking blade out. He said, 'The yids are having it with this.'

We went out the back, we tooled up, we smashed all the pallets up. We had planks of wood, one for every face. Only 30 of us, but it's the right 30. Eventually, Tottenham came; seven o'clock in the evening. They came to the pub, they put all the windows through, right through, and we went out the back, everyone fully tooled up. They let flares into their firm, fired thunderflashes, CS gas, blades, fucking bats.

The 30 of us come out tooled up. And if they'd looked at us and stood, they might have done us, but they were on their toes, they went three ways, left, right and forward. They panicked for whatever reason. But I think if Tottenham would have looked at us and took stock, they could have done better. But as a kid said from Chelsea, no one's gonna fuck with this, and I thought, 'I'm with you, kid, you are right, we should have got fucked.' But they didn't stand on their own manor. Embarrassing for Tottenham.

WHAT IS THE MOST IMPORTANT LESSON YOU LEARNED PERSONALLY DURING YOUR TIME WITH YOUR FIRM AND WOULD YOU DO ANYTHING DIFFERENTLY?

Two things. First – I wouldn't go on the suicide missions, just for the sake of having a fight when you know you're just going to get fucking murdered, it's pointless really. We went to Sheffield Wednesday with a good 80 lads and we went to this pub after the game and had it for what seemed like a good 30 minutes of toe-to-toe running battles. The next season 20 turned up and, after the game, we just knew we weren't going to win it, but we had to go to the pub and front it anyway. And it was like, 'What the fuck are we doing here?' and we got swamped and it got proper scary. No Old Bill and we fucking escaped by the skin of our teeth. We nearly got butchered.

Second – not to wear bright colours as there is a bigger risk of arrest when they pick you up from the CCTV footages. Stick to dark clothing.

WHO WERE YOUR BIGGEST RIVALS BOTH TEAM AND FAN-WISE?

Originally, when I were still at school, it was Blackburn Rovers, both team and fan-wise, because we stayed in the same league for years with each other. But when Manchester City got relegated, now that was meaty. Oldham fans didn't hate Man

United, they hated Man City. They might not like to admit it because we're too small for them, if you like, but originally we were their game. They hated us, and we hated them, and we still do. And that's the team we hate and fight, Man City.

WHO ARE THE TOP FIVE FIRMS OF ANY IMPORTANCE TODAY?

Today? Man United. I believe Hull City are active at the minute. I'll give it Middlesbrough because they turned up at Manchester three times. I'd say Man United, Middlesbrough, Tottenham – they're the only team to come out of London recently. We'll go for Cardiff because they travel about, don't they?

WHO ARE YOUR TOP FIVE FIRMS OF ALL TIME?

Man United, Hibs, Poland, Portsmouth and Arsenal.

WHAT IS THE WORST GROUND YOU'VE EVER BEEN TO AND WHAT IS YOUR FAVOURITE GROUND?

The worst ground was Rochdale, but I think now it might be done up a bit. They might have put new stands up there, but that was a shit-hole. It made Oldham look fucking good. It was these old grass bankings and it was basically a shed.

Hartlepool was another dump. Five of us ran on to the pitch in a night friendly so the police came and made the five of us stand on an open terrace in the pissing rain.

My favourite is the Maricana, Rio, Brazil; the atmosphere and everything. But I say the best actual stadium I've been in with proper facilities and everything would be the Sydney Olympic Stadium in Australia.

WHAT IS YOUR FAVOURITE FOOTBALL FASHIONWEAR AND THE WORST YOU'VE SEEN OR WORN?

I used to like it in the late '80s on the scene when you wore Classic Nuovo, Liberto, Ciao, Valentino, C17s, them labels. I used to like them. You could get away with them then because everybody wore bright colours. Casual dress. But I must admit our Oldham look at the time was all crew cuts, a big Stone Island coat, dark-blue Armani jeans and white Reebok classics. The whole firm dressed like that and looked the bollocks.

The worst, without a doubt, was me wearing a fucking pink NafNaf sweatshirt. There must have been too much Acid House. I can't believe I were walking about during Italy 1990 wearing that. What the fuck I was doing wearing one of them I'll never know, NafNaf and all.

FANS OFTEN TALK ABOUT THEIR FOOTBALL-GOING DAYS AS JUST BEING A LAUGH. ANY EPISODES YOU REMEMBER?

Well, the best laughs are always on your foreign trips. And the best one we got up to was in Amsterdam before England played Holland. We were strolling round the streets and me mate spots this girl just looking in the window, a shop window, and she's got a leather cap on. So he runs up and pinches her cap and puts it on his head. She's quite friendly and that, and she's an Australian backpacker. So they come into the Grasshopper pub with us. And it's me mate who's got her. And so we're all in there having a drink, and me mate and another mate take her up to the hotel. Half-an-hour later, he comes in the hotel, and says she'll have anybody. So everybody just leaves their drinks and runs out.

We get up there in the room and me mate is there with fuck all on but her leather cap, dictating, 'You can do this, you can do that ...' And everybody ended up with sexual favours of one sort or another. It was mental. But the funny thing was, she stayed with us for two days; she must have been on a budget and wanted free digs.

RACISM AND RACE ISSUES HAVE BEEN PART OF FOOTBALL WITH CERTAIN CLUBS AND SETS OF SUPPORTERS AT BOTH CLUB AND INTERNATIONAL LEVEL. WHAT WAS YOUR EXPERIENCE OF THIS?

Well, when I stopped going, Oldham did get that Combat 18 up here. I'm not into all that stuff, but I think Oldham definitely is as racist as any other club I would have thought. Firm-wise now it is; it never used to be.

We used to have black lads who used to come in with our lads, with our firm. Another incident where we stuck up for somebody was a black West Ham fan in Poland (for the England game) and the racist Villa firm pulled him, and we were in the bar and they're at it, 'Nigger, what are you doing in here, nigger?' Proper grief. And he's on his own with one lad. He was folding, he was turning white to be honest, but no wonder. So we stood up and fucking told them, 'Fucking shut up.' And they said, 'Oh, what the fuck are you lot gonna do about it?' So we picked up the fucking tables and chairs and rammed them in their fucking heads. Six of us. Backed them off to the back of the fucking pub.

There was an incident years ago in the late '80s at Oldham's last game of the season. We always used to hire strippers and comedians for the last home game. But this one time it was a pub on the other side of Glodwich and obviously things never remain peaceful at these dos. Because the police shut the place down, around 200 Oldham boys spilled out on to the streets and had to walk back to the town centre down Waterloo Street which is right through Glodwich and it went off to fuck from top to bottom. They all come out the houses and that was probably worse than the actual race riots. But it was 1988 and a lot of Oldham got nicked and escaped jail by the skin of their teeth, about ten of them. No Asians got nicked.

Did they go to the Burnley riots? I don't know. I think some of them got arrested, didn't they, because it were in the paper. I don't know first-hand. After the race riots, the next week Oldham arranged to meet and go into Glodwich and lads come from all over, they come up from London, Stoke, Huddersfield, Stockport, and it was like a truce on. Because Stoke and Oldham have massive rivalries and other firms had massive rivalries, but they get in touch and direct it over the Internet these days. And so there was a lot of lads out. But the police were on the ball that day – they all got apprehended on the way into Glodwich, Section 60 and all that.

HOW HAVE FANS FOLLOWING THE NATIONAL TEAM ABROAD BEEN TREATED, AND WHAT ARE YOUR EXPERIENCES FOLLOWING YOUR CLUB OR NATIONAL TEAM ABROAD?

Following the national team is totally different. Going to watch an England game abroad, you're treated like scum. You get treated bad whether you've done wrong or you're doing right. An incident with me – I was walking with a firm of hooligans in Rome when these two coppers got hold of me and me mate for no reason and they chased us up the road. They grabbed us two out of the crowd, put us on our hands and knees and started whacking us on the back with truncheons. An unmarked car turned up, they threw us in the car, and it sped off to the station with sirens blaring.

Now the opinion was it was mistaken identity, but what the fuck we were meant to have done I don't know, but it could have been serious. And when we were taken to the station, they took our passports off us and threw us in the cells. Half-an-hour later, they gave us our passports back, laughing, and kicked us out. It makes you wonder if we was set up.

I've followed Man United in Europe and it's just totally like, there's no pressure, you don't get that hassle, you can walk about the towns, you can drink where you want, you're not getting followed everywhere. It's totally different. It's relaxing. I think now they can't afford to have any trouble with the tournaments and the money, the FA, and getting kicked out of things, and I think they put that much money and resources into it, they send that much intelligence over and the police abroad think there's going to be an army coming and that's why they probably overreact with you because of the information being fed from the English authorities.

WOULD YOU SAY THE MEDIA 'OVER-HYPE' THE TROUBLE AND CAN YOU GIVE AN EXAMPLE OF THIS?

I don't think they really over-hype it because it happens. But also I think they miss a lot of it. But I think the major off they miss and they make something that was bad sound a bit worse,

...ally, when they miss probably the worst bit. There's certain incidents when you look at Germany and the Italy riots in Rimini and Düsseldorf and that, there's no over-hyping there because they were turned into war zones, weren't they?

HOOLIE MOVIES AND FLICKS – DO THEY GLORIFY VIOLENCE OR CREATE A COPYCAT SYNDROME?

My personal view is, I don't think the films are too realistic, they miss out on certain points. Originally, for myself, when I was still at school I watched the ICF documentary and that made me want to be a football hooligan, so I think, yeah.

HOW WOULD YOU DESCRIBE YOUR FIRM/SUPPORTERS' FAN BASE, AND HAS YOUR FAN BASE CHANGED OVER TIME?

It's real local, but when the FYC were very active football hooligan-wise, we had lads who came from Scotland, especially Edinburgh, we had kids from Merseyside, London, Shrewsbury. But the reason they came was, they said, it's guaranteed violence, 'We know we're gonna have a row with you lot, because you lot look for it, you find it and you have it.' So they come with us. This would be from '91 to nearly '94/95. I'm talking named players from all round the country. And they said, 'We're not Oldham fans,' but we built up a friendship.

EVERY ONE OF TODAY'S KNOWN HOOLIGAN FIRMS HAS A POLICE INTELLIGENCE OFFICER DEDICATED TO IT. HOW DO THE FIRMS TODAY RESPOND TO THAT? DO YOU HAVE ANY POLICE SPOTTER STORIES?

Our intelligence officer, who I won't name, he saved me once against Derby. Steamed into Derby, I was cuffed up on the floor me face in the ground and alone. And he went, 'I'll take care of this man.' He uncuffed me and said, 'Right, Spence, off you pop.'

Another time, we were playing Bolton away in the FA Cup quarter-final. We took a major firm on the train and nobody had tickets, obviously, so we had some problems. But his advice was, 'Let them in … we know where they are. You get rid of them now, you're fucked.'

But Bolton Police didn't listen to him. So he said he had a cash bet evens on the violence, 'My balls in the bag.'

But the Bolton Police sent us back to Manchester. So we hijacked a double-decker bus and we returned. We sat tight and after the game we come up the main drag. We were in Bolton and the police got on us and they split us up. And our spotter ended up with us. Suddenly, Bolton spilled out in the road into the street. We were toe-to-toe and we battered them. Then heard our spotter say, 'I've got a bet on this, I'm not losing. I knew you'd come back, lads, you wouldn't let me down.'

IS THERE, IN YOUR OPINION, A NEXT GENERATION OF HOOLIGAN APPRENTICES COMING THROUGH AND WILL THEY BE ANYTHING LIKE THEIR PREDECESSORS?

I hope they do, but you just don't know, do you? My opinion is, time will tell. In the last England days before I were banned, the new firm were more interested in wearing designer gear than getting stuck in, proper posers. In Poland, they locked the pub doors and left a few of us outside with 100 Poles. But just recently it seems most clubs have a young hoolie firm of which the new breed appear a lot more ruthless, which could be good for the future. Time will tell.

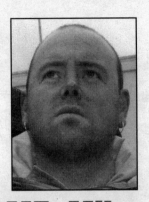

**NAME: Mike
CLUB: Plymouth Argyle
FIRM: The Central
Element**

**'The Element is
a good name for
a rogue sort
of group.'**

BACKGROUND AND MEET

I heard about Mike through a reliable England source and, to be fair, Plymouth have always had their lads on the England scene. It's in their blood as Plymouth is a large port with so much history – Drake, Cook, Raleigh all set sail from its docks, as did the Pilgrim Fathers aboard The Mayflower in 1620 to seek a new world. But bollocks to its well-documented history – you lot want to know about its history as a firm on the football terraces.

From a West Ham viewpoint, I've never really heard a lot, although I've always noticed they've had a big support that travels when you compare their gates with others in the same division. Before the 2004/05 season, they have mainly been in the lower leagues. The first I've really heard about them as players was through Portsmouth 6.57 Crew who basically ruined them to such an extent that the local police force said Pompey's fans were the worst in the land. But that was way back and, in recent years, you kept getting little snippets on the grapevine saying TCE – The Central Element – run-ins and clashes with Cardiff, Bristol, QPR. So, with my club dropping down a league division and Plymouth coming up a division, our teams would meet and it would give me the chance to get down there.

So I called a meet on with Mike to enlighten me about The Central Element boys. It was the weekend after West Ham fans went to Chelsea and played up in the Carling Cup. So policing for this game was massive for what was only West Ham's normal travelling supporters. Helicopters, police motorbike outriders for the coaches, Section 60s for those on the train, plus a Sky news crew following you around – all done with a smile and nice words like, 'Enjoy your time here.'

'Yeah, all right,' as I slipped the escort to join up with Mike, who soon corrected me.

'Cass, that's the norm down here. They've really strangled the scene for the TCE right now.'

Mike was born in 1970; qualifications listed as City & Guilds Carpenter/Shop Fitter. Is sincere and remembers his first game being Plymouth v Blackpool, 1984.

WHAT HAS BEEN THE MOST LEGENDARY FIGHT OR RIOT YOUR TEAM'S SUPPORTERS HAVE BEEN INVOLVED IN?

Basically, we're a smaller club so we don't get involved in the large-scale punch-ups, it's all on a smaller scale. But the best one was Cardiff away in 1996. We travelled up in minivans and cars. Got stopped by the police near the ground, and sent us to this pub which sounded really dodgy.

We get in there, and Cardiff turn up in twos and threes and said, 'Oh, how many have you got?' and they started counting our heads, so they got sort of whacked. Next thing, a massive mob comes down the road, attacks the front door, attacks the back. All the bar staff, the bouncers, they steam into us as well, and we had to fight our way out the pub. Get outside and there's maybe 100-plus Cardiff bouncing down the road now. We sort of stand for a bit, move off, regroup.

About 15 of us stand on this corner and we have a toe-to-toe with them for about five to six minutes. It was a funny scene, really, because there's a woman and a baby come past and the Cardiff lads sort of put a defensive screen around them. The fighting just stops. The scene is just unbelievable. They go past and it just all carries on again, it's like one of those moments in time where you think, 'That's weird.' But fair play to Cardiff, they were good as gold. The lads they were knocking down, they were sitting back up on the wall and saying, 'All right, lads, you'll be all right, ambulance will be here in a minute.' And then they'd carry on to catch the rest of us.

Basically, we're fighting from under this railway bridge, all the way to the ground. We're sort of moving past the coppers and they're standing there thinking, 'What the hell's going on here?' And then you can see the rush of Cardiff lads coming behind us. Get herded into the ground by the police then.

Afterwards, you're thinking, 'Oh no, that's not on, we're gonna go back.' So we started to take two minivans back into the city centre. We get to what was then one of their main pubs, go in, whack a few people about. We get back in the vans, and realised we've left some lads in the city centre. So now we've got a problem; can't leave them, we'll have to send some into the town, go back and find them.

We get back into the town, probably about ten lads go back and look. We were just waiting by the van. Then suddenly the lads are running back towards the vans and we've got another massive mob chasing these lads back to the vans. So we all get in the vans, come out of this car park, but, instead of going left towards Cardiff, we go right into a dead end. We're now confronted with 50–60 Cardiff fans, and there's 20 of us in the vans.

We're thinking, 'Oh Christ.' So we basically drive out and you've got everything coming at the van. You've got bottles, bricks, rocks, everything. All the windows are trashed. People are getting bricks coming through the vans on their heads and we managed to drive straight through them, knock a few over, and then start heading out the city picking up lads on the way who have been stranded.

The police come driving past. What the hell's going on here? We get this escort straight out of Wales with no windows.

That's the most recent one, and everyone remembers that day. We've only gone with 50 and we've taken on a decent mob and got a bit of reward for it.

HOW IMPORTANT WAS THE ROLE OF ALCOHOL AND DRUGS? WAS THERE ANY TIME IN YOUR EXPERIENCE EITHER HAD PARTICULAR INFLUENCE?

Yeah, you do get the occasions in the minivans and the coaches where everyone's like on the coke and whatever. But I tend not to do it myself, I like to keep a clear head at football. I don't even really have a drink because I just think it's another thing that can take it to a further level where you may end up doing something you might regret. Also, it gives the police another sort of leverage. They say, 'You're drunk and disorderly, it's another nicking offence.' Stop you going in the ground, things like that.

WHO WAS THE MOST VIOLENT, CRAZY SET OF SUPPORTERS YOU EVER CAME ACROSS?

Again, because we're a lower league club, you've got to say Cardiff City, really. And they always come to us. We tend to go to them. We've got a good relationship where they've got respect for us, we've got respect for them, and they've always got a good mob.

We've got a main pub called The Britannia which we all used to drink in. They came down with a mob of probably about 50 and they fronted that pub and it's full. But just before they got to it – they'd probably tell this story slightly differently – we had another mob that's left the pub probably about 120-strong to try and encircle them. We thought they were gonna go straight up the road. They didn't. They attacked the pub and they claim they had a result. It's played on our minds because if we'd had the other mob that had got to them, we would have absolutely annihilated them. So, basically, they've played a result against our main boozer. They're pretty good. On that day, we must have had 300 lads out, but they've had a result with that 50, whereas really they shouldn't have.

ARE YOUR FIRM STILL DOING IT?

I think it's like anything now. Our age group ranges from the late 40s right down to about 15. All the 35-plus are not turning out as a firm any more due to the banning orders, convictions, family problems, wife, kids. They tend to take their kids more so they don't really get involved, so it's left to the under-35s downwards to carry it on. And we've got a new, young firm come through who are quite active in themselves, about 40–50-strong, and that's the sort of thing that's keeping us going, really. And a few old heads are sort of joining on the bandwagon as they go. We'll always turn out for a big Cup game, or for our local derbies, but other than that now, the police have nailed it on the head down there.

HOW WOULD YOU DESCRIBE THE SITUATION WITH THE SCENE TODAY? CAN IT COMPARE WITH WHAT HAPPENED IN THE PAST, AND DO THINGS STILL GO OFF IN THE SAME WAY?

It's getting harder all the time. They seem to know your every move down here and it makes it difficult. Every time you take a train to wherever, they're waiting; every time you take a van, they're there waiting. With their intelligence-gathering and the names they know, they just seem to flood the area and you just cannot do anything any more.

Anyone who comes off the train gets escorted straight to the pub and you've got no chance of getting near that escort. The escort on them is so large that you just cannot break through that police line. So, basically, at home it's virtually finished; unless there's a big game, we don't bother going at all now. It's all small skirmishes, really.

Bristol City last season – about 25 of our lads got in a pub. Bristol rang them up and said, 'Where are you ... we'll come to you.' They've attacked the pub, CS gas, bottles, glasses, usual stuff. Our lads have then had to defend this pub against an overwhelming number of lads, which they did quite well. And that's an instance where they've got into a pub quiet, kept out the way, smaller numbers, which is the only way to do it now if you want a proper battle.

HOW DID YOU GET GOING WITH A FOOTBALL FIRM, DID IT HAVE A NAME AND HOW WAS THE NAME ESTABLISHED?

The Central Element was formed in the mid-'80s. It was a group of young lads in their late teens. The old crew used to be called the A38 Crew, after the motorway. That's the old firm. The new lads come along. They virtually merged into one then known as The Central Element. I actually got involved by being whacked by them. I actually live outside Plymouth and I used to dress quite well. I walked through the city one day and they thought I was an away fan, and got assaulted. I just got drinking with them and basically carried on from there. So that's the way it ended up. The 'Central' came from where we used to stand, and away fans had to walk through Central Park, and the 'Element' is a good name for a rogue sort of group, and that's how it was formed.

WHAT WAS THE WORST INSTANCE OF WEAPONS BEING USED?

Basically, down here we don't tend to carry knives or things like that. The worst we've had recently was with Luton's Asians, actually. We went to an away game. We were going for the championship, as were they. We come out the ground and it's their Asian group and we sort of stumbled into their area and they've come at us with axes, hammers, knives, bats, anything else they could get their hands on from their shops and they attacked our group. We were unescorted, having broken away from our escort.

I suppose there were about 50 of us, and about 25 of them. And they just give it us, literally, with weapons. We've had two stabbed, people hit over the head with hammers. Police just completely flooded the area, arrested all our lads, and didn't touch a single one of theirs. This was three seasons ago.

I think, apparently, they attack any away vans that go into their area – the lad who actually did one of the stabbings was one of the biggest drug-dealers in Luton. So the police could never touch him on anything else. And once he did that, they've dawn-raided him and actually arrested him for the offence. Most of our lads weren't arrested for the offence, they were arrested for their own safety, basically. We had something like 25 arrests, I think it was. Luton's paper, The Luton News, said it was the worst trouble since Millwall in 1984.

WHO WERE YOUR BIGGEST RIVALS BOTH TEAM AND FAN-WISE?

Well, Exeter City are our local rivals, so they're our main rivals down this way. Obviously, the nearest big club to us, a middle-sized club, is Bristol City, and Southampton going the other way. But Exeter City's our main rivals.

WHO ARE THE TOP FIVE FIRMS OF ANY IMPORTANCE TODAY?

Personally, for us I've got Millwall, Cardiff, Portsmouth, Stoke and Nottingham Forest, who are still active and doing it at the moment, or the last few years.

WHO ARE YOUR TOP FIVE FIRMS OF ALL TIME?

I've got Chelsea, West Ham, Millwall, Cardiff, Portsmouth.

WHAT IS YOUR FAVOURITE FOOTBALL FASHIONWEAR AND THE WORST YOU'VE SEEN OR WORN?

My favourite is CP Company which is quite subtle, it's not really noticeable and the police don't pick that up. Stone Island is still a big favourite with all the lads, really, that's quite big down this way. Paul and Shark, that sort of stuff.

The worst I've seen lads wearing – I can't stand Tommy Hilfiger.

WHAT IS THE WORST KIT YOU'VE SEEN A TEAM IN AND WHAT WOULD BE YOUR OWN CLUB'S BEST EVER STRIP?

Well, the last few years we had a Scottish manager down here who sort of came from Dundee United and he give us an orange away kit and we always play in green or green-and-white. So when the orange away kit come in, most of the lads weren't very happy about it. Not that we wear replica shirts ourselves, but it didn't seem right for our club.

My favourite – I think the one now's quite nice. The only thing wrong with it is that the shirt sponsors are Ginster's, which is the local pasty company in Cornwall, and it's got 'Made in Cornwall' on it, so everyone assumes that we're a Cornish team, but we're not, we're in Devon, and we're the largest city in Devon.

DOES TODAY'S MODERN FOOTBALL PLAYER HAVE THE RESPECT OF THE FANS?

Certainly in the Premiership. I mean, you've got to respect their skills for what they do, but they're too highly overpaid, really, it's crazy how much money they earn and it's not a working-class game any more, it's becoming middle-class, businessmen are getting in on it. You don't seem to have the loyalty of the players that you used to have years ago to the club, to the fans.

There's too many agents in sport, there's too much money going out the game, which pisses a lot of people off. Down our club, we're quite a home sort of club, a lot of the players are local from this area which is nice and they do seem to have a lot of loyalty for the club. They all work together as a team, play as a team, there's no prima donnas down there, if you know what I mean, it's a good work environment for them all. They all go out drinking, they all go out socialising together.

FANS OFTEN TALK ABOUT THEIR FOOTBALL-GOING DAYS AS JUST BEING A LAUGH. ANY EPISODES YOU REMEMBER?

We get instances – last season we went away to Queen's Park Rangers and it was just one of these days where nothing went right from start to finish. We arrived in London, and a couple of us go and have a look round their pubs. We get collared and, while this is happening, there's a riot going on between our fans and the Met Police. A number of officers get glassed, bottled. Numerous arrests at this pub. So, basically, we're now on a loser from the start from the police point of view. A lot of our lads are arrested. After the game, a group of us get held by the police for about an hour. So we decide we're gonna stay in London for a while, and wait for some of our lads to come out of the nick.

We're waiting for them. We end up in a town called Acton so we're still in West London. We go in the pub, we have a good laugh. We get involved in a massive fight with locals then. So we've now got more lads going to hospital, we've got more lads being arrested. So what turns out as a normal day, we're normally home about nine o'clock at night, we end up getting home about eight o'clock the next morning, which was quite funny. It was just one long day, just a piss-taking day really.

YOUR OPINION ABOUT ALL-SEATER STADIUMS, TICKET PRICES AND THE COMMERCIAL ASPECT OF TODAY'S FOOTBALL INDUSTRY. DO YOU STILL FEEL FOOTBALL BELONGS TO THE FANS?

Basically, our stadium's just been revamped so we've had three new sides. We're lucky that we've still got the old stand with terracing, which I tend to stand on. I grew up on the terraces. I do prefer standing on the terrace to watch football.

Ticket prices are going up now, they've raised our prices every single season. It's within reach of us at the moment. It's only £16 to stand on the terrace which is reasonable for First Division football. They never used to be, but they're getting more considerate to the fans now. The all-seaters do look nice, don't get me wrong, but they just lack the atmosphere; all the singing lads cannot get together and generate an atmosphere any more, they're sporadic around the ground. It does belong to the fans and it doesn't. It is now we've got a new Board of Directors who've come on and they've taken the fans on board and they've taken us to two championships, two in three years, so everyone's happy with that. The club is now playing Coca Cola Championship football and we're holding our own.

RACISM AND RACE ISSUES HAVE BEEN PART OF FOOTBALL WITH CERTAIN CLUBS AND SETS OF SUPPORTERS AT BOTH CLUB AND INTERNATIONAL LEVEL. WHAT WAS YOUR EXPERIENCE OF THIS?

Basically, there are not many ethnics in Plymouth so we've had a few lads come with us at football. We've got a right-wing group who follow England and I would say most of the lads are of a right-wing view, but it's more an English patriotism rather than a racist sort of perspective. Certain individuals are and we don't tend as a majority to go by those principles but there are ones in the group who do have links to these sorts of groups. There's links to the Loyalists, there's links to the BNP, there's links to the National Front, it's various right-wing groups. They don't surface here, it's more following England.

Imagine if Turkey came over, our lads would be looking to

engage in disorder with them on a nationalistic scale rather than racist. Generally, most of the lads are right wing, because we are a white working-class club and I think our tendencies go to the right, not extreme right, but they are English patriots. If there was a large influx of asylum-seekers, which they're starting to bring down this way, people do resent that and it does cause problems. We've had problems in the night-time out on the streets where lads have confronted these lads and the police sort of pick on our lads first and even Marines down here have had problems with the asylum-seekers. There's never been a problem with racism, but the influx of asylum-seekers in the city centre have caused problems.

HOW HAVE FANS FOLLOWING THE NATIONAL TEAM ABROAD BEEN TREATED, AND WHAT ARE YOUR EXPERIENCES FOLLOWING YOUR CLUB OR NATIONAL TEAM ABROAD?

I think England over the years have made a rod for their own back. Years ago, they caused so much trouble abroad that the authorities are on edge wherever they play in the world and they draft in all these extra police resources. They've got the riot police, they've got the horses, the dogs, the water cannons; they're expecting England to play up. So the trouble is, you've got these rival fans from other countries obviously wanting to take England's reputation away, so they're fronting England fans and, of course, England fans being England fans are going to defend themselves and this is where they get themselves into problems. And no one in the government seems to back our fans and say, 'No, this is wrong, your fans are attacking us, do something about them.' They always say, 'No, it's the England fans, we've got a major problem there, we've got to stop them travelling.'

WOULD YOU SAY THE MEDIA 'OVER-HYPE' THE TROUBLE AND CAN YOU GIVE AN EXAMPLE OF THIS?

Yeah, I think they do. On a national scale, if England fans turn up and they're expecting trouble, you get reporters everywhere. There's been instances in the past where they've actually paid some England fans to go and hit some foreigners and actually cause trouble, it's well documented. So, I mean, they do over-hype it and it's good sensationalist headlines for them. At the end of the day, it does sell papers I presume, so it is sensationalist headlines.

The papers don't seem to report on it too much down here. They do try to keep it under wraps; there was a while back they were saying that, if you report it, it seems to antagonise it. So down here, the local press and that seem to put a lid on it. They just use these big sensationalist headlines like '50 banned' due to banning orders or, if there's a big load of arrests, they will sensationalise that and then it is a big front-page headline, or the new security measures that are coming in. But other than that, the minor disorder they tend to keep to the back pages.

DO YOU HAVE ANY VIEW ON BANNING ORDERS? DO YOU KNOW THIS FROM YOUR OWN EXPERIENCE OR THAT OF OTHERS?

Well, this is the new thing that they're bringing down here on a major scale and they do infringe certain civil liberties, really. I mean, you just have to be an associate of someone, speak to someone outside the ground, and we've seen these reports where the lads have been going through these banning orders and the profile they've got on them. I mean, some pages are 100 thick and it's what you've done for the whole day, basically, who you've met, who you've spoken to, what you do, what pub you've been in, what time you leave, and they really are putting so much money and resources into this sort of banning order theme and it is working, it is getting lads off the football, but it's not a fair way to do it.

I mean, no one minds getting banned if you've hit someone outside a ground, or you've actually done something, but these new banning orders just sort of discriminate against people who are probably not into it any more, but just happen to speak to lads outside a ground or meet in the same pub, or use the same transport as the actual firm, and they're getting rounded up and branded as one collective group. In a way, they're not really fair and they're mostly circumstantial, but they are effective if they're used properly. We had the seventh-highest number of arrests in the country last season, so there's been a big crackdown.

HOOLIE MOVIES AND FLICKS – DO THEY GLORIFY VIOLENCE OR CREATE A COPYCAT SYNDROME?

Anyone from my sort of generation, The Firm was always my favourite, everyone likes to think of themselves as a Becksy who was the one to sort of look up to. Football Factory has updated it now to the present day; it has a more modern look to it and it's very good. I mean, it depends on the individual if it encourages them. It's like any film, like a murder film, a psycho film, that sort of thing. If people are that sad that they actually copy what is on telly, that's down to them, but, as far as I'm concerned, it's just a film and it's nice to see something that you've actually been engaged with in the past being put into visual effects.

HOW WOULD YOU DESCRIBE YOUR FIRM/SUPPORTERS' FAN BASE, AND HAS YOUR FAN BASE CHANGED OVER TIME?

The fan-base down here is 99 per cent local to Devon. We've gone from an average of probably 6,000 to 17–18,000. So the crowds will travel and people are enjoying going to watch the football now and there is no trouble any more, the police have seen to that and the crowd measures. It's a friendly sort of club. We've got a large catchment area, it covers the whole of Devon, really, because there's no major club down here, all of Cornwall, even into Somerset and places like that.

EVERY ONE OF TODAY'S KNOWN HOOLIGAN FIRMS HAS A POLICE INTELLIGENCE OFFICER DEDICATED TO IT. HOW DO THE FIRMS TODAY RESPOND TO THAT? DO YOU HAVE ANY POLICE SPOTTER STORIES?

Obviously, we do try and avoid them but you can't because they seem to know exactly what you're doing down here. We used to have two that were very good; one's retired now and he's actually taken over as the Head of Security at Plymouth Argyle, so that's another thing where you've got to watch out, because he obviously knows who you are before you've even got in the ground. The other is an international spotter. He goes with every England game, he's one of 12 spotters nationwide who follow the England scene, so he knows everybody, not just local, but he knows lads we're quite friendly with, Nottingham Forest, Wolves, Cardiff. If you meet up with them at any game, he's clocked you and that's that.

At the end of the day, you've got to remember they're doing their job and they've got a job to do so you've got to watch what you say all the time. Since promotion, there are loads of new ones.

IS THERE, IN YOUR OPINION, A NEXT GENERATION OF HOOLIGAN APPRENTICES COMING THROUGH AND WILL THEY BE ANYTHING LIKE THEIR PREDECESSORS?

Down here, most of our older lads have now packed it in for various reasons, but there are young lads coming through in every firm in the country. We've got a new group coming through down here, about 40–50 strong. They're getting to know the scene, but obviously it's gonna be more difficult for them because, in our day, you had no cameras, you had no police intelligence officers, no spotters. So it's a different ball game now, so they're gonna be picked off by the police and the authorities before they even get a chance to start. They're ranging from 16 up to 22, but I don't think they're gonna last very long. They call themselves The Youth Element and they've got their own website –which I don't personally agree with, these websites – but that's the way they do things now. They will not measure up to the old lads, it's all gone now.

NAME: Eddie Crispin
CLUB: Portsmouth
FIRM: The 6.57 Crew

'It's just an everyday part of life down where we come from.'

BACKGROUND AND MEET

Eddie is here because I didn't have a 6.57 Crew member in *Terrace Legends*. That book was about passionate fans that had made themselves famous as individuals on the football terraces, so it included the likes of actors and eccentric fans that would take that passion to its limits. Portsmouth's most famous fan has got to be John PFC Westwood. Westwood is Westwood – he was never part of the 6.57 Crew. The 6.57 maintained they never had a leader as such, they were a firm. But for this book *Top Boys*, it's more the characters within such firms that interest me.

Today, the 6.57 no longer call themselves that any more. It was all part of the period when the football Casual came along and went out with the rave scene. When the book about the 6.57 Crew came out, Eddie helped with the contributions behind the scenes as he was very much part of that scene back in the day. Now, of course, he is removed from all that, but still goes home and away, and everybody knows him, black book in hand – '... prices include your match ticket, T-shirt, travel and booze'. So would he do the 6.57 Crew chapter for us? 'Not a problem,' he said. 'It's all in the past, but they were interesting days when we all went out as the 6.57 Crew.'

He was born in 1962; qualified with O-levels in History and English. Currently single, working as a self-employed hod carrier, but is also a fitness instructor on evenings and weekends. He has two children and remembers his first game as Portsmouth v Tranmere, third round of the FA Cup, 1970. He adds, 'We lost, of course, so no changes there.'

WHAT HAS BEEN THE MOST LEGENDARY FIGHT OR RIOT YOUR TEAM'S SUPPORTERS HAVE BEEN INVOLVED IN?

There's been a few over the years. QPR always gets written up, but that just came out of nothing, really. QPR away game, everyone went. There was too many Pompey to go in the end so everyone was all round the ground and it sort of kicked off from there.

Coventry was another one a few years ago. Once a season, there seems to be a game that everyone wants to go to. We hadn't played at Coventry for a long time. Got to the station in the morning. Five or six hundred on the train up to Coventry. Came out the station, went into the pub straight outside the station. Drank there for about an hour.

We marched into the town. Got into the boozer and the Old Bill got heavy-handed very quickly, pulling people out. I had my boy with me, he was only about 12 at the time, so we fucked off out of it, got out and went to another couple of pubs. But then the police went in and attacked people in the pub with batons and that. This was about four years ago now, I think. It was quite high-profile at the time, because later the game got held up for 16 minutes in the second half.

At this pub, they then singled about 20 lads out. Told everyone they were getting on buses to be taken to the game, then they stopped 20 from going, put them in a meat wagon and took them to the police station. Didn't actually charge them with anything, just left them in the compound. And I was getting phone calls and they were saying they'd been nicked, and I said, 'You can't be nicked, you've got your phone with you.' And basically they just held them, wouldn't let them go to the game. And then at half-time there was a bit of banter going on between the rival fans, and then some stuff got thrown, and it just went mad for about 15 minutes. I was on the side with the Pompey fans and we were nearer the halfway line and this happened up in the corner, wherever Coventry's end was. I think it started off with a bit of abuse, then some stuff being thrown, and then a few Pompey just got up, jumped over the fence, got into their end, and then everyone went on to the pitch and cleared their end from the corner flag to behind the goal at one point. They all charged into the corner, and their end backed off to the goal from the corner. But then to be fair to Coventry, once the police got there, they did come back and have a go after that and it went on for quite a while.

The second half got held up for 15 minutes because of the fighting in the Coventry end. Pompey had literally jumped over the fence, went into them. About 30 got into their end, I suppose; in the aftermath there was a lot of nickings off the video evidence, but only one person got a jail sentence off it, so it was quite a result all round, really.

And the most recent one, I suppose, would be the Scum (Southampton) game at home last season, although there was nothing against them, you couldn't get near them. But after the game – I mean there's 54 been jailed for that game at the moment, and they're still looking for people now. A lot of them are kids, though. Everyone who was clued up knew what was going on and got out the way. But it started off outside the ground, and we never had police horses at Fratton Park, but they brought Thames Valley mounted police in for that day. They had 400 Old Bill on duty for one game, and they basically kept them in the ground for an hour-and-a-half afterwards while they, as they put it in the paper, 'fought to regain the streets'. And then once they pushed Pompey past Fratton Station, they let the Scummers out the ground.

Then the kids formed a barricade across the street, and then they were running up with wheelbarrows full of bricks, tipping the bricks up, unloading that lot, and then the runners were going back, loading the barrows back up and coming back. It weren't really the old school; a lot of those who were jailed were like 15–16 and stuff. But, basically, the Old Bill just filmed it and they're nicking everyone for it now. Today's hooligan generation – The House of Burberry, as they like to be called.

HOW IMPORTANT WAS THE ROLE OF ALCOHOL AND DRUGS? WAS THERE ANY TIME IN YOUR EXPERIENCE EITHER HAD PARTICULAR INFLUENCE?

There is a bit of drugs at football, but I don't do any drugs myself, through personal choice. I think the drugs scene ruined football violence for a while, when the rave scene took off and everything. A lot of lads who used to go to football used to be up and down and tabbing and stuff like that. Disappear off for weekends and everything. But a few lads have made a decent bit of money out of it.

There's a bit of a drinking culture at Fratton Park. Yeah, there's quite a bit of drinking goes on, but I think it's just an everyday part of life down where we come from. It's the long journeys.

WHO WAS THE MOST VIOLENT, CRAZY SET OF SUPPORTERS YOU EVER CAME ACROSS?

The Polish were pretty mad with England. In the park after the game at Gdansk. Didn't go this year, but it was the second one, I don't know the year. But in the park after the game, I think it was Gdansk, the German who goes with England had arranged it, apparently, but forgot to tell a lot of England that there was going to be 500 mad Poles waiting there with ice picks and scaffold tubes and everything. It was fighting for your life at one point. Two to three hundred England went. Headed off and they came from both sides, pincer movement, if you like. And England went in, obviously stupid thinking, but the mad Poles went toe-to-toe and they were tooled up as well. Couple of Sheffield lads got slashed across the chest and everything. And then you weren't getting any help from the police after.

At home, I think Lincoln were pretty mad when we went there one year in the Fourth Division days, early '80s. Their main shopping centre, you could still drive through the town and we were there, about 17–18 years old in our minibus, thinking we were the bee's bollocks driving through their town giving everyone the wanker sign. Suddenly, the lights turned red and there were two pubfuls of them that came out. 'Quick, get out, they're gonna smash the van up.' And, yeah, that was quite an interesting one. We were outside the van having it with them, and then there was another Pompey geezer, who must have drove up behind us, he was trying to run them over at the same time. And then the lights changed, and we're trying to get back in the van as the lights were changing. Yeah, that was quite a good one at Lincoln.

ARE YOUR FIRM STILL DOING IT?

Well, I wouldn't say it was an active firm now. You still get a few lads going away. If it went off, Pompey would always be up for it, but there's no organised travel or anything now. I think the main heyday was the early '80s, through to about '86, then a few of them got in the rave scene and then a few stopped going. A few lads got quite heavy prison sentences. And then everyone just sort of grew up, didn't they? And you can't get away with it now with the cameras and the surveillance and everything. Coventry was just a mad day. I think it might have had something to do with some of the Colombian marching powder some of them were having.

HOW WOULD YOU DESCRIBE THE SITUATION WITH THE SCENE TODAY? CAN IT COMPARE WITH WHAT HAPPENED IN THE PAST, AND DO THINGS STILL GO OFF IN THE SAME WAY?

No, I wouldn't say it would ever kick off like it used to. You'll never get it where you've got 200-a-side battles going on. A lot of people get on quite well together now, don't they, different teams and that, which I think does the Old Bill's head in, really. You go to an away game and suddenly you walk in the other team's pub and you all have a drink with their boys and that. Spotters can't make it out. There'd be an occasional match where it might kick off, always at a Pompey–Scum game it will kick off, but it's always Pompey taking it to them and I think last season they've really clamped down. I mean, a lot of the kids who got jailed have never even been arrested for anything in their life and they're getting six-month sentences and six-year football bans. So that's going to have a deterrent effect on people, I think.

HOW DID YOU GET GOING WITH A FOOTBALL FIRM, DID IT HAVE A NAME AND HOW WAS THE NAME ESTABLISHED?

When we were young, everybody used to go to football. Portsmouth is like a village, really. So you'd have all your different little areas going. We'd have a couple of minibuses from

Eastney, Stamshaw, get the Cosham Commandos and all the different areas, and everyone would go and then, as we got a bit older, everyone started going on the train. And there was an article in The Face magazine, one of the lads he wrote a letter, a bit tongue-in-cheek, and signed it 'Portsmouth 6.57 Crew', because of the train we used to get to get to London in the morning, and it just stuck from there. First train out of Portsmouth to get you to London for half-eight, and then carry on to wherever we were going. So we took the name off the time of the train.

There wasn't a sort of a meeting and everyone said, 'Right, what we gonna name ourselves?' or anything. And that became recognisable. That would have been around '82/83, something like that.

WHAT WAS THE WORST INSTANCE OF WEAPONS BEING USED?

I don't really agree with weapons being used, but a bad one I saw was Millwall away last time we played them at the Den, and we were drinking in a pub past New Cross. Bit further down from New Cross, there was a pub on the corner, it was called the White Hart, and a few Millwall went by and sussed out Pompey were in there. And then when it kicked off, they came up. There was a big roar, everyone piled out the pub. They come up and they had a geezer at the front with a sledgehammer and a couple with scaffold poles, sort of leading them in, and went toe-to-toe. There was an island in the middle of the road, it went toe-to-toe on there at one point.

I remember the geezer coming up the road banging the sledgehammer on the road as he came along. That was a bit spooky.

WHO WERE YOUR BIGGEST RIVALS BOTH TEAM AND FAN-WISE?

Team-wise, obviously the Scummers, but fan-wise it would be Millwall who are our biggest rivals, because we don't really rate Scum at all. We've had a lot of history with Millwall, especially during the '80s when it was major. We used to play them every season. Always used to go there, they'd always turn up at ours, always go off. And I think there's quite a bit of mutual respect between Pompey and Millwall.

Scummers – we don't rate them as a firm or anything. They're our biggest rivals because they're the nearest club, but we didn't play them a lot really. There's a hatred there, proper hatred. I think it's more on our part than theirs. They go along with it a little bit, when push comes to shove. It stems from the dock strike, whenever it was in the 1800s or something, and they came in and broke the strike in Portsmouth and brought them in from Scumland when everyone else was sticking together. So you can never trust a Scummer.

WHO ARE THE TOP FIVE FIRMS OF ANY IMPORTANCE TODAY?

You don't see many major firms any more, do you? Obviously, you've still got West Ham, Millwall, Birmingham were good for a time. You get different ones, it goes in circles now. Tottenham have been pretty active recently. Middlesbrough were active for a little while. There are teams that will turn out for certain games, but a lot of the lads don't bother. You've got Tottenham, Middlesbrough, West Ham, Millwall, Birmingham.

WHO ARE YOUR TOP FIVE FIRMS OF ALL TIME?

West Ham, Millwall, Birmingham – the only team who really come down to Pompey and took the piss, I would say. Bristol City we always used to have a row with, always, home and away. And that little surprise team again, Lincoln. For the numbers they had and everything, they were superb.

WHAT IS YOUR FAVOURITE FOOTBALL FASHIONWEAR AND THE WORST YOU'VE SEEN OR WORN?

I used to like Adidas Stan Smiths, trainers; Stone Island jeans; nice Armani top or Lacoste.

The worst was when people used to wear those patchwork leather and suede jackets with the criss-cross on the top like the old yellow-and-green Man U shirt and they used to wear them with leg warmers. And do you remember the hair when it was shorter on top and long at the back, like a Brian Robson style? We used to call it a Robson at Pompey and no one in Portsmouth has a 'tash ever, that's a Scummer's thing, or, as we call them, 'wielders'.

WHO'S THE PLAYER AND/OR MANAGER THAT WINDS YOU UP THE MOST?

There's two players that I detest. First, obviously, Matt Le Tissier, the most unambitious person ever to walk the planet. Just stayed there for his life, didn't he, nice and cushy for him, just showed no ambition, and he was a horrible, filthy Scummer. And the other player that I cannot stand and makes watching England horrible when he's playing is Wayne Bridge. We played at Chelsea last year and he was defending in front of the Pompey fans first half, and he was absolutely terrified when he was playing left-back in front of us. Second half, he fucking went and scored, didn't he, two minutes into the second half and went running along in front of the Pompey fans giving it plenty. So he doesn't get my vote.

And manager – I can't stand Alex Ferguson, he's a vile man. Even worse in my eyes is Harry Redknapp, lower than a snake's belly. A guy we all had enormous respect for at Pompey, who we thought was switched on and one of the old school and knew a thing or two about loyalty and passion. He could have gone anywhere else, taken the Scotland job, Argentina job, anything, anywhere except for those vile Scum cunts down the road. In the process he's destroyed his rapport and reputation with the Pompey fans in one act. On the bright side – they say every cloud has a silver lining – Bond went with him!

WORST FOREIGN PLAYER YOU'VE SEEN AND THE BEST FOREIGN IMPORT? YOUR FAVOURITE CLUB PLAYER AND YOUR FAVOURITE OTHER PLAYER?

Worst foreign import I've ever seen is Matt Le Tissier who comes from Guernsey, so we call him a foreigner.

Best player I've actually seen myself as an import is Robert Proseneki at Fratton Park, a Croatian player. What he could do with a football was outstanding, but he was the laziest player going. Used to smoke; if he didn't want to play, he wouldn't play, he was one of those. But when he was on song, he was unplayable. This was about 2000. Mandaric brought him over, he only played one season for us, but he could just win a game on his own.

My favourite player for me in my time of watching Portsmouth has been Kit Symonds. He's now Assistant Manager at Crystal Palace, but when Pompey nearly folded a few years ago and they set up a fund, they had a meeting in the Guildhall and Kit came down – he was playing for Man City or Palace at the time. He came down on a Sunday morning, drove himself down, and he pledged £1,000 of his own money to set the fund up and everything. Whenever he's come to Fratton Park with another team, he's always got a big cheer and that. He didn't want to leave the club when he went to Man City, and I think he's a good example of a loyal player and a loyal person.

Dave Waterman at Pompey – never the greatest player at the club, but someone you'd want with you in the trenches. When he pulled on the shirt, you could see his heart. My favourite player of all time would be Bobby Moore, because he's the only Englishman ever to lift the World Cup. I think he was a good example to everybody and he was loyal to West Ham 'til towards the end of his career. Obviously, when he wasn't good enough to get in, then he dropped down to Fulham.

FANS OFTEN TALK ABOUT THEIR FOOTBALL-GOING DAYS AS JUST BEING A LAUGH. ANY EPISODES YOU REMEMBER?

We had a couple of little famous ones, well, old glory type ones. We had the pushbikes to Cambridge one, when everybody, about 40 of us, turned up at the station all with pushbikes on the train and we went to Cambridge and then we went riding off round Cambridge. I remember West Ham were going to Norwich that day, and Taffy Aldridge was lying on the station bench in the morning when we were at Liverpool Street. He just went, 'This will never fucking catch on Pompey,' but it was just done as a piss-take for the day.

I remember when we got to Cambridge, we all got to this

boozer and chucked our bikes in a heap outside. And I remember we came out and there were American and Japanese tourists standing there with their video cameras which were quite rare in those days. And I went up to them saying, 'Yeah, we're students at the university, this is our modern art project,' and they went, 'Oh great,' and they all got their cameras out and started filming it. Load of pushbikes just chucked in a pile.

And also there was the wedding suits to Cardiff, which was quite a good one. Went to Cardiff, everyone wore Farrahs, blazers, shirt and tie. We heard Old Bill were going to be at the station, so we had some invites printed up inviting us to a wedding in Cardiff and let everyone else get off the train and then pretended that we were going to a wedding. But I think we got sussed after about two seconds.

YOUR OPINION ABOUT ALL-SEATER STADIUMS, TICKET PRICES AND THE COMMERCIAL ASPECT OF TODAY'S FOOTBALL INDUSTRY. DO YOU STILL FEEL FOOTBALL BELONGS TO THE FANS?

No. I went to Bristol City yesterday, and that was like going back in time. You pay on the day, all the lads could sit together. Now it's all season tickets. You sit basically where you're told. You can't get in with your mates any more and have the crack. Premier leagues are all heading for corporate as much as possible, except at Pompey where we try and keep it a bit real, let the away fans get wet in the Milton End.

Some of the new grounds are nice. I like Sunderland's new ground. I think that's the best of all the new stadiums I've been to. I don't really like all-seater stadiums, I think you should have a choice, there should be terrace areas as well. Personally, I like to sit down, but some people like to stand up and sing and that, and I think they should have a chance to do that if they want.

Ticket prices are a rip-off and too many shit players are getting paid too much money. I mean, players in the reserves are getting ten grand a week and they're not going to get a game, they're just there to be in the squad. A day out at Newcastle would be £75 on the train, or £100 if you want to fly, then you got your grub, your ticket which is £40. You're looking at doing

£200 by the time you've had a drink, caught the train and had food and got a programme and got hassled by the police and everything like that. The score at Newcastle last year? We lost 3–0. £200 to be three-quarters-of-a-mile from the pitch, up in the clouds, in the away section at Newcastle and we ended up staying in the bar for the second half because it was better watching it on the telly, you were that far from the pitch. It's just back and high.

RACISM AND RACE ISSUES HAVE BEEN PART OF FOOTBALL WITH CERTAIN CLUBS AND SETS OF SUPPORTERS AT BOTH CLUB AND INTERNATIONAL LEVEL. WHAT WAS YOUR EXPERIENCE OF THIS?

Compared to other clubs, Portsmouth is basically nearly all white supporters. There's a couple of coloured lads who go with us, one who used to go all the time, but he's got a couple of kids and that now. It's just the city, there's not many coloured people in the city.

I don't think anyone's really that racist at Portsmouth. Sometimes there's a few comments aimed at players, but I think you get that anywhere. There's no history, we never had the bulldog paper being sold at the ground or anything like that, nothing like that, no. There was never anything down our way really with the Far Right. I think it's a matter of personal choice for a lot of people, isn't it? I remember when the Wallaces – three brothers that happen to be black – played the Scummers at Fratton Park, there were lots of bananas chucked on the pitch at them. But there was a pig's head thrown on at one of their non-black players as well.

HOW HAVE FANS FOLLOWING THE NATIONAL TEAM ABROAD BEEN TREATED, AND WHAT ARE YOUR EXPERIENCES FOLLOWING YOUR CLUB OR NATIONAL TEAM ABROAD?

We've never been abroad with Pompey. I go away with England quite a bit and I think the treatment of England fans is abysmal when you're away. From the moment you leave your house, you get to the airport, you get questioned, you get stopped, you get searched, you get photographed. You're just not treated like a normal human being, and all you want to do is go and watch the football. You get shepherded about. I don't think it's justified. It's a good jolly-up for the spotters, a good day out for the spotters and everything. I mean, in the last five years going away with England, I wouldn't say I've seen anything happen at all. I know there was that little bit of stuff in Charleloi in 2000, but that could have happened anywhere. And what they reported on in Portugal this summer, they was on holiday, they was nowhere near any of the football and that, and that's what's probably happening in Ibiza every single night of the summer. But because the football was in Portugal, they report it.

WOULD YOU SAY THE MEDIA 'OVER-HYPE' THE TROUBLE AND CAN YOU GIVE AN EXAMPLE OF THIS?

The trouble at the recent Scummers game, our local paper here in Portsmouth has gone so over the top about it, it's unbelievable. Every week they bring the story up. They just pad a story out, but print the same stuff every week. And a ten-year-old boy was involved, the youngest hooligan ever to be convicted in this country. And a 15-year-old girl, and all these children. And they had some policemen in there this week saying, 'We will hunt you down and wreck your lives.' They don't treat paedophiles like that, do they? But the local paper just keeps bringing it up all the time.

I mean, some of these kids who got six months, they're out now, and they've printed all their pictures in the paper this week. They shouldn't be allowed to do it. I actually phoned the paper up and made a complaint about it, but their reporter wasn't very receptive, really.

SHOULD CELTIC AND RANGERS BE ALLOWED TO JOIN THE ENGLISH PREMIERSHIP OR NATIONWIDE LEAGUES?

No. They're Scottish, aren't they; they should stay in Scotland. If Hearts finish above Rangers, should they be allowed to join the English league? We had Celtic in a friendly last year and there was a lot of red hand flags and all that sort of sectarian stuff going on.

DO YOU HAVE ANY VIEW ON BANNING ORDERS? DO YOU KNOW THIS FROM YOUR OWN EXPERIENCE OR THAT OF OTHERS?

I think a banning order is an easy target; they don't actually have to prove anything as far as I can make out. Just the fact that you go to football is enough for them to say, 'Well, he might cause trouble.'

A friend of mine who wouldn't want to be named, we went to Portugal for the friendly in Faro in February. Now bear in mind that Portsmouth Police would have known that we were travelling anyway, so they let us leave at four in the morning, drive to Luton to get there at six o'clock for an eight o'clock flight. Next thing, I walked into the airport, and some of the lads who'd gone on said, 'Your mate's had a tug.'

I said, 'What do you mean?'

Next thing, I'm up against the wall with my mate and we're getting searched and questioned and everything, but they wouldn't let him travel. They brought him back home and tried to get him a three-year football ban, but he fought it by paying for his own lawyer and it was thrown out of court in the end.

Despite that, he goes everywhere with England. He couldn't go to Euro 2004 this year because the court case was still going on. And all the time the court case was going on, they wouldn't let him travel. But there's no apology for it. He can't get any compensation. He's actually turned it over. It cost a lot of money; we had a fund-raising evening for him. Because he won it, he didn't get hammered with court costs or anything, but it was the time off work, the travelling, no legal aid.

HOOLIE MOVIES AND FLICKS – DO THEY GLORIFY VIOLENCE OR CREATE A COPYCAT SYNDROME?

I don't think they glorify violence. I think the Football Factory was a good film, dealt with it quite well. I don't think there's any copycat stuff. The only thing to come out of that was the new catchphrase – 'jog on', wasn't it? I think as long as they're done quite well, which I thought that one was, apart from some of the fight scenes at the end, but then they've got to do that, I suppose, have the two rival mobs baying at each other.

HOW WOULD YOU DESCRIBE YOUR FIRM/SUPPORTERS' FAN BASE, AND HAS YOUR FAN BASE CHANGED OVER TIME?

It's very local, the Portsmouth fan base, and very loyal. Portsmouth's quite small, it's an island. We're 25 miles away from Scum, which is the nearest other team to us, so there is a little bit of a catchment area, but Portsea Island is actually an island and everyone's quite proud of that and loyal. I mean, you go to the park, I think Harry Rednapp said it, you go to the local park, you don't see people going about in Man United and Arsenal shirts and that, everybody's got a Pompey shirt on. So it's very local.

I know Pompey fans who come down from London for every game, and they're Pompey fans because they were born in Portsmouth and moved out or their parents were Pompey fans and things like that. We've got a good little mob who come from Salisbury, even though it would be nearer for them to go to Scum, but they come along, they're all good lads.

WAS YOUR LIFESTYLE WITH THE 6.57 CREW SOLELY CONFINED TO THE FOOTBALL CONTEXT OR WOULD IT HAVE BEEN THE SAME FOR YOU IN EVERYDAY STREET LIFE?

If I didn't go to football, I wouldn't have any dealings with the police at all. I wouldn't be known to the police if it weren't for football. But at the moment, they've got more film of me than Martin Scorsese's got of Robert De Niro, I'd say. You go to have a drink with your mates on a Saturday and you've got a camera shoved in your face. And now they've got a couple who ride round on mountain bikes with cameras in their helmets following everyone round, which is a bit of infringement of civil liberties, I like to tell them.

EVERY ONE OF TODAY'S KNOWN HOOLIGAN FIRMS HAS A POLICE INTELLIGENCE OFFICER DEDICATED TO IT. HOW DO THE FIRMS TODAY RESPOND TO THAT? DO YOU HAVE ANY POLICE SPOTTER STORIES?

The two police spotters at Pompey have got a lot of front after what they done at the Scum game. One of them – he's from a Portsmouth family, he's got two brothers, they all used to go to football. And I've seen him do things when we were kids at games, and he's banging people's kids up now for the same things that he used to do as a kid. They come up and they try to talk to you at away games and that. They're there all the time. But I just say hello and then move on.

IS THERE, IN YOUR OPINION, A NEXT GENERATION OF HOOLIGAN APPRENTICES COMING THROUGH AND WILL THEY BE ANYTHING LIKE THEIR PREDECESSORS?

They just can't do anything nowadays. There was a little firm got together, about two years ago, they were quite good, up and coming. But a lot of them have been jailed for that Scum game. They'd have been a little firm called the House of Burberry and they'd have been about 14–16 years old at the time. A lot of kids from the Eastney area and round that way, they had quite a good little firm. But about six of them got jailed for that game. All the others know they can't get away with it now with the cameras and everything.

There's another little firm, the FUG from Fareham – Fareham Urban Guerrillas, as they like to call themselves – they're quite an amusing little firm. But that's about it really, I think.

**NAME: Gregor
CLUB: Queen's Park
Rangers
FIRM: QPR**

'It'll never be
like it was in
the seventies,
never, never.'

BACKGROUND AND MEET

Gregor was always an interesting call. He's a known character so he had been mentioned to me before but, being a West Ham lad, I was never exactly sure where his loyalties lay. If I can be honest, Mark Gregory was very well connected around London. The only club he wasn't linked to was mine, and I guess the other would be the Gooners. But if you think of QPR's firm, you think of Gregor. He's been on the scene for years and wound up plenty enough rivals in the process. When you get the rival mobs personally name-calling you, then you can take it as read you are a boy and someone that is known.

Funny little firm, QPR, who for one of London's small clubs are well supported, with an ever-growing fan base and very much the new fan and the neutral's choice of club. Within that framework, there is a hardcore hoolie element who have been mixing it for years, comfortably holding their own against some of the rated firms of their time – rows with Man U, Tottenham, Arsenal, Stoke, Leicester, Villa, and even in the book Scally, Everton said QPR. If there is such a thing as a hoolie league, the more publicised antics of the London clubs with bigger mobs, QPR can get overlooked, but from the '80s to the present day, there is a small, tidy and quite violent underbelly over QPR who operate different ends of town.

The guys I originally contacted said, 'Cass, we can't. Everyone is too active around here. If you go down the Bush, you should try Gregor, we think he's on a ban.'

His real name is Mark Gregory, born in 1960. Unemployed, single, and his first game was QPR v Burnley.

WHAT HAS BEEN THE MOST LEGENDARY FIGHT OR RIOT YOUR TEAM'S SUPPORTERS HAVE BEEN INVOLVED IN?

We had a home game with Nottingham. And give them their due, they went into the park, about 150–200. We went into the park after them, shut the gate and they had one mounted policeman who was running into us and Forest were steaming into us and we run back into them behind the Old Bill. It was proper toe-to-toe in the park and the Old Bill was not around in any number; it went for about another three to four minutes in the park. And I'm sure, if any Forest read this, they will understand what I'm saying, it was a good day out for QPR, a good day out for Forest. This was about 1986/87. The numbers were about 200 each.

One Saturday afternoon, we were playing Middlesbrough, about 40 of our top boys, the Naughty Forty at the time, they met in a pub called The Shepherd and Flock. So I've gone up to the green to be nosy to see where 'Boro are, suddenly I've seen on the other side of the green up to about 250 tops, they're all crossing the green. I've run across the green and – I know 'Boro will laugh at this story now and they will know that I'm telling the truth when they read this – I run across the road and I went, 'Oy, you lot, you're going the wrong way.' They'd come back across the green. I've run into The Shepherd and Flock and I've said, 'All right, boys, they're here.'

'How many of them?'

'Blinding … 80 of them, 50 of us, no Old Bill, it'd be good.'

As we've run up the road, they've come round the corner, we've clashed, we've hit them toe-to-toe, back-pedalled them twice. Suddenly, a fella's turned round and said, 'There's only 40 Cockneys … come on, let's weigh into them, let's run 'em, we're 'Boro.'

The next minute, they've chased us for ever, the Old Bill trying to make a stand. One of my friends gassed people, and he gassed all of us. And a chap was running along the side of the road; I was on one side of the road barrier, and he was on the other, and he was chasing me, and he was holding his badge and he went to me, 'I see you, Gregor, you bastard, when I catch you I'm going to make you fucking kiss this badge, you're gonna know you met 'Boro today.'

I hope you appreciate the story, 'Boro. Enough respect.

WHO WAS THE MOST VIOLENT, CRAZY SET OF SUPPORTERS YOU EVER CAME ACROSS?

The craziest that I've ever come across would be Chelsea, West Ham, Cardiff, Millwall. West Ham because I thought they were very organised at the time, back in the '70s and early '80s. Chelsea were the mad lot, and Millwall were very bad, and so were Cardiff. I remember one of the worst ones I ever went to was when West Ham beat Millwall at the Den and it was the closing of the Den and it was the most violent football violence I've ever seen in 25–30 years of going to football; even the Old Bill couldn't control it and the Old Bill got weighed in as well to try and stop both sides hitting each other.

I took a couple of young QPR just to show them, this is the big boys' football, and they couldn't believe what was happening on the day. This was before the game.

West Ham had come along with about 500 but Millwall seemed to turn out with about 1,000. They blocked them off in one road. I remember it clearly because it was outside the school by the away end and West Ham come down one of the side roads, the Bushwhackers come one way and the main older firm of Millwall came the other way and West Ham were stuck in the middle. And I can remember a geezer walking up to Tiny and going, 'You black cunt,' and he turned round and goes, 'It looks like I've got to come out of retirement,' and he started weighing into people. That was one of the last games at the old Den.

ARE YOUR FIRM STILL DOING IT?

We surprise a lot of people at the end of the day and, yeah, they're still going strong and got a good up-and-coming youth firm at the moment, which I think this is the new thing about football at the moment, all the youth firms turning out all over the country right now, so it's getting back a bit like the old days. It'll never be the same because the Old Bill got it sorted out nowadays.

QPR can pull a mob when they want to on the day. Cardiff turned up and we was on our way to the boozer, I believe they was in Ealing at the time. This was a couple of seasons ago. QPR had a phenomenal firm, all the old chaps turned out on the day, and we had a pukka firm, and QPR had it with the Old Bill and it just got a bit mad and we didn't really actually get to meet Cardiff's firm on the day. Pity, as they would have had their work cut out.

HOW WOULD YOU DESCRIBE THE SITUATION WITH THE SCENE TODAY? CAN IT COMPARE WITH WHAT HAPPENED IN THE PAST, AND DO THINGS STILL GO OFF IN THE SAME WAY?

There is today, but sometimes you've got to be fortunate, you've got to be lucky. You might bump into a firm coming round the corner, but more or less the Old Bill have got it all sorted out. But it's nothing like the old days, you'll never compare the old days. We had little rows with Luton because they used to be one of our arch enemies, Men in Gear. I'm not very popular with Luton's firm. We didn't turn up to a pub and give them their due, give them their respect; they did turn up there and we sent a few of our young lot up there and they got back-pedalled. We said, 'Don't turn up without your main boys there,' and we couldn't believe they came to the pub and they come down the road and weighed into QPR, but we didn't have the numbers at the time. But that's not an excuse, we should be there on the day and whatever happens happens.

They got off at least 2?–3 miles away from the ground, told us they were there, and half the people couldn't believe it so a few of them went up there as scouts and realised they were there and it was too late. By the time the chaps have come, they'd already done their work and gained a result.

HOW DID YOU GET GOING WITH A FOOTBALL FIRM, DID IT HAVE A NAME AND HOW WAS THE NAME ESTABLISHED?

Well, I got involved with football because I come from an area called Notting Hill and Ladbroke Grove. It's notorious for gang-related violence and we always stuck together as a family up there and no one runs from each other. We were all going in the Loft end at the time and I watched a game against QPR with Burnley when we needed a point or two to stay up and to win the championship. It was a great day out. I remember it clearly.

It was packed and the next minute I just see the Burnley end empty out for about ten minutes to go and come running round to try and come into the Loft, and everybody goes, 'Here they come, here they come.'

Everybody ran down the stairs. I was going, 'What's happening?'

'Burnley's coming to take our end,' and we went out there and it was just toe-to-toe in the street. This must have been about 1974/75.

With me being a QPR boy for so many years, I know we've had firms like the C-Mob, they used to go everywhere on a coach in the '80s, they went everywhere and they always stuck tight. Then you had the Naughty Forty, then you had the Ladbroke Grove lot, the Notting Hill, and you also had Northolt. But on the day, it was mainly the C-Mob that always went out together.

At one time, I started a thing where we used to call ourselves Ellesley-enders. I used to get the mob and we'd go in the end and pay in the away end and go in the top and then give a roar and a big gap would open up and the Loft would sing, 'Ellesley-enders, Ellesley-enders, do your job.' And we'd have a big toe-to-toe in the end; you could see us running down the terraces, but we done it regular every week. A couple of times it come on top, and a couple of times we done really well by running the terraces across.

WHAT WAS THE WORST INSTANCE OF WEAPONS BEING USED?

The worst instance, we had a really bad run-in with Arsenal. It started back in the day when everyone used to go to the Lyceum with DJ Steve Walsh, and now he's dead, God rest his soul. It was a thing about where the DJ used to go, 'Is there anyone from West London?' And you'd hear a little roar, and it would be East

London, North London, and then we got to where we started having it with North London and it ended up from there. We had a bad rivalry between each other for so many years.

It started at Friday nights at the Lyceum; Pimlico was having a row with North London, we went over to back them up saying we're Ladbroke Grove, we'll have it with you, we'll back you up, Pimlico, and Pimlico half-bolted on us. I've got stabbed in the chest by one of Arsenal's lot and, at the time, no names mentioned, but they've now become well-known, well-established faces at Arsenal. When they read this they'll laugh and say, 'Yeah, he was right, they was the good old days at the Lyceum ...'

At one time, we had about 400 waiting for them to get off and it was like we was all going to the Falklands, we had everything you could think of and they didn't come that way. But give them their due, they did get off after the game about 300–400 and it went through the market and there must have been about 700 people just having it in the market stalls. Everything was going west everywhere and, in the end, it come on top. Arsenal had quite a few black fellas with them which are known faces and I respect them because, every time we bump into them, they've never really backed off, they've stood toe-to-toe with us. So that's why I wasn't really liked at Arsenal because of the Lyceum days and it just went on from there, really.

WHAT IS THE MOST IMPORTANT LESSON YOU LEARNED PERSONALLY DURING YOUR TIME WITH YOUR FIRM AND WOULD YOU DO ANYTHING DIFFERENTLY?

I ain't got nothing really out of it. As I say, I must have 25 previous for football violence going back to the early '70s, but the one mistake that I made was one time when we were messing about and Old Bill walked up and he goes, 'You're nicked for threatening behaviour.'

I went, 'Behave yourself, I ain't done nothing.'

'Well,' he says, 'just go to court, plead guilty and it'll be a slap on the wrist.'

So I went to court, pleaded guilty, and the judge said, 'What did he do?'

So the copper says, 'Well, your honour, this man attacked people with a broom handle and a dustbin lid on the High Road with a mob of supporters.'

And I couldn't say nothing now, because I've already gone guilty. But I shouted, 'Your honour, that's a lie,' and he gives me six months' imprisonment.

I never got to see my kid until she was six months old, because I was sent to prison and she was born four days later. And that was the one regret, I never got to see my baby. It was a hard lesson. Her mother has never forgiven me for not being there.

Something I would like to say – a big sorry to her personally. Sorry. I'll never forget, it was 20 April 1980 and my daughter Nicola was born on 24 April 1980.

WHO WERE YOUR BIGGEST RIVALS BOTH TEAM AND FAN-WISE?

Our rivals were people like Luton, which it always went off mad, they hated us and we always used to think we were better than them; they used to think they were better than us.

Oxford we couldn't stand and they were our real bad rivals. And the likes of Forest always used to love to come to us. People like Chelsea, Millwall, West Ham, they'll always rate people like Forest, but they wouldn't rate QPR. But then Forest would come to us and we'd have toe-to-toe with them and we'd match them pound for pound.

Team-wise, a lot of people can't stand Chelsea, they just love to beat Chelsea; well, I suppose because it's a big club and we're down the road, we're another West London club and I don't think we'll ever get as big as them. But to get a result against them was like getting a victory at Wembley.

WHO ARE THE TOP FIVE FIRMS OF ANY IMPORTANCE TODAY?

Well it's got to be Chelsea, Millwall, Cardiff, Leeds on their day, and Middlesbrough. And I believe Man United are really good; when we've bumped into them here we've had some really bad run-ins with them, but a lot of the time with the Cockney Reds as well, the Cockney Reds and the Mancs together.

WHO ARE YOUR TOP FIVE FIRMS OF ALL TIME?

You've got to put West Ham there, Millwall, Cardiff. At one time, Derby when we used to go to the old Popside, we used to go in their end, they was notorious with us. And I'd say 'Boro, because I'd seen 'Boro turn out massive at QPR.

WHAT IS THE WORST GROUND YOU'VE EVER BEEN TO AND WHAT IS YOUR FAVOURITE GROUND?

The worst ground I think I've ever been to was Mansfield on a cold night and it was quite a bit of a bad experience for me as well. We got there early in the morning and we was with this mad nutter called Gary, he was drunk, and he pulled up in a van only 12-handed. We've gone in this pub, and I went, 'Oops, it's them.' My mate's a bit drunk, so he went out round by Tesco's and walked back in with about 12 fluorescent lights under his arm and started throwing them around like a Zulu in the pub. They was exploding everywhere.

Everyone run out the pub. We went to try and run in our van and they slashed our tyres and we must have got attacked by about 400 and I've never ever been that scared where we'd had to try and hold our own with whatever we could hold our hands to and we just got annihilated, and we ended up hiding in gardens, in trees, everything to get away.

We got a bit more scared when they came back at twelve o'clock at night and the only thing that saved us was a geezer who was a Cockney who happened to be a tyre fixer. He said to me, 'Don't worry about it, we ain't running nowhere now,' and he pulled out a big case and opened it to reveal the biggest spanners and monkey wrenches I've ever seen in my life. He was a Tottenham fan and he lived in Mansfield, but he was a car mechanic.

My best ground is when I went to Old Trafford and when I went there when Kerry Dixon scored a hat-trick with Chelsea. It was just the atmosphere, the surroundings were just unbelievable, and now it's like Chelsea's got to be up there now with their new stadium as well.

WHAT IS YOUR FAVOURITE FOOTBALL FASHIONWEAR AND THE WORST YOU'VE SEEN OR WORN?

My favourite fashionwear was when we used to go to the Lyceum and it was the times of the Gabiccis and the Farahs and the Crocs, the snakeskin shoes, the suede coats and the Burberrys. It was all Burberry and Aquascutum at the time and then it got into the scene where it was the Tacchini tracksuit and my favourite was the Björn Borg tracksuit top. And the Trim Trab trainers as well, and the Forest Hills. The old Casual days, the '80s.

DOES TODAY'S MODERN FOOTBALL PLAYER HAVE THE RESPECT OF THE FANS?

I believe earlier on in the '70s when I used to go, I think they used to love the game more, the likes of Rodney Marsh, Stan Bowles, Bobby Moore, Peter Osgood, Davy Webb and Martin Chivers. But, nowadays, I think a lot of them get too much readies and they're just out there to earn money – not all of them do – but a few of them. It ain't like the old days. The hardcore footballer don't seem to be there like they used to be. They used to like going out there and mixing it and want to win the game no matter what. Nowadays, I think they just put their boots on and get their 50 grand a week. They haven't got the respect of the fans.

FANS OFTEN TALK ABOUT THEIR FOOTBALL-GOING DAYS AS JUST BEING A LAUGH. ANY EPISODES YOU REMEMBER?

I remember one day we was going to Norwich and a friend of mine called Pat was with us who's a Chelsea supporter and I said, 'Come to Norwich for the day.'

In them times, everybody said, 'What, QPR and Norwich?'

We'd reply, 'If you want a proper day out and a proper tear-up, toe-to-toe, come with us to Norwich.'

So he's come out; he used to like wandering about like a sightseer and he's walked up the hill. I said, 'Don't go up the hill, it's about ten to three, they're gonna come bowling down there.'

Next minute, we're in this pub at the bottom of the hill, all looking out the window, and we see Fat Pat running down the hill with about 200 Norwich chasing him and our lot was all going, 'Here he is, your Chelsea mate, he's getting run.'

I went, 'No, leave him, he needs to lose some weight. Let him get right in the boozer first before we come out there.'

And he's shouting down the road, 'Come out, they're here, they're here, they're here, help me out, it's on top.'

The next minute, I say, 'Right, come on, boys, let's get out there.' And we run out the pub and we just run up the hill and it was toe-to-toe and there was him sitting by the side recovering, knackered, sweating and saying, 'You bastard, you fucking let me get fucking run.' And he hates remembering it.

RACISM AND RACE ISSUES HAVE BEEN PART OF FOOTBALL WITH CERTAIN CLUBS AND SETS OF SUPPORTERS AT BOTH CLUB AND INTERNATIONAL LEVEL. WHAT WAS YOUR EXPERIENCE OF THIS?

You always got the banter if you was with a couple of black geezers and they'd say, 'Come on, you coon,' or something like that. But a lot of the black geezers I was with at the time, they didn't give a fuck and, at the end of the day, they'd most probably end up chinning the geezer throughout the day or after the game.

I remember going to Tottenham with my good friend Norman from Ladbroke Grove, he's black, we're standing together and this firm come over to us and one of them chinned one of the black guys. He goes, 'Come on, you black cunt,' and there was about 10–15 of us and they had about 30 and it went toe-to-toe and suddenly the Shelf turned on us. Now I don't know if the Shelf believed that we was another firm that come in to take the Shelf over, but it just went so bad and the black fellas I was with would not budge and we ended up taking on half of the fucking Shelf at the top bit. It just went absolutely crazy.

And the Old Bill didn't know who was who because they believed that they had all the supporters in the away end. But this prime example was a really bad incidence of a white firm having it with a black firm in the end. Tottenham had a little firm of black fellas that were known to be good together. Same as the Arsenal. It was one of my worst memories of a racial thing because I was with the black fellas because they was my pals, and I had to back them up and there was no way I was gonna leave them. It just come out of nothing. This was back in the early '80s. It was really bad in the ground.

Since then, not really. We've got a mix, we don't really get that much. We've never had a problem at QPR and everyone sticks together, no one cares about where they come from or what colour they are.

HOW HAVE FANS FOLLOWING THE NATIONAL TEAM ABROAD BEEN TREATED, AND WHAT ARE YOUR EXPERIENCES FOLLOWING YOUR CLUB OR NATIONAL TEAM ABROAD?

No, it's definitely worse when you're with England because we've got the reputation of being hooligans and we've seen previous televised things that England are notorious for standing up for themselves and for their country. But they do get dug out. I feel sorry for the fans who are proper English supporters that have got nothing to do with football violence whatsoever and they get weighed in by Old Bill through the fact that English are known for being hooligans.

After Heysel, when England went to Italy you saw the Old Bill properly weigh in with truncheons on any supporter that had an England top on or who was an English person at that time. It's not the same when you follow your club. But at the end of the day, if you go away abroad with your club and they know it's a British club – woah, you will get people turn out because you are English and they all think that English clubs have got hooligans, as you can see by the prime example when Millwall went to Hungary and it seemed like the whole of Hungary's hooligans turned out for them, and the same when Middlesbrough went away in the UEFA Cup in 2004. And they said that was really crazy, with about 200 skinheads turning out and 'Boro apparently had about 400 boys.

I heard from one of their boys that at two to three o'clock in the morning, 50–60 of them came running into the hotel and little did they know that 'Boro's all up there 200-handed, Charlied out of their nut, no one going to bed. They've come running through the foyer, and the next minute there's 200 'Boro still awake, ain't gone to bed yet, and they got the shock of their life, got weighed in out in the street at two to three in the morning.

DO YOU HAVE ANY VIEW ON BANNING ORDERS? DO YOU KNOW THIS FROM YOUR OWN EXPERIENCE OR THAT OF OTHERS?

I believe, sometimes, they might know a face of some sort and they ain't been nicked before, but they want to nick him just to make sure that he gets the ban, even though he might not have a lot of previous. But they'll make out at court that he's here, there, he's always been noticeable, and that's when they stitch people up.

I've been banned four times now, this is my twelfth year of being banned. I've just got a three-year ban against Brighton on Uxbridge Road. It's one of them silly ones; the geezer bowled out in the middle of the road at me and where I'd been to football for so long, I just jumped, I bit at it, went across, tried to punch him, totally missed him like a doughnut and ended up getting nicked for it and getting a three-year ban, and a three-year probation and a three-year anger-management course. You have to take that, it's the law. If I don't do the anger management, I go and do bird.

HOOLIE MOVIES AND FLICKS – DO THEY GLORIFY VIOLENCE OR CREATE A COPYCAT SYNDROME?

It does highlight it a bit because everyone gets to look at it and say, 'I remember them days ...' or 'It didn't happen like that, but it did happen like that ...' Now you've got the younger breed coming up thinking, 'Cor, is it really like that?' And that's why I think now you've got the youth firms coming up because it's just a new generation. As you can see, the fashions go round in a cycle and I believe the football, the youth, has made its cycle now back to the late '70s, bringing up youth firms that are back on the bandwagon of the football hooligans. Yeah, there's definitely copycat.

HOW WOULD YOU DESCRIBE YOUR FIRM/SUPPORTERS' FAN BASE, AND HAS YOUR FAN BASE CHANGED OVER TIME?

The support comes from all over – we've got Shepherd's Bush, Ladbroke Grove, Northolt area, Greenford area, and we've always had the same steady support, your average 13,000–14,000, even in Division Two, which was quite good at that time but we've never, over the years, had the 30,000. We used to get it, I believe, earlier on in the '60s ; I believe QPR used to get 35,000 and they used to have a stadium in White City at the time which is not there any more. But we've always had a loyal, solid support of QPR from West London, Middlesex, and they're very vocal to their club. You come to the ground, they're very vocal, they inspire the players on the pitch.

WAS YOUR LIFESTYLE WITH QPR SOLELY CONFINED TO THE FOOTBALL CONTEXT OR WOULD IT HAVE BEEN THE SAME FOR YOU IN EVERYDAY STREET LIFE?

It would be the same in everyday street life for me. All right, you know you got up to your skulduggery and I went with Ladbroke Grove and Notting Hill at the time, they were notorious for gang-related stuff. When we went anywhere together, they'd always say, 'Look, there's that Notting Hill lot,' or Ladbroke Grove, and people was very proud to be from there. But then you took your street cred from there and then you put it on to the terraces which was a different day out, different environment, different sort of violence, totally different because it was football-related it wasn't gang-related now. But it was still the same sort of feel of violence in the culture if you was brought up in Notting Hill.

EVERY ONE OF TODAY'S KNOWN HOOLIGAN FIRMS HAS A POLICE INTELLIGENCE OFFICER DEDICATED TO IT. HOW DO THE FIRMS TODAY RESPOND TO THAT? DO YOU HAVE ANY POLICE SPOTTER STORIES?

We've had a lot of police spotters. I remember one time we was playing, we used to have an old Irish sergeant and it was quite funny at the time when we played Liverpool and we were sitting on the fence, about eight of us. A Scouser come past and he went, 'All right, coon, where's your firm, coon?'

And he said, 'Give me two minutes, mate, I'll be back.'

The next minute, he's come along with 15 of them and the sergeant looked over to me and he went, 'Gregor, behave yourself.'

I went, 'Guv, five minutes. Don't get on the blower for five minutes.'

He went, 'All right, I'll give you five minutes, I'm gonna turn a blind eye.'

The next minute there was eight of us and 15 of them rolling around like a school fight, all punching each other, people jumping on to help each other. And he turned round, he went, 'Gregor, time's up … can I have assistance please, major disturbance at Springbox.'

'We're all going, leave it out, guv.'

'No,' he went, 'I gave you five minutes.'

And he was one of our spotters. And then we used to have one that everybody hated. What I don't like about him, to this day, was the difference between the northern spotters and the London spotters; you go up north and they will back their boys up, but when you come to London, our spotters are digging us out, putting the pressure on us.

IS THERE, IN YOUR OPINION, A NEXT GENERATION OF HOOLIGAN APPRENTICES COMING THROUGH AND WILL THEY BE ANYTHING LIKE THEIR PREDECESSORS?

There's a lot of big youth clubs coming about at the moment. I remember bumping into Sheffield Wednesday last year, and they just had an absolutely massive youth firm, I couldn't believe it when I saw it. It was absolutely massive. They must have had 100–150 youth. All the youth firms in the country now are becoming so big. It'll never be like it was in the '70s, never. You'll never get them mobs again, the Old Bill have got it too tamed now.

QPR have got an up-and-coming youth firm but how long that will last, I don't know. As you know, today the Old Bill have got their ways of sorting people out to lower the numbers nowadays.

**NAME: Steve Parker
TEAM: Rotherham
United
FIRM: Tivoli Crew**

**'In my time,
I never saw a
lot of weapons.'**

BACKGROUND AND MEET

I heard about him through a Blades fan who comes from Rawmarsh, Rotherham. Shaun simply said there were a few lads I could consider for the book. He also said, as a firm, on their day they can put a few out. He said they showed that when Cardiff came down a few seasons back. He then went and contacted Steve Parker for me, who I went to interview at his home.

As Steve rolled back the years for me, I found him an honest man and very much a man of his word. Obviously not a player of today, and I didn't want that because, in one of his answers, he said the difference today is that there aren't any real characters around any more. And, to some extent, he would be very right on that, and just to emphasise it, we went outside and I watched Steve roar out the garage on his Harley Davidson.

He was born in 1950; left school to work in the steelworks, and achieved a City & Guilds in Engineering. He still works in the steelwork industry today, is married and remembers he went with his father to his first game way back in 1956.

WHAT HAS BEEN THE MOST LEGENDARY FIGHT OR RIOT YOUR TEAM'S SUPPORTERS HAVE BEEN INVOLVED IN?

Well, basically, time erases your memory. I'd have to go back to probably season '81/82, Chelsea at home. We actually beat them 6–0, and after the game they weren't very pleased and there was a big set-to outside ground down towards the centre of town, a big set-to. That's the biggest I can think of in the past few years because, obviously, we've dipped since then, we've dropped divisions. It was a league game. First time we'd played them for, I imagine, 30 years, but I can't remember. We got promoted, they came down, they fetched a big following, most of whom had probably never been to Rotherham, never heard of it. Everybody turned out, big set-to. Running battles from ground down to a big island, a big set-to on there and then into town, and it followed on into town. It was a stalemate, everybody sort of dispersed eventually, they went back to station and we all drifted off. I got a clout for me troubles. They still talk about that one as far as I know.

Another one is probably Newcastle. We played them, they beat us 5–1, Kevin Keegan played. There were quite a few of them; they had a go at them in town as well, but that were probably a little bit more sporadic.

WHO WAS THE MOST VIOLENT, CRAZY SET OF SUPPORTERS YOU EVER CAME ACROSS?

In my opinion, it's Millwall. Obviously, again, it's the divisions we've been in, we've never been in the top flight, so I can't really compare them with Man U or Liverpool, we've only ever played them in Cup games over the years. But from a point of view of those we've played, I've found them the worst, Millwall.

They came to Rotherham just after that documentary was on TV about them many years ago. They had little surgical masks on. They turned out in force, and their reputation obviously preceded them. Everybody was very wary of them. And, to us, they seemed above our level, if you understand me, a level above what were normal at that time. But, again, I think they're no different to any others, it's levelled off. They were the worst, especially at Millwall. It was intimidation and the way they looked as well, the way they dressed, they were intimidating. Certainly, when you go to Millwall you know exactly what you're up against; that to me is one of the most intimidating places I've ever been.

ARE YOUR FIRM STILL DOING IT?

No. Rotherham still have an active firm. I believe they go under the name of Section 5 because of a couple of disorder offences, they took their name from that. I know that they are active; obviously, they're all 20-odd years younger than what we were, but I do know some of them and I know that they play an active part, so they are still going, it hasn't died off.

HOW WOULD YOU DESCRIBE THE SITUATION WITH THE SCENE TODAY? CAN IT COMPARE WITH WHAT HAPPENED IN THE PAST, AND DO THINGS STILL GO OFF IN THE SAME WAY?

Again, going back to when we were young, it was a sort of spontaneous thing where groups met. Today, there's such things as mobile phones, which I think play a very big part, I think it's a lot more organised, it's not anywhere near the ground any more. It always used to be near the ground because there was no such things as phones or communication, really. To put it in a nutshell, I don't think it's spontaneous any more, it's arranged, isn't it, sometimes weeks in advance.

When I were younger, people just went to matches and it'd kick off in a pub or we'd have it in the ground and there were no pre-set time or meeting, it just happened, or it didn't happen, whatever.

HOW DID YOU GET GOING WITH A FOOTBALL FIRM, DID IT HAVE A NAME AND HOW WAS THE NAME ESTABLISHED?

When I was in my teens, the Rotherham element didn't have a name; I don't think anybody did in the late '60s. I, just like all kids, followed on, stood on Kop and followed everybody. First of all, it were more of a Mod thing – Mods and Rockers, because if me memory serves me right, the first sort of gang I can remember seeing at Rotherham were what I would term 'Rockers'. They had leather jackets and ice-blue jeans, whereas on the other side of the coin we classed ourselves as Mods. It were just two groups that stood on the Kop.

In my opinion, I would say that the dominant ones were the Rockers at that time, definitely. It changed with the skinheads; I would say that that's where these come along, who eventually called themselves Friday Crew and the EDM. Skinheads started coming in. And that was sort of the next lot. Then, after that, it sort of drifted into what I call 'casual wear' for younger people and then they moved on to the Section 5.

WHAT WAS THE WORST INSTANCE OF WEAPONS BEING USED?

In my time, I never saw a lot of weapons. I can remember Rotherham playing Blackburn at home and a guy, some Blackburn fan, actually came up Rotherham Kop with a big sheath knife and actually stood waving it round. There was no segregation then, they let in everybody. A mate of mine sort of jumped on him and thumped him and police come and took him away then.

Other than that, the only other instance I can recall is in 1972 we played Tottenham in the FA Cup at White Hart Lane and there were odd skirmishes, but at the end of the game everybody seemed to move rapidly away at one point, and there were some guys from Tottenham in front of me and they all had knives, and that was the first time I'd seen anything like that; you'd never seen all that here.

WHAT IS THE MOST IMPORTANT LESSON YOU LEARNED PERSONALLY DURING YOUR TIME WITH YOUR FIRM AND WOULD YOU DO ANYTHING DIFFERENTLY?

I don't think there's a learning curve in it. Perhaps you learn a bit about self-preservation probably, but it didn't really teach me anything. The only thing as I see it now as a 50-odd-year-old, and again it's a personal opinion, I would have loved to have been more involved at the front of things rather than being just sort of part of things, I would like to have been more involved in leading and sorting and organising. But again, you don't know if you could have done it or not. We can all sit back later in life and say, 'I could have done this ...' we don't know. But if I had me time again, that's what I would like to do.

WHO WERE YOUR BIGGEST RIVALS BOTH TEAM AND FAN-WISE?

As a youngster, I would have to say in my teens Barnsley were our rivals. Both Sheffield teams were then as they were First

Division clubs, so we very rarely come across them. Barnsley, Doncaster Rovers to some extent. Then, in the late '70s, the biggest rival started, and that was Sheffield Wednesday, and they've been our rivals now for a long, long time, 20–30 years. It is a big rivalry, definitely.

I don't seem to have a problem with Sheffield United, we seem to get on reasonably well, but Sheffield Wednesday definitely. The main reason I can give any outsider for that is, if you walk round Rotherham on a Saturday afternoon, there are more Sheffield Wednesday shirts than there are Rotherham, and that has antagonised everybody for a long, long time. And that's why I think there's this big thing with Wednesday.

WHO ARE THE TOP FIVE FIRMS OF ANY IMPORTANCE TODAY?

Again, I've had to think about things because we've not been involved at top level. A team that always spring to mind for me is Lincoln. Lincoln's a small place, but they've a real following, some real lads there. I've noticed Sheffield's had a lot of trouble with them. Ours have only been little skirmishes, really. For a small place that you don't associate as a footballing area, they seem to have a really good set of lads.

As for me top five today, I'd have to go for West Ham, Millwall, Stoke, Sheffield United. And I've gone for Middlesbrough; they seem to be quite active.

WHO ARE YOUR TOP FIVE FIRMS OF ALL TIME?

Again, I'm going for West Ham, Chelsea, Millwall. I've got Birmingham City because they used to have a hell of a following, I've had experience of them at Rotherham. Well, just sheer numbers, but their reputation preceded them. They'd been to Blackpool the week before and broke into the ground and they actually dug some of the pitch up. So the following week, when Rotherham played them, there was a massive police presence, video cameras, it really was over the top. And they've always had the numbers.

Me other one would be Newcastle; they've always seemed to have had a massive following.

WHAT IS THE WORST GROUND YOU'VE EVER BEEN TO AND WHAT IS YOUR FAVOURITE GROUND?

This question stumped me. I thought about it for a long time. I've been to probably 80-odd grounds. As a dump, I've got to be honest, there isn't many worse than Rotherham. All I can think of that are worse that springs to mind straight away is Chesterfield and Wrexham and Doncaster, they're not very good grounds at all.

I went to Hartlepool in 1968 and there was a big scrap there and their ground was awful. But I've been since, only four year ago, and they've done it up smashing, it's a lovely little stadium. So I can't say it's a dump, because it i'nt.

Now, as for intimidation, I'd go for Millwall and Birmingham. The best one I think I've been to is Old Trafford when we played Man United in a Cup game. It was 1988 when I went there and I sat, me and our kid, and we just sat and said, 'Imagine what this is like to come here every week to a stadium like this.'

And I'm a big fan of Wembley, I loved Wembley for what it was and what it did for me. It's everything I think of in football, it's great and I can't wait to go to the new one. But I still believe, and I think everybody in your book would probably agree, that them twin towers should have stayed, I really do believe that. That were our heritage, it belonged to us, the people.

WHAT IS YOUR FAVOURITE FOOTBALL FASHIONWEAR AND THE WORST YOU'VE SEEN OR WORN?

For me, I'd have to say denim in '70s. And, at that time, I had hair, lovely long hair, so everything went into place. Everything was denim. We played Northampton away. In New Musical Express there was an advert for a shop in Northampton that sold jackets and jeans made up from patchwork old Levis, you couldn't get them. So when we played Northampton away, I went and found the shop and bought myself a lovely jacket. And I swanned around, I was only one who had one of them in Rotherham and I thought I was Jack the Lad for a while.

As for the worst, I couldn't stand the Bay City Rollers-type gear. I thought that was awful. Scarves round their wrists.

WHO'S THE PLAYER AND/OR MANAGER THAT WINDS YOU UP THE MOST?

Maradona, the famous one. I just can't stand the man.

Manager-wise, I had to think about this. Alex Ferguson came into me reckoning, because of the way he seems to rule referees' timing of the game, but I've also got down here he's an excellent manager, so I sort of put him to one side. And I've got Rudi Voller. I don't like him, he's German, I can't stand his hairstyle. He just looks to me like somebody I'd love to punch.

WORST FOREIGN PLAYER YOU'VE SEEN AND THE BEST FOREIGN IMPORT? YOUR FAVOURITE CLUB PLAYER AND YOUR FAVOURITE OTHER PLAYER?

The worst one I've ever seen, it was a guy called Gisbert Boss from Holland, who Rotherham signed a few years ago from Lincoln City and he was an absolute joke. He couldn't kick a ball. And the managers talk about him – 'He can't kick a ball, he can't run, and he can't head a ball, but other than that, he's not bad.' He was an absolute joke. How he got here in the first place I don't know.

Me favourite import is Thierry Henry of Arsenal. I think he's an excellent footballer.

My favourite club player is Dave Watson by a mile. He went to Sunderland and then he went on to captain England, so probably the best player Rotherham's ever had. My favourite other player of all time is Bobby Moore, simply for what he was, he was everything I thought a footballer should be.

FANS OFTEN TALK ABOUT THEIR FOOTBALL-GOING DAYS AS JUST BEING A LAUGH. ANY EPISODES YOU REMEMBER?

In 1968, I went to Brighton. I was only 17 years old, probably about 8st. And I'd never seen a skinhead, only heard about them. And I came face-to-face with one in Brighton football ground. There was no segregation. And I looked round, he were about 6ft 4in, no teeth, and he stood behind me and I remember to this day he looked at me and he went, 'I'm gonna fucking break your teeth, mate.' And I ran as fast as I could. He chased me all over the ground, and I ended up hiding in one of the stands. So that stood out.

Another incident occurred when we went to away to Hove. We stopped in a pub in the village and a friend of mine, John, was eyeing up the landlady who had two little Yorkshire terriers. He convinced her he was a top dog breeder and, within half-an-hour, he was upstairs giving her one.

YOUR OPINION ABOUT ALL-SEATER STADIUMS, TICKET PRICES AND THE COMMERCIAL ASPECT OF TODAY'S FOOTBALL INDUSTRY. DO YOU STILL FEEL FOOTBALL BELONGS TO THE FANS?

I don't think it belongs to the fans any more; I think more and more we're treated like shit, especially in the higher divisions, i.e. the Premier League. They're moving more towards corporate hospitality and that's all they're interested in. Some guy sits with his wife at Old Trafford and she asks which colour are Manchester United, they've never stood in rain, they're never served their time, and it's all moving towards that.

Stadium-wise, they're excellent to look at and sit in, but there's no atmosphere, there's nothing, it's all gone. It just seems to me as if I would imagine at some grounds it's like going to a theatre to watch a play, there's just no atmosphere. Ticket prices – even a club as low as Rotherham have an ABC category, so if we were playing Sheffield United, a good local derby, tickets are dearer than if we were playing Gillingham at home, which I think is wrong.

RACISM AND RACE ISSUES HAVE BEEN PART OF FOOTBALL WITH CERTAIN CLUBS AND SETS OF SUPPORTERS AT BOTH CLUB AND INTERNATIONAL LEVEL. WHAT WAS YOUR EXPERIENCE OF THIS?

I've never known a racist element among the supporters. I've been to grounds obviously where there have. Years ago,

Blackburn were well known for that, for racism, very bad. So were Newcastle and Leeds at one time. But in Rotherham, I would say no, I've never come across it.

I'm of the opinion I don't care what colour anybody is, if they score for Rotherham or England, I don't mind. They can be yellow, green, whatever, if it wins us the World Cup, I'm happy. Again, as a club who'd never played Chelsea, I just had this view that they were all skinheads and BNP, probably they're not. That's the view you get through the press.

HOW HAVE FANS FOLLOWING THE NATIONAL TEAM ABROAD BEEN TREATED, AND WHAT ARE YOUR EXPERIENCES FOLLOWING YOUR CLUB OR NATIONAL TEAM ABROAD?

I'll never be following Rotherham abroad; we can't get Premier Division, never mind getting into Europe. But I've been abroad with England and I fully 100 per cent believe that English supporters are treated like shit. One example was Rome, a World Cup qualifier in '97. We were herded into the ground an hour before kick-off. We had cigarettes, lighters, any money taken off us. For the full hour before kick-off, missiles were thrown, including seats, bottles, everything, and nothing was done about it. And yet the police were hitting English people, which I found every time I've been abroad. You're treated, to me, just like a second-class citizen.

The police outside the ground had dustbins about 3ft high at the turnstiles full of change. They searched everybody and hit everybody. And I don't know how much money was in those dustbins, but they had a nice little tipple.

After the game, we were kept in the ground for four hours. It was two-thirty in the morning when we left the ground. Then we were put on these 'hoolie buses'. They put everybody on, shut the doors and windows and then left us for three-quarters-of-an-hour. It was like being in a sauna.

I haven't been abroad many times, maybe eight or nine with England, and I've found that everybody treats you the same, wherever you go, you're treated as an animal. Again, the hype before it, they don't regard you as a person, they judge it on what they've been told and read.

SHOULD CELTIC AND RANGERS BE ALLOWED TO JOIN THE ENGLISH PREMIERSHIP OR NATIONWIDE LEAGUES?

I would like to see them in our football set-up. I'd like to see just how good they really think they are, because they keep saying they can beat English teams. OK, Celtic have done in it in Cup competitions, but I think, come the season, they would find they're playing in the best division in the world, our Premier League.

On the other side of it, will they then bring sectarian violence with them? Obviously, Celtic and Rangers are very bigoted, although they won't admit to that. We all know Celtic are Catholic and Rangers are Protestant. Every football fan knows that.

DO YOU HAVE ANY VIEW ON BANNING ORDERS? DO YOU KNOW THIS FROM YOUR OWN EXPERIENCE OR THAT OF OTHERS?

I've no experience personally, but I've listened to other people. They're obviously effective because the law makes sure of that. But what I picked up is that it can also be very unfair, because they go on hearsay.

For example, you have a row with your neighbour or a guy in a pub, he can phone the police up and say so-and-so is now organising trouble at a match on Saturday and, purely from hearsay, they can put you away or ban you to your house, whatever, and I don't think that's fair because there's no evidence and you're not allowed to speak on your own behalf.

EVERY ONE OF TODAY'S KNOWN HOOLIGAN FIRMS HAS A POLICE INTELLIGENCE OFFICER DEDICATED TO IT. HOW DO THE FIRMS TODAY RESPOND TO THAT? DO YOU HAVE ANY POLICE SPOTTER STORIES?

I actually do have a story and it involves my wife and I. We went to Scarborough to watch Rotherham years ago. We met up with a guy we'd met on holiday, so we had a drink with him. I'll admit I'd had a few beers. We went and got a taxi to the ground. I didn't speak to anyone, I didn't shout, I didn't make any gestures. My wife walked on my arm towards the ground. There were people drunk, falling all over, from Rotherham. The stewards moved forward and said to me, 'You can't come in.' So I said, 'Why?' And he looked over my shoulder and pointed, and there behind me was a Rotherham spotter, and he said, 'He says you can't come in.' And I'd done nothing wrong. My wife was with me, she would witness that. I didn't even speak to anyone.

I eventually got in the ground in a different part and, after about ten minutes, I were arrested, which really upset my wife, but it's only part and parcel of what we expect in this day and age. But I'd done nothing wrong.

As for spotters in general, I've noticed that they seem to be on first-name terms, it seems to be very friendly, although there might be an undertone to that of trying to glean information from lads. But I've heard lads call policemen by their first names and policemen call lads by their first names. It just seems to be a cat and mouse game that they play every week.

IS THERE, IN YOUR OPINION, A NEXT GENERATION OF HOOLIGAN APPRENTICES COMING THROUGH AND WILL THEY BE ANYTHING LIKE THEIR PREDECESSORS?

I always think there will be lads coming through. I think it's part of our lifestyle in Britain. I don't think there are any characters today. I believe that I look at some of the young lads today, they all seem to dress exactly the same, they're all in Burberry, etc. Perhaps they thought that about us when we were young, I don't know. But I don't seem to see individual characters.

I also believe that today they're very much more into using weapons and drugs, and that has become a prominent part of their lives. The individuals I've met in my time were some real characters from different clubs. You could sit and listen to them for hours, but again, they're all older lads. You don't seem to see individual characters any more. Yeah, OK, they might be lads, but they're just lads, they haven't got any stories to tell or depth. You couldn't have a conversation with them. They'd probably just say, 'I fought so-and-so on Monday ...' and there's just no stories of life. Generally, they don't seem to have 'owt.

NAME: Tony Cronshaw
CLUB: Sheffield Wednesday
FIRM: Ex-East Bank Republican Army

'Who says that the hooligans are not true football supporters.'

BACKGROUND AND MEET

I literally bumped into the Wednesday chapter on the strip in Albufeira down on the Algarve. It was a case of either walking into him or going around him and ending up in the middle of the street. The man was huge and his pals were distinctly from 'oop norf' and all looked lumps. I thought, 'Here we go,' as the bottom end of the strip is usually where the trouble was each night. But, lo and behold, the huge man was none other than Tony Cronshaw, author of Wednesday Rucks & Rock 'n' Roll and, to the bemusement of his pals, me and Tony stood on the corner having an authors' chin-wag.

Now you have only to read his book to see Tony's heart is of the old school, a true hardcore football fan, who has had the crack following Wednesday up and down every bloody division. It is true his football club once saw better days, though, sadly, it is remembered now mostly for football's greatest tragedy – Hillsborough – unless you're a Wednesdayite die-hard like Tony, who can recall every game he ever went to, every beer along the way and, of course, the rucks. And if we are looking on that side of things, Wednesday as a mob have a pedigree going back to the late '60s–'70s, and big numbers. Since then, like their team, things got a little inconsistent, particularly going into the '90s. During the '80s they managed to rampage their way round grounds and back into Division One. Today, it's a younger outfit that is calling it on – guess it comes with the pedigree.

He was born in 1955; first job was as a shop lad. He's been married 21 years, and his first game was Sheffield Wednesday v Arsenal in 1964.

WHAT HAS BEEN THE MOST LEGENDARY FIGHT OR RIOT YOUR TEAM'S SUPPORTERS HAVE BEEN INVOLVED IN?

The Oldham riot in 1980 was the most infamous day in the history of Sheffield Wednesday for the explosion of violence that was directed at anyone who stood in the way on that day. Wednesday took a massive following that day, including all the factions that made up the East Bank Republican Army from all the estates in and around Sheffield.

The start of the 1980/81 season had the boys taking on Newcastle United at Hillsborough, and this led to many arrests and fighting from well before the game until early evening. All the lads were bang at it for well over eight hours. It was Wednesday's first season back in the Second Division and, with Chelsea and West Ham to come, this was the start we'd been waiting for.

Once at the ground, the lads got on to the Oldham Kop but were rumbled and made a hasty retreat, but the odds were stacked against them. Once we'd got into the Wednesday end, fighting was breaking out all over the ground and you could sense the atmosphere changing. It all kicked off when Terry Curran was sent off and all hell let loose – fans were raining missiles down on to the police and others were trying to get on to the pitch. Even Jack Charlton could not calm the situation and he was God to most Wednesdayites. The terracing was torn to pieces and anything that could be thrown was directed at the police.

Wednesday received a massive fine and ban for their supporters which would see them banned from four away games and also the terracing was to be closed for a further four matches.

During the 1975/76 season, Wednesday supporters caused havoc in Chesterfield after a league game when they went on the rampage smashing up the town centre on the way back to the train station. There was also rioting in Southend on the opening day of the season when Wednesdayites had running battles with the police on the seafront until late in the evening.

Wednesday's visit to Charlton Athletic in the FA Cup saw the East Bank lads having it with Millwall inside the ground and after the game; cars were overturned and windows were smashed in nearby properties.

A couple of years after the Oldham riot, Wednesday were once again on the offensive at Oldham because, as the police kept the fans inside the ground, outside Oldham fans were turning over vans and minivans belonging to the Sheffield Wednesday fans. This resulted in the Owls storming the gates to get out and running battles ensued in the Oldham car park.

WHO WAS THE MOST VIOLENT, CRAZY SET OF SUPPORTERS YOU EVER CAME ACROSS?

My own personal view was a minibus trip to Millwall in 1976 when we played them in the League Cup. We parked the bus under a railway bridge on the Old Kent Road behind another bus. We got into the ground and were immediately showered with missiles from all directions. It was the most hostile reception we'd ever encountered. Wednesday lost the game 3–0 but now we had to get back to the bus. I was walking with two mates. As we approached the bus, a group of about eight lads were stood bang opposite the bus, so we proceeded to walk past. But we'd been sussed; they squirted ammonia in the face of my mate and he fell to the floor. My other mate was kicked and punched, but I managed to get to the other side of the road with the gang in pursuit. How I managed to keep on my feet I'll never know.

I ran straight through the door of a boozer and one of the Millwall mob followed me in. He picked up a pool ball and I thought, 'Here we go, now it's my turn for some good old Cockney hospitality.' But before he could launch the ball, one of the blokes playing pool cracked him over the head with the pool cue. He picked himself up and made for the door, while the man playing pool asked his mate where to put the ball on the table.

The landlord ushered me out the back door which backed on to the most uninviting housing estate I'd ever seen, so I declined his invitation and went out the front door and wandered back up the road towards the van. I was informed by a police officer that my mates were holed up in a boozer opposite the bus. When I walked in, they told me that one of the lads had gone to Guy's Hospital, so we proceeded to see how he was.

Over the next four hours, they cleaned out most of the ammonia, but on the journey home we had to stop every 30 minutes to put drops in his eyes. Thankfully, he made a full recovery and, to this day, does not wear glasses so his eyesight was not permanently damaged.

ARE YOUR FIRM STILL DOING IT?

The lads that I went with on a regular basis during the '70s and early '80s, most had packed it in by 1981, but some carried on until the end of the '80s when the changing face of the football hooligan was transformed from the rampaging mobs of the '70s to the more tightly knitted firms that you have today. In my opinion, Wednesday on their day can still put a massive firm together when the occasion arises and, over the past few years, they have turned out in force for trips to Derby County and Leicester City.

HOW WOULD YOU DESCRIBE THE SITUATION WITH THE SCENE TODAY? CAN IT COMPARE WITH WHAT HAPPENED IN THE PAST, AND DO THINGS STILL GO OFF IN THE SAME WAY?

As they say, where there's a will there's a way. But it's becoming increasingly harder for the present day lads to have it off, but it's not all doom and gloom because, only last season, Wednesday and Bristol City had it off on the outskirts of Sheffield. This must have taken a lot of planning to get well over 100 like-minded souls to a pub car park at least ten miles from Hillsborough and, by all accounts, it was like an old-fashioned set to until the police broke up the party.

Personally, you can't even have a quiet drink with your kids before someone's pointing a video camera in your face, but you just soldier on and hope they can find other duties for the heavy police presence you witness every Saturday afternoon.

HOW DID YOU GET GOING WITH A FOOTBALL FIRM, DID IT HAVE A NAME AND HOW WAS THE NAME ESTABLISHED?

I started going on a regular basis with the lads around 1974/75 when Wednesday were at an all-time low and were languishing at the bottom of the Second Division and the likes of Manchester United and their Red Army were rampaging round the country. The name East Bank Republican Army was taken because that's where everybody stood on a Saturday afternoon, our massive uncovered end where you'd get piss wet through. Also, it was at the time when the Owls had sunk to the depths of the Third Division and, at most games, the away Wednesday following would outnumber the home fans. At those away games at the time, everybody travelled independently and our favourite mode of transport was the good old Transit van. But once at your destination, all the lads from the different parts of Sheffield would come together as one and we all know what the '70s were like.

WHAT WAS THE WORST INSTANCE OF WEAPONS BEING USED?

During my time travelling the country watching the Owls, weapons were rarely used, but on the odd occasion when your backs were against the wall, you'd know that one of your party would be tooled up in case it came on top. The only time I was on the receiving end was after an away game at Luton in 1981. We had met some lads from Leamington Spa and Hatfield on holiday during the summer, so we decided to have a bit of a reunion after the game. Wednesday put in a brilliant performance to send us to the top of the Second Division, so we were on a roll as we headed for Hatfield.

We met the lads in their boozer but it was a bit of a dump, sorry to say. So we asked if there was anywhere with a bit of life. They told us The White Hart was swinging on a Saturday night, but it was a bit rough. We told them we'd be OK, thinking that because we were with them there'd be no trouble. Unfortunately for us, Wednesday were on Match of the Day and some of the locals did not take too kindly to a bunch of northerners cheering on their football team. Our driver came in to tell us that three of the tyres to our van had been slashed and that we were going nowhere. We got all the lads to the van and started to break up all this furniture in the back of the van. We also asked the Hatfield lads not to get involved as they had to live amongst our aggressors.

Then it happened. A rampaging mob came for us, slinging bottles and pots in our direction. How we were not cut to pieces I'll never know. Once they ran out of weapons, we went on the offensive and, for a short while, we held our own, but the numbers were overwhelming. We were thinking that the Old Bill must surely be on their way because we'd been at it for a good ten minutes. Now, that's a long time to be under the cosh like we were that night. We were defending ourselves the best we could.

Then – WHAM – I was struck with a bottle, sending me crashing to the floor. Before they could put the boot in, my good friend Shaun went at them while the lads dragged me to the van. My head was spinning and I was throwing up for England. They had fractured my skull and I spent two weeks in the Queen Elizabeth in Welwyn Garden City. By all accounts, the rest of the boys looked a sorry sight when they eventually got back to Sheffield Sunday evening and our driver failed to get back the £40 deposit he had had to leave with the hire company. But I'll say one thing – it was a bloody good day out.

WHAT IS THE MOST IMPORTANT LESSON YOU LEARNED PERSONALLY DURING YOUR TIME WITH YOUR FIRM AND WOULD YOU DO ANYTHING DIFFERENTLY?

The most important thing I learned was the sense of togetherness you got when you travelled around the country because you'd know that eventually you'd come unstuck. Following your team in the '70s and '80s was, on occasions, a dangerous pastime when you visited London, Manchester, Merseyside and the North-East, to name but a few, but anywhere in the country could give you a nasty wake-up call. I still go to the matches with the lads from those days, but now we are usually outnumbered by our kids. And who says that the hooligans are not true football supporters? In my day, our team was that crap it was only the hooligans that travelled away.

WHO WERE YOUR BIGGEST RIVALS BOTH TEAM AND FAN-WISE?

Sheffield United, in my day, and they are still our closest rivals. But during my time in the '70s, we rarely played them in a league game because we were languishing in the Third Division. But when we did play in a County Cup game or testimonial, Wednesday would have the upper hand because the Owls just happened to have the better hooligans.

WHO ARE YOUR TOP FIVE FIRMS OF ALL TIME?

Manchester United for the antics of the Red Army for their rampaging of the 1970s; Chelsea for the times we've had it at Hillsborough and Stamford Bridge; West Ham for their organisation home and away; Millwall, just like Chelsea, for the times we've crossed swords; and finally Sheffield Wednesday, because they're my team and I'm making the choice.

WHAT IS YOUR FAVOURITE FOOTBALL FASHIONWEAR AND THE WORST YOU'VE SEEN OR WORN?

My all-time favourite fashion has got to be the good old Crombie and the Doc Marten's of the '70s, but of the new generation, the Stone Island wear is the best, but I hate the Burberry.

YOUR FAVOURITE BAND OR MUSIC DURING YOUR FOOTBALL-GOING DAYS?

The first single I ever bought was Gary Glitter's 'Rock 'n' Roll: Parts One and Two' about 1972, but I'll have that on my conscience for the rest of my days. I thought the punk scene which started in 1976 was a breath of fresh air and, by the start of the 1977/78 season, I'd seen quite a few bands, the first being The Ramones who were supported by Talking Heads and it cost 75p to get into the Outlook Club in Doncaster.

By Christmas 1977, I'd seen the Jam, Boomtown Rats (if only

for 20 minutes, because someone threw a bottle and it hit Geldof so they pissed off), the Stranglers and – my all-time favourites – The Clash. One of my mates, Trigg, spent most of 1977/78 touring with The Clash as a roadie. The highlight of 1977 was seeing the Sex Pistols at Huddersfield on Christmas Day, and they were excellent.

During 1978, we were once again in the Outlook Club to see the band Sham 69 and they did not disappoint and became a firm favourite with the lads. During a concert in Sheffield, my mate Shaun asked if they needed a hand with the gear and we helped out as unpaid roadies. This took us to Glasgow, Edinburgh and Sunderland, where we met the West Ham lads for the first time. Out of the four of us that travelled regularly up and down the country helping out the band, I was the only Owl and the only one whose team was in the Third Division, but they never took the piss.

During this period was when the hooligans left the terraces and invaded the concert halls. At one particular gig in Cleethorpes, Grimsby Town fans were giving the concert-goers a hard time. Jimmy Pursey stopped the gig and asked if anybody wanted to fight, please remain in the centre of the dance floor and everybody else move to the side. All the Grimsby boys stayed put and, once again, the West Ham/Sheffield contingent had them on their toes so that the show could go on.

I can remember one occasion in 1980 when Wednesday travelled to Upton Park and we had a Special laid on to take us to the game and we were met with a hostile reception from The Queen's pub as we made our way to the ground. As I got to the away end, I saw some of the Sham lads stood opposite. I went over for a chat, only to be politely told it was football today and not music, so I, for once, was the enemy. They bade me farewell with the words 'I hope you get home in one piece' ringing in my ears.

Towards the end of the '70s, the emergence of the Two Tone scene even proved more popular with the lads than punk. With the likes of Madness and The Specials, the music scene was thriving. That period in time, from 1976 until 1981, was, in my opinion, the best ever time to be a lover of football, fighting and music.

YOUR OPINION ABOUT ALL-SEATER STADIUMS, TICKET PRICES AND THE COMMERCIAL ASPECT OF TODAY'S FOOTBALL INDUSTRY. DO YOU STILL FEEL FOOTBALL BELONGS TO THE FANS?

There's no real atmosphere in the stadiums any more with the over-zealous stewarding and policing. Unless your Chairman happens to be Sam Hamman of Cardiff City, you try to engage in banter with rival fans at Hillsborough and you've got some jobsworth telling you to sit down or some copper who thinks he's Jeremy Beadle and sticks a camcorder in your face.

All-seaters? I wouldn't mind if you were allowed to stand in one section like they do on the Continent. As for ticket prices, they're well over the top. I mean, we're paying over £20 for Third Division football. Most of the lower league clubs need a good commercial side to survive these days, after the greedy Premier League has taken all the money.

Most of the fans these days, especially in the Premier League, are soon on their bike once they drop out of the top flight. Take, for example, Leeds United: 29,000; Sunderland: 24,000; Derby County: 23,000. Where are the missing thousands that jumped on the bandwagon? I'll tell you where – they've gone back to shopping or the theatre of a Saturday instead of staying with their club.

Wednesday have a hardcore of around 20,000 who, at the moment, are sticking by the club, but, on the other hand, the away following has not changed for 20 years – you still see the same old faces you first set your eyes on in the late 1970s.

RACISM AND RACE ISSUES HAVE BEEN PART OF FOOTBALL WITH CERTAIN CLUBS AND SETS OF SUPPORTERS AT BOTH CLUB AND INTERNATIONAL LEVEL. WHAT WAS YOUR EXPERIENCE OF THIS?

Racism has always been in football, from the rampaging mobs of the '70s through to the Casual era, but also racism can be found in the home and work and everyday life, but it's not as bad as the '70s. Take, for instance, the 1970s when all the black players were getting abuse. Some clubs like West Brom were cheering on their coloured players while abusing black players from another club.

Wednesday's first black player was Tony Cunningham, around 1983, and he was cheered along with the others that followed like Thompson, Chamberlain, Atkinson, Anderson and Palmer, but that didn't stop opposing black players getting stick from the Hillsborough crowd. Everybody has a prejudice, some more than others, and it's not all white on black.

Me, personally, I have mates from all ethnic backgrounds and Wednesday have had more than their share of coloured supporters in the past who I have fought at the side of. But I would be lying if I said I'd never hurled abuse at an opposing coloured player, but that does not make me a racist.

HOW HAVE FANS FOLLOWING THE NATIONAL TEAM ABROAD BEEN TREATED, AND WHAT ARE YOUR EXPERIENCES FOLLOWING YOUR CLUB OR NATIONAL TEAM ABROAD?

I have two experiences of following England abroad. First was in France '98 and then Portugal '04. In France '98, attending the Romanian game in Toulouse without a ticket, we tried all day without success, so we made our way as close to the ground as possible, to be met by a massive line of police at the other side of the bridge. As you needed a ticket to proceed any further, we just hung around on the bridge.

At this point, a journalist came up and said he would pay good money if anyone would launch missiles at the lines of police, so he and the photographer could get a story. Unfortunately, it was him who the England fans turned on, and his cameraman's bag was pinched and was last seen floating down the river.

After this, we headed for the boozer, but it was packed and the ticketless England supporters were milling outside. The police come in force and what they did next was unbelievable. They cordoned off the road so that tables could be brought outside so we could all see the game – now that was never reported. The day had been a great success apart from the result, and the journey back to the Costa Brava gave us plenty of time to sober up.

Next was the visit to Portugal and our stay in Albufeira for Euro 2004. We arrived just after England had beaten Switzerland

and we headed for the strip that had been on the news before we had left England. It was pretty quiet that night, but the following evening the Portuguese Police were really heavy-handed, playing up to the cameras that lined the overseeing buildings. Horses were brought out and were paraded up and down the strip. Most of the England fans congregated outside two bars and banter was exchanged between the two sets. As we were all-inclusive, we never ventured out of our hotel until after 11.30pm. It was now about 12.30am and one or two lads were being dragged off, to the delight of the waiting media, but, in all, no more than half-a-dozen lads were led away. We left the area at about 4.30pm and the Portuguese Police could have done with a bit of guidance from the plod in France who knew how to treat people.

The next day, the wife was on the phone saying that there'd been rioting on the strip again and were we all right. I asked her which riot she was talking about, and she said it had been on the news the following morning. I informed the good lady that half-a-dozen drunk English lads having a bit of banter is no riot.

The remainder of our stay was enjoyable because the police relaxed a bit and put away the horses. We enjoyed a great day out in Lisbon when we beat Croatia, and even after we'd lost to Portugal it was still a party atmosphere on the Algarve. I think travelling abroad and being English is an occupational hazard because everybody hates us.

DO YOU HAVE ANY VIEW ON BANNING ORDERS? DO YOU KNOW THIS FROM YOUR OWN EXPERIENCE OR THAT OF OTHERS?

Banning orders do not stop and will not stop trouble at football. Wednesday have had a fair share of banning orders over the years, but it has not stopped the trouble. Only last season, there was trouble home and away with Bristol City, and trouble at Stockport, and I bet this season there'll be trouble between Wednesday, Bristol City, Hull City and Bradford City. I was reading just recently that a Walsall supporter got a three-year ban for turning up at Chesterfield pissed. Banning people for trivial offences only puts the police in a bad light when you see what goes on in the real world. If more effort was put into ridding the streets of the real menace, like drugs and the crimes that are associated with it, instead of waging war on the football supporter all the time, things might get better.

I personally received a six-month ban in 1990 after being found guilty along with 13 mates of consuming alcohol on the way to a football match. It was Wolverhampton in the FA Cup and we'd organised a bit of a reunion and got a bus and driver to take us to the game. We set off with one or two cans on board and we stopped off at one or two pubs on the way. At no time was there any trouble, but once reaching the ground we were arrested and banged up, finally getting let out mid-evening. When we finally got to court, the prosecution stated that 95 discarded ring pulls were found on the bus. I wondered how long it took the copper to gather them up. The magistrate did not take too kindly to our outrageous behaviour that day and we all received a £100 fine and a six-month banning order.

HOOLIE MOVIES AND FLICKS – DO THEY GLORIFY VIOLENCE OR CREATE A COPYCAT SYNDROME?

I think the first hoolie film I saw was The Firm which was on TV, followed by ID, then the recent one, Football Factory. Personally, it may sway a very small percentage to carry out what they've seen on the screen, but hooliganism had been around for a long time before it made the movies.

HOW WOULD YOU DESCRIBE YOUR FIRM/SUPPORTERS' FAN BASE, AND HAS YOUR FAN BASE CHANGED OVER TIME?

When I became involved round about 1974, our little firm was just starting out and we were just a small part of the wider picture. When I was asked to do this about my club, I made it clear I was no terrace legend, but just part of the scene that swept the terraces at the time. During the 1975/76 season, Wednesday were in the Third Division for the first time in their history and I've stated before that Wednesday had a massive away following and trouble flared up every week. Our fan base was mainly from the Sheffield estates of the Manor, Arbourthorne, Darnall, Wybourn, Hillsborough, Parsons Cross and Southey; this, plus outlying districts like Stocksbridge, Mosborough and Killamarsh, plus the Owls from Doncaster, Rotherham and Barnsley, and the pubs and clubs like The Windsor, Park and Arbourthorne, Friery Fred, Woodbourne and The Gate and Travellers from Hillsborough, these were the hardcore of the East Bank Republican Army. But it did not matter whether you travelled in your hundreds from one particular area or 12 of you jumped into a transit van, you were all together as one.

It was not until the start of the punk scene, when the lads who frequented town and the pubs up and around West Street joined our little band, that we joined with the lads from the other side of the city and coaches would leave from the Crazy Daisy for excursions down south, sometimes leaving after the club had closed at 2.00am. We've had some great days out in London and Portsmouth after setting off in the early hours.

The scene today has completely changed, with the boys being very wary of new faces, unlike the days of old, but who can blame them with all the snide surveillance that goes on today.

IS THERE, IN YOUR OPINION, A NEXT GENERATION OF HOOLIGAN APPRENTICES COMING THROUGH AND WILL THEY BE ANYTHING LIKE THEIR PREDECESSORS?

Even with the clampdown, it's still going strong, but it's more a lower league thing with the Premier League being swamped by the prawn sandwich brigade. Moving into the millennium, lads are still fighting at football, but they are being closely watched and it is the beginning of the war through the civil courts and being guilty by association, while the banning orders are being dished out at an alarming rate. The year is now 2004 and lads are still fighting at football.

Many of the faces you've seen over the years have moved aside, but can still be found cheering on their team on Saturday afternoon. The next generation have stepped in, the boys who were at primary school when most of our generation were at it; today it's the kids of lads that went before. But they are facing a more heavy-handed police presence than we ever did; if we stepped out of line, we'd get a crack with the truncheon or a boot up the arse. Today, it's a different ball game and the rules have changed. But I have every confidence that, come my sixtieth birthday in the year 2015, we will still be reading about trouble at football, if the game as we know it is still alive and well and we're not watching some crap European League for the fat cats of English football. So to answer the question, I think the lads that are coming through will measure up to what went before, but it will be a different ball game.

NAME: Cola
CLUB: West Bromwich Albion
FIRM: Section 5

'We took the name
from the police
charge sheet.'

BACKGROUND AND MEET

I heard about this mysterious Cola from the 6.57 book author, Rob Silvester. Upon hearing of his exploits and reputation, I wanted to meet him. Normally, I got to interview the person I sought in a quiet pub and met a few of the lads, but Cola invited me around to his house. He had someone else there he'd like me to meet. So I drove over to Cola's, shook hands and did the interview.

After, I met a man called Johnny Payne, bit of a West Brom legend and what I call proper old school. And how we talked about the old days! We were like a couple of war veterans – the scrapes, the laughs, and I thought it was a shame that I didn't have Johnny in one of the books. But he just said, 'Don't want none of that. Leave that to today's lads. They're all right.' Then he carried on talking about the good old bad days.

Cola was born in 1968, and qualified with an HNC in Carpentry and Building. He's self-employed with his own business; single, but with a partner of 12 years.

WHAT HAS BEEN THE MOST LEGENDARY FIGHT OR RIOT YOUR TEAM'S SUPPORTERS HAVE BEEN INVOLVED IN?

We had a right ding-dong with Blues [Birmingham City] away earlier in the season; revenge was awaiting. We were well prepared, plenty of gas; we all chipped in and got some flares from a local boat shop. We heard Blues were in West Brom at the

Lewisham pub. They came out and showered us with bottles and glasses, so we opened up with the flares. It was like the parting of the Red Sea as the rocket-like flare went through the middle of them Zulus. Then we went into them, each mob was about 150-strong. It was mental.

Blues were probably one of the best firms in the country at the time and we wasted them; I recognised the lads who'd gassed me and tried to cut me up at their place, and I got revenge proper. It went on for ages. The only copper there was on a motorbike; even he got gassed and came rolling off his bike. It was a proper ruck.

HOW IMPORTANT WAS THE ROLE OF ALCOHOL AND DRUGS? WAS THERE ANY TIME IN YOUR EXPERIENCE EITHER HAD PARTICULAR INFLUENCE?

Beer and drugs go together like football and violence. Best experience of that was when I went to Scotland, first leg of England's Euro 2000 qualifier. Fifty of us arrived in the East End of Glasgow around seven in the morning, after travelling up on a coach full of lads that were a right drinking crew. It could have gone off straight away – we bumped into Blues, but we thought they were Wolves. As it was still seven and early, a little truce was established with one of our major rivals.

We set up base in a pub I hated. Had pictures of Gerry Adams placed around. It was a Taig hole [Celtic], but it was open and, after a few beers and lines of Charlie, the lads started trying to set the pub on fire. The fire extinguisher came over and Old Bill came in and moved everyone on.

Within five minutes of being in the city, we came across Hibs Casuals and it was great wasting them until Old Bill arrived; they blocked off both ends of the road to enclose everybody in, putting the lads under a police escort for the day. Half-a-dozen of us managed to get clear. Never bothered going to the game, found a Yates's bar, had a few beers and what have you. Next, we heard our mate had got glassed bad in another pub. He was celebrating England scoring, Jocks come up to him and put a glass in his face, got terrible scars. So when we learned about that lot, we was fuming.

All the Jocks were coming out of the pubs on to the street after we beat them 2–0 and we were at it straight away, just six of us, we were pumping, having a row on every street corner and these coppers would just come in and move you to another street corner, where we was rowing again. I remember these English lads from Blackburn shouted out, 'Who are you? Who are you?'

'We're Albion,' we said. 'Come on, let's get into them.'

We were famous that day. Good result, felt like 'The Untouchables'. It was the Charlie. It's a regular part of the scene today, all the kids have gone into it now.

WHO WAS THE MOST VIOLENT, CRAZY SET OF SUPPORTERS YOU EVER CAME ACROSS?

Me, personally, it's Millwall, they're just loonies. We played them midweek in a Cup game, they was in the Third Division and we was in the old First Division. About 70 of them came into our end [the Rainbow] and played up like fuck, people running about on top of the executive boxes. I was only a kid myself, but it was at that stage when I got the bug for it. Albion had a right go at them, but with this Millwall mob they was just a different league to us.

In the return leg, five coaches left for Millwall, only two arrived at the old Den 'cos they was either hijacked on the services or smashed up when they went under bridges.

ARE YOUR FIRM STILL DOING IT?

Still doing it for the big games. Season 2002/03 saw us in the Premiership for the first time and we were making a lot of noise, playing up all over the place. Derby games against Blues and Villa always got the lads out and loads of good kids joined us. We don't half miss the Wolves fixture, though. Old Bill have really come down on Albion with banning orders.

HOW WOULD YOU DESCRIBE THE SITUATION WITH THE SCENE TODAY? CAN IT COMPARE WITH WHAT HAPPENED IN THE PAST, AND DO THINGS STILL GO OFF IN THE SAME WAY?

It will never be as good as it was, but so many lads have

other firms' mobile numbers, meetings can be sorted out away from the grounds and the Old Bill, but some of the best rows happen unplanned.

HOW DID YOU GET GOING WITH A FOOTBALL FIRM, DID IT HAVE A NAME AND HOW WAS THE NAME ESTABLISHED?

Went to college with Eamonn and he used to tell stories of the rows he had at the football and I wanted to be a part of it. Eamonn introduced me to his brother, Johnny Payne, Albion's top lad and I got into it that way. I was 16 and proud to be part of a unit and never let the lads down. Section 5 Squad was our firm; we took the name from a police charge sheet they used to give you in the '80s.

WHAT WAS THE WORST INSTANCE OF WEAPONS BEING USED?

Blues away. Went to the Old Crown and smashed it up. They all came out and we got stuck into them. We was doing well until about another 300 joined the 100 that was already there, and they had blades, gas and hammers. We stood our ground the best we could, but they were well on top. We had a few casualties that day, but revenge was sweet when we played them at our place later in the season.

WHAT IS THE MOST IMPORTANT LESSON YOU LEARNED PERSONALLY DURING YOUR TIME WITH YOUR FIRM AND WOULD YOU DO ANYTHING DIFFERENTLY?

Sticking together with your mates and forming a unit that you can trust 'cos, when you're rowing, you don't want to be looking over your shoulder to see if your mates are still there.

In 2000, England played Holland in a friendly in Amsterdam. The Dogheads [Wolves] joined up with Plymouth and came into our boozer. There were about 60 Albion in there and this scruff came into the middle of us screaming out his name and yelling he's Wolves. My mate clattered him all over the pub. They threw a few glasses and we run them out of the pub.

To be fair, that infamous Wolves main lad stood his ground but a sweet right-hand put him on his arse and he was fucked. All his mates had left him. After a kicking, my mate said, 'Kick him in the cut [canal],' and, as he looked up with those sad puppy eyes, he bleated out, 'Don't let them throw me in the cut,' so I called it off and saved him. It's the biggest regret that I've got.

WHO WERE YOUR BIGGEST RIVALS BOTH TEAM AND FAN-WISE?

There's a few because of the way we've moved up and down the divisions. As a kid, it was always Villa, until we got relegated, and then it was Blues. It was always good against Blues during the '80s, but since the '90s it's been the Dogheads.

WHO ARE THE TOP FIVE FIRMS OF ANY IMPORTANCE TODAY?

Wolves has got to be the most important rivals and, after them, Villa. Banged it off with Cardiff, give it to them. Man U, they always turn up, don't they? Blues. So it's Wolves, Villa, Cardiff, Man U and Blues.

WHO ARE YOUR TOP FIVE FIRMS OF ALL TIME?

Millwall, Chelsea, West Ham, Arsenal and Man United.

WHAT IS YOUR FAVOURITE FOOTBALL FASHIONWEAR AND THE WORST YOU'VE SEEN OR WORN?

Lacoste or Burberry, but I don't like Burberry check. I had this Tacchini rollneck and wore it with a yellow Lacoste V-neck jumper. I thought I was the bollocks. I'm talking the '80s now, but even today it's still nice to have a bit of Lacoste gear, coat or something, they haven't changed much.

As for the worst, it's after Christmas when you see these plastic lads dressed up with Burberry check looking more like Rupert the Bear.

WHAT IS THE WORST KIT YOU'VE SEEN A TEAM IN AND WHAT WOULD BE YOUR OWN CLUB'S BEST EVER STRIP?

About 10–12 years ago, Bury had a pink home top with 'Birthday' written across the front and Coventry had a chocolate-brown away top.

Albion's best shirt was 1979/80 season with W.B.A. scroll written on the shirt – the Big Ron Atkinson days.

HAVE YOU EVER WORN A REPLICA FOOTBALL SHIRT TO A GAME AND NAME A CLUB THAT'S ALL SHIRTERS AND SCARFERS?

No. Having said that, I used to be a ball boy for Albion when I were about 12 and we had this Albion tracksuit, 'WBA' down the side. It was really good. I used to sit behind the main stand which is all the old fans. Some of the lads used to sit in various positions round the ground, some of the lads used to sit in the visitors.

West Ham and Leeds were terrible. They just used to gob and spit all day. Every game, these poor kids, my mates, used to come back with ... It was the old terraces then, so it was all coming over.

The club of shirters is Wolves. Gold-and-black all over the place. And I tell you what, I've got to tell you this because it sticks out – they go to work in them, they go to the match in them, they go to weddings in them, funerals in them, they go to bed in them, in the same one. They've got it and they just wear it out, they really do.

I went to Newcastle in '86 when England played Scotland in the qualifier for the European Championship. It was the game when Gascoigne put that ball over the top of Hendry's head to score that goal. Anyway, we turned up off the Metro and I could not believe what I saw – Newcastle black-and-white tops, that's all you could see. Kids, old men, old women, and it wasn't even a match day. It wasn't a Newcastle match day and there was just black-and-white. I could not believe that all these people were wearing black-and-white tops.

DOES TODAY'S MODERN FOOTBALL PLAYER HAVE THE RESPECT OF THE FANS?

Footballers generally don't respect the club or the fans. Modern-day footballers are too money orientated. After scoring a goal, they kiss the club's badge, misleading the fans that they love the club – it's not genuine.

WHO'S THE PLAYER AND/OR MANAGER THAT WINDS YOU UP THE MOST?

For me it's Stan Collymore, 'cos he always scored against us for whatever club he played for. He's made millions out of football. With the talent he had, he has achieved nothing, he's an absolute prick who deserves a slap (or two).

Graham Rix came out of jail for sex with a minor and his first job back in football was manager of Pompey. His first game was against the Albion. The Albion singers had his life that day. I don't know where they get their chants from, but everybody seemed to know the words. They must print song sheets or go to college or something 'cos they totally embarrassed him, and rightly so.

WORST FOREIGN PLAYER YOU'VE SEEN AND THE BEST FOREIGN IMPORT? YOUR FAVOURITE CLUB PLAYER AND YOUR FAVOURITE OTHER PLAYER?

Worst foreign player is Savo Milosevic; when he played for Villa, he was terrible.

Best club player is Tony Brown; he played in midfield, scored 279 goals in 704 top-flight appearances, had England caps and was never been booked or sent off in his career. A total gentleman and a credit to football. My favourite other player is Zinedine Zidane, a perfect and complete player.

FANS OFTEN TALK ABOUT THEIR FOOTBALL-GOING DAYS AS JUST BEING A LAUGH. ANY EPISODES YOU REMEMBER?

Played Villa and smashed up their top boozer. As they were coming out, my mate picked up an oil drum from a shop next door which was outside a butcher's. He raised the drum above his head before throwing it through the pub's Georgian window and all this offal fell out of the drum on top of his head and all over his clothes. He still went to the game, standing on his own with a big gap around him because he stunk so bad. He was obviously the brunt of all jokes that day.

YOUR OPINION ABOUT ALL-SEATER STADIUMS, TICKET PRICES AND THE COMMERCIAL ASPECT OF TODAY'S FOOTBALL INDUSTRY. DO YOU STILL FEEL FOOTBALL BELONGS TO THE FANS?

All-seater stadiums have taken the atmosphere away from the game. There should be a section in every ground for standing and it's your choice if you want to stand there. Attendances are falling because of the price of match-day tickets and travelling away makes it more expensive, as the genuine fan finds it harder, the lining of the pockets of the Board always seem to get bigger. Even though it's more comfortable and the facilities are better, I still prefer the old days on the terraces.

RACISM AND RACE ISSUES HAVE BEEN PART OF FOOTBALL WITH CERTAIN CLUBS AND SETS OF SUPPORTERS AT BOTH CLUB AND INTERNATIONAL LEVEL. WHAT WAS YOUR EXPERIENCE OF THIS?

Football brings together people with different opinions on race issues. I think within every firm there is a right-wing element. There are pockets of lads who have their own personal view, whether racist or not. But when rowing, our firm has no prejudices, black and white stick together as one unit. Race doesn't make a difference.

If you're in a ruck and see your mate having a bit of a kicking, you don't see black or white, you only see Albion and help him out. There's no internal racism in our firm. Blacks and whites get on because we are all there for the same thing, that's to represent West Brom. It's bizarre to think it's all right to have black Albion players but when opposing teams have black players, opinions change. It's strange to see lads giving monkey chants to opposing black players, but have blacks playing for their club and say nothing.

HOW HAVE FANS FOLLOWING THE NATIONAL TEAM ABROAD BEEN TREATED, AND WHAT ARE YOUR EXPERIENCES FOLLOWING YOUR CLUB OR NATIONAL TEAM ABROAD?

When going away with England, the foreign coppers definitely treat England fans disrespectfully and more aggressively and that's down to the influence and tactics of the English Police. Foreign coppers do what they want, when they want. It's their day out when the English are out there.

WOULD YOU SAY THE MEDIA 'OVER-HYPE' THE TROUBLE AND CAN YOU GIVE AN EXAMPLE OF THIS?

Yeah, the media do over-hype it. It sells newspapers. There was a time when we went to France '98, I think we played Morocco, and the media was paying the England fans with a bellyful of beer to go into them, to go in and cause a ruck. The media was paying them.

It was the same when we was in Charleroi, all day these journalists kept out of the sun; they had the laptops, the mobile phones, this, that and the other. And then come five o'clock, six o'clock, after everybody had been drinking all day, they come out and they were provoking, got the cameras ready and they was asking the English fans, 'Are you gonna let them get away with that? The Germans are only over there.' They were in this one big square and they're provoking them. It if hadn't been for the media egging you on, it wouldn't have gone off. It was provoked.

I don't know if it's just the English press. Although it's going off all the time, it doesn't get reported. When it's gone off recently, you couldn't get it in the paper, whereas in the '80s it was front page, pull-outs, but now you're lucky to get a little bit there. They try not to glamorise it.

SHOULD CELTIC AND RANGERS BE ALLOWED TO JOIN THE ENGLISH PREMIERSHIP OR NATIONWIDE LEAGUES?

I think they should be in the Premiership because every firm in England would be up for bashing the Taigs. Fixtures involving Celtic would always involve violence.

DO YOU HAVE ANY VIEW ON BANNING ORDERS? DO YOU KNOW THIS FROM YOUR OWN EXPERIENCE OR THAT OF OTHERS?

Depends what details are in the banning order. My mate had a three-year banning order for trying to leave the country to watch England away. It didn't affect him 'cos he was out on every match day, he just missed the game. In fact, it made him worse because he was in the pub getting tanked up while we were watching the game.

HOOLIE MOVIES AND FLICKS – DO THEY GLORIFY VIOLENCE OR CREATE A COPYCAT SYNDROME?

Hoolie films glamorise football violence. Lads watch it and think, 'Fucking hell, I'll have some of that.' They come into our world on a Saturday and are hooked.

WHO'S YOUR TOP FELLOW – SOUND AS A POUND – FROM YOUR OWN SUPPORTERS, WHY HE IS NOMINATED AND WHAT DID HE DO FOR YOU?

Johnny Payne, without a doubt. As I mentioned earlier, the first game against Blues, we went up there. I was more frightened of him than the Blues that day, 16 years old. He was saying, 'Anybody who don't perform when we get back to West Brom, I'll do you.' So you had to perform. He's got the full respect of everybody, he's a legend. I had heard of him before I met him, because I'd heard what everybody told me about him, also knew his brother, so I was more worried about not performing.

And the week after we went up to Birmingham and, as he went to get on the bus, he muttered, 'Cola.'

'What?' I said.

'You done all right last week.'

For the top man to say that to you, I tell you what, it didn't half give you a buzz. When you're recognised at 16–17, fucking hell, he knows my name. He's always looked out for me, he really has always looked out for me. And, together, we've got Clem, PG, Eamonn and Bale, who are top fellows.

WAS YOUR LIFESTYLE WITH SECTION 5 SOLELY CONFINED TO THE FOOTBALL CONTEXT OR WOULD IT HAVE BEEN THE SAME FOR YOU IN EVERYDAY STREET LIFE?

Saturday match day brings the same way of thinking as Friday nights; if it's there, you don't walk away from it. It's just violence, nothing else!

EVERY ONE OF TODAY'S KNOWN HOOLIGAN FIRMS HAS A POLICE INTELLIGENCE OFFICER DEDICATED TO IT. HOW DO THE FIRMS TODAY RESPOND TO THAT? DO YOU HAVE ANY POLICE SPOTTER STORIES?

We try to avoid them, me personally as much as possible, but some of the kids keep talking to the Old Bill. They lull them into a false sense of security, make them vulnerable to the copper's own need and that's to gain information. There is a lad who got nicked recently and he was offered a deal. They said they wouldn't charge him, but in return they would pay for his match ticket home and away, his transport costs to games and even give him beer money, so long as he told them where the lads were on a match day, who was there and also give details of any trouble. To the lad's credit, he took the charge and told them to fuck the deal.

IS THERE, IN YOUR OPINION, A NEXT GENERATION OF HOOLIGAN APPRENTICES COMING THROUGH AND WILL THEY BE ANYTHING LIKE THEIR PREDECESSORS?

Our young lads coming through are very good and are a match for any firm, but they will never experience the violence of the

'80s. Hoolies in the past seemed to involve proper hard men, not like some other firms who are just Stone Island-clad muppets.

NAME: Bunter
TEAM: West Ham United
FIRM: The Inter-City Firm (ICF)

'The Teddy Bunter firm was well established at West Ham.'

BACKGROUND AND MEET

When Bunter had his fiftieth, all the old stories came out – the time he ran on the pitch and smacked Willie Donachie, the pitch invasions, the end-taking, the famous Teddy Bunter firm, the songs, the banter, the fights – they were all retold again as all the boys turned out in his honour. I knew right then who would be the West Ham chapter for this book. Bit of an Upton Park legend and someone who has given his life up for the claret-and-blue, you don't ask someone like that for their CV, we all know about Bunter – now you will, too.

Someone said there ain't no characters today going to football. Well, look no further than the Bunters; the whole family go and each member is respected by each generation. I remember getting carried away with the whole occasion and getting pissed in Metz when West Ham took a fantastic amount of support away for the two-bob Cup Final. I entered the ground, and temporarily forgot I had brought me son with me. I didn't have time for the frantics, before Ma Bunter cut me dead with music to me ears, 'We've got him, he is with us. The boys will keep an eye on him.' That's typical West Ham – one big family.

Later, I asked me boy how he enjoyed the company of the Bunters. 'Dad, Dad, I see this massive fight.' Well, this was news to me as everyone was remarking how trouble-free the day had been. 'No, Dad, the fight was the young Bunters. They were arguing amongst themselves, then started fighting each other, right in the middle of the square. Proper row, Dad.'

Well, folks, I can't speak for everybody else's firm but we still have some real characters over the Hammers, and one in particular we just call 'Bunter' nowadays.

He was born in 1951. His first game was West Ham v Sunderland, 1965, which the Hammers won 2–0. He's married with four children and three grandchildren and is a warehouse foreman.

WHAT HAS BEEN THE MOST LEGENDARY FIGHT OR RIOT YOUR TEAM'S SUPPORTERS HAVE BEEN INVOLVED IN?

There's several – Harry Cripps's testimonial in the '70s was one, and another was Man United in the Cup when we took liberties up there in the '80s, fighting before the game, after the game.

We all got up there early. They wonder what hit them, basically. When Chrissy Harris got a whack off Sammy the Engine, it just went off from there. It was all over the place. I think a few West Ham took their pub on the corner, I forget the name of the pub, but it was fighting everywhere, before the game in the town centre near the station, and after the game in the streets just outside the ground. The Old Bill didn't have a clue. It just kept going and going.

Birmingham – that was the FA Cup, 1984, pitch invasion and all that. Plenty of fights before the game again and afterwards, mainly in the town centre again with the Zulu lot. I went with my mate Dave. They went early, but I met them up there in the pub, and it just went off from there. My mate Dave, who ain't a fighter, was shitting himself all the way through the game. I said, 'Well, you'll have to stay with me because I'm with Ted and all that lot now.' I didn't get on the pitch, but most of the others did. We was in the side of the ground, but the main West Ham was behind the goal. I don't think there was any fighting on the pitch, because I don't think Birmingham got on the pitch, but there were plenty of fights after the game.

Chelsea – that's when they was fighting in three parts of the ground and the Shed on the west stand. I think you was involved in that. It was all in the corner with the ICF lot and that's when all the police horses come on the pitch. Took half the

Shed. Canning Town was in the west side, but, when the fighting went off, all the West Ham up the other end, the visiting end, all was on the pitch trying to get up and help everyone else. It just went off all round. The police horses stopped it by forming a line across – they put all West Ham in the fucking corner and I can't remember exactly if they escorted them all out or made a big gap like they used to in the old days. But they stopped the game for a little while and I've never seen nothing like it at a football match, the fighting.

HOW IMPORTANT WAS THE ROLE OF ALCOHOL AND DRUGS? WAS THERE ANY TIME IN YOUR EXPERIENCE EITHER HAD PARTICULAR INFLUENCE?

Once, I ran on the pitch at Upton Park and confronted Winnie Donachie from Man City. The reason I did that was because he'd just fouled Alan Devonshire, but I was so pissed I punched him. He then punched me, and Mark Doyle, the wanker, kicked me. I was so drunk I didn't know what I was doing. It was all in the papers the next day.

The first we knew of this was when a bus conductor kept looking at me and, as we got off the bus, on the back of the newspaper he was reading there was a picture of me and the headline saying, 'Do you know this man?' It also appeared on A Question of Sport, What Happened Next?, and it was also on Match of the Day that Saturday night after the game. On the match highlights, they showed that incident when I was on the pitch. I think that's how the BBC got it for A Question of Sport several years later.

WHO WAS THE MOST VIOLENT, CRAZY SET OF SUPPORTERS YOU EVER CAME ACROSS?

Well, Stoke when we played them in the Cup semi-final, '72 I think. The first game was up there. We went up in cars – me, Ted, Big Fat Ronnie, Simmo and all the others, and we were all boozed up apart from the driver. We all met up in the pub up there, and then went in their end because it was pay on the turnstiles. We were running up the stairs, shouting and hollering, and I remember getting a golf ball on me head. I fell backwards, and someone picked me up, but I can't remember who. I had a fucking big lump on me head from the golf ball thrown by a Stoke supporter. But it went off big time up their end, which we took. I'll always remember that one. But nothing happened at our ground in the second leg or any of the replays.

We had Burnley away. They used to have a side, a great big side, and we all went in there, one side. Then it all went off big time in their ground. It didn't last because we took their fucking end or side, whatever you call it, and we took liberties up there. I think that was in the '70s. I do rate them.

After the game, they came looking for us and they wanted it. Any other team apart from Stoke and Burnley, I don't think they had the bottle in them days, but Stoke and Burnley had a fucking mob and we had a mob, and they wanted it and we wanted it.

ARE YOUR FIRM STILL DOING IT?

Yeah, a few old members still go and turn out for the big ones, but the majority of them just married and moved away and don't keep in touch. You might see them at the odd game, Man United and Millwall, or Chelsea. All of them turn out.

When we was at Old Trafford the other year, people I ain't seen for fucking years – the game where Di Canio got the winner – that was a big reunion.

Millwall last season. Took a big mob over there and showed our faces, and some old faces turned up as well. Even me, 50 years old, and some others there, late forties and fifties, like Ted and Bill, all turn up.

HOW WOULD YOU DESCRIBE THE SITUATION WITH THE SCENE TODAY? CAN IT COMPARE WITH WHAT HAPPENED IN THE PAST, AND DO THINGS STILL GO OFF IN THE SAME WAY?

When we played Birmingham on the last game of the season the year we went down; I didn't go, but I've heard plenty of stories from my sons and me friends and all that. A close pal, his boy got bitten by a police dog up there, and got compensation of £500 which was fuck all. He's got a great big scar.

It's just not happening now. I think Birmingham knew they got fucking shown up and all on their own manor again. I think the police suss a lot of it out quite well. West Ham turned out at Millwall last year with people meeting at Stratford and Poplar at seven in the morning. The pub's open, there's fucking 500 people in there, and it only wants a neighbour to phone the Old Bill up, you know what I mean?

The police are very clever at the moment. You might get the occasional 20 against 10 round the fucking back who don't go to football, like me, three miles away or something like that before and after the game, but there ain't no fucking 600 v 600 no more, none of the heavyweight stuff.

HOW DID YOU GET GOING WITH A FOOTBALL FIRM, DID IT HAVE A NAME AND HOW WAS THE NAME ESTABLISHED?

Quite a few people met in pubs in Leytonstone and Stratford, but mainly it was the Plough and Harrow where we met. People come from Leytonstone, Stratford, Dagenham. They was all West Ham supporters and made a firm up and called ourselves the Teddy Bunter firm, which was made up of me, Bunter, Big Ted and about 30–40 boys. We all had a go and never bottled anything. This has got to be 1970.

It got bigger and bigger and other people joined in. Got well known over West Ham. Bill Gardener, he weren't a member of Teddy Bunter, he just wanted to be himself. I don't think Bill was in any firm, but he's well established, the same way the Teddy Bunter firm was well established at West Ham, and had a hefty reputation.

WHAT WAS THE WORST INSTANCE OF WEAPONS BEING USED?

There was Harry Cripps's testimonial, a night match. Mile End and our firm joined up together, and none of our firm were tooled up, but we didn't know the Mile End was. Apparently, they broke into a railway workman's hut, took all their fucking big tools and everything. Come out the station, they was all there waiting for us, and I've never seen nothing like it, smashing everyone over the fucking heads with everything and Millwall just scattered.

In the ground, we was up their end, all at the back before the game. We was all creeping in, but they knew who we fucking was. I don't think nothing major happened in the ground. I can remember being stuck up in the corner of the Cold Blow Lane end, running back and forth, but it was before the game and after the game that saw the real action. Good firm Millwall, for a testimonial. But, if it was a league game, West Ham would have more boys out. But we didn't need no more than the Mile End/Teddy Bunter firm that night. We were all up for it. I reckon there was a good 100–200 West Ham there. I've never seen a firm so tooled up as that night. And when we see them all tooled up, we was all up for it and all.

WHO WERE YOUR BIGGEST RIVALS BOTH TEAM AND FAN-WISE?

Well, team-wise it's got to be Millwall or Man United. Fan-wise, it's got to be the same two, I would have thought. Could put Spurs in there, too, but for me it's Millwall because of the incidences over South London. It goes back a long while. I was brought up to hate them. Me aunt and uncle had pubs in Canning Town and they didn't like people from South London. And, as for the football, the docks were involved. Millwall and West Ham old boys used to work in the docks together and fucking hated each other.

WHO ARE THE TOP FIVE FIRMS OF ANY IMPORTANCE TODAY?

Spurs, Chelsea, I don't know about Millwall because they ain't really played no one apart from Bournemouth, little teams like that. There's a couple of teams come down to West Ham – Cardiff, they like to put themselves about. I don't think Man United are doing all that much at the moment. Newcastle like a row still.

All the others are usually out of the First Division. They hate the big clubs. Got to be Stoke in there, I reckon, Stoke or Burnley. They brought a few firms down. And maybe Wolves.

So – Spurs, Chelsea, Newcastle, Cardiff and Stoke.

WHO ARE YOUR TOP FIVE FIRMS OF ALL TIME?

Millwall, Chelsea, Spurs – they always had a row but never took any end in our place – Man United. I've got to go with Everton; we had a fucking row up there. They've had a row down here and all. So – Millwall, Chelsea, Spurs, Man United, Everton.

WHO'S THE PLAYER AND/OR MANAGER THAT WINDS YOU UP THE MOST?

Well, I've already punched one player and that's Willie Donachie, but the other one is Robert Pires of Arsenal. Gets away with it when he appears to be diving. You've seen it on telly. Phil Neville, the ugly cunt, and his brother Grant. I call him Grant after Grant Mitchell on the fucking telly. And Ferguson, you watch him when he's losing 1–0, or Wenger keeps moaning, 'I never saw that tackle, blah, blah.' Ferguson and Arséne Wenger are the managers, and Robert Pires is the player.

WORST FOREIGN PLAYER YOU'VE SEEN AND THE BEST FOREIGN IMPORT? YOUR FAVOURITE CLUB PLAYER AND YOUR FAVOURITE OTHER PLAYER?

The worst foreign player, it's got to be Marco Boogers of West Ham, because he's fucking crap. He fucked off. He got sent off the first game against Man United. Didn't live up to his reputation, was just fucking crap – Sunday-morning footballer.

The other geezer, Florin Raducioiu, fucked off shopping when he's supposed to be injured.

Best foreign import has got to be Di Canio. He was magic, weren't he? He either had a bad game or a fucking brilliant game.

My favourite other player has got to be Thierry Henry, the Arsenal player. Still don't like him, though.

FANS OFTEN TALK ABOUT THEIR FOOTBALL-GOING DAYS AS JUST BEING A LAUGH. ANY EPISODES YOU REMEMBER?

When we was the Teddy Bunter firm and all that, we went to Chelsea, took the Shed again. We were fighting all through the first half. Would have been '77, I would have thought. I was warned twice by the same copper in the Shed to calm down. The beer had took its toll on us all again by the way. Half-time we took their bar, kicked the fuck out of them again. I was after this fella who I'd had a fight with before on the terraces. He was in the bar. Kicked off with him, and I got nicked by the same copper. He said, 'I warned you several times,' and they took me to the nick where I was put in a cell.

I thought, 'Fucking hell, I'll sober up here.' But when I got in, I saw Big Ted in there.

He went, 'Fucking hell, you got done?'

'Yeah,' I said, 'it went right fucking off and … I got nicked.'

They took me boots off me as they were steel toecaps, because I'd been to work in the morning. Big Ted said, 'Fucking hell, Bunter, your feet fucking stink,' which they did. I'm glad to say I don't have this problem now, thank God.

Me and Ted went to court several days later. He said to me, 'Bunt, plead guilty, I only got fucking £30 fine.'

So me, silly bollocks, went in and pleaded guilty. I got a week in custody in Pentonville Road at Christmas. It was a shock getting bird because it was a woman and all on the fucking bench. She must have just come on or something.

When I come out, Ted and Bill met me. Got me a big card from West Ham, fucking hundreds of signatures on it, massive card, and quite a few of us went out that night up to The Tower Pub at Tower Hill. Loads of us there, all the Teddy Bunter firm, Bill, too many to name. I'd been to the Tower Hill pub before because my mate Johnny Green from the Mile End mob was a bouncer on there, he let us all in for nothing. He heard I'd done a bit of bird over Christmas. We had a good time.

YOUR OPINION ABOUT ALL-SEATER STADIUMS, TICKET PRICES AND THE COMMERCIAL ASPECT OF TODAY'S FOOTBALL INDUSTRY. DO YOU STILL FEEL FOOTBALL BELONGS TO THE FANS?

Yes and no. Yes, because all-seaters are good when you get to my age, but no for the younger fans, i.e. my son, etc. All-seater does make a difference to the atmosphere, I think that's the reason why. But talking about the atmosphere, you've only got to think of when we had Ipswich in the play-offs, semi-final over West Ham. The fucking atmosphere was brilliant, and that was an all-seater. But that's because we were winning this important game. I think the true fan's been priced out the game, so no, the game doesn't belong to the fans or any of us any more.

RACISM AND RACE ISSUES HAVE BEEN PART OF FOOTBALL WITH CERTAIN CLUBS AND SETS OF SUPPORTERS AT BOTH CLUB AND INTERNATIONAL LEVEL. WHAT WAS YOUR EXPERIENCE OF THIS?

It hasn't really figured, really. You have your chants at football at West Ham. I've so many coloured friends, some in the Teddy Bunter firm, like Turkish Carlos, Singhy the Paki, Cass, Matthew, I could go on and on. There was Sammy Skyes of Spurs, old Skyesy, he near got a kicking when he was coming back from a Spurs game by train. He's on his own, he was about to get done in. I stepped in. I said, 'Leave him alone, I know him.' I hope Sammy remembers me for that. West Ham were gonna do him.

HOW HAVE FANS FOLLOWING THE NATIONAL TEAM ABROAD BEEN TREATED, AND WHAT ARE YOUR EXPERIENCES FOLLOWING YOUR CLUB OR NATIONAL TEAM ABROAD?

I reckon the police abroad are all the shit cunts anyway. They like hitting the English fans with batons. Don't touch their own fans. The Dutch Old Bill are fair because our country helped them against the Krauts in the war. They haven't forgotten. Some of the Old Bill over here are also unfair, except our spotters at West Ham, at least they talk to you about problems, not like some of the others.

DO YOU HAVE ANY VIEW ON BANNING ORDERS? DO YOU KNOW THIS FROM YOUR OWN EXPERIENCE OR THAT OF OTHERS?

Well, I think it's crap myself, because if they want to fight and they can't go near the ground for three miles, they can still meet and have a fight fucking three miles from the ground. So I think it's bollocks myself. I know fucking plenty who got nicked and they got banning orders; everyone from last season against Cardiff at home got banning orders. I think if they want to do a banning order, they should do it after the court case, not before. And what happens with the season-ticket holders? Do they get their fucking dough back? No, of course they don't. It's another load of old bollocks. I don't think they're fair. If it were done fair, if a supporter done it and he got a banning order, I think 95 per cent of them would accept it.

HOOLIE MOVIES AND FLICKS – DO THEY GLORIFY VIOLENCE OR CREATE A COPYCAT SYNDROME?

To tell the truth, I ain't seen a lot of hoolie movies, but me sons have seen one and they reckon it glorifies the Chelsea and Millwall fans causing a copycat syndrome, like the firm in Football Factory walking around like they're the bollocks. But I ain't seen it myself. I've seen the documentaries on the telly. I couldn't sit and watch the hoolie movie because it's a fucking movie, but I like the proper documentaries on the telly – proper fucking films, not made-up ones.

HOW WOULD YOU DESCRIBE YOUR FIRM/SUPPORTERS' FAN BASE, AND HAS YOUR FAN BASE CHANGED OVER TIME?

Not really, a lot come from Essex now. In the '70s and early '80s and that, a lot of them come from Stratford, Leytonstone, Dagenham and Barking. But now I think the majority is all Essex. I know a load come from Cambridge and all round. Former EastEnders. I think a lot of them are now from outside East London. It's not a localised spot no more. Half the players, some people don't even fucking know who they are. I know people who live in Nottingham who support West Ham, they're not even Londoners, and further afield. It's not a close-knit community any more. It used to be in the old days, an East End thing, I reckon it was anyway.

EVERY ONE OF TODAY'S KNOWN HOOLIGAN FIRMS HAS A POLICE INTELLIGENCE OFFICER DEDICATED TO IT. HOW DO THE FIRMS TODAY RESPOND TO THAT? DO YOU HAVE ANY POLICE SPOTTER STORIES?

Well, I ain't got no police spotter stories, but there is a couple at West Ham. There's a couple over West Ham we have banter with, but I wouldn't tell them too much because I don't trust them, really. But, yeah, you have to talk to people and I think they try to find out where they're meeting and who they're meeting and where. Like last season, before the Millwall game at Stratford, our Old Bill come up and said, 'Where's the boys meeting?'

I said, 'I can't tell you that, you know what I mean?' which I didn't. But it didn't take long to find out where 500 people were. They soon shot up there.

IS THERE, IN YOUR OPINION, A NEXT GENERATION OF HOOLIGAN APPRENTICES COMING THROUGH AND WILL THEY BE ANYTHING LIKE THEIR PREDECESSORS?

Yeah, like my three sons. Most of my mates from the '70s and '80s have sons. They're a young firm, like Birmingham and Spurs. They remind me of the young ICF when they started out. All come from Walthamstow, Chingford, Higham Park, yeah, Yids' area. Ha-ha!

NAME: Jela
CLUB: West Ham
United
FIRM: The Under Fives

'I can't put into
words how
fucking good
going to
football was.'

BACKGROUND AND MEET

I basically had to persuade little Jela to do the Under Fives chapter – personal interest, really. Back in the day, I knew every firm that came along over West Ham. The one firm that naturally escaped me, yet fascinated me, was the Under Fives. They were quite young, which is not unusual in itself. What was different was the fact they moved around as an individual group quite independent from the main firm. Very vulnerable, I thought to myself, but there again, the places we had to go, the main mob wouldn't want its youth wrapped around them. You just didn't want to be coming up against it thinking half your firm behind you was bastard kids. It's more than enough trying to look after yourself in certain situations without having to fight anyone else's corner because the kids have fucked off and left you.

I needn't have concerned myself, for the Under Fives were the new breed of kids that had grown up with football violence; it was a way of life open to them. Thatcher's children, is how I viewed this generation. The attitude was, if they want it, they are just going to take it. A few older West Ham would mock them as being the Under Fives.

Any underestimation from me ended when I once saw what can only be described as a kid in a diamond Pringle jumper, but this kid, I swear, drew out a blade the length of his torso. I thought, 'Fucking hell, he can't be more than 10–11 years old.' I later found out he was just that, and he went by the name of Jela. When the ICF were at their peak, I watched these ruthless young boys skip school to go and learn about thieving right across Europe. It was these lads I got my first Armani from. While back on the home front, they introduced a new tax system on London's Underground. They were just kids with fresh faces, but you couldn't help but notice that there were that many with Mars bars on their cheeks you were no longer shocked at the sight of seeing someone's slashed face. They had made it the latest must-have accessory, like part of the designer wear.

Little Jela was very much a mascot prodigy of this violent youth academy to graduate from the terraces of Upton Park.

His real name is Djelal Ispanedi, and he was born in 1969. Never had a job, now disabled. He is single and remembers his first away game being at Liverpool.

WHAT HAS BEEN THE MOST LEGENDARY FIGHT OR RIOT YOUR TEAM'S SUPPORTERS HAVE BEEN INVOLVED IN?

I think the most significant for me would be at Highbury, 1982; the Under Fives were a really big firm at the time and we went into the North Bank. We had a really good mob. We met up at Canning Town, we went to Highbury Corner. Everyone got into the North Bank without being detected until we actually let off an orange smoke bomb and this was like a second before three o'clock, they was just about to kick off.

It was stated in the paper that it was the worst football disturbance ever in history because a lot of the boys come in from the top and they threw the orange smoke bomb and everyone fled out the way to come down to the front and I was in a mob of about 15–20 of us positioned nearer the front and we was fighting them back towards the others. Everyone's gone on the pitch and we stayed up in front of them, above them, so then I went up with the other mob at the top and we stayed there the whole game. We had them all round us, all the Gooners, all their top boys were all round us. And through the whole game, we was just like slagging them off and it kept going off. We was so well organised and there'd be different groups of us. We had so many police round us, we really took the piss that day. I don't think I can remember nothing else like that, apart from Chelsea.

When I was at Chelsea, I was in the West Stand and the West Ham were in the Shed as well and there was a mob of Canning Town opposite me in the other seats. This was also in the papers. And the whole seats on my side were fighting and running along underneath where the tunnels go down the steps, they were fighting down there, and it started in the seats as well. But we was fighting underneath and it was really chaotic, but you could look across at the Shed and the same thing was happening there, and the same thing was happening opposite us on the East, and up the North Stand was all the West Ham away supporters. And it was really synchronised – everyone done it all at the same time. And there weren't mobile phones in them days, it was just different mobs with different plans, and everything sort of worked out well that day. The police couldn't really do what they had to do so a lot of Chelsea fans will remember that day because they got mullered and that is what counted.

HOW IMPORTANT WAS THE ROLE OF ALCOHOL AND DRUGS? WAS THERE ANY TIME IN YOUR EXPERIENCE EITHER HAD PARTICULAR INFLUENCE?

I was ever so young when I was going to football, but that was my drug – violence, that was my drug. 1983 – I was 13 years old at the time and I was down Epping Country Club, it was all the Under Fives and a guy named BJ had a birthday party, it was his 21st. I was involved in a fight and I got lumped over the head with a stump you put in the ground to make a fence. I received a blood clot on the brain and a fractured skull and I was in a coma for six weeks. I was 13 and I should never have been there, but I should never have been running into grown men without fear. I didn't care, I was really fearless. But I done that.

And when I come out of this coma, I couldn't walk. I was paralysed down the left side and I couldn't talk because I'd had a tracheotomy with all tubes coming out me throat. I had to learn to walk and talk again and that's when I really picked up drugs because I couldn't substitute the violence with anything else but drugs. And I eventually moved on to hard drugs and, at the moment, I'm staying away from them and I wish I could have the football, as nothing compares to the buzz I got from football. I was always trying to take more and more drugs to achieve the buzz, because when I used to go to football it weren't just the match on a Saturday, it was my way of life. Everything revolved around West Ham, it was really passionate.

When I was a kid, I was took into Hamley's (the only place what sold Fila my size) and put on what I wanted and I had the Under Fives boys around me and then I felt safe, with the boys, and it was like being part of a family. We all stuck together as best as we could. When the football all come to an end, I had an experience with drugs – every drug under the sun I took to extreme and they weren't doing nothing to me. It's unreplaceable the way it was, it's indescribable as well, the aura around that West Ham era, and the passion. That was what kept me going, football violence was my life, my life revolved around it.

WHO WAS THE MOST VIOLENT, CRAZY SET OF SUPPORTERS YOU EVER CAME ACROSS?

I remember we was going to Crystal Palace and everyone got off at New Cross and we had a really good mob. We weren't ready for what happened. There was this pub with a right handy firm of Millwall, every single one of them had a heavy-duty weapon on them, like machetes, baseball bats, and I think I saw a petrol bomb. This is going back a few years – early '80s.

I jumped on a bus and I met a guy who was clinging on to the bar and he had had his earhole cut off; he felt safe to come off the bus with me and go to the Old Bill, but a lot of people got hurt that day. It was scary, but at the time it was just like part of football. We rarely got run and that day we did turn and run from the Millwall, the Bushwackers. They're the biggest opposition I've ever seen. Most teams, they'd be a bit wary of coming into West Ham, but Millwall just didn't care, they was really expecting us, and we weren't even playing them, we was playing Crystal Palace, but they knew we'd show. And we had a really good firm but we weren't tooled up, though.

ARE YOUR FIRM STILL DOING IT?

Everyone's still around, they still go over there, it's like a kind of reunion, but you can't expect too much to happen. When we went to Man United a few seasons back, everyone showed up and it was just a great day to be with everyone, not how it used to be, but just to be together and see all them old faces. We lost 6–0, but I really really enjoyed the day out, though, and it brought it all back to me, but nothing happened, we was just escorted there, being humiliated by the Manchester Police, and it's just changed so much, it's just so well policed now. But being together is still part of the buzz, but you're not getting the full thing, it's just not happening. It's a social occasion. We had a drink and talked about all the old days and what we did then.

HOW WOULD YOU DESCRIBE THE SITUATION WITH THE SCENE TODAY? CAN IT COMPARE WITH WHAT HAPPENED IN THE PAST, AND DO THINGS STILL GO OFF IN THE SAME WAY?

I think there is, which is a hell of a surprise. There's people that use phones and all that, so it is a bit hard to compare it with our past. I started to go into the visiting supporters at Upton Park and we was very young. I mean, I was about eight or nine when I started to go to West Ham and I weren't even a teenager when I was going to football and doing the things that the other older lot were doing. But we got a little group of us, we was like the ICF Under Fives.

We used to take knives, I always had a knife on me, I was ten years old. And all the others they just grew and grew and grew, and our main passion was football and clothes and trying to earn a buck. It will never be like it was; it's a time that's gone and it'll never come back.

HOW DID YOU GET GOING WITH A FOOTBALL FIRM, DID IT HAVE A NAME AND HOW WAS THE NAME ESTABLISHED?

I can't remember who actually come up with the Under Fives as the name, but it was accepted straight away. Nobody was a leader. It was like Under Fives jokingly sort of saying it and it just stuck, and we just grew and grew. And there was a lot of Under Fives and my friend, Johnny Reid, he said if you got caught by the ICF, you'd probably get a punch in the mouth and a kick up the arse and that would be it, but if you got caught by the Under Fives you'd probably get cut and get all your clothes and money stolen as well at the same time, because that was to humiliate you more than anything else. We was terrible people, we was really really intimidating.

When the season weren't on, we used to just go down Oxford Street and the West End looking for people shoplifting or buying clobber because it was all about clobber in the early '80s, and we just used to attack people all day long. If we saw other fans that had got the clothes, like the hooligan uniform – we used to have Pringles, Filas – and you see someone standing out like a hooligan, we'd just set about them, and really ruin them, beat them up, nick their money, nick their clothes, make sure they knew who we was, and they'd be scared to go out of their houses or go to earn money in the West End.

We was from all over, but I could go to Canning Town and there'd be Under Fives, I could go to Stratford and there'd be Under Fives, I could all over, Hounslow, all round London and there's different Under Fives. If anyone's had trouble in one of these areas, then it'd be all Under Fives for each other more or less. I was never in one area at the same time. Most of us were still either at school or just leaving school, at that age. I was the youngest, definitely the youngest, who stuck there so long. The oldest might have been about 17–18.

WHAT WAS THE WORST INSTANCE OF WEAPONS BEING USED?

It was actually the West Ham fans fighting each other, Canning Town and Stratford, and it was in the back streets of Upton Park. It was before the game, I can't remember, but I know a gun was pulled out and it was shot off just the once. It was down to something that happened between Stratford and Canning Town, either a Canning Town got hurt in Stratford – can't remember – but I went over there and they was fighting each other with guns and that's another side of what West Ham fans are about.

WHAT IS THE MOST IMPORTANT LESSON YOU LEARNED PERSONALLY DURING YOUR TIME WITH YOUR FIRM AND WOULD YOU DO ANYTHING DIFFERENTLY?

They give me all my life skills. I remember before I was a teenager, I was hanging about with young men that were like master criminals, they went to New York and travelled across country to Mexico City and then went to the World Cup in Mexico City and, because I was so young, I'd like to have done all that. I could have done it all but I was so young I didn't go; I didn't want to take the piss out of me mother, me dad died and I had more respect for me mother. She wouldn't let me go out the country, so she called the Old Bill when I tried to go out the country and they stopped me at Dover because I was going to go thieving abroad and I got pulled in and the Old Bill went to me mother and said, 'Do you know he's going abroad?' And she said, 'No, I don't.' And that's what stopped me from going away with that lot. But every week they'd be away in Europe doing really well, getting a lot of money, and I only went once or twice with the Inter-Rails, but I loved travelling. Going to football and travelling is what I thrive on, and I don't seem to do it now.

WHO WERE YOUR BIGGEST RIVALS BOTH TEAM AND FAN-WISE?

Well, I'm gonna say Millwall because we're East London and they're South London. I mean, I've been in discos in the West End before the Es and all that come out and it'd be South London versus East London and it come down to West Ham and Millwall, basically, because they're representatives of them areas, like Bermondsey, and we're from Forest Gate, Stratford and Canning Town, and that's a part of being in your team.

WHO ARE THE TOP FIVE FIRMS OF ANY IMPORTANCE TODAY?

Well, I did see some things in the papers about hooligans and they had a table and Cardiff was at the top – they've had the most arrests and that. So they're still doing things. Portsmouth, they've got a really good firm. A lot of West Ham go Portsmouth.

Millwall and Chelsea as well. Out of London, Everton fans I would rate.

WHO ARE YOUR TOP FIVE FIRMS OF ALL TIME?

Millwall, because I see their firm come to Upton Park, they're big, but it's so well policed now it would never happen. They've always been able to pull out numbers because it's their area against our area, like I said earlier.

Arsenal in the '80s, we had so much trouble with them, everywhere they'd turn up and we'd have a fight with them down Bethnal Green in all the nightclubs, and they had a bit of a tasty firm.

Everton, because I always found with Liverpool that it would be a straight run at them and that would be that, but we did actually have a fight with Everton down in Scotland Road and that was one of our biggest fights there, and Everton really did come at us.

I think Man City more so than Man United, they're proper Manchester up there. You'd always get a fight with them, but Man United weren't really much to talk of, they was all over the place, they weren't together at all.

Sheffield Wednesday had quite a good firm when we went there. All them northern teams, they'd always be expecting you, it was either Sheffield United or Sheffield Wednesday – probably both of them.

There's also Leeds, they had a good crew. But they'd be at home and they wouldn't travel around, they would never turn up at Upton Park.

To tell you the truth, the biggest mob I've ever seen at West Ham was Wigan, but they didn't do nothing. This was when we played them in the Cup, this was in the '80s. They were all along Green Street, the whole road, from the station right up to the ground, over 1,000 of them.

Birmingham City, out of all the Birmingham teams, they had a little mob that was always there, wherever Birmingham were, they were there. From that era, they were consistent, it was always the same lot.

So Millwall, Arsenal, Man City, Everton and Birmingham City.

WHAT IS THE WORST GROUND YOU'VE EVER BEEN TO AND WHAT IS YOUR FAVOURITE GROUND?

Well, the most intimidating ground has got to be the old Den, when it was all standing. Every ground was like it at that time. I went to Millwall–West Ham and it was a night game and you really didn't know what was gonna happen. There was quite a lot of trouble there, it was pretty hairy. But I went to a football match in Northampton and their ground was one stand and a rope round the other end of it, so Millwall's ground's tasty.

My best – when I went Man U the other year, the atmosphere in that Old Trafford Theatre of Dreams was electric, but they weren't even singing or nothing. West Ham were losing 6–0 and there was just no atmosphere. When it was standing, it was so much different. I've never been in a stadium like that before.

WHAT IS YOUR FAVOURITE FOOTBALL FASHIONWEAR AND THE WORST YOU'VE SEEN OR WORN?

Well, I used to like Georgio Armani. When I was going to football, I had five different Georgio Armani jumpers and that Georgio Armani is so expensive, but we just used to want to have the best clobber, be the top firm. I used to go up north, and they'd be in ski jumpers and tight jeans and big man trainers, you could tell us apart. But a lot of the gear, they've even started to sell Trim Trab again. A lot of it's all retro now. People want what we was wearing in them days, so I reckon it's all coming back. It's fascinating to see it, because the clothes were quality what we used to wear. That's all I can say, it was top quality, top gear, and we just robbed it, we robbed everything.

The worst is up north, you get the boys up there, it's just Woolybacks sort of fashion, they had this big old furry jumper on and really the tightest pair of jeans you ever seen in your life and a big old pair of shoes hanging out, and that was them being smart.

DOES TODAY'S MODERN FOOTBALL PLAYER HAVE THE RESPECT OF THE FANS?

I think that actor Ray Winstone's got the right idea. He won't pay to go over West Ham because he don't want to put money in their pockets because it's just a fucking joke. We've got the most loyal fans in the country who spend their money and where is their money going?

When I used to go to football, everyone was getting nowhere near the money they are getting now and people used to play their heart out because their heart was in the game and now it's all money and who's got what and who's got this, and it's just not appealing. If anyone who goes to football now could see it how it was, compared to how it is now, they'd just think you're being had, being ripped off.

WHO'S THE PLAYER AND/OR MANAGER THAT WINDS YOU UP THE MOST?

I think it's got to be pretty much all the Manchester United team, because they're like their shit don't stink. I've seen so many conflicts with them and they've sort of like walked away. It's like yesterday there was a big fight in the tunnel. They obviously think they're the best because they've got so many expensive players. But every time I watch Man United, they disgust me.

The manager – he's got his attitude as well. He ain't on the pitch, he's telling them what to do, how to go about it, so he's part of their team, it's the whole lot of them.

WORST FOREIGN PLAYER YOU'VE SEEN AND THE BEST FOREIGN IMPORT? YOUR FAVOURITE CLUB PLAYER AND YOUR FAVOURITE OTHER PLAYER?

You see, I'm terrible with names, I can never remember people's names. Well, I could say that the best player I have a lot of respect for was Paolo Di Canio and he was like one of the old school players, he was like playing with his heart in his fucking shirt pocket and he was dedicated, really dedicated to his game. And you just don't see it, the passion, no more.

My favourite club player is Trevor Brooking, Alan Devonshire,

David Cross, hard to split because they gave their all. Best other player? I think Beckham's got a lot of fucking talent, no one can take that away from that geezer. He's got so much talent.

FANS OFTEN TALK ABOUT THEIR FOOTBALL-GOING DAYS AS JUST BEING A LAUGH. ANY EPISODES YOU REMEMBER?

I have got plenty, but one stands out. We got off at Crewe. For some reason or other, the train got stopped there and we all went up to the chip shop which was on the bridge at the top of the station. And this guy Barry, he's ordered 200 bags of chips and when she's gone to him, 'Right, that'll be £50,' or whatever, he's gone, 'Right, you're knocked,' and everyone's walked away with their chips. That was funny. But another time we were stranded, the lines went down, and we've all got off. All it was was a platform and a car park with a load of coaches. And we've all jumped on this coach and this guy Johnny, he started the coach up with us lot in the back and he's driven it through a garden and hit the front window. And everyone's jumped off and had a laugh, it really was funny, it was hilarious.

Yeah, the lines went down on the way up north, so we had to go back. There was coaches laid on to take us elsewhere so we just turned round and said, 'Right, we're Arsenal fans, we want to go to Luton,' because they was playing Luton and it weren't really far away from where we'd stopped, Bedford or somewhere. They took us by coach, the whole lot of us, and diverted us to Arsenal and they started putting us in their end because the game was on. So we've had it off with Arsenal at Luton.

As I was going in the ground, I turned round and I saw all the Gooners' main lads, and they're saying, 'What you's doing here?' They were just so amazed. But it was hilarious. Now I find it funny, but it was deadly serious. That was the sort of thing we did.

YOUR OPINION ABOUT ALL-SEATER STADIUMS, TICKET PRICES AND THE COMMERCIAL ASPECT OF TODAY'S FOOTBALL INDUSTRY. DO YOU STILL FEEL FOOTBALL BELONGS TO THE FANS?

Definitely not. When it was terraces, everyone was jammed in together and you're not segregated as much. When the terraces disappeared, it took everything out of football. But I suppose from a Health and Safety point of view it had to happen – because if you've got people like us running around doing what we was doing, then it don't give anyone else a chance to enjoy the game, they've always got to worry about that. And now I've grown up and matured a lot, I can see how it's done, but it's all money.

Entertainment is money, and it's so overpriced. I used to go to football with no money, go and see the game, come back and have money in me pocket and eat like a king, that was part of going West Ham. I went to Liverpool, I didn't have nothing, so all the boys had a whip round for me. No one would let me go home without going to football because I had a passion for it and that's what we're breeding. We want youngsters to come and go to football with the boys and be part of it all because it's so fucking good; at the time, it really was.

RACISM AND RACE ISSUES HAVE BEEN PART OF FOOTBALL WITH CERTAIN CLUBS AND SETS OF SUPPORTERS AT BOTH CLUB AND INTERNATIONAL LEVEL. WHAT WAS YOUR EXPERIENCE OF THIS?

I was a skinhead over West Ham and when we started the Under Fives there were a few of us that were skinheads, but then we went to being Casuals and we've ended up turning on the skinheads because of their bad reputation for racism. But, as for us, that didn't really come into it because there were so many black boys with our gang, they was just West Ham, and we didn't look at them as black boys or white boys, it was West Ham and that was that. The skinheads put that uniform on to represent racism with their swastikas and all that, and it's not fucking on. And we turned on them, we got rid of them all.

When I was a skinhead there was Judge Dread, he was like a poetry sort of reggae artiste – he was in the '70s – but we went to their concert in the Bridgehouse in Canning Town. And we just went in there and battered all the skinheads who were at the concert that night. Not for any reason, it was just that everything was violence. We did it for no particular reason, they represented violence, so we stuck it on them and that was that.

DO YOU HAVE ANY VIEW ON BANNING ORDERS? DO YOU KNOW THIS FROM YOUR OWN EXPERIENCE OR THAT OF OTHERS?

Well, a banning order, it don't mean you're banned. I'm banned from certain shops in the West End. It don't mean I can't go in there, but, if I go in there and I'm arrested for stealing, I'm trespassing, I shouldn't be going in there. So that's what a ban is, for an individual not to be allowed near a ground. It teaches people to be careful. If you've got persistent offenders, rather than putting them in jail, the banning order in the judge's eyes is a way of preventing people going back and reoffending. So I think it is a good way of curbing stuff.

HOOLIE MOVIES AND FLICKS – DO THEY GLORIFY VIOLENCE OR CREATE A COPYCAT SYNDROME?

Films like Football Factory do glorify violence; people fighting over a game of football is intriguing to some people, but I done that when I was very young and I wouldn't like fucking things that happened then to happen nowadays. I could get that buzz, I see a bit of violence and I want chaos, but I'm really trying to draw myself away from it.

There's a video called The Firm which is based on West Ham. OK, it's a bit like it, but, until you've actually done it, it seems a bit silly because you can't see the whole picture from a film, the way everything was.

HOW WOULD YOU DESCRIBE YOUR FIRM/SUPPORTERS' FAN BASE, AND HAS YOUR FAN BASE CHANGED OVER TIME?

It weren't one area, we come from nationwide. We had so many people coming along just to be part of this buzz, from everywhere, the suburbs of London. We had a guy from Milton Keynes, he used to come up a lot, all the time he was there, a Northampton geezer. The main supporters come from

Newham and Tower Hamlets. It was East End and the backdrop of Essex, Barking onwards, pretty much West Ham territory. We had a lot of people from Romford, Harold Hill, a lot of people from that area, they were there all the time. It's changed a lot today.

A lot of people that I went to football with ain't showing at these little games because we're in the First Division, we're being fucked off by the fucking Board. They're still from Canning Town, Barking Road and Essex way. Their kids are coming now.

WAS YOUR LIFESTYLE WITH THE UNDER FIVES SOLELY CONFINED TO THE FOOTBALL CONTEXT OR WOULD IT HAVE BEEN THE SAME FOR YOU IN EVERYDAY STREET LIFE?

Every single day. Even if the season weren't on, we'd all be in a gang, in our mob. We'd go out of our way to intimidate other fans, go to their nightclubs, we'd go to where they do their grafting. We'd pull some guy's market stall out into the middle of the road just to teach him a lesson. We really did take it too far. We'd go to the ends of the earth just to fucking really humiliate someone that we knew was one of Tottenham's boys or one of Arsenal's boys. You know, he's working there, we'll all go down there. And you'd see his face, like, 'Oh no, look at all this lot that's turned up here.' That's what we'd do to humiliate you and to see that expression on someone's face, like, 'Fucking hell, what am I gonna do, there's too many of them.'

And we did get hold of people, it weren't just a slap and a kick, it was really fucking hurting people with lumps of wood and all that. It could never happen like that again. It was so passionate, because we wanted to be the best, that was the whole thing of it. West Ham come up and they fucking done this, that, and we was legendary.

People don't forget things like pulling stalls on to the road because he's a Chelsea fan. 'Next time I'm going to see you on your fucking stall, don't worry about that, I know where you work, you cunt,' and it'd be all that through the game. 'We know where you live,' and things like that. And we'd show as well, it wouldn't be idle threats, it'd be, 'Oh, they're gonna come for me, they do know where I live.'

EVERY ONE OF TODAY'S KNOWN HOOLIGAN FIRMS HAS A POLICE INTELLIGENCE OFFICER DEDICATED TO IT. HOW DO THE FIRMS TODAY RESPOND TO THAT? DO YOU HAVE ANY POLICE SPOTTER STORIES?

I think it's all done by camera now because when I was at Millwall–West Ham at Upton Park last season, I was sitting next to a guy and he had his kids with him and the Millwall fans were going, 'You fat bastard, you fat bastard,' and the geezer's sitting there with his kids. One of the main Millwall fans who was standing up and saying, 'You fat bastard,' fell off his chair. So I jumped up and I've gone, 'Good, you fucking wanker,' like that, nothing menacing, I did it because he was doing it to this geezer who was fucking innocent. About ten stewards come round me and said, 'If you do that again, you're out.' God knows how they was all watching me, but that's sort of being spotted, isn't it?

Fuck that, I couldn't fucking pay to go and get that done to me. It's only because someone took me in on a complimentary ticket that I went in there. But I can't enjoy myself. A lot of people go to football to let their anger out, but you can't shout and do what you used to do in the terraces, it's just monitored, you're closely monitored all the time. I must have been monitored, because I weren't looking round me to see who was looking. They just spot people and watch reactions from other people all the time and see trouble spots.

IS THERE, IN YOUR OPINION, A NEXT GENERATION OF HOOLIGAN APPRENTICES COMING THROUGH AND WILL THEY BE ANYTHING LIKE THEIR PREDECESSORS?

Anyone who really, really loves their football team and is a proper supporter will fucking have a row for their team, I think. Whatever the circumstances, whether they're in a mob, on their own, getting pissed on by someone saying their team's shit, you'll retaliate because it's insulting. So, obviously, there's gonna be scraps and all that, but it could never ever measure up to anything remotely like it used to be, because I've written it myself how it's changed – I can't put into words how fucking good going football was, how fucking much I really, really enjoyed going West Ham every week. It was my whole life until I got done over the head and it stopped me in me fucking tracks. I'd still be going, I wouldn't have dropped out. And that's it, really.

Conclusion

Times change ... we change with them.